Law, laity
and solidarities

MANCHESTER
UNIVERSITY PRESS

SUSAN REYNOLDS

Law, laity and solidarities

❦

Essays in honour of Susan Reynolds

❦

edited by
Pauline Stafford, Janet L. Nelson and Jane Martindale

Manchester University Press

Manchester and New York

distributed exclusively in the USA by Palgrave

Copyright © Manchester University Press 2001

While copyright in the volume as a whole is vested in Manchester University Press, copyright in individual chapters belongs to their respective authors, and no chapter may be reproduced wholly or in part without the express permission in writing of both author and publisher.

Published by Manchester University Press
Oxford Road, Manchester M13 9NR, UK
and Room 400, 175 Fifth Avenue, New York, NY 10010, USA
http://www.manchesteruniversitypress.co.uk

Distributed exclusively in the USA by
Palgrave, 175 Fifth Avenue, New York,
NY 10010, USA

Distributed exclusively in Canada by
UBC Press, University of British Columbia, 2029 West Mall,
Vancouver, BC, Canada V6T 1Z2

British Library Cataloguing-in-Publication Data
A catalogue record for this book is available from the British Library

Library of Congress Cataloging-in-Publication Data applied for

ISBN 0 7190 5835 X *hardback*
0 7190 5836 8 *paperback*

First published 2001
10 09 08 07 06 05 04 03 02 01   10 9 8 7 6 5 4 3 2 1

Typeset in 10/12pt Minion
by Graphicraft Limited, Hong Kong

Printed in Great Britain
by Bell & Bain Limited, Glasgow

Contents

List of contributors	*page* vii
Introduction *Pauline Stafford, Janet L. Nelson and Jane Martindale*	1
Writing about Charles Martel *Paul Fouracre*	12
Peers in the early Middle Ages *Janet L. Nelson*	27
Stepmothers in Frankish legal life *Brigitte Kasten*	47
Political ideas in late tenth-century England: charters as evidence *Pauline Stafford*	68
Medieval mentalities and primitive legal practice *M. T. Clanchy*	83
The problem of treason: the trial of Daire le Roux *Stephen D. White*	95
Between law and politics: the judicial duel under the Angevin kings (mid-twelfth century to 1204) *Jane Martindale*	116
Local custom in the early common law *Paul Brand*	150
'Slaves of the Normans'? Gerald de Barri and regnal solidarity in early thirteenth-century England *John Gillingham*	160
Kinsmen, neighbours and communities in Wales and the western British Isles, *c.*1100–*c.*1400 *Rees Davies*	172
Lay kinship solidarity and papal law *David d'Avray*	188
Laity, laicisation and Philip the Fair of France *Elizabeth A. R. Brown*	200
Lay solidarities: the wards of medieval London *Caroline M. Barron*	218
Language, laughter and lay solidarities: an inquiry into the decline of pilgrimages and crusading *Charles T. Wood*	234

Lay/clerical distinctions in early India   *Romila Thapar*   249

A bibliography of Susan Reynolds's work (to 1999)
   compiled by Pamela Taylor   262

Index of topics   *compiled by C. P. Lewis*   269

Contributors

David d'Avray is Professor of Medieval History at University College London. His publications on medieval religious and cultural history include *The Preaching of the Friars* (1985) and *Death and the Prince: Memorial Preaching Before 1350* (1994). He has edited *Medieval Marriage Sermons: Mass Communication in a Culture without Print* (2001).

Caroline Barron is Professor of Medieval History at Royal Holloway University of London. She co-edited *Medieval London Widows* (1994) and has written the chapters on 'The Reign of Richard II' for the New Cambridge Medieval History (1999) and on 'Later Medieval London' for the *Cambridge Urban History of England* (2000).

Paul Brand is a Fellow of All Souls College Oxford. He is the author of *The Origins of the English Legal Profession* (1992) and of numerous articles on the practitioners and users of medieval English law.

Elizabeth A. R. Brown is Professor Emeritus at Brooklyn College and the Graduate School, City University of New York. Two collections of her papers, *Politics and Institutions in Capetian France* and *The Monarchy of Capetian France and Royal Ceremonial*, appeared in 1991.

Michael Clanchy is Professor of Medieval History at the Institute of Historical Research in the University of London. He is the author of *England and its Rulers, 1066–1272* (1983), *From Memory to Written Record* (2nd edn 1993), and *Abelard: A Medieval Life* (1997).

Rees Davies is Chichele Professor of Medieval History at the University of Oxford. Among his publications are *Conquest, Co-existence and Change (1987)*, *Wales 1063–1415* (1987) and *Domination and Conquest. The Experience of Ireland, Scotland and Wales 1100–1300* (1990), *The First English Empire: Power and Identities in the British Isles, 1093–1343* (2000).

Paul Fouracre is Reader in History at Goldsmiths' College University of London. He is co-author of *Late Merovingian France: History and Hagiography 640–720*

(1996), and co-editor of *The Settlement of Disputes in Early Medieval Europe* (1986) and *Property and Power in the Early Middle Ages* (1995). His *The Age of Charles Martel* appeared in 2000.

John Gillingham is Professor Emeritus at the London School of Economics, University of London. His publications include *The Angevin Empire* (2nd edn, 2001), *Richard I* (1999), and a collection of papers, *The English in the Twelfth Century* (2000). In 1997, he was awarded the Prix Guillaume le Conquérant for the French translation of *Richard the Lionheart* (revised edn 1989).

Brigitte Kasten teaches medieval history at the University of Bremen. She has published *Adalhard von Corbie* (1986), and *Königssöhne und Königsherrschaft. Untersuchungen zur Teilhabe am Reich in der Merowinger- und Karolingerzeit* (1997).

Chris Lewis is a lecturer in the School of History at Liverpool University and editor of the *Victoria County History* of Cheshire.

Jane Martindale taught Medieval History at the University of East Anglia and is a Life Member of Clare Hall, University of Cambridge. She has published articles on many aspects of early medieval French history and a collection of her papers *Status, Authority and Regional Authority: France and Aquitaine (9th to 12th Century)* appeared in 1997.

Janet L. Nelson is Professor of Medieval History at King's College London. She is the author of *Charles the Bald* (1992), and of numerous papers on earlier medieval politics and ritual. She co-edited *The Medieval World* (2001).

Pauline Stafford is Professor of Medieval History at the University of Liverpool. Her publications include *Queens, Concubines and Dowagers* (1984, reprinted 1998), *Unification and Conquest: A Political and Social History of England in the Tenth and Eleventh Centuries* (1989), and *Queen Emma and Queen Edith: Queenship and Women's Power in Eleventh-Century England* (1997).

Pamela Taylor is the author of the Introduction to *Little Domesday Book* (Alecto 2000) and has published papers on the history of the churches of St Albans and St Martin le Grand and St Paul's cathedral in London.

Romila Thapar is Professor Emeritus of History at Jawaharlal Nehru University, New Delhi and is a Corresponding Fellow of the British Academy. Her works include *A History of India*, vol I (1996), *Ancient Indian Social History: Some Interpretations* (1978), *Interpreting Early India* (1993).

Stephen D. White is Professor of Medieval History at Emory University, Georgia. He is the author of *Custom, Kinship and Gifts to Saints* (1988), and of many articles on the legal and cultural history of western Europe in the central Middle Ages.

Charles T. Wood is Professor Emeritus of Medieval History at Dartmouth College. He is the author of *Joan of Arc and Richard III: Sex, Saints and Government in the Middle Ages* (1988). He co-edited *New Verdicts on Joan of Arc* (1996), and has published widely on medieval cultural and political history.

Introduction

Pauline Stafford, Janet L. Nelson and Jane Martindale

This collection of essays is dedicated to Susan Reynolds and celebrates the work of a scholar whose views have been central to recent reappraisals of the position of the laity in the Middle Ages. It is arranged chronologically but is bound together by a series of themes and concerns. Those themes and concerns are hers: a medieval world in which the activity and attitudes of the laity are not obscured by ideas expressed more systematically in theoretical treatises by ecclesiastics; a world in which lay collective action and thought take centre stage. For her this has meant the rejection of over-simplified notions of progress, but above all of teleological explanations of the past which have often led historians to try to fit their findings into a framework of interpretation that was devised in the sixteenth century and elaborated in the seventeenth and eighteenth. So this is a world without 'the image of feudalism' 'composed syncretically to fit a thousand years of the history of all Europe'.[1] Instead she has insisted on a careful reading – indeed often a rigorous rereading – of sources without presuppositions based on anachronistic concepts.

Susan Reynolds has written her own Middle Ages, especially in her innovative book *Kingdoms and Communities* whose influence can be seen in so many of the essays here. It is a world of overlapping communities or, as she would prefer it – eschewing the comfortable and comforting notions of harmony conjured up by that word – of 'collectivities' and 'solidarities'. She has presented us with collective action as a spontaneous, ubiquitous and essential part of secular life. It was characteristic of every level of society and touched every sphere of life, from peasant villages to kingdoms. Such action sometimes occurred in response to the pressures of lordly or kingly power, but was in no sense a simple product of the exercise of superior authority and her version of the dynamic of this activity has frequently gone against the grain of traditional interpretations. As Rees Davies points out here, this has often corrected earlier historiographies, in particular those exclusively concerned with state-building and political unification, which overemphasise vertical authority and royal or seigneurial source material.

---

[1] S. Reynolds, *Fiefs and Vassals* (Oxford, 1994), pp. 2 and 9.

The medieval world of *Kingdoms and Communities* is not dominated by the clergy, nor is it unthinkingly presented as an 'age of faith'. Elsewhere she has drawn attention to the incidence of religious doubt and scepticism among the laity, and she has consistently questioned whether medieval society should be principally viewed through the eyes of the intellectuals – most of whom were clerics – who created the theoretical texts. Instead she has recognised the widely diffused existence of complex thought in medieval society, and emphasised that the ideas and ideals of the laity are not always to be found either in the elaborately developed ideas of clerical intellectuals or in self-conscious pronouncements. They may be better revealed in charters, accounts of lawsuits, and in narrative histories and literature. In other words she has insisted on the need for a detailed reappraisal of documentation and on a readiness to use familiar sources to ask novel questions and with different ends in mind. These convictions have provided powerful stimulus for many of this volume's contributors, as can be seen, for instance, from Pauline Stafford's analysis of late Anglo-Saxon charters, and from Peggy Brown's reappraisals of the records of the French monarchy in the early fourteenth century. Stephen White's discussion of 'fictional' treason trials, too, reveals how early verse romances in French can be used to throw light on secular attitudes towards questions of lay solidarity, fidelity and the law. Paul Brand, by contrast, has used the records of the common law courts of England to illuminate the ideas of 'ordinary' laymen and women towards issues of pressing importance, such as the inheritance of land or the apportioning of dower.

In Susan Reynolds's Middle Ages, thought was no monopoly of the traditionally educated clergy. All thought, all thought rationally and all thought in a sophisticated way. That conclusion calls into question the notion of progress which still underpins much historical research and writing. As Michael Clanchy suggests here, the prevalent model of progress envisages transitions and temporal developments as proceeding from barbaric or savage to civilised or (implicitly) modern, implying a clear dichotomy between irrationality and rationality, orality and literacy. This is a 'top-down model of cultural diffusion'. First those at the top begin to think in a complex way; then those modes of thought are transmitted, in a simplified way, to others lower down. This grand narrative of progress stems largely from the Enlightenment, and perhaps also more insidiously from the optimistic views of the nineteenth century; but it is also based on terms whose loaded meanings have been questioned by Susan Reynolds – 'irrational', 'primitive', 'rational'. While others were whoring after the false gods of medieval difference, she has constantly maintained that medieval people are like us in essential ways – and especially in their capacity for intelligent and thoughtful management of law and government. Along with many other historians and anthropologists concerned with such issues, Susan rejects the idea of the primitive and with it especially the condescending view of the medieval laity. Again as Clanchy puts it, she has cut to the heart of this notion of difference by distinguishing a Middle Ages which is strange, in the sense of unfamiliar, from one which is strange in the sense of irrational or pre-rational. The latter should be rejected, the former

Introduction

accepted as an inevitable consequence of the distance between the historian and the past.

In her challenge to these views Susan Reynolds's work has mounted a coherent set of attacks along a broad front. She has shown an unremitting determination to distinguish between words and things, to revisit key sources and terms and to tackle misconceptions. She has subjected to critical examination the conceptual frameworks and terminology we apply to the past, urged us to unpick myths, for instance of race and nation, and to resist teleology. Her work has been remarkable for its breadth, ranging from Italy to England – correcting, as Rees Davies points out, a view both of English exceptionalism and of paradigms which are largely a result of French historiography, even of a handful of great and influential studies of French regions, and the notion of a 'feudal society' substantiated largely by French historical sources. France supplied historians with the chronological narrative of a progressive privatisation of power during the early Middle Ages (at any rate in the post-Carolingian world), and the concept of 'feudalism' reinforced the preoccupation with hierarchical structures and with vertical rather than horizontal bonds. Such versions of medieval development have tended to marginalise or even ignore areas – like most of western Britain – which the models do not fit. Some contributors have confronted these problems head on, like Rees Davies with his 'western British but mainly Welsh . . . additamentum to Susan Reynolds's great book' and Paul Fouracre's exposé of how mistaken was the old conclusion that Charles Martel's 'response to the repression he faced . . . was "feudal" reorganisation', and the seizure of the lands of the Frankish church. Other contributors have approached these topics more obliquely as Janet Nelson has done with her revelations of the importance of horizontal bonds of parity in the ninth century, or John Gillingham with his development of the view that 'an equality of oppression' apparently united many of the ethnically distinct peoples within the English kingdom in the twelfth and early thirteenth centuries, and so helped produce that 'regnal solidarity' of which Susan Reynolds has written.

Collectivities, solidarities and collective action are everywhere in these essays, as Susan Reynolds has shown us to expect them to be. They can be traced in the false monasteries of seventh-century Galicia (Nelson), and they are expressed in pilgrimage and crusade (Wood). They existed in medieval Wales and western Britain (Davies); in tenth-century England and early fourteenth-century France (Stafford, Brown); even in authoritarian, centralising common law England, where they recalled and defined local custom (Brand). They formed horizontal bonds which crossed the hierarchical divides of medieval society: of lord and peasant in Gillingham's regnal solidarity against oppression; of cleric and lay, who met together to counsel and debate within a common culture (Brown, Stafford); of the men of lords in the courtrooms of White's romances – where the vertical tie of lord and man itself produced a horizontal collectivity, a community of judgement among peers. Indeed judgement, peers and collective action appear as intimately linked. Davies points to the community of judgement of the 'good men' who carried local knowledge, who knew how a local society worked, and how judgement had to be given in order to ensure its continued working. For Nelson, the very notion of peers and parity is tied up with association from the ninth century if not before. Jane Martindale, too, brings out the importance of parity for laymen expecting to be challenged to fight duels in the courts of the Angevin kings of England. However, Davies provides the most comprehensive account of collective action. He is aware, as we all must be, of its structural place in society, but also of its varieties and ad hoc quality. His were communities of culture and entertainment, of shared memory – and of competing memories – as well as of agricultural cooperation and dispute resolution. A society where kinship was strong, and defined identity as well as sometimes action, nonetheless needed and produced wider groupings. These were necessary to resolve issues among neighbours which kinship and lordship could not, those too which kinship and lordship might produce. David d'Avray takes that insight into the unlikely world of high medieval papal thinking about incest regulations. Wider collectivities were a positive desideratum to break down the tight cohesion of the clan divisions of medieval Italy.

Association was everywhere, but not necessarily always easy and not necessarily always a sign of harmony. Collective action was carried out often in pursuit of social peace, but it existed precisely because there was discord. Nor should we be carried away by ideas of collective *bonhomie*. Vertical differences remained. Drink dissolved them in Nelson's Francia, lubricating and easing a recognition of parity, but Nelson's essay also warns us that association, solidarity and collective action could be threatening. Military action produces a sense of collectivity, and bands of armed men and criminal gangs have to be included as forms of collective action. As Davies makes clear, authoritarian governments were not sympathetic to collectivities, and nor were many modern historians to what they saw as medieval localism and disorder: witness the evident preference for the smack of firm government evinced alike by the hard-headed, institutional, legalistic, authoritarian, centralising Anglo-Norman and later medieval English kingdoms and the historiographical traditions which have mapped them. Attempts to enforce sobriety in the ninth century as in the nineteenth were aimed at collective action as well as individual morality. Davies's communities of entertainment in medieval Wales may not always have been as dry as some of their modern Welsh successors. If governments mistrusted association, whether in medieval Wales or in late eighth- and ninth-century Francia, they may often have had good reason.

What is clear is that collective action and community were neither primarily nor necessarily responses to lordship and government. They were part of the functioning of lay – and of lay/clerical – society, and not only at times of crisis. They were part and parcel of everyday needs. In ninth-century Francia they provided mutual aid and security, against fire or shipwreck, which no government could hope to give its subjects. Government, however, could itself make use of the strong tendency to associate. In Ottonian Germany and Alfredian England fortifications were built on the strength of it; in early tenth-century England beer-drinking associations helped keep King Athelstan's peace. Strong centralising government and local association could coexist, although Martindale's Poitevin barons who refused to fight men who were not their peers were using their social and political solidarity to rebuff the pretensions of King John. Brand's Kentish knights, remembering Kentish custom, were only the most obvious groups of men making collective claims and showing a strong collective will in the face of the centralising English common law. Their claims were formalised in a charter of liberties, as were such claims against the English government in late medieval Wales. One might question how different Kentish knights and Welsh 'good men' (*boni homines*) were in their fundamental assumptions about law and government. Davies, on the other hand, sees the Welsh charters emerging out of traditions of collective action unlike those in England, and he evokes a communal movement sweeping much of Europe in the Middle Ages to which England seems the significant exception. Yet Susan Reynolds's own work has suggested that the shire and urban customs of Domesday Book already show signs of collective activity in face of strong royal power in eleventh-century England. England certainly had its medieval solidarities. She has recognised many different forms of collectivity, including what Rees Davies finds the 'very serviceable notion' of regnal solidarity, expressed, for example, in Magna Carta. The notion of regnal solidarity raises its own questions about identity, and especially about national identity, which have exercised Davies and Gillingham in other contexts. Gillingham returns to the issue here. He explores a particular instance of the notion of Englishness in the early thirteenth century, aligning Gerald de Barri with the barons of Magna Carta in his awareness of a wider solidarity cutting across vertical hierarchies to unite in a sense of regnal identity – and producing an early version of the idea of the 'Norman Yoke'. There was much interest in 'Englishness' after the Norman Conquest of 1066, present in the primary sources but brought out especially in Gillingham's recent work. Here especially he makes clear how far these questions of national identity may be inseparable from a sense of regnal community, united by a sense of common oppression.

Of the narratives and interpretative frameworks with which Reynolds's work has been concerned, this collection has least to say directly on the debate over feudalism. This is perhaps because the full impact of her book *Fiefs and Vassals* is only beginning to be felt; *Kingdoms and Communities* on the other hand has now been influential for a considerable time. Paul Fouracre addresses the questions raised by *Fiefs and Vassals* most explicitly. By writing about Charles Martel he engages with a period seen as formative in the story of classic feudalism. For a reorganisation of landholding driven by feudal arrangements, he substitutes another shift, equally fundamental and critical, and couples it with the process of acculturation which we now recognise as the conversion of Western Europe to Christianity. Charles Martel was not an author of these historical changes but an actor strengthened and threatened by them. In Fouracre's rereading, Charles Martel loses his role in making feudalism the basis of landholding. His myth is unpicked. Removing the feudal blinkers also allows White to see the full complexity of treason and its definition, a cluster of problems in which loyalty was perceived as central and where feudal contracts appear irrelevant. Other narratives, old and more recent, are challenged here. The hypothesis that medieval society witnessed a transition from kinship to lordship is specifically questioned by White for twelfth-century France, and implicitly by Davies for the entire history of medieval Wales. The last century of Anglo-Saxon England, which saw the emergence of the authoritarian English state, ended in a decade in which political debate was still dominated by kinship's values (Stafford). The inexorable trend towards laicisation and the secular state, a theme beloved of some later medievalists, is shown to be of limited utility in understanding the critical period of the reign of Philip the Fair (Brown). A twelfth century which allegedly saw a shift to concern with intention and a growing legal ambiguity will not survive scrutiny of the *Roman de Thèbes* and the *Chanson de Roland*. Both texts reveal these attitudes, and discuss them in pressing detail, in the first half of the century (White).

The narrative of change from irrationality to rationality, from primitive to complex and sophisticated, is one with which many of the essays here take issue. Clanchy raises important questions about the growing use of writing. What part does writing play in rationality? Is the development and diffusion of written forms a straightforward story of progress, or have we been so mesmerised by literacy that we have devalued the symbolic and the ritual as methods of communication in some ways more sophisticated than the written word? Did literacy and writing denote progress, or do they merely allow us to see a complexity which orality was already able to accommodate and address in social practice? Wood throws sidelights on this question as he reflects on the capacity of relics as symbols to substitute for words, and to express the duality of earth and heaven, holding together a doubled meaning in which the physical object can still evoke laughter whilst its supernatural significance remains untouched. Clanchy explicitly invites us to rethink or at least re-examine our categories, specifically the rational/irrational distinction. Both Martindale and White approach the dilemma less directly, but show how difficult it is to solve since, despite frequent criticism of ordeals as 'irrational' and offensive methods of reaching legal judgement, the judicial duel survived; and was regarded by many laymen as an honourable means of establishing justice, embedded still in perfectly rational legal mentalities. Equally, symbol and ritual, with their enactment and use of body language, can convey much more than the written word, which itself may be the simplifier. 'Primitive mind-sets', like 'the medieval mind', must be expunged from historians' vocabulary. Instead they must address not only the issues Clanchy raises, but also sharpen their analytical tools, as David d'Avray does. He refers us to Weber for aid in thinking about the great postmodernist question of relativism, and its challenge to historians to identify the differentness of the past, the historicity of rationality itself, the problem of whether rationality is culturally specific. By following Weber in distinguishing instrumental rationality (ends/means) and value rationality, d'Avray presents the first as universal, and the second as culturally specific, in all cultures setting the framework of instrumental rationality, defining objectives, setting 'no-go areas', affecting 'common-sense reasoning'. This allows not merely a subtle reading of papal intentions in rules on incest, but offers insight into, even if it leaves unresolved, the deeper philosophical question of whether some values themselves are universal. Rationality is not simple – nor are signs of it as obvious as was once thought.

If there is no straightforward story of progress from irrationality to rationality, nor is there one of naïve to sophisticated. Lay thought, always present, was always complex. It had its quandaries and dilemmas. Davies's local judges used local knowledge to ensure that legal judgement could be made in such a way as to ensure the continued working of local society. In White's detailed literary accounts of court cases, nobles argue through the sorts of dilemmas which Stafford's English charters of the 990s suggest must have faced their earlier counterparts in Æthelred's reign. What type of conduct defined good and bad lordship or kingship, how should good counsel be distinguished from bad? In no case were the questions and issues which faced the lay nobility simple ones; in no case could they have been resolved without sophisticated distinctions and elaborate thought. As Susan Reynolds would delight to point out, norms and values conflicted as much as they reinforced each other. For White there are at least two discourses in play in these texts: the legal one of classifying conduct, and the fluid one of negotiating the boundaries between honour and shame. It is, to be sure, a non-professional legal thought which we see grappling with these problems, but it is certainly not simple or unsophisticated.

We see White's cases presented from the perspective of the participating nobles, 990s England from that of legitimising, royal documentation. In both, new questions, here concerning lay thought and ideology, are asked of well-known sources. White's reading here follows other important work in this area, not least his own. It is part of a significant trend to reread these literary sources for lay ideas and practice. Similarly the rich early sources from western Britain, most notably the legal and literary ones, provide a very different picture of Welsh society from the world dominated by lordship which readily emerges from documents of English administration (Davies). Yet, as Stafford's essay suggests, even royal documentation can be reread for evidence of common ideas and shared ideals, as Nelson's does, and Gillingham's.

The narratives of the Middle Ages have to some extent been shaped teleologically: at their most extreme by a caricature of medieval people trying to be us. There is still something to be said for the notion that medieval people were different, because that difference allows them to be themselves. The past is to be respected on its own terms. There is, by contrast, no defence of teleology, which Fouracre and Brown rightly resist. Thus Fouracre rereads Charles Martel as his career unfolded in the early eighth century not as he was rewritten first by his Carolingian descendants, then by later generations of nationalists and latterly by historians of feudalism. Charles responded to his own present; he was not planning an unknowable future. Brown makes clear how modern states and their self-image as secular and rational have shaped the narrative of a past which leads inexorably towards the nineteenth- or twentieth-century present, and in which points are awarded to those historical actors who appear to advance that process most. Yet Philip the Fair and his contemporaries can only be understood on and in their own terms. They were not creating the modern secular state: they were living in a medieval kingdom, which drew no sharp distinctions between lay and cleric. Importing such a distinction into interpretation of that world can be seriously distorting. We might, for instance, misjudge as mere evidence of increasing secular rationality the preservation of records, although Clanchy suggests that this may owe at least something to the prevalent idea of the Last Judgement. A number of essays here warn against this over-sharp clerical/lay distinction. Romila Thapar warns that in 'medieval' India something like it may have existed but that it was not necessarily drawn in the same way, or as sharply (or even at all?) in the different religious traditions of the sub-continent. She explores how and whether that distinction is drawn, but in specific circumstances which illuminate other questions of social stratification. And she reminds us that relations between lay people and religious shrines and institutions produced their own sorts of community, and potentially far-reaching ones. The parallels with and differences from medieval cultic communities are striking. Her essay provides a comparative perspective which will provoke European medievalists to reconsider the implications of gift-giving to churches. How far should we follow Susan Reynolds in her view of the age of faith as yet another myth? Were there such oppositions as sacred/secular; this worldly/next worldly? Ordained/unordained was certainly a recognised medieval distinction, but, as Peggy Brown stresses, the line was blurred. Cleric and lay worked together in early fourteenth-century France. They occupied the same thought world in late tenth-century England. As Susan Reynolds herself has pointed out, the clergy were born lay and retained lay links.

'We cannot amputate lay consciousness from the influence of the church.' D'Avray reminds us of this in his discussion of the importance of the church's kinship system for all medieval people. Kinship has not been as central to Susan Reynolds's rethinking of the Middle Ages as it has proved to be in some other recent rereadings of the period. But kinship lay at the heart of secular life, and of the laity's thought and preoccupations, whether in later tenth-century England or in twelfth-century romances. It comes as no surprise that issues of inheritance and dower were among the customs which thirteenth-century English shires struggled to preserve. Although kinship did not start out as an explicit and overt theme of this volume, it emerges as a leitmotiv, perhaps in part because when feudalism is removed, kinship is thrown into sharper relief. Brigitte Kasten makes it her central concern as she probes the stereotype of the stepmother in legal theory and Frankish family practice. Once again it is Rees Davies who has taken up the central challenge of showing how kinship, collectivities and lordship interacted together; and just as he makes us aware of both the inevitability and the often improvised quality of collective action, so too he highlights not only the centrality of kinship, but also its inadequacies. Kinship was a source of identity as much as of action. Crucial as it was, it was unable to provide an all-purpose social bond to the exclusion of all others, and it left a need for collective action to deal with issues beyond its scope. There was only one universal kinship system in the Middle Ages: that provided by the church and its rulings. The anthropologist, Jack Goody, has produced one of the few attempts to explain that system. David d'Avray, whilst recognising the importance of Goody's work, offers alternative explanations of the system and its motivation, and especially of the incest taboos which formed a central part of it.

He argues that the system was rational, conceived in a context both Christian and Italian. A major aim was the encouragement through exogamy of wider collectivities and solidarities, and the social peace they brought, which kinship, especially in its Italian clan form, could threaten. He offers an explanation which works, at least for the high and later Middle Ages. Fouracre is concerned with kinship as essential to any understanding of medieval high politics. His essay, like Stafford's, underscores the recent recognition that the working of medieval politics cannot be understood without reinstating the family at its heart.

These essays engage with many of the themes of Susan Reynolds's work, but also pursue some of the issues which are currently prominent in re-examinations of the medieval world, and particularly in studies of the medieval laity. Their breadth of coverage, chronologically from early Carolingian dynastic politics to the decline of medieval pilgrimage in the sixteenth century, reflects something of the scope of her own interests, but scarcely matches her own mastery of European-wide sources and the interpretations placed on them. The topics included are inevitably determined to some extent by the interests and expertise of individual contributors. There are some regrettable omissions: Germany is scarcely represented here, as is Italy; the Iberian peninsula, as in so much medieval scholarship, is almost totally ignored. There is no coverage of Eastern Europe, nor Byzantium. Scandinavia and Iceland are a particular loss. Always identified as amongst the most 'Teutonic' of European societies, they provide interesting points of comparison with Rees Davies's 'Celtic' Britain. Iceland, at least, was another society where kin and neighbour were more important than lord and king.

If there are geographical omissions, as well as strengths, there are also thematic ones. It is noticeable that Susan Reynolds's own contribution to urban and civic history is reflected in one essay only, that of Caroline Barron. However, since that is devoted to the solidarities established in a London ward, it is directly concerned with the theme of collective action. The peasantry too – an essential part of Susan's analysis of collectivities – appears only incidentally as part of larger unities (Nelson, Davies). In one respect this volume does reflect the range of Susan Reynolds's work fairly accurately. It is lay *men* rather than the laity (in a gender-inclusive sense) whose norms, values and actions are considered here, as they were in *Kingdoms and Communities*. It might, of course, be argued that any collection which centres on collectivities and solidarities would almost exclude women by definition, so that, despite the bulk of recent work on medieval women, their absence would not be surprising. Nelson highlights this omission. Her own study suggests that, although a Carolingian bishop might assert that women should be their husbands' peers, this egalitarian pronouncement seems to have had no practical consequences in the spheres of public life, where peers remained firmly male.

Nelson argues that women were not involved in much collective action. It constituted one of the medieval public spheres, from which women were excluded. It would thus be no accident that they crop up in essays largely involved with family and kinship, with family and politics, as for instance in Fouracre's account of Pippinid family politics, in Brigitte Kasten's essay on stepmothers, and in Stafford's analysis of English politics in the 990s. In the cases of Fouracre and Stafford, women appear in the context of power relations where it was 'impossible to separate family affairs and politics'. In the early Middle Ages, perhaps less so later, power was channelled through families not institutions; it is women's household and familial activities and power which Kasten sees as focusing fear on the evil stepmother rather than her male equivalent. The inseparability of family and politics gives cause for hesitation before accepting the generalisation that women were automatically excluded from collectivity and solidarity as a medieval public sphere. The public and the private were drawn differently then. Interesting women speak out in Stephen White's romances. Although his extensive analysis of the trial of Daire le Roux shows that *Le Roman de Thèbes* was shot through with the values of lordly and kingly (public?) power and authority, its narrative allots important parts to women who give counsel on issues of law and justice as well as on marriage alliances. They might be seen as arguing the values of family as opposed to lordship: they counsel the defence of children or propose marriage as a solution to political problems. But does this indicate separate spheres of family and lordship or, more subtly, conflicting lay values, the different aspects of noble honour, expressed by women? The fact that women are portrayed as expressing opinions on these issues in public, in court, in the king's camp, as well as in the home, may be a warning to historians. Romila Thapar's Buddhist donors included many women. Her essay raises questions about how far one strong sense of difference, cleric/lay, may interact with another, male/female. And since here donors became part of a collectivity centred around the shrine itself, she forces us to think again about women's involvement in such groups in a European context. Perhaps we should question and probe rather than simply accept women's exclusion from the medieval collective, and certainly we should rethink the laity from a gendered perspective. Those would be themes for another collection of essays! And in raising such unsettling questions we would follow, yet again, Susan's example – not here asking her questions, but emulating her courage in a readiness to pose them.

This particular collection, we hope, has themes enough and offers its readers rich possibilities, which do show the depth of Susan Reynolds's influence on its contributors. The broader themes which link them have already been discussed, and other issues emerge with a surprising clarity to throw further light on Susan's studies of 'Lay Collective Activity in Western Europe'. The law as practised and presented in the twelfth century, for instance, seems infinitely more flexible than it is often portrayed as being, as emerges from White's literary treason trials and Martindale's judicial duels. Clanchy too reveals how older practices could survive alongside the newer procedures established in the wake of English legal so-called 'reforms'. The human body appears as a striking metaphor for early fourteenth-century collectivities in the French kingdom (Brown), but also for change and development in the troubled England of the late tenth century (Stafford). Its language was an essential, if now too often lost or ignored, part of communication (Nelson). The notion of 'patria' recurs again and again: in tenth-century England (Stafford) as in the later English common law texts (Brand): it was the task of

Charlemagne's peasant warriors to defend their 'patria' (Nelson), and 'patria' was a powerful image in medieval Wales (Davies). Interestingly medieval England can also be viewed in wider perspective. By exploring the impact of 1066 and the Norman Conquest in a setting which includes both the western and cross-channel neighbours of the English kingdom, both Rees Davies and John Gillingham have shown how much the changes in the Anglo-Norman and Angevin world contributed to the formation of English identity and the political and social evolution of the British Isles. It would, however, be presumptuous to give too much advice on how to read these essays, and, in the polysemic world of postmodern discourse, futile.

This collection is a tribute to the distinction and inspiration of Susan Reynolds's work. Its authors have learnt from her in many contexts: as her pupil, colleagues – on both sides of the Atlantic and as far afield as India – and as co-seminarists at the Wednesday seminar at the Institute of Historical Research. All of them have benefited from stimulating conversations with her – productive of their own medieval solidarities – and from the counsel and aid with which she is so generous. We hope that as a collection, these essays have taken further some of the insights and questions raised by Susan Reynolds's own work. It is central to the current study of the Middle Ages and, we confidently affirm, will have an enduring impact on the study of medieval history in the twenty-first century.

Writing about Charles Martel

Paul Fouracre

In the night of Saturday, 20 July 1991, a group of far-right extremists calling themselves variously the 'groupe', 'club' or 'commando Charles Martel' firebombed an Algerian social club in the drab Paris suburb of Bondy. The attack was, it seems, the last of several similar outrages that this nasty little group perpetrated in Marseilles and Paris between 1973 and 1991.[1] In each case the intended victims were people of North African origins. It is to be assumed that the group called themselves after Charles Martel because this early medieval figure, who died in 741, is famous in the popular imagination as the leader who saved France from conquest by the Arabs. In 732, or 733, somewhere between Tours and Poitiers, Charles Martel defeated a Muslim force from Spain. In medieval tradition, this would be remembered as a crushing victory, in which three hundred and seventy-five thousand Arabs were killed, and which, in the words of Bede (Martel's almost exact contemporary), turned the tide of war against 'the dreadful plague of Saracens'.[2]

What, one wonders, did the 'groupe' really know about Charles Martel, apart from the fact that he was the victor of the battle of Tours/Poitiers? Did they know, for instance, that his tomb lies less than ten kilometres from Bondy, in the abbey of St Denis? They may not, however, have been aware of the tradition which portrayed their hero as an enemy of the church, and of the legend that maintained that his tomb in St Denis was empty. For when it was inspected, all that could be seen were the scorch marks of the dragon which had dragged Charles Martel off to hell.[3] What he had done wrong in the eyes of the church was to take its land for his own

---

[1] *Le Monde*, 23 July 1991.

[2] *Bede's Ecclesiastical History of the English People*, ed. and trans. B. Colgrave and R. Mynors (Oxford, 1968), V, ch. 23, pp. 556–7. On Charles Martel in later medieval tradition, U. Nonn, 'Das Bild Karl Martells in mittelalterlichen Quellen', in J. Jarnut, U. Nonn and M. Richter (eds), *Karl Martell in seiner Zeit*, Beihefte der *Francia*, 37 (Sigmaringen, 1994), pp. 9–21.

[3] The legend has its origins in a vision attributed to Eucherius, bishop of Orléans, who was one of Charles Martel's victims. The vision of the empty tomb was first reported in the *Vita Rigoberti*, ed. W. Levison, *Monumenta Germaniae Historica, Scriptores Rerum Merovingicarum* VII (Hanover and Leipzig, 1920), pp. 58–80, ch. 13, p. 70. It seems almost certain that it was the author of this late ninth-century work, Hincmar archbishop of Rheims, who composed the account of Eucherius's vision.

use. Charles Martel thus emerges as a historical figure with contrasting reputations, as both hero and villain. The time in which he lived (c.688–741) is also seen as a crucial period of development in Western Europe, with changes in social, political and economic organisation being brought about by Charles Martel himself. This last view was developed by the great German legal historian Heinrich Brunner, and it was a brilliant resolution of the hero/villain contradiction. Charles Martel, argued Brunner in 1887, took land from the church in order to provide for his army. That army, now largely a cavalry force, then had the resources to beat the Arabs. In the process of taking land and leasing it out again in return for military service, performed by mounted warriors, 'feudalism' was born, and 'feudalism' would transform European society.[4] Historians have seen the period as a watershed in other ways too. It was the period in which much of Germany was converted to Christianity and brought within the fold of mainstream European culture. And it was, of course, Charles Martel who laid the foundations for the rule of the dynasty which bears his name, the Carolingians. It was supposedly under the Carolingians that Europe would be defined as a single cultural space in terms of its religion, language and political geography. Charlemagne, the most impressive of these rulers, would in his own lifetime actually be referred to as the 'father of Europe'.

The task in writing about Charles Martel is to set the record straight.[5] It is thus necessary to unpick both sides of his reputation and to confront the massive implications of the Brunner thesis, which means examining very carefully the grounds on which this period is seen as a watershed. On all three counts, the work of Susan Reynolds can never be far from mind. Susan Reynolds demands that we take misconceptions seriously for the damage they can do. Her most recent thinking comprehends the horrific consequences of letting myths about nation and race go unchallenged.[6] The murderous activities of the 'groupe Charles Martel' are a chilling reminder of those consequences. Susan Reynolds has, of course, much to say about 'feudalism'. Where Charles Martel is concerned, her work is the spur to revisit even the most familiar sources to check the terminology of landholding, lordship and clientage to see whether early medieval authors used the words and terms associated with 'feudalism', which modern historians read into them. And she is very nearly always right: only very rarely is any so-called 'feudal' terminology to

---

[4] The seminal article is H. Brunner, 'Der Reiterdienst und die Anfänge des Lehnwesens', *Zeitschrift der Savigny-Stiftung für Rechtsgeschichte, Germanistische Abteilung*, 8 (1887), 1–38.

[5] Although there has been much work on the different aspects of this subject in recent years, as demonstrated by the generally excellent essays in the collection *Karl Martell in seiner Zeit*, no attempt has been made to pull these studies together into a coherent account. J. Deviosse, *Charles Martel* (Paris, 1978) did treat the whole subject, but his is hardly a scholarly work for it actually feeds on some of the myths one might have hoped to see exploded. P. Fouracre, *The Age of Charles Martel* (London, 2000) represents a fresh attempt to discuss the career of Charles Martel in the light of recent scholarship. The present essay reflects on the some of the issues raised in the writing of this book, and as they relate to Susan Reynolds's work.

[6] See, for example, S. Reynolds, 'Our Forefathers? Tribes, Peoples, and Nations in the Historiography of the Age of Migrations', in A. C. Murray (ed.), *After Rome's Fall. Narrators and Sources of Early Medieval History* (Toronto, 1998), pp. 17–36.

be found in eighth-century sources, that is to say, in the period in which in which 'feudalism' was supposedly born.[7] As for the watershed, and the pivotal role of the new dynasty, she teaches us to resist teleology, and calls for each moment to be properly understood in its own terms. In all of these areas of study there have, of course, been great advances since Brunner's day, but Susan Reynolds's message is that misconceptions remain potent even when the premises upon which they rest have been formally refuted. What follows aims to point to areas in which our understanding of the career of Charles Martel has changed significantly, that is, to draw attention to the recent refutation of old views and misunderstandings. I shall then go on to ask whether such rethinking can bring us any closer to understanding the figure and career of Charles Martel himself. For how can we approach the biography of a figure whose personality is the product of myth and imagination? How do we determine the significance of a career when the identification of widespread social and political change with a single person now seems to us inadmissible, and when it would seem at best naïve to explain history simply in terms of decisive events and the deeds of heroic leaders?

Remarkably little was written about Charles Martel in his own lifetime. The most valuable references, not more than a few passages, come from the Neustrian chronicle the *Liber Historiae Francorum*, and they are valuable because this work was complete by the year 727, and thus not subject to the hindsight which so dominates Carolingian writing.[8] Only six charters issued on behalf of Charles survive, and of these five come from the years 718–23.[9] There are in addition two papal letters written to Charles, and a handful of references to him in the correspondence of the English missionary Boniface.[10] The bulk of our information on his career comes from the *Continuations of the Chronicle of Fredegar*, the relevant section of this work being written up probably in 751.[11] As Roger Collins has recently demonstrated, the *Continuations*, the first section of which was commissioned by Charles Martel's half-brother Childebrand, are fiercely partisan in their interpretation of events.[12]

---

[7] S. Reynolds, *Fiefs and Vassals. The Medieval Evidence Reinterpreted* (Oxford, 1994). Chapter 4 ('Gaul and the Kingdom of the Franks') deals with the material discussed here.

[8] *Liber Historiae Francorum*, ed. B. Krusch, *Monumenta Germaniae Historica, Scriptores Rerum Merovingicarum* II (Hanover, 1888), pp. 241–328, chs 43–53, trans. with commentary P. Fouracre and R. Gerberding, *Late Merovingian France. History and Hagiography 640–720* (Manchester, 1996), pp. 79–96.

[9] The essential guide to the charters issued by Charles Martel and his family is I. Heidrich, 'Titular und Urkunden der arnulfingischen Hausmeier', *Archiv für Diplomatik*, 11/12 (1965–6), 17–279.

[10] Two letters from Pope Gergory III to Charles Martel, sent in 739 and 740 begged for his help against the Lombards. They form the first two letters of the *Codex Carolinus* drawn up at Charlemagne's request in 791, *Codex Carolinus*, ed. W. Grundlach, *Monumenta Germaniae Historica, Epistolae* III (Berlin, 1882), pp. 476–653, nos 1–2, pp. 476–9. Two letters in the Boniface correspondence, both from the year 724, are of direct relevance to Charles Martel: *Sancti Bonifatii et Lulli Epistolae*, ed. M. Tangl, *Monumenta Germaniae Historica, Epistolae Selectae* I (Berlin, 1955), nos 22, 24.

[11] *The Fourth Book of the Chronicle of Fredegar with its Continuations*, ed. and trans. M. Wallace-Hadrill (London, 1960).

[12] R. Collins, 'Deception and Misrepresentation in Early Eighth-Century Frankish Historiography. Two Case Studies', in *Karl Martell in seiner Zeit*, pp. 227–47.

The account in the *Continuations* in effect does two things. First, it denigrates all of Charles Martel's opponents, leaving them looking weak and foolish. The narrative of events leading up to the battle of Poitiers provides the clearest example of distortion in this way.[13] Second, the account plays down the opposition Charles faced within his own family, thus giving us the impression that this family was the very base of his power. This viewpoint was set out in a much more articulate and cogent manner in the *Earlier Annals of Metz*, a work composed in 805 by someone with close links to Charlemagne's court, which explained the family's history in the light of their recent triumphs and which carefully justified their rise to power.[14] Like Einhard in his *Life of Charlemagne*, the author of the *Earlier Annals of Metz* set the family's ascent to the Frankish throne in the context of a failing Merovingian kingship, which was effectively defunct by the time the Merovingians were ousted by the Carolingians in 751. As reported by the *Continuations of Fredegar*, it was the pope who advised Charles Martel's son Pippin to take the throne for himself. Later, in the *Royal Frankish Annals*, it would be spelled out that the pope thought that it was morally right that there should be a change of dynasty, for strong kings would better protect the Christian people than puppets, however venerable.[15] The picture of the family sticking together, doing its duty by fighting off dangerously foolish opponents and finally taking royal power to honour its moral obligations, is persuasive but fundamentally misleading. Matthias Becher has shown that the Carolingian family was anything but united before the year 754. Charles Martel had fought to make himself head of the family, and this meant killing some of its members. According to Becher, who sets contemporary charter and letter evidence against later Carolingian narratives, Pippin's seizure of the throne in 751 was the culmination of a similar campaign to exclude other members of his family from power, and this involved imprisoning nephews, hounding one brother to death, and keeping another under arrest until he died.[16]

Under Pippin's son Charlemagne (768–814) the Carolingian regime massively strengthened its authority. It conquered the pagan Saxons and Avars, and presented itself as the leading Christian power. Charlemagne's court circle articulated a programme of moral reform and religious correction. Charlemagne, having taken over the Lombard kingdom in northern Italy, built upon his close personal ties with successive popes to become the papacy's protector. He was, of course, crowned emperor in Rome in 800. It was this triumphal background that the *Earlier Annals*

---

[13] Collins, 'Deception', pp. 235–41.

[14] *Annales Mettenses Priores*, ed. B. von Simson, *Monumenta Germaniae Historica, Scriptores Rerum Germanicum in usu scholarum separatim editi* (Hanover and Leipzig, 1905), section 688–725, trans. with commentary Fouracre and Gerberding, pp. 350–70. On the depiction of Charles Martel's family in this work, I Haselbach, 'Aufstieg und Herrschaft der Karolinger in der Darstellung des sogennanten *Annales Mettenses Priores*', *Historische Studien*, 406 (1970), 1–208.

[15] *Continuations of Fredegar*, ch. 33, p. 102. *Royal Frankish Annals*, trans. B. Sholz, *Carolingian Chronicles* (Ann Arbor, 1972), s.a. 749, p. 39.

[16] M. Becher, 'Drogo und die Königserhebung Pippins', *Frühmittelalterliche Studien*, 23 (1989), 131–53, and idem, 'Neue Überlieferungen zum Geburtsdatum Karls des Grossen', *Francia*, 19 (1992), 37–60.

of Metz reflected. By now the Carolingians had thoroughly crushed all their enemies and there was virtually no writing in opposition to them. But in the generations after Charlemagne some elements in the church were clearly becoming restive, for the rulers, including Charlemagne, had put pressure on church resources. Some abbacies and bishoprics had been used as political rewards. The lay abbot became a familiar figure. The need to provide troops for Carolingian armies had impoverished some churches, and others had been forced to accept unwelcome tenants on their estates. Quite apart from these losses, churches in general seem to have had trouble in keeping control of their estates and there was general complaint that land had been 'lost' to laymen. After the middle of the ninth century, such losses would increasingly be blamed on Charles Martel. How he came to be so blamed seems clear.

It was Hincmar, the highly influential archbishop of Rheims (845–82), who stated that 'of all the princes of the Franks' Charles Martel 'was the first to take property away from the church and to divide it up'. This claim Hincmar made in a letter sent in 858 from the Synod of Quierzy to the kings Louis the German and Charles the Bald, and his aim was to encourage these rulers to help him recover church lands.[17] Hincmar seems to have picked on Charles Martel because it was said in the *Life of St Eucherius*, composed *c*.738, that Charles had exiled Eucherius bishop of Orléans along with his kindred and had taken their lands and positions (*honores*) to give out to his own followers.[18] Hincmar then quoted a vision, the one we have already met, in which Eucherius saw that Charles's tomb in St Denis was empty, Charles having been dragged off to hell for his depredations. It is highly probable that Hincmar himself was the author of this vision text. There was a further connection here with the church of Rheims itself. In the time of Charles Martel, Rheims had been held by one of his chief supporters, Bishop Milo, who was castigated as a typically bad bishop by the missionary Boniface.[19] What Boniface meant by 'Milo and men like him' was bishops who were warlike, adulterous and prone to help themselves to church property. Hincmar thus saw in Milo the author of the losses suffered by Rheims. But there was another good reason for using Charles Martel as a stick with which to beat his descendants. He was one of the few Carolingians who had already been the target of hostile writing. The *Life of Eucherius* was the last in a long line of saints' lives which criticised rulers and claimed sanctity for their opponents or victims. In other words, Hincmar had to go back to the time of Charles Martel in order to find material which portrayed a Carolingian as unjust. It

[17] Hincmar, *Epistola Synodali Carisiacensis ad Hludowicum Regem Directa*, ed. A. Boretius and V. Krause, *Monumenta Germaniae Historica, Capitularia* II (Hanover, 1897), pp. 427–41, at p. 432.

[18] *Vita Eucherii*, ed. W. Levison, *Monumenta Germaniae Historica, Scriptores Rerum Merovingicarum* VII, pp. 46–53, ch. 7, p. 49.

[19] *Bonifatii Epistolae*, no. 87, a letter from Pope Zacharias to Boniface which referred to the missionary's complaints about Milo. The seminal essay on the letter and on the background to Boniface's grievances is E. Ewig, 'Milo et eiusmodi similes', in *Sankt Bonifatius Gedenkengabe zum zwölfhundersten Todestag* (Fulda, 1954), pp. 412–40, reprinted in E. Ewig, *Spätantikes und Fränkisches Gallien*, Beihefte der *Francia*, 3, pt 2 (Zurich and Munich, 1979), pp. 189–219. For the view that Boniface really did see Charles Martel as a 'seculariser' of the church, T. Reuter, ' "Kirchenreform" und "Kirchenpolitik" im Zeitalter Karl Martells. Begriffe und Wirklichkeit', in *Karl Martell in seiner Zeit*, pp. 35–59.

was also helpful to Hincmar's representation that while Charles was the progenitor of the dynasty he had not actually been a king, which made him a more vulnerable figure. Hincmar's *Vision of Eucherius* became the key text in establishing Martel's reputation as a despoiler of church lands, and in the histories of the various bishoprics and abbeys which were produced in the later ninth century Charles invariably figures as the person responsible for each institution's losses.

Even such a brief account of the way in which writing about Charles Martel developed is sufficient to indicate how the Brunner school got it so wrong. For what Brunner and the great F. L. Ganshof and many others did was to assume that when the various texts portrayed Charles Martel as both hero and villain they did this because they faithfully reflected the different and conflicting pressures which determined his actions. And the context for these actions was taken from a literal reading of the Carolingian sources, which furnished a picture of the family's solidarity and their dutiful behaviour in first propping up an ailing Merovingian regime and then catching it when it finally fell. What we would now say is that Charles Martel's contradictory portrayal is not related to what he actually did, but is a reflection of the changing nature and focus of history-writing under the Carolingians. We must remember that more than a century separates the writing of the first section of the *Continuations of Fredegar* from the letter of Hincmar of Rheims. The change in Charles Martel's reputation, from Old Testament-like hero in the *Continuations*, to the despoiler of the church in Hincmar, is a strictly post mortem development, and as such can have little or no bearing on the man himself. On the other hand, when we strip Charles Martel of his later reputation, we find that we know very little about him. He was perhaps as old as twenty-seven when the first reference to him appears.[20] If the sources are silent about his early life because he was at this stage relatively unimportant, then this is information which does directly affect our understanding of his career. We shall return to this point, but first let us examine more closely the question of Charles Martel and 'feudalism', for this is prime Reynolds territory.

The issue of 'feudalism' turns on the idea of leasing out land, here church land, in return for military services. Historians have identified these kinds of leases in grants referred to in documents as *precaria*.[21] *Precaria* were grants made at the request of a beneficiary or, more rarely, of a third party, the term being derived from the verb *precari*, to ask for. What, in theory, was being asked for here was church land to be given out to Charles Martel's followers. In Ganshof's classic

---

[20] On the lack of information about the early life of Charles Martel, Fouracre, *Age of Charles Martel*, pp. 55–6.

[21] The granting of *precaria* is discussed in detail in Fouracre, *Age of Charles Martel*, pp. 137–45. Susan Reynolds commented on the first draft of that discussion and, typically, demanded greater precision in order to avoid common misconceptions. For her own comments on the origins of Frankish *precaria*, *Fiefs and Vassals*, pp. 78–9. Also important as a demonstration of the nature of leases is I. Wood, 'Teutsind, Witlaic and the History of Merovingian *Precaria*', in W. Davies and P. Fouracre (eds), *Property and Power in the Early Middle Ages* (Cambridge, 1995), pp. 31–52. On Charles Martel and the question of 'feudalism', see also H. Wolfram, 'Karl Martell und die fränkische Lehenswesen', in *Karl Martell in seiner Zeit*, pp. 61–78.

account of the origins of feudalism, these followers were increasingly described as 'vassals', that is followers who had pledged themselves to serve a lord, particularly to provide him with military services, and the land they received was their reward or 'benefice' (*beneficium*). It was, in Ganshof's view, the union of vassalage and benefice which gave birth to feudalism.[22] As we have already seen, the evidence for Charles Martel using land in this way is late, and relates to conditions of the ninth, rather than the eighth, century. There is, of course, the famous contemporary reference to Charles Martel giving the lands of the bishopric of Orléans to his followers, but we cannot generalise from this one incident, as Hincmar did. Charles Martel did drive out other bishops too and sometimes replaced them with laymen, but in these cases the exiles were his enemies, and it was necessary to replace them with trusted warriors in order to hold down hostile areas. This is not the same thing as systematically despoiling or 'secularising' church lands. Boniface's complaints about the care of the church generally being given over to laymen or unsuitable clerics come in the context of disputes he had with the bishops of Cologne and Mainz who contested the missionary's ecclesiastical jurisdiction in areas east of the Rhine.[23] Boniface cannot be taken as a reliable witness to the state of the Frankish church as a whole. As for Ganshof's vassals and benefices, the former are hard to find in the sources, and the latter are so ubiquitous that it is clear that the term *beneficium* had a multiplicity of meanings. It is quite natural that a term that carried the general sense of 'a good deed' should have been in common use when social relations revolved around the giving and receiving of gifts and favours.[24] And as for the conviction that Charles Martel developed new kinds of cavalry forces in order to combat Arab invaders, there is simply no evidence to support this. Even the account of the battle of Poitiers in the *Continuations of Fredegar*, which has often been thought to describe a cavalry charge through the Arab camp, turns out to be a paraphrase of a passage in the Book of Numbers, where the spirit of the Lord rushed into the tents of Israel.[25]

There were basically three kinds of *precaria*. The first, *precaria verbo regis*, were made when rulers asked that a church lease land to their followers. This kind is regarded as the essential vehicle through which rulers utilised church land for their own benefit, and while it is true that in the ninth century churches complained bitterly about such involuntary leases, they are in fact relatively rare, and almost unknown until after the death of Charles Martel.[26] The second kind of *precaria*

---

[22] F. L. Ganshof, *Feudalism*, trans. P. Grierson (London, 1964), pp. 3–50, esp. pp. 40–3 for the 'Legal Union of Vassalage and Benefice'.

[23] Ewig, 'Milo', pp. 199–200.

[24] *Beneficium* is in fact the largest single entry in J. Niermeyer's *Mediae Latinae Lexicon Minus* (Leiden, 1984), pp. 91–6, which recorded forty-one different ways in which the term was used.

[25] *Continuations of Fredegar*, ch. 13, pp. 90–1. On this passage, and Wallace-Hadrill's mistranslation of it, Fouracre, *Age of Charles Martel*, pp. 148–9.

[26] Wood, 'Teutsind', pp. 34–9, shows how in one case, that of the monastery of St Wandrille, the land that was the subject of complaint about involuntary leases amounted only to a small fraction of the institution's total holdings.

involved churches making temporary grants of land to their own friends and clients, and are more common. But the third, and by far the most common, form was when individuals or families made gifts to a church and then requested that they might retain the use of the land until they died, thus receiving it back on a temporary lease. There were of course lots of other ways in which land could be held, donated or exchanged, and Susan Reynolds is absolutely right to insist that we should not impose our own notions of ownership and possession on the property relations of the early Middle Ages. Her demonstration that these relations were often messy and confused provides an important insight both into the situation in the time of Charles Martel and into the way in which modern historians tend to tidy up the past by 'clarifying' terminology and by sweeping information into neat categories.

As Reynolds explains, by the mid-eighth century the church had acquired more land than it could manage, hence the need to let some of it out to suitable tenants.[27] Tenancies tended to be handed down the generations. Those who had rights over extensive lands often failed to keep control of them, especially when that land lay in distant provinces. There was confusion between lease and gift, and a great variety of ways in which land could be held. In these conditions it was, and still is, hard to draw distinctions between the ownership and possession of property. The growing use of different kinds of *precaria* in our period might well have been a response to this messiness. For *precaria* of all kinds generated written records which stated clearly who had the ultimate right over the land and on what terms someone else was allowed to use the land on a temporary basis.

So, far from being occasioned simply by the need to increase military resources, the spread of *precaria* should be seen as part of a wider process of reorganisation in which churches themselves took a leading part. This took place across the spectrum of landholding. Great estates were broken down into smaller holdings in which peasant households were grouped around the land of a lord to whom they owed labour services and rent in cash and/or produce. This process historians often term 'manorialisation'. At the other end of the spectrum, lesser noble or free landholders gave their land to the church and became its tenants partly to gain spiritual benefits, but also to avoid the fragmentation of landholding which tended to occur when land was divided at times of inheritance. Such tenants could reasonably expect to have their leases renewed, undivided, over generations. That this was the desired outcome was sometimes spelled out in precarial agreements.[28] The

---

[27] Reynolds, *Fiefs and Vassals*, pp. 77–8

[28] In two separate essays focusing on South German leases, W. Hartung and the late J. Jahn have argued convincingly that giving to the church in this way became a common strategy for the maintenance of undivided inheritances, and one which changed the whole pattern of landholding. This important argument remains to be properly tested in other areas of early medieval Europe. W. Hartung, 'Adel, Erbrecht, Schenkung: die strukturellen Ursachen der frühmittelalterlichen Besitzübertragungen an die Kirche', and J. Jahn, 'Tradere ad Sanctum: politische und gesellschaftliche Aspekte der Traditionspraxis im agilolfingischen Bayern', both in F. Seibt (ed.), *Gesellschaftsgeschichte. Festschrift für Karl Bosl zum 80 Geburtstag* I (Munich, 1988), pp. 417–38 and pp. 400–16.

result was, again, manorialisation. The distribution of charters across time and space gives the impression that this shift in landholding patterns spread outwards from the core area of the Frankish lands, that is, the area between the Loire and the Rhine, into the outlying regions, and there are good reasons for thinking that this impression is a fair one.

It is in the core area that there were the greatest concentrations of large estates, held both by churches and by kings. It is with land in this area that the bulk of the earliest surviving charters (mid-seventh century onwards) are concerned. And it is here that we find the first signs of manorialisation, although it is only later, in the ninth century, that we have the detailed surveys ('polyptychs') which show exactly how estates were organised in this way.[29] Charter evidence for Toxandria (the lower Meuse valley) first appears at the very end of the seventh century, and for central and southern Germany only in the mid-eighth century. In the mid-seventh century, the lands east of the Rhine were areas where there were no mints, no counts, no bishops and no monasteries. Charters, that is, all kinds of documents concerned with property, not just *precaria*, appear in these regions only when the church became organised and when monasteries were founded. The spread of charters does not just mark these developments, it directly affected the way in which land was held by helping to define property rights, and by recording property transactions. Property rights could now be defended in law courts through the witness of charters, and the general effect of keeping a written record of rights in this way was to stabilise property relations. The context for this change is our other eighth-century watershed, the conversion of Germany to Christianity.

Although historians still sometimes use the term 'conversion', rarely do they mean by it a simple rejection of paganism in favour of Christianity in the way, say, that Bede described the conversion of various Anglo-Saxons. Conversion or, better, 'christianisation' is now understood as a lengthier process of cultural transformation in which Christian burial customs, symbols and sacraments slowly worked their way into a mass of existing custom and practice. The evidence of archaeology, of place names, of charters, and of saints' lives concurs to show that it was the elite that led the way in this cultural transformation. In particular, what has been termed the 'Merovingian burial community' broke up as leaders founded churches and had themselves and families buried in or near them, thus separating themselves off from the rest of the community. It was such leaders who sometimes gave their names to settlements, and the settlements themselves were regrouped around the hall of

---

[29] It is generally accepted by historians that it was this reorganisation of estate farming, especially on church lands, which led to that increase in production which allowed markets to develop and which in turn led to a growth in economic activity. See W. Bleiber, *Naturalwirtschaft und Ware–Geld-Beziehungen zwischen Somme und Loire während des 7 Jahrhunderts* (Berlin, 1981), J.-P. Devroey, 'Réflexions sur l'économie des prémiers temps Carolingiens (768–877): grands domaines et action politique êntre Seine et Rhin', *Francia*, 13 (1985), 475–88, and G. Depreyot, *Richesse et Société chez les Mérovingiens et Carolingiens* (Paris, 1994), pp. 37–62.

the leader.[30] We can therefore say that conversion was associated with, or indeed stimulated, the development of a social elite. These are the leaders who appear in charters as donors or witnesses, and it was their social predominance which charters helped to reinforce. Missionaries only come into the picture when the process was already well advanced, and, although the 'lives' of the various missionary saints speak of their heroes preaching to the pagans, in more concrete terms what their work involved was the organisation of a fledgling church into bishoprics, and the foundation of monasteries, in both cases with the material support of local or regional leaders.

The *Earlier Annals of Metz* claimed that areas on the periphery of the Frankish realm such as Frisia, Bavaria and Alemannia had once been subject to the Merovingian rulers but had broken away because those kings had been so indolent.[31] It was Pippin and his son Charles Martel who forced them back into line. The picture now looks rather different. We have just seen that the conversion of these areas was part and parcel of a process of elite formation. The establishment of bishoprics and the foundation of monasteries also marked a degree of acculturation to Frankish ways. Eventually the lands east of the Rhine would have counts too and, finally, mints. It is in this sense that one can describe the spread of Frankish culture from core to periphery, but in the first half of the eighth century there was much violent conflict between centre and outlying regions. This was not because the peripheral regions had 'broken away', but rather that they resisted Charles Martel and his sons on the grounds that the Carolingians had no right to rule them.

Thuringia, Bavaria, Alemannia and, west of the Rhine, Alsace, Aquitaine and Provence were all ruled by ducal families who derived their authority from the Merovingian kings. Thuringia and Alsace seem to have accepted Carolingian rule, but there was fierce resistance to it in the other regions, and some evidence from Bavaria and Provence that opponents of the Carolingians from elsewhere in Francia

---

[30] For the shift in settlement and burial patterns in Toxandria (the lower Meuse valley), F. Theuws, 'Landed Property and Manorial Organization in Northern Austrasia. Some Considerations and a Case Study', in N. Roymans and F. Theuws (eds), *Images of the Past. Studies on Ancient Societies in Northwestern Europe* (Amsterdam, 1991), pp. 299–407. This is a particularly useful study because Theuws investigated settlements for which there is early charter evidence, and he was thus able to show how settlements were reorganised in the process of becoming incorporated into a monastic estate. For a conspectus of 'conversion period' archaeology in Germany, see H. Steuer, 'Archäologie und die Erforschung des germanischen Sozialgeschichte', in D. Simon (ed.), *Akten des 26 Deutschen Rechtshistorikertages, Studien zur Europäischen Rechtsgeschichte*, 30 (Frankfurt, 1987), pp. 443–53. For settlement patterns in southern Germany, F. Damminger, 'Dwellings, Settlements and Settlement Patterns in Merovingian South-West Germany and Adjacent Areas', in I. Wood (ed.), *Franks and Alemanni in the Merovingian Period. An Ethnographic Perspective* (Woodbridge, 1998), pp. 33–89. On southern Germany, elite formation and development of place names, F. Prinz, 'Frühes Mönchtum in Südwestdeutschland und die Anfänge der Reichenau', in A. Borst (ed.), *Mönchtum, Episkopat und Adel zur Gründungszeit des Klosters Reichenau, Vorträge und Forschungen*, 20 (Sigmaringen, 1974), pp. 37–76, esp. pp. 40–6.

[31] *Annales Mettenses Priores*, s.a. 691, trans. Fouracre and Gerberding, pp. 359–60.

joined the fight against them.[32] What made their resistance more effective was the social and cultural transformation we have just been discussing, that is to say, the emergence of a better-organised and better-resourced nobility in these regions gave them the means to fight the Franks. The region which put up the most effective resistance was Aquitaine which was very much on a par with Francia in terms of resources and military organisation. It was in fact Arab invasions from Spain which weakened Aquitaine at a crucial time of Frankish pressure. Until the Aquitanian duke, Eudo, was distracted by these invasions, it looked as if it might be he, not Charles Martel, who would emerge as the strongest leader of all. Eudo did win a crushing victory against the Arabs at Toulouse in an early encounter with them, but later tradition switched the magnitude of this victory (the three hundred and fifty thousand Arab dead) to Charles Martel's triumph at Poitiers, and painted Eudo as a foolish traitor.[33] It was not until 769 that Aquitanian resistance to the Carolingians finally ceased. Alemannia was finally overwhelmed in 746. Bavarian independence lasted to 788. It is very striking, however, that once these regions were finally conquered, they became so fully integrated into the Frankish polity that it would be hard to point to any political, social, cultural or religious feature which distinguished them from other regions. Acculturation may have been a factor in their ability to resist the Carolingians, but it also meant that by the time they gave up the struggle, Alemans, Aquitanians and Bavarians were very little different from Franks.

Having looked at Charles Martel in the wider frame, let us now look at the background to his career in terms of family and politics, before returning to the question of whether the reinterpretation of our sources can bring us any closer to understanding him. The early history of Charles Martel's family (known as the 'Pippinids' before Charles) can be pieced together from the *Chronicle of Fredegar*, completed *c.*660, from the *Liber Historiae Francorum*, from the *Life of Gertrude* (a late seventh-century work) and from charters.[34] The account of the family's rise to power in the *Earlier Annals of Metz* drew principally on the first two of these sources. The *Annals* devoted a surprising amount of space to the seventh-century history of the family, and to one event in particular, the victory of Charles Martel's father, Pippin, over the Neustrians at the battle of Tertry in 687.[35] It is in fact this view of Tertry which down to the present has persuaded historians of its importance. As we have seen, the author of the *Earlier Annals of Metz* explained the family's rise to power in relation to the declining power and stature of the Merovingian kings. Victory at Tertry was portrayed as the moment at which Pippin became leader of all the Franks, and after which the kings became mere figureheads. The initial concentration on Pippin

---

[32] On Bavaria, H. Wolfram, 'Der Heilige Rupert und die antikarolingische Adelsopposition', *Mitteilungen des Instituts für österreichische Geschichtsforschung*, 80 (1972), 4–34, and for Provence, P. Geary, *Aristocracy in Provence. The Rhône Basin at the Dawn of the Carolingian Age* (Stuttgart, 1985).

[33] Nonn, 'Das Bild Karl Martells', pp. 11–12.

[34] *Vita Geretrudis*, ed. B. Krusch, *Monumenta Germaniae Historiae, Scriptores Rerum Merovingicarum* II, pp. 464–71, trans. with commentary Fouracre and Gerberding, pp. 301–26. Gertrude was Charles Martel's great-aunt.

[35] *Annales Mettenses Priores*, s.a. 689, trans. Fouracre and Gerberding, pp. 355–60.

also served to integrate Charles Martel into the family's earlier history by making him the heir to Pippin's triumphs, and thus carrying on a family tradition of leadership which stretched back to the mid-seventh century.

It is now clear that this picture is severely distorted. Most obviously, the *Earlier Annals of Metz* chose not to mention that the Pippinid family fell from power in the 660s. The author must have known this because it is the *Liber Historiae Francorum* which tells of it.[36] Secondly, the Merovingians were by no means done for in 687. The *Liber Historiae Francorum* lauds one post-Tertry king whom the *Annals* imply was powerless, so we must conclude that this distortion was again deliberate.[37] That Pippin had to share power with the Neustrians even after he had beaten them is something that our author genuinely may not have realised, for this impression is one drawn largely from the reading of charters.[38] On the other hand, the way in which the work's narrative structure links Charles Martel into the family's earlier history, and makes him the heir to Pippin's power, was clearly designed to deal with a fact which the author could not ignore: that Charles Martel had been excluded from the family after Pippin's death at the end of 714. The story of Charles's fight for power with Pippin's widow, Plectrude (for which the original source was again the *Liber Historiae Francorum*), was too well known to brush aside. But another reason for dragging Charles Martel's family history back into the seventh century might simply have been that the author knew little or nothing about his origins, about his mother, or about the first twenty-seven years of his life.

It is in the *Continuations of Fredegar* that we find the name of Charles Martel's mother.[39] The author of the work should have known this since it was commissioned by Charles Martel's half-brother, Childebrand. She was called Alpaida, and referred to as Pippin's 'wife' in the *Liber Historiae Francorum* and in the *Continuations*. Later tradition had it that she was Pippin's concubine. Though historians have thought hard about who she might have been, and where she might have had family and lands, this is all we know about Alpaida.[40] Charles was born sometime after

---

[36] *Liber Historiae Francorum*, ch. 43, trans. Fouracre and Gerberding, pp. 87–8. On the family's vicissitudes in the later seventh century, Fouracre, *Age of Charles Martel*, pp. 37–40.

[37] *Liber Historiae Francorum*, ch. 50, trans. Fouracre and Gerberding, p. 94, referred to King Childebert III (694–711) as 'the famous and just lord, King Childebert, of good memory'. Compare the *Annales Mettenses Priores*, s.a. 693, trans. Fouracre and Gerberding, p. 362, which tells of Pippin making Childebert king, adding that 'giving to these men the name of kings, he [Pippin] kept the reins of the whole realm and governed with the highest glory and honour'.

[38] For such a reading, P. Fouracre, 'Observations on the Outgrowth of Pippinid Influence the "Regnum Francorum" after the Battle of Tertry (687–715)', *Medieval Prosopography*, 5 (1984), 1–31.

[39] *Continuations of Fredegar*, ch. 6, p. 86.

[40] R. Gerberding, *The Rise of the Carolingians and the Liber Historiae Francorum* (Oxford, 1987), pp. 116–34, and idem, '716: A Crucial Year for Charles Martel', in *Karl Martell in seiner Zeit*, pp. 203–16, imagines that Alpaida's family was powerful and had lands in the Liège area. She was, Gerberding argues, the source of Pippin's power in Meuse valley and it was her landed base which was the first source Martel's power too. There is, however, no information at all about her landholding, and, with one possible exception, we cannot identify any other member of her family. For an alternative view of how Charles Martel might have come to power in 716, Fouracre, *The Age of Charles Martel*, pp. 58–62.

688, and was at least twenty-five years old in 714, by which time he was married and had a son. In 707 his half-brother, Pippin's son Drogo, died, and in 714 Grimoald, another son of Pippin was murdered. Pippin himself died at the end of 714. On none of these three occasions, apparently, did Charles receive any kind of promotion within the family. Each time it was the grandsons of Pippin and his wife, Plectrude, who were preferred, even though they were much younger than Charles. The impression must be, therefore, that he was a relatively insignificant member of the family. There may, of course, have been other adult sons of Pippin (but not of Plectrude) who were in a similar position. Perhaps Childebrand was one of them.

After Pippin's death, Plectrude assumed power on behalf of her grandsons and imprisoned Charles Martel. But then she was assailed on all sides by Neustrians, Frisians and Saxons. Charles escaped from prison and emerged in 716 as a military leader in the Liège area. After his first, and only, defeat, he began to drive back the three groups of invaders and in 717 went on the offensive against them. In the same year he defeated Plectrude and acquired the family's treasure. He then set up his own king and became master of all Austrasia. By 720 he had conquered Neustria and then came his relentless campaigning against the outlying regions which lasted until 740 when he finally became ill, dying in 741. What had happened, it seems, was that the death of Pippin and of his eldest son in 714, followed in the next year by the death of a Merovingian king who had no adult heir, unleashed a general struggle for power in Francia. No *bona fide* adult Merovingian was available to bring the warring factions to peace, as had happened in the past, and so the conflict was fought out to its bitter end. First Charles Martel battled for survival. He then fought to capture the Neustrian king and the royal palace, and then, when resistance to him continued in the peripheral duchies, he campaigned against them. And, of course, he fought the Arabs too. It was in the course of this relentless fighting that the king (it was Theuderic IV, 724–37, who ruled for much of this period) lost face as politics gave way to military conflict, and as Martel became a supremely successful military leader. After Theuderic's death, Charles actually ruled without a Merovingian king, although his sons would enthrone another one in 743.

We have seen how writing about Charles Martel shifted the focus from his career as a military leader to his supposed depredations of church lands. We have noted how the historical conjecture placed upon this shift in emphasis was fundamentally wrong in imagining that 'feudal' reorganisation was Charles's response to the pressures he faced. Change and development in the ways in which land was held and exploited there certainly were in this period, and, as we saw, there was a cultural transformation and degree of elite formation in those regions which were christianised at this time. We cannot, however, directly relate Charles Martel's career to these developments as cause and effects. When we strip the figure of his traditional associations in this way, we are left with just three elements: his initial obscurity; his struggle to establish himself within his own family; and his extraordinary success as a military leader. But if a re-evaluation leads us away from the view that Charles was a decisive figure in European history, and means that there is less to say about him, it also allows us to make much better sense of what elements remain.

After the balance of power in Francia had been violently upset in 714–15, it was very likely that a military strongman would emerge, and if that person could draw on the combined resources of Neustria and Austrasia, it was equally likely that he would be able to dominate other regions. There were in fact several leaders who might have risen to predominance in this way. There was Eudo duke of Aquitaine, and Ragamfred mayor of the palace in Neustria. There was also another Austrasian family, the so-called 'Gundoinings' who had long contested Pippinid domination, and the Gundoinings had links with the powerful Agilolfing family which ruled Bavaria. Charles Martel emerged supreme because he defeated all of these people. He was, simply, the most effective military leader in Francia. Although we know nothing of his early life, it is safe to assume that by the time he first appeared on the scene he must have acquired a great deal of military experience and skill. The only strictly contemporary remarks about him as a person (coming again from the *Liber Historiae Francorum*) were that he was handsome and an outstanding leader.[41]

The fact that he rose to power from a subordinate position in the Pippinid family is likely to have affected his behaviour thereafter. With Charles Martel, as with his descendants, it is impossible to separate family affairs and politics. Fighting outsiders was also a way of maintaining a hold over the family. Individual women feature prominently in the narratives and in the charters of this period because power was channelled through families as well as expressed through political institutions. The importance of Plectrude is obvious. After Charles Martel had broken her power and that of her grandsons, he reshaped the family around himself and his three sons by two (successive) wives, Chrotrude and Swanahild. Of Chrotrude we know no more than her name and that she died in 725. About Swanahild, we know enough to see that she played a crucial role in the career of her husband. She had links with the Agilolfings of Bavaria and Alemmania, and possibly also with Plectrude's family.[42] Charter evidence shows that she acted as regent for Charles in the all-important Paris region. After Charles died in 741 Swanahild was driven out by the sons of Chrotrude, and her son Grifo was incarcerated. But first she engineered the flight of Chrotrude's daughter Chiltrude to Bavaria where she married her lover the Agilolfing duke. For this act, and for her attempt to protect the interests of her son Grifo, Swanahild's memory would be damned in Carolingian writing. Modern historians have tended to follow suit.[43]

Although Charles Martel's *curriculum vitae* reads as a string of military triumphs, he never actually conquered Aquitaine, Alemannia, Bavaria or Saxony. His career ends on a note of unfinished business. What his intentions were, other than to pass on his power to three of his sons, we have no idea. From 737, when Theuderic IV died, until his own death, Charles ruled as mayor of the palace without a king.

---

[41] *Liber Historiae Francorum*, ch. 49, trans. Fouracre and Gerberding, p. 93. Fouracre and Gerberding translate the term *elegans* as 'well educated', but, on reflection, 'handsome' is the more likely meaning.

[42] J. Jarnut, 'Untersuchungen zur Herkunft Swanahilds, der Gattin Karl Martells', *Zeitschrift für bayerische Landesgeschichte*, 40 (1977), 254–9.

[43] On Swanahild and Charles, Fouracre, *Age of Charles Martel*, pp. 161–7.

It has often been assumed that this interregnum was somehow a preparation for taking the throne. It is, however, just as likely to have other explanations. The raising of a new king might have provided a dangerous opportunity for enemies to rally against Charles. We have one very clear late seventh-century example of how this could happen.[44] If Charles made himself king, to whom would he pass on the throne? It would have been difficult to divide the kingship three ways soon after a change of dynasty. There was, though, precedent for the institution of three mayors of the palace in Francia. During the interregnum Charles continued to rule through the palace, and charters were still dated with reference to Theuderic, according to the years since his death. If this system was working satisfactorily, there may have been no need to do anything about replacing the king. Interestingly, no Carolingian sources ever refer to the interregnum, although one might expect them to have done so, since they are so eloquent on the subject of Merovingian powerlessness. Did their authors even know, one wonders, that there had been no king in these years? Again, we come back to the point that later Carolingian writers actually knew very little about Charles Martel. It would be a very Reynolds-ish conclusion to say that we may not know what was in Charles Martel's mind at this time, but we may guess that he was far more likely to be responding in a pragmatic way to immediate problems than planning for future constitutional change.

We have replaced the old view of Charles Martel and the invention of 'feudalism' with a different big picture, that of the spread of core culture to the periphery, and of a reorganisation of the way in which land was held and exploited. Neither was much to do with Charles Martel. These changes would, however, benefit his descendants in giving their empire a large degree of cultural and social homogeneity, and by helping to increase the resources available to rulers. It was the success of Charles Martel's grandson, Charlemagne, making the most of these favourable conditions, which drew attention down on Charles as the progenitor of the new dynasty and which made him into an author of change. Ironically, what cultural and social changes there were at this time are likely to have worked as much against as for Charles Martel in that they strengthened his enemies. What little we do know about him is that he had many enemies, that his career consisted of an endless fight against them, and that though he fought them to a standstill, they were back again the moment he died. Susan Reynolds is not very interested in political history for its own sake, nor has she written on biography. But by following her lead in analysing the background to the career of Charles Martel and in setting out once again the misconceptions, both ancient and modern, in what has been written about him, we can arrive at a much more realistic appraisal of both the career and the man.

---

[44] In 673 the powerful mayor of the palace Ebroin was deposed when the magnates met to raise up a new king. The incident is described in detail in the near-contemporary *Passio Leudegarii*, ed. B. Krusch, *Monumenta Germaniae Historica, Scriptores Rerum Merovingicarum* V (Hanover, 1910), pp. 282–322, trans. with commentary Fouracre and Gerberding, pp. 191–253. Here, chs 4–6, pp. 220–3.

Peers in the early Middle Ages

*Janet L. Nelson**

The earlier Middle Ages are generally thought of as a period when there was no such thing as equality. Near the beginning of his fine book, *Lebensordnungen*, Heinrich Fichtenau writes: 'the absolute necessity of a hierarchical order ... resulted from the medieval reception of Neoplatonic thought'. Thus there was ranking of churches, of cities, of orders, of dignities, of seating arrangements; rank operated within monasteries ... and in secular life (where they were not so *au fait* with Neoplatonism).[1] Even though, in Fichtenau's view, feudalism was too unsystematic to present much of a hierarchy, and anyway tended towards a personal rank ordering that was constantly contested and quite untidy, still, assumptions of hierarchy and rank were ubiquitous.[2] Geoffrey Koziol's account of rituals of requests for pardon and favour assumes a world of unequal dyadic pairs.[3] Feudal relations are alleged to have been generalised by Carolingian rulers to reinforce kingship.[4] Power descended.[5] Law-codes differentiated the value of persons by their status and condition.[6] Recent work on the three orders of society, a ninth-century discovery (or

---

[*] I owe warm thanks to my fellow editors for comments on a draft of this essay. It began life as a lecture (one of the 1999 Carlyle Lectures in the University of Oxford), to an audience that included Susan Reynolds. Then, as for a good many years before, and since, Susan has been an unfailing source of inspiration, constructive criticism, and practical help. The substantially rewritten version of this essay is an inadequate token of gratitude.

[1] H. Fichtenau, *Living in the Tenth Century: Mentalities and Social Orders*, trans. P. Geary (Chicago and London, 1991), pp. 21–9. Cf. D. Luscombe, 'Conceptions of hierarchy before the thirteenth century', in *Soziale Ordnungen im Selbstverständnis des Mittelalters, Miscellanea Mediaevalia* 12.1 (Berlin and New York, 1979), pp. 1–19.

[2] Fichtenau, *Living*, pp. 7, 29.

[3] G. Koziol, *Begging Pardon and Favour. Ritual and Political Order in Early Medieval France* (Ithaca, NY and London, 1992).

[4] F. L. Ganshof, *Feudalism*, trans. P. Grierson (London, 1964).

[5] W. Ullmann, *Political Ideas in the Middle Ages* (Harmondsworth, 1967); idem, *The Carolingian Renaissance and the Idea of Kingship* (London, 1969); idem, *Law and Politics in the Middle Ages* (London, 1975).

[6] Cf. the penetrating comments on F. W. Maitland of P. Wormald, *The Making of English Law: King Alfred to the Twelfth Century*, vol. 1, *Legislation and its Limits* (Oxford, 1999), p. 17.

possibly rediscovery), shows that in earlier medieval thinking, specialisation of function was bound up with distinction of rank.[7] Though subtler gradations of wealth and status nuanced the stark polarity between powerful and powerless, *potens* and *pauper*, early medieval man, like Indian man, was *homo hierarchicus*.[8]

There is some truth in all the above. But in this essay for Susan Reynolds, who insisted we view kingdoms and communities within one medieval frame, I intend to qualify that verticality: or rather, to set alongside it, and initially to highlight, evidence of ideas about horizontal relationships – ideas which sometimes explicitly, and often implicitly, contained a whiff of egalitarianism, not, for the most part, in the universalistic, modern, sense but in reference to the members of a particular group. Such ideas were clearly articulated, and in secular contexts, in the eleventh century, for instance when *c.*1025 Count Odo of Blois told the king whom he suspected of planning to confiscate his benefices that 'it was not fitting to pass such a judgement on him without an assembly of his peers' (*sine conventu parium suorum*).[9] Almost exactly contemporary is the case of Duke Godfrey of Lotharingia, adjudged *a contubernalibus* as liable to forfeit his benefices to the emperor.[10] Such groups were quite restricted in terms of their members' status and often also in terms of geography (members were neighbours), but within those limits they exercised collective judgement and embodied a perception of equality. When the flow of royal and princely charters and privileges became a flood in the twelfth century, peers, whether as Latin *pares* or romance *pairs*, appeared more frequently. What had begun as an adjective had become a noun, perhaps indicating that an idea had acquired substantiveness, and clearer embodiment in actual groups. Charlemagne and his Twelve Peers (twelve being a symbolically significant number) from now on exemplified the ideal relationship of king and nobility – and, as Susan Reynolds has noted, that was *not* one of *primus inter pares*.[11] Kingship stood outside, and above, the aristocratic group: a fact which highlighted the distinction between vertical and horizontal bonds even while those bonds coexisted, often intertwined, in reality.

---

[7] G. Duby, *The Three Orders. Feudal Society Imagined*, trans. A. Goldhammer (London, 1980); cf. D. Iogna-Prat, 'Le baptême du schéma des trois ordres fonctionnels', *Annales ESC* 41 (1986), 101–26; G. Constable, *Three Studies in Medieval Religious and Social Thought* (Cambridge, 1995), Part III.

[8] L. Dumont, *Homo Hierarchicus. The Caste System and its Implications*, trans. M. Sainsbury (London, 1970). For the earlier medieval West, see K. Bosl, '*Potens* und *pauper*. Begriffsgeschichtliche Studien zur gesellschaftlichen Differenzierung im frühen Mittelalter', in *Alteuropa und die moderne Gesellschaft. Festschrift für Otto Brunner* (Göttingen, 1963), pp. 60–87, repr. in *Frühformen der Gesellschaft im mittelalterlichen Europa: Ausgewählte Beiträge zu einer Strukturanalyse der mittelalterlichen Welt* (Munich and Vienna, 1964), pp. 106–34; J. Martindale, 'The French aristocracy in the early Middle Ages', *Past and Present* 75 (1977), 5–45, repr. in her collected papers (London, 1997), ch. 4; and recently G. Constable, 'Was there a medieval middle class? *Mediocres (mediani, medii)* in the Middle Ages', in S. K. Cohn and S. A. Epstein (eds), *Portraits of Medieval and Renaissance Living. Essays in Honour of David Herlihy* (Ann Arbor, MI, 1996), pp. 301–24.

[9] Fulbert of Chartres, Ep. 86, ed. F. Behrends, *The Letters and Poems of Fulbert of Chartres* (Oxford, 1976), pp. 152–4.

[10] *Annales Altahenses* s.a. 1044, ed. E. von Oefele, MGH SSrG 4 (Hannover, 1891), p. 38.

[11] *Kingdoms and Communities in Western Europe 900–1300*, 2nd edn (Oxford, 1997), pp. xlvii, 258–9.

It would be a bad case of terminological teleology if the recurrence of a word were to be mistaken for the continuity of a thing,[12] and that thing mistaken for equality in the modern sense. Nevertheless, parity, however circumscribed by particularity, is attested in enough contexts, and in sufficiently many terms, to demand serious attention as an aspect of social relations and political thinking in the earlier Middle Ages. My focus will be on the period before 900, though I shall occasionally gaze beyond it. This essay will have justified its existence if read as a little prelude, *après la lettre*, to the masterwork that is *Kingdoms and Communities*.

In Philippe Buc's *L'Ambiguïté du livre*, there is a striking insistence both on the role of the Bible as a source of legitimacy in the Middle Ages, and on the possibility of egalitarian readings of Holy Writ. Not that Buc means 'egalitarian' in the universalistic sense of the Enlightenment. But he notes that for some twelfth-century Bible commentators, ecclesiastical authority was legitimately and normally wielded by local clergy rather than the pope, while, whatever courtiers might claim, the power of the king had been established for wrongdoers only: hence, *ubi non delinquimus, pares sumus*: 'where we don't commit any offence, we are equals'.[13] This twelfth-century gloss on Genesis 9:2 has several possible sources. In theory Ambrose or Augustine are possible contenders. But those who wrote of parity between the seventh century and twelfth found their inspiration first and foremost in Gregory the Great. In Gregory, parity might be called an anthropological concept: *omnes . . . homines natura aequales sumus*.[14] Robert Markus has found here 'a strong streak of egalitarianism'.[15] 'Strong', that is, by comparison with Augustine. For whereas Augustine had pushed equality back to the Garden of Eden, for Gregory it constituted 'a moral demand in the here and now'.[16] The inequalities Gregory observed in his own world arose, he thought, from individuals' varied sins, hence varied deserts, and from the mysterious working of divine providence: *sed variante meritorum ordine, alios aliis dispensatio occulta postponit*. Gregory was, after all, commenting on the Book of Job. For Gregory, rectors or pastors constituted a divinely picked meritocracy, placed above others. Yet *condescensio*[17] was a pastor's key virtue: the pastor 'came down to join' those for whom he was responsible, recalling his subjects to be *in sui comparatione equales*: equals when com-*par*ed with him (the force of that *par* should survive translation).[18]

---

[12] Cf. the warnings of S. Reynolds, *Fiefs and Vassals* (Oxford, 1994), pp. 12–14.

[13] P. Buc, *L'Ambiguïté du livre* (Paris, 1994), pp. 338–50. This is a book for anyone interested in the ways that culture shapes political thought.

[14] Gregory the Great, *Moralia in Job* xxi, 15 (22–4), ed. M. Adriaen, Corpus Christianorum 143A (Turnhout, 1979), pp. 1082–3.

[15] R. A. Markus, 'The Latin Fathers', in J. H. Burns (ed.), *The Cambridge History of Medieval Political Thought* (Cambridge, 1988), p. 121.

[16] Ibid., cf. M. Reydellet, *La Royauté dans la littérature latine de Sidoine Apollinire à Isidore de Séville*, Bibliothèque des Écoles françaises d'Athènes et de Rome 243 (Rome, 1981), p. 465.

[17] *Moralia in Job* vi. 35, CC 143, 323–4, xix, 25, CC 143A, 990–1; cf. Markus, *Pope Gregory the Great* (Cambridge, 1997), pp. 27, 29.

[18] *Moralia in Job* xx, 14 (27), CC 143A, 1024; *Regula Pastoralis* iii, 5, ed. B. Judic, F. Rommel and C. Morel, 2 vols, Sources chrétiennes 381–2 (Paris, 1992), ii, pp. 282–4.

Gregory's words are significant in themselves; but additionally so for those of us interested in the centuries after Gregory. In *A History of Medieval Political Theory in the West,* A. J. Carlyle quoted not only Gregory, but a string of earlier medieval writers who either paralleled (for Gregory's own immediate source was a Roman jurisconsult) or, more often, borrowed from him.[19] Gregory was appropriated by Alcuin in the moral handbook he wrote for Count Guy of the Breton March in 799: in his high office, the count must practise humility, recalling that entry into the kingdom of God is available to all *aequaliter,* according to merit.[20] Theodulf in his poem of advice to judges warned that

Pauperibus quicumque praeest, mitissimus esto
Teque his natura noveris esse parem.[21]

Karl Bosl commented, 'there is nothing subversive here'.[22] Well, not perhaps if you can keep morals and politics apart. But Theodulf – and Charlemagne – did not mean them to be kept apart. The notion of *pauper* and *iudex* as *natura pares* informed Charlemagne's whole reform programme.[23] Theodulf's poem was intended to be read, indeed read out, before a royal court that agonised over justice, and before men who as judges would confront *pauperes* in their own courts.

The decrees of the Council of Chalon, one of five great councils summoned by Charlemagne in 813 to put reform in place, were very probably Theodulf's work.[24] C. 51 commented on differences of 'condition' between men, but insisted that superiors show mercy to inferiors, 'remembering that they are all brothers, because they are all sons of one Father'.[25] More than one ninth-century bishop borrowed this clause in giving advice to priests and laity.[26] Jonas of Orléans in his *Rule for the Lay Way of Life* – another handbook written for a *potens,* a count – adapted Gregory's original formula: 'Those whom [lords] see in this world to be lowly and abject in their demeanour (*cultus*), and unequal to them in bodily appearance and wealth (*cutis et opes*), they should recognise to be by nature their

---

[19] R. and A. J. Carlyle, *A History of Medieval Political Theory in the West,* 6 vols (London, 1903–36), vol. I, pp. 114, 127, 199–200.

[20] Alcuin, *De virtutibus et vitiis,* PL 101, col. 638. In the mid-ninth century, Marquis Eberhard of Friuli owned a copy of this book. The noblewoman Dhuoda evidently did too, for she drew heavily on the work in composing her own Handbook for her son in the early 840s: cf. below, n. 94.

[21] Theodulf, *Paraenesis ad iudices,* (ed.) E. Dümmler, MGH Poetae I, 516, ll. 895–6: 'Whoever is in charge of those lacking power, let him be most gentle / for you know that you are by nature equal to those.'

[22] Bosl, '*Potens* und *pauper*', p. 82.

[23] See P. J. Fouracre, 'Carolingian justice: the rhetoric of improvement and contexts of abuse', *La Giustizia nel'alto medioevo, Settimane di Studio del Centro Italiano di Studi sull'alto medioevo* 42 (Spoleto, 1995), vol. 2, pp. 771–803.

[24] E. Dahlhaus-Berg, *Nova Antiquitas et Antiqua Novitas. Typologische Exegese und isidorianische Geschichtsbild bei Theodulf von Orléans* (Cologne and Vienna 1975), p. 233.

[25] Council of Chalon, c. 51, ed. A. Werminghoff, MGH Concilia II, 1, pp. 283–4.

[26] Wulfad of Bourges, MGH Epp. VI, no. 27, p. 191: lay *potentes* are to understand that the members of their *familiae, quamvis potestate minores sint, fratres eorum sunt,* following Rodulf of Bourges, Statutes c. 23, ed. R. Pokorny and M. Stratmann, MGH Capitula episcoporum, Part II (Hannover, 1995), pp. 251–2.

peers and equals (*natura pares et aequales sibi*).[27] *Cultus, cutis* and *opes* meant a lot in terms of external signs of status: Jonas pitted *natura* against them. He recycled this same passage in his 'Mirror for Princes', which in turn was reused in the decrees of the Council of Paris (829).[28] These were texts with a wide readership, lay and clerical, and long-lasting influence. By contrast, Hincmar of Rheims's *The Person and Office of a King* probably did not reach an audience wider than Charles the Bald's court, but it did so at a time, 873, when much hard political thinking was going on there: 'Saving the authority of government, let us bring back constantly to our heart [Hincmar and the king were to think this through together] and assiduously reflect on this, that we are made equal with other men, not that in this temporal world we are set above them . . .'[29] Such ideas did not add up to a theory, for they were not integrated into a coherent structure; but they were directed at the thinking of kings and magnates, key political actors, and to contexts – courts and law courts – in which those men took political action.[30]

The clergy constituted an *ordo* and church councils displayed that order acting as a horizontal group. Bishops routinely legislated *pari consensu, pari voto*.[31] Hence it was hardly surprising that bishops who organised and presided over assemblies that elected kings – as happened from the ninth century on – asserted that the choice had been made *pari consensu*.[32] Though bishops could think of themselves as a kind of tribe (*gens*), the institutional heirs of Aaron and Levi, some bishops were certainly more equal than others: a capitulary of *c*.780 distinguished between *potentiores, mediocres* and *minores* among bishops, parallelling a threefold ranking of counts.[33] In the case of leading churchmen, wealth and power could not be taken for granted, however, and in the newly sensitised atmosphere of the 790s could indeed become grounds for criticism – an Achilles heel. In 799, Archbishop Elipand of Toledo, who lived in straitened circumstances under Muslim rule, attacked Alcuin, his theological opponent, in a letter intended for wide circulation: 'See and beware! Are you not one of those known to have 20,000 serfs: therefore inflated by riches, remember what Scripture says: "Did not God choose poor men in the world, men who were rich in faith?" '[34] Having 20,000 *servi* (and Alcuin didn't deny it) constituted a moral, hence political, slur that was difficult to rebut. He replied,

---

[27] Jonas, *De institutione laicali* ii, 22, PL 106, col. 213: 'Eos vero qui in hoc saeculo infimos abjectosque cultu, et cute et opibus se impares [domini] conspiciunt, natura pares et aequales sibi esse prorsus agnoscant'.

[28] *De institutione regia*, c. 5, ed. A. Dubreucq, Sources chrétiennes 407 (Paris, 1995), pp. 204–11.

[29] *De persona et ministerio regis*, PL 125, col. 836: 'Servata autem auctoritate regiminis, ad cor nostrum sine cessatione redeamus, et consideremus assidue, quod sumus aequaliter cum ceteris conditi, non quod temporaliter caeteris praelati . . .'

[30] Cf. Markus, *Gregory*, p. 24, on 'the courtroom of the heart'.

[31] E.g. Councils of Paris (829), cc. 17, 20, and Tribur (895), prologue, MGH Capit. II, pp. 35, 40, 212.

[32] Synod of Ponthion, 876 (Charles the Bald), Council of Mantaille 879 (Boso), Council of Pavia, 889 (Guy of Spoleto), MGH Capit. II, no. 279, pp. 348 and 351; no. 284, p. 368; no. 222, p. 106.

[33] MGH Capit. I, no. 21, p. 52.

[34] MGH Epp. IV, Ep. 182, p. 302: 'Vide ne tu sis ex illis, qui viginti milia servorum habere dinosceris, et ideo diviciis inflatus . . . memento quod scriptura dicat: Nonne Deus pauperes elegit in mundo, divites in fide?'

invoking Gregory, that everything depended on the frame of mind in which a man possessed this world. 'It is one thing to possess it, another to be possessed by it. There is the man who has wealth yet does not have it, just as there is he who does not have it, yet has it. Never have I acquired any man for my service, rather do I desire to serve all the servants of Christ my God . . .'[35] For Alcuin, lord of the lands of St Martin, Tours, and representative of an imperial church, Elipand's attack was subversive. It was an attack that Charlemagne himself took up a few years later on a broader front. The moral problems of inequalities in the church in the world were clearly recognised as such. That they became political problems suggests that the egalitarian streak in Gregorian thinking was alive and well, not just among Mozarabs in Al-Andalus, but in some quarters of the Frankish church. Later in the ninth century, Hincmar of Rheims would remind his colleagues that the Christian bishop in Cordoba lived among his flock off tithe income, without support from a ruler's patronage.[36] For conscientious churchmen, misgivings about disparities in the church, even though not driven, to be sure, by egalitarianism in the modern sense, were inseparable from a sense of New Testament demands for justice and charity.[37]

Below the level of the communion of saints, or the Old Testament *gens*, or the priestly order, the church ceased to offer much in the way of horizontal terminology. The word *pares* does not occur in the Vulgate Bible.[38] A few learned men – Alcuin, Lupus of Ferrières – could find a source for the language of natural equality in Cicero, not in his works on the state and on law, which were known only at second-hand and barely cited, but in those on old age and friendship.[39] The political sense of late Roman republican *amicitia* was congenial to scholars busily representing themselves to each other as a professional elite. Friendship did not abolish, but could transcend, inequality.[40] Lupus of Ferrières slightly misquoted Cicero in a

[35] MGH Epp. IV, Ep. 200, p. 332: '. . . quo animo quis habeat saeculum. Aliud est habere saeculum, aliud est haberi a saeculo. Est qui habet divitias, et non habet; est qui non habet, et habet. Hominem vero numquam ad meum conparavi servitium, sed magis devota caritate omnibus Christi dei mei famulis servire desiderans.'

[36] Hincmar, *De iure metropolitanorum*, PL 126, col. 228.

[37] Cf. Nelson, 'Making ends meet', *Studies in Church History* 24 (1987), 25–36, repr. in Nelson, *The Frankish World* (London, 1996), ch. 8; Nelson, 'The voice of Charlemagne', in R. Gameson and H. Leyser (eds), *Belief and Culture in the Middle Ages. Studies Presented to Henry Mayr-Harting* (Oxford, 2001), pp. 76–88; cf. M. Innes, 'Charlemagne's will: politics, inheritance and ideology in the early ninth century', *English Historical Review* 112 (1997), 833–55.

[38] The adjective *par* does occasionally appear in the practical sense of an equal measure. The Apocryphal book of Ecclesiasticus 13: 19–20 offers the proverbial passage: 'omnis animal diligit sibi simile, sic et omnis homo proximum sibi. Omnis caro ad similem sibi conjugetur et omnis homo simili sui sociabitur . . .', while I Maccabees 12: 50, tells how the people of Israel encouraged one another before going out to battle. Nor as we'll see were these verses forgotten in the earlier Middle Ages. But I don't think they can be said to have directly evoked much of the horizontal thinking that certainly went on then.

[39] Cicero, *De senectute*, c. 7, cites a proverbial saying, *pares cum paribus . . . facillime congregantur*; and *de Amicitia*, c. 32, says true friends are *pares in amore et aequales*.

[40] Alcuin on *amicitia* as a relationship between equals, *Disputatio Pippini cum Albino*, PL 101, col. 978; *Liber de virtutibus et de vitiis* c. 36, PL 101, col. 638; see A. M. Fiske, 'Alcuin and mystical friendship', *Studi Medievali* 2, 3rd ser. (1961), 551–75, at 566–9.

letter to Abbot Altsig of York requesting *amicitia: pares ad pares facile congregantur*.[41] Alliances of more or less political kinds were part of the everyday experience not only of clerical elites but of laymen. You would have *genealogiae vel regionis consortes* – fellows by kin and/or region – fellowship of both kinds constituting the ties you would exploit if your *consors* was well placed *in palatio*.[42] The *ministri* who ran the Aachen palace apparently saw themselves as a group of *pares*.[43] Men could identify each other as *conpalatini*, a group whose members were bound in and by long-term experience of shared life and work.[44] Now it is true that whatever parity was involved in such bonds of association was qualified in practice by disparities of rank and influence, yet it was not wholly compromised.

Something similar could be said of marriage, through which, as Jonas of Orléans said, alliances were made that produced consanguineous bonds between families, and nobles married their *pares* to reinforce nobility.[45] Marriage itself was an alliance, for which both law and liturgy supplied a language of equality. Spouses as such were *pares*, and would live in a *consortium*, a *societas*, a *foedus*, with *pares animi*, and *par concordia animorum*.[46] Jonas of Orléans, somewhat optimistically, demanded *par pudicitiae [et par] conjugalis thori fides* of husband and wife.[47] In practice, gender constituted a major disparity, whatever the woman's rank. Nevertheless, parity in Christian marriage transcended, in principle, the distinction between slave and free. J.-P. Devroey argues that this in the Carolingian period was an important factor in the decline of slavery.[48]

Associations (*Genossenschaften*) have often been seen as not only fundamentally different from vertical bonds of lordship and service, but as peculiarly Teutonic.[49] Yet one of the earliest bits of evidence of groups of earlier medieval people living together in associations, and holding property in common, comes not from Germany but from Galicia. The *Regula communis* agreed by an assembly of abbots in *c*.660 denounced 'false monasteries' constituted by illicit associations, and instead imposed a 'proper' Rule. The local conditions that evoked these groups were peculiar to Galicia (though perhaps in important respects their associations were not so different from Bede's false monasteries), but it is worth noting, first, that these were not *Ur-Genossenschaften*, timelessly existing, but rather had been created at a

---

[41] Lupus, Ep. 62, ed. P. Marshall (Leipzig, 1984), p. 68, also quoting Eccl. 13: 19; cf. above nn. 36 and 37.

[42] Hincmar of Rheims, *De ordine palatii*, ed. T. Gross and R. Schieffer, MGH Fontes Iuris Germanici antiqui (Hannover, 1980), c. IV (= c. 18), p. 66.

[43] Capit. De disciplina palatii, *c*. 1, MGH Capit. I, no. 146, p. 298; Capit. de Moneta, c. 5, counts have *pares suos*, MGH Capit. I, no. 147, p. 300.

[44] S. Airlie, 'Bonds, of power and bonds of association in the court circle of Louis the Pious', in P. Godman and R. Collins (ed.), *Charlemagne's Heir* (Oxford, 1990), pp. 191–204.

[45] Jonas, *De institutione laicali* II, 8, PL 106, col. 183.

[46] Sacramentary of Fulda, 'Nuptialis actio', ed. G. Richter (Fulda, 1907), pp. 324–7; Augustine, *De bono conjugali*, 1, PL 40, col. 373; Council of Verberie (758/68), c. 6, MGH Capit. I, p. 40.

[47] Jonas, *De institutione laicali* II, 4, PL 106, col. 177.

[48] J.-P. Devroey, 'Men and women in early medieval serfdom', *Past and Present* 166 (2000), 3–30.

[49] Reynolds, *Kingdoms and Communities*, 2nd edn, Introduction, xxv–xxxii.

specific moment *suo arbitrio*, by persons bound by mutual oaths; and second, that whatever we make of the Suevic conquest of that part of the world, these groups were not Germanic, or Teutonic, but composed of indigenous people – Galicians. These were people looking for collective security by adapting, more or less successfully, to structures available within the church. For though the *Regula* denounces these groups in their unlicensed form, it proposes to supervise them, and the very arrangements it establishes assume the persistence of what Pablo Diaz has called an 'original assemblyism': 'if anyone of us [i.e. the members of a village monastery] is accused of murmuring against the Rule, then let us have the power to assemble, all of us, in one body and . . . publicly assess the [extent of] guilt' (*tunc habeamus potestatem omnes in unum congregare et . . . culpam publice probare*).[50] Is this to say that in the beginning all the world was Galicia? I would claim no more than that assemblyism, or, echoing Susan Reynolds, a propensity to collective association, was something continually reinvented and rethought in various contexts in various parts of early medieval Europe. Though, given 'the hierarchical temper of the times',[51] associations as such were by no means straightforwardly egalitarian, and though elements of hierarchy were present in Galician and other varieties, characteristic features of parity may nonetheless be seen in voluntary and public adherence to the group by oath-swearing, and collective monitoring of a member's ongoing commitment to group regulations.

Earlier medieval judgements on the desirability or otherwise of such associations were determined not by the extent of parity within them but by the ends for which they were formed. Men joined *in contubernio*, or *in conpanio* (in the Merovingian period), or *collectae* (in Charlemagne's reign), or *caballarii* (in the mid-ninth century), comparable to the *hloth* (armed band) of Anglo-Saxon law or the *arschild* of Lombard law, were negatively depicted, therefore.[52] All too familiar was the disruptive group activity of bands of men, criminal gangs, assumed to be all-male. 'Thus do men, not women', said the Lombard king Liudprand. The comment was in fact made à propos an exceptional case of group violence by women (who had

---

[50] *Regula communis, Pactum*, PL 87, col. 1128; see C. J. Bishko, 'The pactual tradition in Hispanic monasticism', in his *Spanish and Portuguese Monastic History* (London, 1984), ch. 1, pp. 1–43 (a paper published for the first time in this collection of Bishko's essays), esp. pp. 17–25, definitively countering the arguments for 'a strong Germanic stamp' put forward by I. Herwegen and U. Stutz early in the twentieth century (and revising Bishko's own line of thinking in 1951, reprinted in ch. 3 of the same volume); see further P. C. Diaz, 'The role of the monasteries in a peripheral area: seventh-century *Gallaecia*', in M. de Jong and F. Theuws (eds), *Topographies of Power* (Leiden, 2001 forthcoming). I am very grateful to Pablo Diaz for letting me read this paper in advance of publication.

[51] *Kingdoms and Communities*, p. 29, in the context of collective judgement; cf. ibid., '. . . people of higher status . . . would dominate deliberations . . .'

[52] Pactus Legis Salicae cc. XIV, XLII, XLIII, LXIII, ed. K. A. Eckhardt, MGH Legum Sectio I, Leges nationum Germanicarum IV, 1 (Hannover, 1962), pp. 66, 162, 165, 229; MGH Capit. I, no. 20, c. 17, p. 51 (Herstal, 779), no. 68, c. 2, p. 157 (801 × 813); Hincmar of Rheims, Ep. no. 126, ed. E. Perels, MGH Epp. VIII (Berlin 1939), p. 63; Laws of Ine, cc. 13, 1; 14, ed. F. L. Attenborough, *The Laws of the Earliest English Kings* (Cambridge, 1922), p. 40; *Leges Langobardorum*, ed. F. Beyerle (Weimar, 1947), Leges Liutprandi 134, p. 300.

perhaps been put up to the deed by menfolk intent on evading legal penalties – hence the need for royal equity).[53] By contrast, groups that upheld the law and kept the peace by working together in local courts were entirely respectable. When *rachimburgii* gave judgements together, they worked as *pares*.[54] So too, no doubt, did *viri sapientes* and *boni homines*. Wherever charter evidence is thick enough, groups of landowners can be found in the regions acting repeatedly together as attesters of charters for each other and/or for common lords. When we find them also as colleagues in religious endowments, we can infer that some sense of group identity had developed.[55] We do not often know what they called themselves collectively. The name matters less than the thing. In a few cases, we hear of local land holders, sometimes clearly peasants, acting as groups. At Risano in Istria in 804, 172 *homines capitanei* from several places, united 'in great oppression and grief' (*in grandi oppressione et dolore*), denounced to Charlemagne's *missi* the 'violent acts (*forcia*) of the *dux* of the region, whom hitherto they had not dared resist 'on account of fear' (*propter timorem*). Before the *missi*, the *dux* prudently acknowledged the law of their forefathers, and gave pledges to make amends.[56] At Antoigné in the Touraine in 828, it was a group of *pares* represented by four named men who protested to King Pippin I of Aquitaine that their lord, the monastery of Corméry, had imposed heavier payments and renders upon them than their *lex* allowed.[57] The peasants lost their case.

An apparently larger group, neighbours still, but from a wider area, in the Allgäu, appear in 853 in a charter of Louis the German: the *populus . . . circumquaque posit[us]* vis-à-vis the monastery of Kempten, again, put up a legal fight against a powerful church, this time over land newly brought into cultivation.[58] The Allgäu

---

[53] Leges Liutprandi 141 (734), p. 310; cf. R. Balzaretti, ' "These are things that men do, not women": the social regulation of violence in Lombard Italy', in G. Halsall (ed.), *Violence and Society in the Early Medieval West* (Woodbridge, 1998), pp. 175–92.

[54] Edict of Chilperic c. 8, MGH Capit. I, no. 4, p. 9: where seven *rachimburgii* determine the extent of a lawful delay permitted (*sunia*, cf. Medieval French *essoin*) before an accused must appear in court, 'si VII venire non potuerint . . . tunc veniant III de ipsis qui . . . pro paris suos sunia nuntiant'.

[55] Cf. W. Davies, *Small Worlds. The Village Community in Early Medieval Brittany* (London, 1988), pp. 109–28; M. Innes, *State and Society in the Early Middle Ages. The Middle Rhine Valley 400–1000* (Cambridge, 2000), pp. 125–8.

[56] C. Manaresi (ed.), *I Placiti del 'regnum Italiae'*, vol. 1 (Rome, 1955), no. 17, p. 55. Some of the alleged *forcia*, so Duke John claimed, had been done under the impression that those woods and pastures were the public property of the lord emperor (*a parte domni imperatoris in publico*); cf. H. Krahwinkler, *Friaul im Frühmittelalter* (Vienna, Cologne and Weimar, 1992), pp. 199–243. Susan Reynolds drew this text to my attention some years ago (and told me that Walter Goffart had drawn it to hers) when we used it in teaching about early medieval dispute settlement to classes at the Central European University in Budapest: academic life would be unimaginable without such *consortia*.

[57] L. Levillain, *Actes de Pépin I, roi d'Aquitaine* (Paris, 1926), no. 12, pp. 46–7. Cf. Nelson, 'Dispute-settlement in West Francia', in W. Davies and P. Fouracre, *The Settlement of Disputes in Early Medieval Europe* (Cambridge, 1986), pp. 45–64, repr. Nelson, *The Frankish World* (London, 1996), pp. 51–74, at pp. 54–7, 71–2.

[58] Louis the German, Diploma 66 (?853), ed. P. Kehr, MGH Diplomata regum Germaniae ex stirpe Karolinorum (Berlin, 1934), p. 92. Eric Goldberg's forthcoming book on Louis's reign will illuminate this episode, and I am grateful for the chance to read it in advance of publication.

men too lost. Their punishment was to come on foot before an assembly near Regensburg, and all publicly carrying saddles on their backs. Did the punishment break or reinforce the group's identity? A group of peasants at Limonta, on Lake Como, *servi homines . . . ac consortes suorum*, and their descendants, maintained their resistance to their monastic lord's demands across a century.[59] The pressures of powerful ecclesiastical lords may themselves sometimes have produced, and exploited, a sense of parity, and superiority, on the part of village elites. The village of Mitry, for instance, was split in 861 between *coloni* and *servi*, the latter denying their servile status: their common lord, St Denis, used the *coloni* as witnesses against the *servi* and coerced the latter. Sant' Ambrogio may have tried something similar against the Limonta *servi homines*. The thinking of these groups is recorded indirectly, always by their opponents and/or superiors. Yet its basic features emerge clearly: men had customary rights, and groups defended these at law; they had some sense of equality of status, and of group identity; also of some confidence in courts, in royal agents, even in kings themselves, as protectors of that status. These were not, in Eric Hobsbawm's phrase, 'primitive rebels': their thinking, like that of the Galician associates, was not 'pre-political', surely, but political, for they sought to maintain what they saw as fair social relations through collective action, and they acted within, not outside or against, existing power structures.[60]

Other evidence for more or less horizontal groups comes from prescriptive sources. Charlemagne's capitularies contain several references, the earliest of them in the Capitulary of Herstal (779) which forbids the mutual swearing of oaths *per gildonia*. 'Although men may otherwise form *convenentiae* concerning their alms-giving or fire or shipwreck, let no one presume to swear to these.'[61] The Double Edict for *missi* (789) prohibits 'those sworn associations which they make by St Stephen or by us or by our sons'.[62] *Coniurationes per nos*, that is, by the name of Charlemagne, sound royalist enough, but they may have been intended to challenge or bypass lordly authority, hence aroused royal concern as well, while competing associations focused on either Charlemagne or (one of) his sons could have been seen as threatening to open up dangerous fault-lines within the royal family.[63] As for St Stephen, oaths taken on his saint's day, 26 December, were perhaps associated with the excessive conviviality of the Christmas season.[64]

---

[59] R. Balzaretti, 'The monastery of Sant'Ambrogio and dispute settlement in early medieval Milan', *Early Medieval Europe* 3 (1994), 1–18.

[60] E. Hobsbawm, *Primitive Rebels* (Manchester, 1959), esp. pp. 153–62. Cf. below, p. 40.

[61] Capit. of Herstal c. 16, MGH Capit. I, no. 20, p. 51: 'De sacramentis per gildonia invicem coniurantibus, ut nemo facere praesumat. Alio vero modo de illorum elemosinis aut de incendio aut de naufragio, quamvis convenentias faciant, nemo in hoc iurare praesumat.'

[62] Double Edict for *missi*, MGH Capit. I, no. 23, c. 26, p. 64: 'Omnino prohibendum est omnibus ebrietatis malum, et istas coniurationes quas faciunt per sanctum Stephanum aut per nos aut per filios nostros prohibemus. Et praecipimus ut episcopi vel abbates non vadant per casas miscendo.' The association of material here indicates that a *coniuratio* involved hard drinking, that the venue was a private house, and that clergy could be participants.

[63] See Nelson, 'Charlemagne: *pater optimus*?' (forthcoming).

[64] See below, p. 37.

At Thionville (805), particularly savage punishments were decreed 'concerning conspiracies (*de conspirationibus*) which have been confirmed with an oath (*quicumque facere praesumpserint et sacramento quamcumque conspirationem firmaverint*), when evil has been perpetrated: the ring-leaders are to be put to death while those who aided them are to be flogged, one by another, and to cut off each other's noses'.[65] Such a punishment was, at one and the same time, an exemplary public act of permanent dishonouring,[66] a negation of that mutual support which was the acceptable face of *convenentia*, and a ghastly demonstration of parity misused.[67]

To see why Carolingian authorities (and perhaps others too) worried about groups, and collective action, their anxieties need to be put in context.[68] First, there is the matter of drunkenness: the Apostle (Gal. 5: 19) had classed this among the works of the flesh, but the legislation of 789 linked it explicitly with the forming of *conjurationes*. Hincmar of Rheims in c. 16 of his episcopal statutes, 'on those associations called in the vulgar gilds or confraternities . . . formed for religious and charitable purposes', and including women, depicted gild meetings as occasions for *pastus* and *comessationes*.[69] Hincmar, anxious about the involvement of priests, recognised that 'if such associations should have to meet because someone has a grievance against his fellow member (*contra parem*) and they cannot be reconciled unless the priest and the others have a meeting', then the priest would have to attend, but he was to 'touch only a single drink – not a drop more!' To my mind, suggestions that drinking in guild-brotherhoods was a way 'to enter into communion with supernatural forces'[70] or 'a passport to mystical experience'[71] are fanciful. The drinking has more to do with easing social relations, creating community,

---

[65] Capit. of Thionville, c. 10, MGH Capit. I, no. 44, p. 124: '. . . adiutores vero eorum singuli alter ab altero flagellatur et nares sibi invicem praecidant'.

[66] P. Bourdieu, *Outline of a Theory of Practice* (Cambridge, 1977), ch. 1; V. Grubner, 'Noses and honour in the late medieval town', *History Workshop Journal* 40 (1995), 1–15; cf. K. Schreiner and G. Schwerhoff (eds), *Verletzte Ehre: Ehrkonflikte in Gesellschaften des Mittelalters und der frühen Neuzeit* (Cologne, 1995), the editors' introduction to this interesting collection, pp. 1–28.

[67] Cf. Lothar as ruler in Italy, in the Capitulary of Olonna (822/823), c. 4, MGH Capit. I, no. 158, p. 318: 'Volumus de obligationibus ut nullus homo per sacramentum nec per aliam obligationem adunationem faciat; et si hoc facere praesumpserit, tunc de illis qui prius ipsum consilium incoaverit aut qui hoc factum habet in exilio ab ipso comite in Corsica mittatur, et illi alii bannum componant; et si talis fuerit qui non habeat unde ipsum bannum conponat, LX ictus accipiat.' Here Lothar refers to laws of the Lombard kings Ratchis and Liutprand.

[68] In the Carolingians' case, there was the extra drive to reform the clerical and monastic orders and detach them from worldly ties: hence prohibitions on gatherings where clergy might be involved, Double Edict of Commission, MGH Capit. I, no. 23, c. 26, p. 64: 'bishops and abbots must not go mingling with [lay]people in their homes' ('. . . non vadant per casas miscendo'), or on clergy or monks forming *conspirationes* against their own superiors, *Admonitio Generalis*, c. 29, MGH Capit. I, no. 22, p. 56: '. . . ut nec clerici nec monachi conspirationes vel insidias contra pastorem suum faciant'.

[69] Hincmar, *Capitula* c. 16, ed. Pokorny and Stratmann, MGH Capitula episcoporum, II, 43–4.

[70] M. Rouche, 'The early Middle Ages in the West', in P. Ariès and G. Duby (eds), *A History of Private Life*, vol. I (London, 1987), p. 432.

[71] E. John, *Reassessing Anglo-Saxon England* (Manchester, 1996), p. 23.

transforming (perhaps literally) the vertical to the horizontal,[72] which is not to say that disputes might not, and according to Hincmar often did, break out over a few drinks too many. Insistence on sobriety could be seen as social discipline[73] but it was not only a matter of control by the authorities of church and state: Charlemagne's intent was to involve *patresfamilias* even at the level of the *vulgaris populus* in his great project of creating a culture of sober *conversatio* from top to bottom.[74] Patriarchy, an association of male household heads, thus operated in horizontal as well as vertical ways.

Secondly, Charlemagne was determined to use oaths of fidelity more vigorously, it seems, than his predecessors ever had, as crucial instruments of his regime.[75] Here verticality may seem clearly opposed to horizontality. Sometimes the very same capitularies that are concerned with oaths to the ruler, or to other lords, are those which prohibit oath-swearings of the mutual kind. Thus in 805, a clear distinction was made between on the one hand, *sacramenta*, oaths sworn 'to us and someone's own lord for our benefit and that lord's', or by one man to another *iuste secundum legem*, that is, as part of legal procedure, and, on the other hand, oaths sworn *in conjuratione*, or *in conspiratione*. The second kind of oaths were clearly linked with political subversion.[76] Nevertheless, horizontality was not unacceptable in itself: peer-group associations such as *convenentiae* for charitable or insurance purposes, so long as they did not involve mutual oaths, had Charlemagne's approval. Further, while capitularies stressed the obligation to obedience of each individual faithful man, and the oath of fidelity was thus dyadic, between *dominus* and *homo*, the actual circumstances of oath-swearing – the gathering at the local assembly, presided over by count or *missus*, of both indigenous neighbours (*pagensales*) and outsiders endowed by the ruler with local land 'in vassalage', the mutual witnessing of the ritual act, and the *missus*'s inscribing of the names of those oath-swearers, followed perhaps by a reading-out of the names, and his taking of the list to Charlemagne[77] – were calculated to engender a group of *fideles* in a given locality. Fidelity would thus have been experienced as a collective as well as an individual thing, reinforced by ongoing legal, administrative, and military activity: *fideles* were also *pares*.

---

[72] Cf. Hobsbawm, *Primitive Rebels*, pp. 153–4.

[73] Cf. M. Foucault, *Discipline and Punish* (English translation London, 1975) cited in P. Rabinow, *The Foucault Reader* (London, 1991), pp. 169–213, esp. p. 206, on discipline as a ' "physics" of power'.

[74] MGH Capit. I, no. 64, c. 7, p. 153: 'De ebrietate, ut primum omnium seniores semetipsos exinde vetent et eorum iuniores exemplum bonae sobrietatis ostendant'; and cf. ibid. c. 17: 'De vulgari populo, ut unusquisque suos iuniores distringat, ut melius ac melius oboediant et consentiant mandatis et praeceptis imperialibus.'

[75] M. Becher, *Eid und Herrschaft. Untersuchungen zum Herrscherethos Karls des Grossen* (Sigmaringen, 1993), esp. pp. 16–17, 195–212.

[76] Capitulary of Thionville (805), cc. 9 and 10, MGH Capit. I, no. 44, p. 124: c. 9: 'De iuramento, ut nulli per sacramentum fidelitas promittatur nisi nobis et unicuique proprio seniori ad nostram utilitatem et sui senioris; excepto his sacramentis quae iuste secundum legem alteri ab altero debetur . . .'; c. 10: 'De conspirationibus vero . . . de caetero in regno nostro nulla huiusmodi conspiratio fiat, nec per sacramentum nec sine sacramento.'

[77] *Capitulare missorum* (789) c. 4, MGH Capit. I, no. 25, p. 67.

Peers in the early Middle Ages

Early medieval horizontal groupings have been the subject of illuminating papers by Otto Gerhard Oexle.[78] Oexle is surely right to highlight the common trait of group action. Nevertheless, it is possible to exaggerate the similarity between different types of group: not all groups involved mutual oaths, and when they did, not all members may have sworn such oaths (I know of no evidence that women ever did even when they belonged to *gildoniae*, though Oexle assumes so[79]). Moreover Oexle distinguishes so sharply between horizontal and vertical bonds as to make them mutually exclusive, or substitutes for each other. Thus he correlates the formation of associations of equals with the failure of post-Roman regimes to defend their people against a second wave of barbarian invasions.[80] In *c.*820, for instance, the inhabitants of Flemish maritime regions made *conjurationes* that were clearly a form of self-defence against Vikings – and a form of self-help necessary because of the state's incapacity.[81] So too the *conjuratio* by the *vulgus promiscuus* between Seine and Loire in 859 made *incaute* (that is, on my reading, seen by those with regional power as potentially subversive) was a case of local action where the inertia of king and counts and bishops had left a void. Bishop Prudentius commented laconically: 'they were easily slain by our more powerful people'.[82] Oexle cites these examples and observes that these associations offered security 'in epoch-making disorders, in conditions of disorganisation'.[83] This is not the only scenario that makes sense of the earlier medieval evidence for associations of peers (and the like) in general. In the last part of this essay, I want to offer, not an alternative account, but a complementary one. There is some evidence to show how the horizontal and vertical coexisted and interpenetrated: how kings and peers cooperated, and how persons from lower strata exploited the parity of peers above them.

On Oexle's reading, the 'culture of the *coniuratio*' entailed values, mentalities, forms of social action, 'group-specific objectivisations (rituals and institutions)' in

---

[78] 'O. G. Oexle, 'Gilden als soziale Gruppen in der Karolingerzeit', in H. Jankuhn (ed.), *Das Handwerk in vor- und frühgeschichtlicher Zeit*, Teil I (Göttingen, 1981), pp. 284–354; idem, 'Conjuratio und Gilde im frühen Mittelalter', in B. Schwineköper (ed.), *Gilden und Zünfte. Kaufmännische und gewerbliche Genossenschaften im frühen und hohen Mittelalter* (Sigmaringen, 1985), pp. 151–214; idem, 'Die Kultur der Rebellion', in M. T. Fögen (ed.), *Ordnung und Aufruhr im Mittelalter* (Frankfurt, 1995), pp. 119–37; idem, 'Gilde und Kommune. Über die Entstehung von "Einung" und "Gemeinde" als Grundformen des Zusammenlebens in Europa', in P. Blickle (ed.), *Theorien kommunaler Ordnung in Europa*, Schriften des Historischen Kollegs Kolloquien 36 (Oldenburg, 1996), pp. 75–97.

[79] 'Oexle, Gilden als soziale Gruppen', pp. 349–50, but cf. below n. 95; Oexle, 'Gilde und Kommune', p. 85 offers no further evidence.

[80] 'Oexle, Gilde und Kommune', pp. 86–9.

[81] Capit. missorum (821), c. 7, MGH Capit. I, no. 148, p. 301: 'De conjurationibus servorumquae fiunt in Flandris et Menpisco et in caeteris maritimis locis volumus ut per missos nostros indicetur dominis servorum illorum ut constringant eos ne ultra tales coniurationes facere praesumant.' See S. Epperlein, *Herrschaft und Volk im karolingischen Imperium* (Berlin, 1969), pp. 42–50.

[82] *Annales Bertiniani*, s.a. 859, ed. F. Grat et al. (Paris, 1965), p. 80; cf. Nelson trans., *The Annals of St-Bertin* (Manchester, 1991), p. 89. These *potentiores* were not always inert, then.

[83] Oexle, 'Gilde und Kommune', p. 89, 'in epochalen Umbrüchen, in Verhältnissen der Desorganisation'.

which can be heard the voices of the 'Others' constantly repressed by the countervailing culture of 'the ranked society' (*Ständesgesellschaft*).[84] The problem here is not a historical, but a sociological one. Given the evidence for earlier medieval collectivities, Oexle is absolutely right to challenge a modern assumption that 'modern' traits could not be found before the twelfth century. But why assume, instead, that only social disaster could elicit peasant self-help? After all, the Capitulary of Herstal's reference to *convenentiae* (c. 16: *de illorum elemosinis aut de incendio aut de naufragio . . . convenentias faciant*) suggests that peasants normally had their own organisations to provide collective social security. It's anachronistic, surely, to suppose that the Carolingian state could ever have provided benefits for destitute families, let alone fire insurance or travel insurance. As for the parallel Oexle draws with Hobsbawm's primitive rebels,[85] that is, with workers' associations in the nineteenth century: yes, there are interesting similarities, in, for instance, the use of oaths to strengthen horizontal bonds, and likewise the use of strong drink. But were the *vulgus promiscuus* of 859, or the members of the *gildoniae* of the Rémois *c*.870, rebels – any more than were the masons or oddfellows or (mostly) the trade unionists of nineteenth-century Britain? Were these associates not *part of* the culture that surrounded them?

Charlemagne's government, like any reasonable regime, worried about the military implications of parity, about the danger to internal peace posed by bands of armed men within the realm and ill-controlled.[86] From the last years of Charlemagne's reign, increasing external attacks meant a new call for defensive war, hence the need to call up peasant soldiers.[87] Warriors on the march through the realm to reach enemies *beyond* the frontier had long been considered a likely danger to social order.[88] When there were more warriors, including peasant warriors, marching to counter enemies *on* the frontier or actually *within* the realm, the risks of disorder increased. Yet there were other kinds of risk too when groups of peasant peers had to equip one of their number to go and serve in the royal army:

---

[84] Oexle, 'Gilde und Kommune', p. 89, points to 'the appropriation by the group of a social/universal norm', for instance, *fraternitas*, and the crucial role of the oath, denoting a voluntary act in a society 'certainly not without a state but without a monopoly of legitimate force'.

[85] As cited above, n. 53.

[86] Capitulary of Herstal (779), c. 14, MGH Capit. I, no. 20, p. 50: 'de truste faciendo nemo praesumat'; Lothar, Capit. of Olonna (822/823), MGH Capit. I, no. 158, c. 5, p. 318: 'Volumus ut cum collecta vel scutis in placito comitis nullus presumat venire; et si praesumpserit, bannum componat'. Cf. above, p. 34 and n. 52.

[87] For the significant distinction between offensive and defensive warfare, see T. Reuter, 'The end of Carolingian military expansion', in Godman and Collins (eds), *Charlemagne's Heir*, pp. 391–405. The distinction is made by a ninth-century Rheims supplier of additional material to Ansegis's Collection in MS Paris BN 10758, Mordek, *Bibliotheca capitularium regum Francorum manuscripta. Überlieferung und Traditionszusammenhang* (MGH Hilfsmittel 15, Munich, 1995), pp. 587–605; P. Wormald, *The Making of English Law* (Oxford, 1999), pp. 59–60.

[88] See Nelson, 'Violence in the Carolingian world and the ritualization of ninth-century Frankish warfare', in G. Halsall (ed.), *Violence and Society in the Early Medieval West* (Woodbridge, 1997), pp. 90–107.

while the picked man served, his property back home might be stolen by one of his *pares*.[89] A capitulary of 811 dealt with problems arising 'when one man has refused to help another on the march or in the army where he ought to be doing something for the defence of . . . the *patria* . . . Very frequent disputes arise when one man seeks to take what he sees is the property of his peer.'[90]

From such capitulary references, it's clear that there was also an important military context to parity. Between men who fought together, or might fight together, there had to exist a sense of solidarity. Rulers, especially Charlemagne, were concerned that men should not suffer by their absence on military service, and concerned, therefore, to reinforce the bonds of solidarity between *pares*, to check the envy of *par contra parem*. True, some forms of solidarity had to be discouraged: 'When in the army let no one ask his peer . . . to drink.'[91] But this evidence shows a regime not so much anxious *about* these particular horizontal groups, as anxious to support them. Everything depended on the nature of the group. Though unauthorised armed bands (*collectae*) could be dangerous,[92] groups of *pares in hoste*, following the same banner-man (*guntfanonarius*), were an essential part of the *lantweri*, the realm's defensive capacity.[93]

Two mid-ninth-century writers show the importance of similar bonds of solidarity in the context of military retinues at elite level, evoking earlier Frankish evidence for *antrustiones contubernales* but adopting a more clearly (if conditionally) positive view of such warrior-bands. Dhuoda, in 841–2, adds a strongly moral emphasis when she writes to her son William among his *commilitones* at the court of Charles the Bald, calling them his *pares et fideles amici*, and offering him examples of *subditi, pares et minores* joined 'in the gluing-together of

---

[89] Capitulare Aquitanicum (768), c. 7 (cf. c. 6: 'quicumque in itinere . . .'), MGH Capit. I, no. 18, p. 43: 'quicumque homo super suum parem dum ad nos fuerit aliquid abstraxerit aut exfortiaverit, secundum suam legem tripliciter componet'; Capit. missorum de exercitu promovendo (808), c. 2, MGH Capit. I, no. 50, p. 137: 'Volumus atque iubemus . . . quicumque fuerit inventus, qui nec parem suum ad hostem suum faciendum secundum nostram iussionem adiuvit neque perrexit, haribannum pleniter nostrum pleniter rewadiet . . .'

[90] Capitularia tractanda . . . (811), cc. 2–3, MGH Capit. I, no. 71, p. 161: 'Quae causae efficiunt ut unus alteri adiutorium praestare nolit, sive in marcha sive in exercitu ubi aliquid utilitatis defensione patriae facere debet'; [c. 3]: 'Unde illae frequentissimae causationes in quibus unus alteri quaerit, quicquid parem suum viderit possidentem'; Capit. of Boulogne (811), c. 5, MGH Capit. I, no. 74, p. 167: 'Quicumque ex his qui beneficium principis habeat parem suum contra hostes communes in exercitu pergentem dimiserit et cum eo ire vel stare noluerit, honorem suum et beneficium perdat.'

[91] Capit. of Boulogne (811), c. 6, MGH Capit. I, no. 74, p. 167: 'Ut in hoste nemo parem suum vel quemlibet alterum hominem bibere roget. Et quicumque in exercitu ebrius inventus fuerit, ita excommunicetur, ut in bibendo sola aqua utatur, quousque male fecisse cognoscat.' Cf. cf. Capitulare missorum (803), c. 16, MGH Capit. I, no. 40, p. 116.

[92] Cf. above, n. 88.

[93] MGH Capit. II, no. 274, c. 13, p. 331, and cf. Nelson, 'Legislation and consensus', in P. Wormald (ed.), *Ideal and Reality in Frankish and Anglo-Saxon Society. Studies presented to J. M. Wallace-Hadrill* (Oxford, 1983), pp. 202–27, repr. in Nelson, *Politics and Ritual in Early Medieval Europe* (London, 1986), pp. 91–116, at pp. 123, 126.

love'.[94] Nithard writes of Charles the Bald's *comitatus*, of which he himself was a member, in similarly moralistic terms. 'They swore to die nobly rather than betray or abandon their king.'[95] The sentiment here may or may not echo a traditional Germanic ideal, but the quotation is from the II Maccabees 14: 42.[96] *Nobilitas* is confirmed by what we might call peer-review when Nithard describes the military exercises performed with 'such great nobility' by the men of Charles and Louis.[97]

'In the West Frankish kingdom, the rapid evolution of a whole discourse of *fideles* acting politically as a truly collective entity vis-à-vis the king can be traced during the reign of Charles the Bald. In 843 at Coulaines in Neustria, the king first dealt with each *fidelis* individually, promising each his *lex* and *honor*, but then dealt with all the *fideles* collectively: they had made a *convenientia*, after coming together in a single thing (*venientes in unum*), each encouraging one another. The citation from I Maccabees 12: 50 signalled the cross-reference to Israel, a collectivity if ever there was one. The second and perhaps most remarkable set of texts were addressed by the king in 856 to rebels who had been his *fideles*. Through envoys, Charles told them that he and they were bound in a pact (*pactum*): if he, though human weakness, should breach it, by treating any one of them 'against his law', they should none of them abandon their peer, but bring the king back to right reason; but should any one of them breach it, he would be 'sent to give an account of his actions before his peers', and if he remained recalcitrant, he would be liable to exile 'from the association of us all' (*a nostra omnium societate*).[98] In a second message, the king bade each *fidelis* exhort his peers to fidelity.[99] In a final message, the

---

[94] Dhuoda, *Liber Manualis*, ed. and trans. P. Riché (Paris, 1975), III, 8, p. 166; III, 9, p. 170; III, 10, p. 174: '... licet inter comilitones minimus esse videaris in formam, tamen sensu tenax vigorum et formam exemplis magnorum ... attentius intueri et sequi ne pigeas ortor ... Magnos ut sublimes, aequales ut altos, consimiles praepone, ut tibi una cum illis profectum dignitatis adquiri possis maiorum; omnibus namque per subiectunum humilitatis exempla tuis praelatos esse congaudeas ...'; III, 10, p. 184: 'Quid tibi in exemplis subditorum parumque et minorum in dilectionis conglutinatione valeam aut possim ostendere?' The editor does not pick up the Augustinian echo (*Enarrationes in Psalm.* 62: 17), but does note Dhuoda's citation, III, 10, p. 178, of Augustine, *Enarr. in Psalm.* 41: 2–4, where stags who cross rivers each with head and antlers supported on the back of the one in front are read as a model of *fraterna compassio*. At IV, 4, p. 216, Dhuoda urges William to show fear and love, 'ex fidelitatis industria ... circa optimates ducum et cunctos pares tuos, maiorumque sive iuniorum'. Parity could be accommodated with rank. I owe to Rachel Stone the observation that *commilito* is Pauline (Philem. 1: 2), and also many incisive comments on guidance for lay conduct in the Carolingian period.

[95] Nithard, *Historiarum Libri IV*, II, 4, ed. E. Müller, MGH SS rerum Germanicarum in usum scholarum (Hannover, 1907), p. 16.

[96] The members of Louis the German's following are ascribed a hardly less admirable motivation (though not explicitly termed noble), Nithard, *Hist.* II, 10, p. 25: 'lest they should leave to those who came after an unworthy memory, they preferred to die rather than lose their unconquered name' (*ne posteris suis indignam memoriam relinquissent ... morti potius subire quam nomen invictum amittere*).

[97] Nithard, *Hist.* III, 6, p. 38. The famous Strasbourg oaths, however, though the *populus* of each brother acts in effect as a group, were sworn by each individual to his lord's brother: each man bound himself to give no help to his own lord should that lord act wrongly towards his brother.

[98] MGH Capit. II, no. 262, c. 10, p. 281.

[99] MGH Capit. II, no. 264, c. 4, p. 284.

Peers in the early Middle Ages 43

king promised to them all security *contra pares vestros* (these bonds of association were fissile) and bade them 'expel any defector unanimously from your fellowship' (*e vestro consortio . . . unanimiter*).[100]

These texts present the men of the realm as a collectivity of peers, each of whom is liable for every other's conduct – to support him when in the right, but to caution and if needs be, punish and expel him if in the wrong. The peers of his realm constitute the group with whom the king literally engages in dialogue, and with whom he is bound in a pact. King and peers together form a *societas* of mutual obligation and mutual help, even while the king reserves the right to aid one against others. The relationship between the peers themselves was ideally supportive, but in practice often anything but. Hincmar of Rheims addressed the assembly of Pîtres in 862 on behalf of the participants:

> now let us repair ourselves . . . because through discord, we have almost lost both this damaged temporal kingdom and also an eternal kingdom, because neither can we all be kings (*nec omnes reges esse possumus*) nor have we been able to bear having the king set over us by God for as the Apostle said, 'there is no power but of God . . .' . . . The archangel who is now the Devil fell from heaven with his minions because he refused to be subject to his maker and scorned to be an associate (*socius*) with his fellow angels in the equality of charity. In a like manner those who refuse to be subject to the power constituted by God . . . and will not bear to have peers and equals in the realm, through which due subjection and equal equality they might have been friends of God and sharers with the angels, are [now] made subject to the Devil and enemies of God.[101]

While by 862 it had become a commonplace that leading subjects were part of a collectivity of peers and equals, and Hincmar himself put true peers on the side of the angels, aristocratic factions at times seemed impossible to contain within the new ideal framework of the realm. Nor was this always to the king's disadvantage, as Charles the Bald himself, an archetypical divider and ruler, spotted in 856.

The role of the high nobility in what I will call mature Carolingian regimes put some contemporaries in mind of the late Roman republic. Nithard, like Sallust,

---

[100] MGH Capit. II, no. 265, p. 285. Cf. Tusey, 865: 'se confirment ad . . . regni utilitatem et illorum commune adiutorium et salvamentum'. If any of these *fideles* should hear that 'his peer and our *fidelis*' (*par suus fidelis noster*) was in danger, they were not to wait but go immediately to his aid ('ad suum parem in nostra fidelitate adiuvandum'). The kings ordered that, if the area for which they were responsible should be attacked, *missi* were to raise troops from church lands: bishops, abbots and abbesses were to send 'their men with a banner-man (*guntfanarius*) who . . . has a list of their peers' ('homines cum guntfanario, qui de suis paribus cum missis nostris rationem habeat') and when urgently required, 'all must come [to the help of] . . . their own peers' ('ad missos nostros et ad pares suos occurrant'), MGH Capit. II, no. 274, cc. 1, pp. 329, 330, and c. 13, p. 331; c. 14, p. 332.

[101] MGH Capit. II, no. 272, p. 305: '. . . nunc reparemus nos . . . quia per discordiam et regnum istud temporale imminutum et pene desertum et aeternum regnum perditum habemus, quia nec omnes reges esse possumus nec regem super nos a Deo constitutum . . . habere sustinemus. . . . Et sicut archangelus, qui nunc est diabolus, cum suis sequacibus, quia per humilitatis subiectionem conditori suo subditus esse noluit et per aequalitatem caritatis coangelis suis socius esse despexit, de caelo cecidit, ita et illi, qui potestati a Deo constitutae propter Deum et in Deo subjecti esse nolunt et pares et coaequales in regno habere non sufferunt, per quam debitam subiectionem et parilem aequalitatem Dei amici et angelorum consortes poterant, subiecti diabolo et Dei inimici constituuntur.'

condemned the egoism of great men who threatened the *res publica*.[102] But Nithard also wrote of nobility, even the nobility, in an entirely positive sense when it served the Carolingian regime. Far more widely read in the ninth century than Sallust was Justin's *Epitome* of Pompeius Trogus's history of the ancient world up to Augustus.[103] Justin's work may have struck a chord with ninth-century readers, including lay readers, not just because of history's general appeal, but precisely because *this* history showed how discord between great men had riven the mighty empire of Alexander, once he himself had died, and had brought the downfall of the Roman state until Augustus finally reharnessed the nobility firmly to the public interest.[104]

Regino of Prüm's famous entry s.a. 888 is intelligible only in light of his use of Justin. Writing of the troubles that followed Charles the Fat's death, Regino said that wars had been aroused,

> not because there were lacking *principes* of the Franks who could have ruled the *regna* in nobility, fortitude and wisdom, but because the equality between them of birth, rank and power increased discord, for no one excelled the rest so far that they would deign to submit to his overlordship. For Francia could have engendered many *principes* suitable to control the government of the realm, had not fortune armed them with a rivalry of manly qualities (*virtus*) [which led] to their mutual downfall.[105]

The passages about equality and fortune are borrowed from Justin, and they are remarkable just for being there at all. This is the *only* time in the main section of his Chronicle (from 813 on) that Regino ever cites an ancient author. In other words, he must not only have seen the events of 888 as deeply significant (he was writing with hindsight from the early tenth century), and deeply disturbing too, for the context of Justin's remarks was the death of Alexander the Great, but must have wanted to put across a particular judgement on them in the most telling way he knew. Regino, like Hincmar, recognised the qualities of the *Franci*; but you could have too much *aequalitas* and a ranked society was not enough. What was

---

[102] Nithard, *Hist.* I, 3, 4; III, 2, IV, 2 and IV, 6, pp. 3–6, 29, 39, 40, 41, 49.

[103] R. McKitterick, 'The audience for Latin historiography in the early Middle Ages', in A. Scharer and G. Scheibelreiter (eds), *Historiographie im frühen Mittelalter* (Vienna, 1994), pp. 96–114, at p. 103, noting that there are over 200 medieval manuscripts of Justin's *Epitome*, beginning with a number of ninth-century ones.

[104] Augustine, *De civitate dei*, IV, 6 quotes Justin at length for early kings down to Ninus.

[105] Regino, *Chronicon*, s.a. 888, ed. F. Kurze, MGH SS rerum Germanicarum in usum scholarum (Hannover, 1890), p. 129 (with the quotations from Justin in italic): '... regna quae eius ditioni paruerant, veluti legitimo destituta herede, in partes a sua compage resolvuntur et iam non naturalem dominum prestolantur sed unumquodque de suis visceribus regem sibi creari disponit. Quae causa magnos bellorum motus excitavit; non quia principes Francorum deessent, qui nobilitate, fortitudine et sapientia regnis imperare possent, sed quia *inter ipsos aequalitas* generositatis, dignitatis et potentiae *discordiam augebat, nemine tantum ceteros precellente*, ut eius dominio reliqui se submittere dignarentur. *Multos* enim idoneos principes ad regni gubernacula moderanda Francia genuisset, *nisi fortuna eos aemulatione virtutis in pernitiem mutuam armasset.*'

needed, as Hincmar had invited the peers of his generation to see, was someone acknowledged as excelling the rest. The Augustans had been right. Hincmar and Regino looked to monarchy, a new Alexander, to channel all that talent, suitability and nobility.[106] Peers and monarchy needed each other.

In O. G. Oexle's view, associations were in principle inimical to state authority. Yet Oexle himself identified a more collaborative relationship in the context of Ottonian Germany. Henry I's *agrarii milites in urbibus* and their *confamiliares* together built, manned, serviced and supplied the new fortifications of these places, and Henry planned ritual support for these groups: they were to have *concilia et omnes conventus atque convivia in urbibus* as well.[107] So, like higher-level *pares*, peasant associations could be compatible with monarchy. (There is no evidence, incidentally, that the *agrarii milites* were bound by mutual oaths, and Oexle may have exaggerated the importance of that feature.) Here the history of Wessex offers an apt comparison. The regime of Alfred showed, already in the 880s and 890s, the key value of fortifications in defensive and counter-offensive warfare, hence too the vital importance of enrolling local groups in the common enterprise. The *burgware* who manned Alfred's burhs and made them work did so in conjunction with king's thegns, and with the king himself.[108] As in war, so in peace, in Athelstan's reign (924–39), the peace-guild of London was an association of not merely Londoners but landowners, 'both nobles and commoners', from the surrounding counties. Their hundredmen and tithingmen assembled monthly under their own steam ('and it might happen that the beer-butts were being filled') but reported their doings to the king and were intimately involved in, and their reeves literally pledged to, Athelstan's larger project of repressing crime.[109] Here are associations of local

---

[106] Interestingly, Hincmar in 881 had evoked Alexander (and his tutor) for the benefit of the young West Frankish king Carloman in the prologue to his revised version of *The Government of the Palace*, citing Quintilian via Jerome: *De ordine palatii*, ed. T. Gross and R. Schieffer, MGH Fontes Iuris Germanici Antiqui (Hannover, 1980), p. 34 with n. 12 for the source.

[107] Widukind, *Rerum gestarum Saxonicarum libri tres*, ed. P. von Hirsch and H.-E. Lohmann (Hannover, 1935), pp. 48–9. On the wider implications of Henry's arrangements, see K. Leyser, 'Henry I and the Saxon Empire', in *History* 50 (1965), 1–25, repr. in his collected papers, *Medieval Germany and its Neighbours* (London, 1982), pp. 11–42. I part company with Oexle on one point: these *convivia* don't seem to me to involve the same people as the *conventicula* of honourable (*honesti*) men and women for whose *loca privata*, according to the *Miracula S. Wigberti*, Henry ordered fortifications to be built, Oexle, 'Gilden als soziale Gruppen', pp. 349–50, *Miracula S. Wigberti*, c. ed. G. Waitz, MGH SS IV (Hannover, 1841), p. 225. Those *conventicula* sound to me like convents, or small family-monasteries. The point matters, because Oexle seems to make it his key argument for the full participation of women in sworn-associations, which I myself think implausible.

[108] R. Abels, *Alfred the Great* (London, 1998), pp. 198–207.

[109] The citations are from the preface and c. 8, 1 of VI Athelstan, ed. F. L. Attenborough, *The Laws of the Earliest English Kings* (Cambridge, 1922), pp. 157, 163. Essential commentary is now to be found in Wormald, *Making of English Law*, pp. 296–9, 306, 323 ('a blend of royal and local directions'). Cf. also S. Keynes, 'Royal government and the written word in late Anglo-Saxon England', in R. McKitterick (ed.), *The Uses of Literacy in Early Medieval Europe* (Cambridge, 1990), pp. 226–57, at pp. 239–40. Oexle, 'Conjuration und Gilde, p. 186 briefly refers to this text but gives no detail about how the London peace-gild actually worked.

men cooperating with royal government. Perhaps even the allegedly 'modern' traits that Oexle finds in early medieval groups, namely, 'free will, equalisation, and the construction of autonomous rules of procedure',[110] acquired new force with the greatly increased role of the *lantweri* in the ninth and tenth centuries. Enhanced they may have been, yet the traits themselves were old. At peasant level and princely level alike, the assumption that associations of peers were a normal part of social and political life was already a characteristic feature of earlier medieval thinking. Far from representing an alien culture in a ranked society, parity belonged where horizontal and vertical structures of thought and practice coexisted and interlocked, in communities and kingdoms.

[110] Oexle, 'Gilde und Kommune', p. 96: '. . . Freiwilligkeit, Egalisierung, und Ausbildung autonomer Verfahrensregelungen'.

Stepmothers in Frankish legal life*

Brigitte Kasten

The evil reputation of stepmothers is among those social phenomena that transcend space and time. The Greeks and Romans already included the 'stepmother-poisoner' among stereotypes of wicked women. Walahfrid Strabo's *noverca venefica* in the ninth century replicated Seneca's in the second. Fairy tales like 'Cinderella', 'Snow-White' and 'Hansel and Gretel' represented stepmothers as murderesses and witches.[1] Step-families were hybrids in sociological terms, and in political terms, they were firmly labelled 'secondary', since the children of the two pairs of parents were never treated on a par with full blood relations.[2] The neglect of children, which actually happened in families of both kinds, was generally believed to be much more likely in a step-family. In popular speech, 'stepchild' has come to stand, metaphorically, for anything neglected (we speak of 'a stepchild of politics', for instance). Anyone who behaves in a harsh and unjust way is said to be acting 'like a stepmother' (never 'like a stepfather').

The starting point for this essay is the question of why crimes within families and in society at large are, and have been, laid at the door of stepmothers, whereas the slur of wickedness has never clung to stepfathers to anything like the same extent.[3]

---

* This essay is dedicated to Susan Reynolds in admiration and friendship. We share an enjoyment of legal sources, and we both favour the critical reappraisal of early medieval feudalism. My thanks go to Jinty Nelson for translating this contribution to Susan's *Festschrift*.

[1] Walahfrid Strabo, *De cultura hortorum*, MGH Poetae latinae II, ed. L. Traube (Berlin 1884), p. 342, ll. 204–7 (stepmothers as makers of poisons); and see further P. A. Watson, *Ancient Stepmothers. Myth, Misogyny and Reality* (Leiden, New York and Cologne 1995), pp. 90–102.

[2] Stepfamilies present a growing problem in modern societies with high divorce rates: 33 per cent for families in general, 50 per cent for step-families: *Frankfurter Allgemeiner Zeitung* 21 July 1997, 35–6. See H. Giesecke, *Die Zweitfamilie. Leben mit Stiefkindern und Stiefvätern* (Stuttgart 1987); S. Ritzenfeldt, *Kinder mit Stiefvätern. Familienbeziehungen und Familienstrukturen in Stiefvaterfamilien*, Diss. Heidelberg 1997 (Weinheim 1998). Families with stepfathers are much commoner than those with stepmothers, since the children of divorced parents normally stay with the mother.

[3] Etymologically, the word-element *step*-[mother] means 'deprived', 'defeated', cf. the OE verb 'be-stiepan', 'to rob [parents or children]' (and similarly cf. modern German *Stief*-[mutter] and OHG 'bi-stiufan', 'to rob'). Latin *noverca* simply means 'the new one'. The derivation of Latin *vitricus*, 'stepfather' is uncertain, as are Latin *privignus*, *privigna*, 'stepson', 'stepdaughter', while Latin *filiastra*,

The question is particularly urgent, because the findings I shall present on the basis of research into early medieval legal norms point, in part, to the opposite conclusion. As regards the number and content of legal regulations on second marriages (and further ones), the object was to protect children of a previous marriage against the step*father* and his potential threat to their inheritance and to their mother's property. The man's possession of power, whether as *pater familias* among the Romans, or *Muntwalt* (wielder of protection) among the Germans, thus had to be subjected to legal restraints if he married a widow with children. Stepmothers are mentioned in the legal evidence in the context of two distinct areas: incest and remarriage. 'The problem of the stepmother' was thus part of the complex of problems surrounding marital rights to property and guardianship. The stepmother's bad reputation was clearly linked with social attitudes to remarriage.

Late Roman and early medieval legal texts

In the Theodosian Code (438/443), regulations on second marriage concentrate on the case of the widow, scarcely ever the widower. Thus they deal with the potential stepmother, that is, the widow or divorcee who might remarry a man with children from a previous marriage. It was not only out of respect for the deceased husband, but, still more, from a desire to protect the inheritance rights of a posthumous child, that the mourning period for both widow[4] and *pater familias*[5] lasted for a year before any remarriage could take place, if the woman was not to incur the social and economic consequences of *infamia*. Late Roman legislators' concern for young children is reflected in numerous regulations on guardianship and care. Two of these are worth highlighting: one, the obligation of a widow with under-age children to prepare an inventory, the other, the widow's loss of her guardianship rights over her children if she remarried.[6] The main object of such legislation was to protect the children of a first marriage, and their inheritance, from a stepfather.

In the Justinianic Code (534), the rules about second marriage had clearly become more detailed and more comprehensive.[7] They came to include all conceivable situations, extending their range to cover men who remarried and also third and even further marriages. In some matters, husband and wife were treated as on

---

filiaster, 'stepdaughter', 'stepson', are derived from *filia, filius*: *Oxford Latin Dictionary*, ed. P. G. W. Glare (Oxford 1982), s.v.; *A Latin Dictionary*, ed. C. T. Lewis and C. Short (Oxford 1879), 2nd edn 1966, s.v. See also M. Beth, 'Stiefeltern', in *Handwörterbuch des deutschen Aberglaubens* 8 (Berlin and Leipzig 1936/37), cols 448–80.

[4] Codex Theodosianus 3, 8, 1 (30 May, 381) = Breviarium Alaricianum 3, 8, 1, ed. T. Mommsen, 2nd edn (Berlin 1954); cf. Codex Justinianus 5, 9, 2, ed. T. Mommsen and P. Krüger (Berlin 1877). See M. Kaser, *Das römische Privatrecht*, 2, Abschnitt: Die nachklassische Entwicklungen, Handbuch der Altertumswissenschaften, 10 Abt., 3 Teil, Bd 2 (Munich 1959), p. 114.

[5] Digest 3, 2, 1.

[6] Cod. Theod. 10, 11, 1–4 (10 July 439). See also 3, 17, 1–4, and on this, F. Pellaton, 'La veuve et ses droits de la Basse-Antiquité au haut Moyen Age', in M. Parisse (ed.), *Veuves et veuvages dans le haut moyen âge* (Paris 1993), pp. 51–97, esp. p. 87.

[7] Kaser, *Privatrecht*, p. 124, especially on the significance of usufruct.

a par, with the result that in the process of improving the rights of women the stepmother was now mentioned expressly. Stepmothers too had sufficient economic control, if in a temporary way, to cheat their stepchildren, thus to be 'wicked'.

While the Theodosian Code dealt with stepmothers exclusively in the context of inheritance law, in the Justinianic Code the ethical aspect of forbidden or incestuous unions entered the picture, even if in a rather marginal way.[8] This would become a major theme in the early Middle Ages. But it is already mentioned in the digests (i.e. jurists' commentaries) on the Justinianic Code, which generally had greater relevance than legislation proper for the legal practice of the early sixth century. The jurists mention forbidden marriages in the context of degrees of relationship, including those of in-laws, and also of step-relations.[9] Sex with a stepmother or stepdaughter was incest.[10] The jurists were probably responding to the moral requirements of Christianity.

Widow remarriage, taken for granted in the late Roman legal codes, was frowned on, by contrast, in public opinion, both in pagan Roman society and, especially, in the views of the Church Fathers. Widows who remarried made themselves potential stepmothers and, still more, widows who already had children brought stepfathers into their homes as potential enemies of their own children.[11] Such women were accused of disloyalty to their dead husbands and lack of responsibility towards the children they had had together. This social and familial disapproval of widow remarriage was not completely without foundation. Jens Uwe Krause's study of widows and orphans in the Roman Empire has shown that the large number of widows aged between twenty and forty was a considerable social problem, and it was in practice extremely difficult for most widows to secure their own and their children's future by remarriage. An increased *dos* for the new husband could help matters only at the cost of reducing the inheritance of the children of the first marriage, and hence became a source of accusations and complaints.[12] Remarriage was really possible only for a fairly well-off widow. Widowers had other socially acceptable options (slaves, concubines) if they wanted to maintain their households and provide care for their children, and they were thus able to evade the

---

[8] J. Gaudemet, 'Du droit romain tardif aux conciles mérovingiens: les condamnations de l'inceste', *Zeitschrift der Savigny-Stiftung für Rechtsgeschichte*, Kan. Abt. 113 (1996), pp. 369–79, at p. 370–1.

[9] Dig. Iust. 38, 10, 4 (Modestinus), *Digesta Iustiniani augusti*, ed. T. Mommsen and P. Krüger (Berlin 1870), vol. II, ibid. 38, 10, 7: 'Hos itaque inter se, quod adfinitatis causa parentium liberorumque loco habentur, matrimonio copulari nefas est'. See further Institutiones 1, 10, 7, *Corpus iuris civilis*, text and translation on the basis of the edition of Mommsen and Krüger, trans. O. Behrends, R. Knütel, B. Kupisch and H. Hermann Seiler, 2nd revised edition (Heidelberg 1997).

[10] Dig. Iust. 48, 5, 39 (1; 5) (Papinianus).

[11] See esp. Jerome, *Ad Furiam de viduitate servanda*, Saint Jerôme, *Lettres*, vol. III, ed. and trans. J. Labourt (Paris 1953), pp. 25–41. See K. *Ritzer, Formen, Riten und religiöses Brauchtum der Eheschliessung in den christlichen Kirchen des ersten Jahrtausends*, Liturgiewissenschaftliche Quellen und Forschungen, 38 (Münster 1962), pp. 33–109; F. Rädle, 'Einige Bemerkungen zur Bewertung der Witwenschaft in der patristischen und frühmittelalterlichen Theologie', in Parisse ed., *Veuves et veuvage*, pp. 17–30; and, for further examples, see J. U. Krause, *Witwen und Waisen im römischen Reich*, 4 vols, III, Rechtliche und soziale Stellung von Waisen (Stuttgart 1995), vol. 3, pp. 32–6.

[12] Krause, *Witwen*, vol. 3, pp. 37–40.

problem of giving their children a stepmother.[13] Increased moral reservations about widow remarriage never became established as law.[14] It was among pagan peoples that social rejection of such remarriage was allegedly sometimes carried to the extreme of the burning or killing of widows.[15]

In the early medieval kingdoms constructed on Roman models, law-codes, some of them produced in the pre-Justinianic period, offer a perspective on the social relations of free men and women. These codes deal with stepmothers as part of the problems arising from inheritance and the protection of the rights of heirs. An enactment ascribed to the Visigothic king Euric (*c*.475) states that 'if a man after his wife's death brings a stepmother into his house, whatever property was left by his first wife must be transferred to all the children, so that, while those children with their property move into another household, they may not be vexed by the injuries of the stepmother'.[16] Interestingly, it is the children's removal that apparently exposes them to their stepmother's malignity. The position of lady of the household confers on the stepmother the power to act 'wickedly'. It is striking that social mistrust of a stepmother's wickedness emerges even in a legal text. Whether or not she had children of her own, she was automatically assigned evil intent towards her stepchildren and their maternal inheritance – though nothing is said here of the obvious corollary, that the stepmother could endanger their paternal inheritance as well.

King Recceswinth in his *Liber iudiciorum* (*c*.654) legislated for the converse case, where a widow, by remarrying, gave her children a stepfather. The rules, again, seem very down to earth: essentially, it was encouraged by the law, and regarded as honourable in economic terms, that a widow should not remarry.[17] But if she should

---

[13] Krause, *Witwen*, vol. 1, pp. 58–66.

[14] B. Kötting, 'Die Beurteilung der zweiten Ehe in der Spätantike und im frühen Mittelalter', in N. Kamp and J. Wollasch (eds), *Tradition als historische Kraft. Interdisziplinäre Forschungen zur Geschichte des früheren Mittelalters* (Berlin and New York 1982), pp. 43–52; B. Jussen, 'Der "Name" der Witwe. Zur "Konstruktion" eines Standes in Spätantike und Frühmittelalter', in Parisse (ed.), *Veuves et veuvages*, pp. 137–75, at pp. 137–46; P. L. Reynolds, *Marriage in the Western Church. The Christianization of Marriage during the Patristic and Early Medieval Periods*, Vigiliae Christianae, suppl. 24 (Leiden 1994), pp. 179–212.

[15] For cases from antiquity, see Krause, *Witwen*, vol. 4, pp. 122–3. For the pagan Wends, see Boniface, Ep. 73 (746–47), in M. Tangl (ed.), *Die Briefe von Bonifatius und Lullus*, MGH Epistolae selectae I (Berlin 1916), 150: 'Et Uuinedi, quod est foeditissimum et deterrimum genus hominum, tam magno zelo matrimonii amorem mutuum observant, ut mulier viro proprio mortuo vivere recuset. Et laudabilis mulier inter illos esse iudicatur, quia propria manu sibi mortem intulerit et in una strue pariter ardeat cum viro suo.' See Pellaton, 'La veuve et ses droits', p. 55. Cf. Thietmar of Merseburg, *Chronicon*, VIII, 3, ed. R. Holtzmann, MGH SSRG (Berlin 1955), p. 494, on the non-Christian Poles.

[16] *Codicis Euriciani fragmenta*, ed. K. Zeumer, Leges Visigothorum, MGH Leges I (Hannover and Leipzig 1902), c. 321, p. 22: 'Qui autem novercam superduxerit, omnes facultates maternas filiis mox reformet; ne, dum filii cum rebus ad domum transeunt alienam, novercae suae vexentur iniuriis.' See also *Liber iudiciorum sive Lex Visigothorum edita ab Reccesvindo rege (c.654)*, 12, 13 (Recc.), MGH Leges I, p. 179.

[17] *Liber iudiciorum* 3, 1, 7 (Recc.), p. 130; 4, 3, 3 (Recc.-Ervigius), pp. 190–2; and 4, 2, 14, p. 182; cf. *Codex Euricianus* c. 322, pp. 22–3.

remarry, she had to pay the penalty of seeing *potestas* over the children of her first marriage pass to an adult son or to a paternal uncle; and even if an inventory of property existed, *tuitio* over it would also pass to an adult son.[18] Should she remarry without observing the full mourning period, she forfeited to her children half the property she had from her first marriage.[19] Man and wife were here treated similarly, as required in the Code of Euric, in that the widower who remarried had immediately to forfeit to the children of his first marriage their maternal inheritance and lost *patria potestas* over them.[20] But, thanks to Christian influence (the models of David and Solomon are explicitly mentioned), this evenhandedness changed later in the seventh century, perhaps under King Wamba, in favour of the widower: even on remarriage, he now retained his *patria potestas* over the children of a first marriage, and control over their maternal inheritance, though he must treat this as a guardian.[21] The danger posed by the stepmother to her stepchildren was regarded as a lesser risk than impairing the father's paternal rights, 'quia valde indignum est, ut filii, patris gubernatione vel potestate relicta, in alterius tuitionem deveniant'.[22]

In the law of the Burgundians, the *Liber Constitutionum* (late fifth century, with additional *novellae* down to 517), sexual intercourse with a stepmother was not included among incestuous relationships.[23] The Burgundians tolerated not only second but also third marriages for widows, but clearly saw the greatest danger arising here in relation to stepfathers, not stepmothers, since legal and economic penalties like those of late Roman law were laid on the remarried widower with children, with the aim of protecting the latter. A law of 10 June 517 assigned a widow with one son the usufruct of a third of her dead husband's property, but she was to lose all this if she remarried except for her *dos* which she could keep for life, with the inheritance to pass to the son. If she remarried, the *wittimon* (analogous to the Roman *donatio ante nuptias*) reverted to the dead husband's kin, yet, if she were again widowed and married a third time, she would retain the second *wittimon*. Once widowed, mother and stepmother were in a similar position in so far as both retained the use of the same legal share of their living children's inheritance.[24]

The Lombard, Alamannic, Bavarian and Frisian laws all treated the problem of stepmothers exclusively as a moral one, from the point of view of incest, though penalties varied. The Edict of Rothari (643) required the disinheritance of a son who 'sinned with his stepmother against his father', a marriage between a stepson and a stepmother was immediately null, with the man paying 100 *solidi*, the woman half

---

[18] Ibid., 3, 1, 7, p. 130, and 4, 3, 3, pp. 190–2.
[19] Ibid., 3, 2, 1 (Recc.), p. 133.
[20] Ibid., 4, 2, 13 (Recc.), pp. 178–9.
[21] Ibid., 4, 2, 13 (Nov. ad Recc.), pp. 180–1.
[22] Ibid., 4, 2, 14, p. 181.
[23] *Leges Burgundionum*, ed. L. R. von Salis, MGH LL II, 1 (Hannover 1892), *Liber Constitutionum* tit. 26, p. 69.
[24] Ibid., tit. 24, 1, pp. 61–2, tit. 59, p. 92, tit. 62, 1–2, p. 93, tit. 69, 1–2, pp. 96–7, tit. 74, 3, pp. 95–6.

her property, as compensation to the king.[25] The Lombard prince Arichis II of Benevento (758–87) forbade gifts to children born of incestuous marriages involving stepmothers.[26] The laws of the Alamans and Bavarians (dating from the first half of the eighth century) required the marriages of incestuous couples to be declared null and all their property to go to the fisc.[27] Frisian law (802/3) enshrined the decision of Wlemarus that while incestuous marriages were null, both parties might lawfully remarry.[28] The *Lex Saxonum* (802/3) prescribed that a sonless widow was to pass under the guardianship of her stepson (that is, a son of her dead husband by a previous marriage).[29] All these laws accepted widow remarriage, but had nothing further to say on stepmothers. The *Lex Baiwariorum* provided against the 'wicked' stepfather, however, imposing heavy penalties on theft from widows, committed with the aim of acquiring stepchildren's property.[30] In Bavarian law, widows retained control of their *dos* and of their own property. In Alamannic law and practice, by contrast, a widow who remarried retained scarcely more than her *Morgengabe*, with only usufruct of her *dos*, so that a stepfather would have no incentive to cheat his stepchildren.[31]

Frankish marriage law is more explicit on widow remarriage. It looks as if with the change from the Merovingian to the Carolingian dynasty, kings withdrew from this whole area of law. Such a conclusion confirms the impression given by the other early medieval codes. There is correlation between a code's increasing divergence from late Roman models, and a more self-conscious new royal dynasty. In other words, the further removed in time and space a kingdom was from the former Roman Empire, the less it involved itself with regulating widow remarriage and guardianship. The *Lex Saxonum* is to some extent an exception, explicable in terms of the special circumstances of the Frankish conquest and Charlemagne's intentions after 802.[32] Otherwise, the Franks in the early ninth century stayed with their customary legal arrangements regarding the family and marital property, and this had consequences for the legal and economic position of women. In comparison with Justinianic law, there was privatisation, in the sense that secular law-makers left the regulation of remarriage to the families concerned.

[25] *Edictus Rothari*, Leges Langobardorum, revd edn, ed. F. Beyerle, *Germanenrechte*, neue Folge, Westgermanisches Recht 8 (Witzenhausen 1967), c. 169, p. 44, c. 185, p. 49.

[26] *Aregis Principis Capitula*, c. 8, *Leges Langobardorum*, p. 208.

[27] *Leges Alamannorum*, ed. K. Lehmann, MGH Leges nationum Germanicarum 5, 1 (Hannover 1888), tit. 39, pp. 98–9; *Lex Baiwariorum*, ed. E. von Schwind, MGH Leg. nat. Germ. 5, 2 (Hannover 1926), tit. 7, 1, pp. 347–8.

[28] *Lex Frisionum*, ed. K. A. Eckhardt and A. Eckhardt, MGH Fontes iuris Germanici antiqui 12 (Hannover 1982), tit. 77, p. 96.

[29] *Lex Saxounum*, in *Leges Saxonum*, ed. C. Freiherr von Schwerin, MGH Fontes iuris Germani antiqui (Hannover and Leipzig), 1918, c. 42, p. 28.

[30] *Lex Baiuwariorum*, tit. 8, 7, pp. 356–7. On the social and economic problems behind prohibition of abduction, see F. Siegmund, 'Pactus Legis Salicae title 13: Über den Frauenraub in der Merowingerzeit', *Frühmittelalterliche Studien* 32 (1998), 101–23.

[31] D. Hellmuth, *Frau und Besitz. Zum Handlungsspielraum von Frauen in Alamannien (700–940)* (Sigmaringen 1998), pp. 37–8, 104–5, 107–8.

[32] *Lex Saxonum* c. 43, p. 29.

In *Lex Salica* and the *Pactus legis Salicae*, there is no mention of the stepmother as such. *Lex Salica*, title 79 (*Pactus*, title 44) dealt with widow remarriage in general, but the remarried widow would become a stepmother only if her new husband already had children by a previous marriage. The compilers of these laws did not concern themselves with this special case. *Lex Salica*, title 79, laid down that the remarriage of a widow had to be performed according to a precisely described legal procedure in the local assembly (*mallus*), with 'ring-money' (*reipus*) of 3 *solidi* going to the new husband and one denarius to 'kin' (whether of the dead first husband or of the women herself is a matter of scholarly debate).[33] Title 79, cited by Pippin in his *Recensio* of c.763/4, certainly belongs to the oldest parts of the law of the Salian Franks, dating from the fifth and early sixth centuries. A later addition to this title, datable to c.555/8, provided for the special situation of a widow with children entering a second marriage: after the second husband had paid the ring-money, as the law required, the woman had to consult the kin of her deceased first husband, and if her original *dos* had been worth 25 *solidi*, she had to pay 3 *solidi* to his closest relatives, that is, parents, brother, or nephew, or, in the absence of such relatives, the second husband acting in the assembly could place her under the king's protection.[34] Here again the lawgiver was not concerned with the woman as a potential stepmother but rather with the new husband as stepfather to the children of her first marriage. Part of the resources of the first husband's family that had gone into the original *dos* were to be retained for that family; and their right to be consulted must have been intended to secure the well-being of the children of the first marriage and their rights to their mother's *dos*.[35] Though the ring-money was a relatively insignificant sum, it apparently often gave rise to such 'dispute (*scandalum*) in our realm' that King Chilperic I (561–84) decreed that it should go in its entirety to his followers rather than to the royal fisc.[36]

Lex Salica seems to reflect tension between conflicting customary rules regarding widow remarriage. Louis the Pious, probably soon after 819, issued a capitulary prescribing a new rule: 'if a man wished to marry a widow, this should not happen according to the terms of *Lex Salica*, but with the consent and will of the kinsfolk, as their ancestors have done up to this day'.[37] Thus the old ring-money was finally done away with, and the widow's remarriage placed firmly within the control of the families concerned, regardless of whether or not there were children by her first marriage. All the early barbarian codes had retained Roman law's emphasis

---

[33] *Lex Salica*, ed. K. A. Eckhardt, MGH Leges nationum Germanicarum 4, 2 (Hannover 1969), title 79, 1, p. 126. See S. F. Wemple, *Women in Frankish Society. Marriage and the Cloister 500 to 900* (Philadelphia 1981), p. 37 and n. 56 (p. 220); G. von Olberg, *Die Bezeichnungen für soziale Stände, Schichten und Gruppen in den Leges Barbarorum* (Berlin and New York 1991), p. 62. A comparable regulation occurs in the Edict of Rothari, c. 182, pp. 47–8.

[34] *Capitula legi Salicae addita – Capitulare 3 = Pactus legis Salicae*, ed. K. A. Eckhardt, MGH Leges nationum Germanicarum 4, 1 (Hannover 1962), tit. 100, 1, p. 256.

[35] *Pactus legis Salicae*, tit. 101, 1, pp. 256–7.

[36] *Edictum Chilperici pro tenore pacis, Pactus legis Salicae* tit. 107, p. 262.

[37] *Capitula legi Salicae addita*, ed. A. Boretius, MGH Capitularia I (Hannover 1883), no. 142, c. 8, p. 293.

on public aspects of widow remarriage (the action in the *mallus*, the affirmation of the king's residual rights), just as they insisted on royal protection of widows and orphaned girls in general, prevented the woman's kin from denying her remarriage with a man of her own rank, and excluded forced marriage that in practice would have been threatened by fathers. Louis the Pious's alteration of the law revealed the ongoing existence of competing conceptions. Did Salic law represent successful royal attempts to override pre-existing 'private' customs, and did Louis's capitulary therefore represent a royal retreat? And/or did Salic law embody the customs of the Neustrian Franks (Chilperic's 'realm'), which diverged from those of the Austrasian Franks, that is, from those of the Carolingians themselves and their new elite? Did Salic law on widow remarriage reflect late antique legal notions, prevalent in Neustria where Franks and Romans lived side by side, about the limiting of family power (but not paternal power!) by the public authority of the state, whereas such ideas were foreign to the Austrasian Franks, and does that explain Louis's decision? *Lex Ribuaria*, the law of the Austrasian Franks around Cologne, datable to the early seventh century but with eighth-century additions, has nothing to say about widow remarriage, suggesting that this was the legal business of family groups, not kings.[38]

What is certain is that the Carolingians caused a form of Frankish custom to become widespread which stressed familial consent as the sole norm governing widow remarriage, and which must therefore have disadvantaged widows, hence potential stepmothers. From now on, only the widow who lived in chastity was under royal protection together with a special legal protection that was enjoined ever more insistently on judges, counts and bishops. The problem of the stepmother faded out of the complex of laws concerned with remarriage, and instead acquired great significance in the moral sphere of incestuous, hence forbidden, marriage. Secular lawgivers now opened themselves up to ecclesiastical teachings and made those norms their own. The prohibition of a man's marriage with his father's wife entered Salic law with a decree of 1 March 596 ascribed to Childebert II: the crime was to be punished by death, in accordance with the harshness of late Roman penalties for incest.[39] But legal interpretation was needed to determine whether this decree covered stepmothers too, and whether it still applied after the father's death.[40]

Ecclesiastical norms and regulations for controlling them in the Frankish Empire

Ecclesiastical marriage legislation, including the establishment of the prohibited degrees, and the prohibition of incest, in conciliar decrees, capitularies and

---

[38] On the dating of *Lex Ribuaria*, see M. Springer, 'Riparii – Ribuarier – Rheinfranken nebst einigen Bemerkungen zum Geographien von Ravenna', in D. Geuenich (ed.), *Die Franken und die Alemannen bis zur "Schlacht bei Zülpich"* (Berlin and New York 1998), pp. 200–69, at p. 224–5.

[39] *Lex Salica, Decretio Childeberti* 1, 2, p. 176.

[40] J. Freisen, *Geschichte des kanonischen Eherechts bis zum Verfall der Glossenliteratur* (Aalen 1963), p. 443; P. Mikat, *Die Inzestgesetzgebung der merowingisch-fränkischen Konzilien (511–26/627)* (Paderborn, Munich, Vienna and Zurich 1994), pp. 133–4.

penitentials, has been very thoroughly studied for the Frankish Empire.[41] It will be enough here, then, to highlight certain aspects and to amplify those that relate to stepmothers. Jack Goody claimed that the extension of prohibitions on marriage to the fourth degree of relationship, and to affines and spiritual kin, was a strategy devised by the church to put obstructions in the way of marriage in order to favour the transfer of property to churches in default of heirs.[42] David Herlihy's critique of this argument is surely correct, not least because, as he points out, the incest prohibition was applied in particular to women living under the patriarchal authority of a male household head, its object being to preserve the stability of the household community through a 'virilocal marriage system'.[43] It is difficult to assess whether, and if so how extensively, such clearcut rules actually affected Frankish social life.[44] A link has recently been proposed between secular legislation on the abduction of women and ecclesiastical incest legislation: Frank Siegmund draws attention to the very limited possibilities that would have been open to a free man in the Merovingian period to enter a legitimate marriage, had the official rules prohibiting incest been applied.[45]

The origins of the church legislation on marriage go back to the third and fourth centuries.[46] The basis for the view that sexual relations, or marriage, with a stepmother were incestuous is to be found in Mosaic Law (Leviticus 18: 8), according to which the father's wife is taboo because she is of the flesh of the father. It was rather a long time, however, before Frankish church councils expressly imposed the incest prohibition on marriage with a stepmother, and the earliest such decree dates from 517.[47] Carolingian conciliar and capitulary legislation contained frequent prohibitions on incest, but rather few references to stepmothers in this

---

[41] F. L. Ganshof, 'Le statut de la femme dans la monarchie franque', in *La Femme, Receuils de la Société Jean Bodin pour l'histoire comparative des institutions* 12, ii (Brussels 1962), pp. 5–58; *Il matrimonio nella società altomedievale*, Settimane di studio del centro italiano di studi sull'alto medioevo 24, 2 vols (Spoleto 1977); Wemple, *Women in Frankish Society*; K. F. Drew, *Society and Kinship in Early Medieval Europe* (Princeton 1986); J. Gaudemet, *Le mariage en occident: les mœurs et le droit* (Paris 1987); M. de Jong, 'To the limits of kinship: anti-incest legislation in the early medieval West (500–900)', in J. Bremmer (ed.), *From Sappho to de Sade. Moments in the History of Sexuality*, vol. 1 (London 1989), pp. 36–59; F. J. Felten, 'Konzilsakten als Quellen für die Gesellschaftsgeschichte des 9. Jahrhunderts', in G. Jenal (ed.), *Herrschaft, Kirche, Kultur. Beiträge zur Geschichte des Mittelalters. Festschrift für Friedrich Prinz* (Stuttgart 1993), pp. 177–201; R. Weigand, 'Die Ausdehnung der Ehehindernisse der Verwandtschaft', *Zeitschrift der Savigny-Stiftung für Rechtsgeschichte*, Kan. Abt. 111 (1994), pp. 1–17; Reynolds, *Marriage in the Western Church*.

[42] J. Goody, *The Development of the Family and Marriage in Europe* (Cambridge 1983), esp. pp. 134–46.

[43] D. Herlihy, 'Making sense of incest: women and the marriage rules of the early Middle Ages', in Herlihy's collected papers edited by A. Molho, *Women, Family and Society in Medieval Europe. Historical Essays, 1978–1991* (Oxford 1995), pp. 96–109, esp. pp. 103–5. For other criticisms of Goody, see Krause, *Witwen*, vol. 4, pp. 105–6, and A. Angenendt, *Geschichte der Religiosität im Mittelalter* (Darmstadt 1997), p. 290.

[44] Gaudemet, 'Du droit romain tardif', p. 379.

[45] Siegmund, '*Pactus Legis Salicae* title 29', pp. 115–22.

[46] Reynolds, *Marriage in the Western Church*, pp. 144–51.

[47] Mikat, 'Inzestgesetzgebung', pp. 96–120, presents the evidence.

context.[48] In principle, sexual relations with a stepmother counted as incest, but in practice things were less clearcut, notably, when lists of incestuous relationships were given without any mention of stepmothers, as was the case with many sets of episcopal statutes.[49] Many bishops, like Haito of Basel, seem to have surrendered in the face of the huge number of cases of incest they confronted, and so decided simply to omit any reference to sex with a stepmother.[50] Theological debates and uncertainties over biblical exegesis made also have played a role here, however. Hrabanus Maurus in his treatise *De consanguineorum nuptiis* interpreted Leviticus 18: 8 as meaning that the prohibition on relations with the father's wife related specifically to a stepmother, and came into force specifically after the father's death (had it applied only in the father's lifetime, it would have been superfluous to command that no other woman should be desired).[51] That some interpretation was required is clear from a number of canonical questions addressed to Hrabanus, among them those of Bishop Humbert of Würzburg and Chorbishop Reginbald of Mainz. Only Hrabanus's answers have survived, and in them he makes clear that relations with a stepmother constitute incest and are sinful.[52] Jonas of Orleans in his treatise *De institutione laicali*, written for Count Matfrid of Orleans, includes union with a stepmother among incestuous marriages.[53] Lists of incestuous relationships never omit sex between stepfather and stepdaughter. Ecclesiastical legislation would indicate, then, that the opprobrium of wickedness ought to have attached more to the stepfather than to the stepmother. Yet in social reality, it was only in the case of a stepmother's incest with her stepson that the penalty of disgrace was exacted.

Not every conciliar decree contains a punishment for the offence. In the Merovingian period, the view seems to have prevailed that incest with a stepmother, like forbidden marriages in general, carried the penalty of anathema. If such a crime was evident, the couple were made to part, and in cases of resistance or recidivism, were excluded from the community of the church, while dispensations to marry

---

[48] Pippin I, Capitulary of Verberie, MGH Capit. I, no. 16, c. 10, p. 41; Council of Arles (813), MGH Conc. II, i, no. 34, c. 11, p. 251; Council of Rome (826), MGH Capit I, no. 180, c. 38, pp. 376–7; Council of Mainz (847), MGH Conc. III, ed. W. Hartmann, Hannover 1984, no. 14, c. 29, p. 175; Council of Rome (857), MGH Conc. III, no. 32, c. 38, p. 329; Councils of Aachen (862), Worms (868), and Douzy (974), MGH Conc III, no. 9D, p. 81, no. 25, Anhang c. 63, p. 287, and no. 40 A, p. 585.

[49] MGH Capitula episcoporum I, ed. P. Brommer (Hannover 1984), Capitula Treverensia (830/900), c. 4, p. 55; Capitula Silvanectensia prima (830s/840s), c. 5, p. 81; Capitula Trosleiana (909), c. 3, p. 144; MGH Capitula episcoporum II, ed. R. Pokorny and M. Stratmann (Hannover 1995), Capitula of Isaac of Langres (860 or later), c. 4, 1, p. 207.

[50] Haito of Basel, Capitula (806–23), MGH Capit. episcoporum I, p. 218.

[51] PL 110, cols 1087–96, esp. 1091–2. Cf. also Hrabanus, *Enarratio super Deuteronomium libri quattuor* (834), PL 108, cols 837–998, at III, 6, col. 929, with a metaphorical reference to Christ as father and the church as the father's wife.

[52] Hrabanus Maurus Epp. nos 29 and 30, ed. E. Dümmler, MGH Epp. V (Berlin 1899), pp. 445–6, 450–1. Cf. also Ep. 31, 455–62.

[53] Jonas of Orleans, *De institutione laicali*, II, 8, PL 106, cols 183–4. See H.-W. Goetz, *Frauen im frühen Mittelalter. Frauenbild und Frauenleben im Frankenreich* (Weimar, Cologne and Vienna 1995), pp. 182–90; P. Depreux, *Prosopographie de l'entourage de Louis le Pieux (781–840)* (Sigmaringen 1997), pp. 276–7, 329–31.

were reserved only for the newly baptised.[54] In the Carolingian period too, the church could be willing to compromise in missionary regions, such as the diocese of Paulinus of Aquileia, which was greatly expanded in 796 by the inclusion of areas of Avar settlement. A council summoned by Paulinus at Cividale in 796/7 decreed that if people had entered into a forbidden marriage unwittingly, they had to separate, but under certain circumstances each partner could marry again, and the children of that subsequent union could be recognised as legitimate.[55] An eighth-century penitential apparently used in the Frisian mission area stipulated that a Christian who married his stepmother, and specifically his father's widow, would have to part from her, and both man and woman would have to perform ten weeks' penance, but thereafter each was free to marry someone else. If they had married as pagans (*gentiles*), they could remain married after conversion to Christianity, for all their sins would be forgiven them through baptism.[56]

The penalty for marrying a stepmother varied in the different penitentials. Fundamentally, it was at the bishop's discretion to fix the punishment, taking into account the information of the parish, the findings of the local priest, and the gravity of the individual case. A penitential from northern Italy, of the first half of the ninth century, punished any man who slept with his stepmother by a ten-year pilgrimage, or an annual payment of 12 *solidi*.[57] The penitential of Halitgar of Cambrai (817–31) recommended anathema as punishment for marriage with a stepmother.[58] In episcopal statutes asignable to Cambrai in the 820s, incest was considered a mortal sin and punished by anathema and excommunication.[59]

The Council of Cividale (796/7) is worth returning to for several reasons. First, it reveals some reservations about the permissibility of remarriage tolerated because of 'unsuitability for continence' or through 'desire for children'. The statements of various Frankish theologians on the subject of remarriage make it clear that the church of the Carolingian period never really managed to reach a unified position on what was evidently a widespread practice among noble families, including the royal dynasty itself.[60] Churchmen were willing to accommodate lay attitudes to the

[54] Council of Orleans (533), c. 10, ed. C. de Clercq, *Concilia Galliae, 511–695*, Corpus Christianorum Series Latina 148A (Turnhout 1963), p. 100; Council of Orleans (538), c. 11, p. 118.

[55] MGH Concilia II, 1, no. 21, Council of Friuli, c. 8, p. 192.

[56] Paenitentiale Oxoniense II, c. 3, in R. Kottje with L. Körntgen and U. Spengler-Reffgen, *Paenitentialia minora Franciae et Italiae saeculi VIII–IX*, vol. 1, Corpus Christianorum Series Latina 156 (Turnhout 1995), p. 191. Cf. Kottje, 'Ehe und Eheverständnis in den vorgratianischen Bußbüchern', in W. van Hoecke and A. Welkenhuysen (eds), *Love and Marriage in the Twelfth Century* (Louvain 1981), pp. 18–40.

[57] Paenitentiale Merseburgense a, c. 43, in *Paenitentialia minora*, ed. Kottje et al., pp. 139–40. Cf. P. J. Payer, *Sex and the Penitentials. The Development of a Sexual Code 550–1150* (Toronto and London 1984), p. 53.

[58] Halitgar of Cambrai, *De vitiis et virtutibus et de ordine poenitentium*, IV, 22, PL 105, col. 685.

[59] Capitula Cameracensia, MGH Capitula episcoporum I, c. 8, p. 338.

[60] See the genealogies in R. Le Jan, *Famille et pouvoir dans le monde franc (VIIe–Xe siècle). Essai d'anthropologie sociale* (Paris 1995); see also those in E. Hlawitschka, 'Die Vorfahren Karls des Grossen', in W. Braunfels (ed.), *Karl der Große. Lebenswerk und Nachleben*, vol. I (Düsseldorf 1965), pp. 51–82 and K. F. Werner, 'Die Nachkommen Karls des Grossen bis um Jahr 1000', in *Karl der Grosse*, vol. IV, pp. 403–84.

extent of allowing second marriage. Halitgar of Cambrai, for instance, cited a penitential which permitted both man and woman to remarry after the death of their first partner, but allowed a third marriage to be atoned for only after a penance of three weeks' fasting, and a fourth or fifth marriage only after twenty-one weeks' fasting.[61] Herard of Tours simply forbade third marriages for the laity.[62] Hincmar of Rheims advised Lothar II that second marriages for lay people were not forbidden, for there were different rules for sheep and shepherds.[63] Also in the context of Lothar's divorce case, a number of bishops at the Council of Aachen (862) considered a consequence of divorce, namely, that the remarriage of either party would result in a step-family. Citing Ambrose, the bishops took a negative view of children's receiving a stepfather or a stepmother: under a stepmother, they would lead an *inliberalis vita* (unfree life).[64] Yet in this case, the stepfather came in for no less criticism than the stepmother: he commanded more powerful resources to inflict dishonour on his stepchildren. At the Council of Compiègne (757), Pippin had wished to protect stepdaughters from forced marriages imposed on them by stepfathers.[65]

Widows who took the veil as a sign that they rejected remarriage were highly regarded.[66] In Carolingian wills, the testator might leave his wife as immediate heir to his property on condition that she kept her bed chaste for the rest of her life.[67] Yet in practice, remarriage remained common. In both Merovingian and Carolingian dynasties, serial marriages were frequent, partly through repudiation, partly through the early deaths of wives (Carolingian wives tended to die between the ages of twenty-five and thirty-nine).[68] In nearly every generation, therefore, there were stepmothers. From a canonical point of view, the marriages of Charles the Bald's daughter Judith were especially problematic. Her second marriage had been to her stepson Æthelbald king of Wessex, and after his death, she had returned to Francia and lived there as a closely guarded widow until she married for a third time, with Baldwin of Flanders her new husband.[69]

[61] PL 105, col. 705: De poenitentia trigamorum.

[62] Capitula episcoporum II, p. 151.

[63] Hincmar of Rheims, *De divortio Lotharii regis et Theutbergae reginae*, ed. L. Böhringer, MGH Conc. IV, Suppl. 1 (Hannover 1992), Responsio 2, p. 127; cf. Responsio 4, p. 134. See now K. Heidecker, 'Why should bishops be involved in marital affairs? Hincmar of Rheims on the divorce of Lothar II (855–969)', in J. Hill and M. Swan (eds), *The Community, the Family and the Saint. Patterns of Power in Early Medieval Europe* (Turnhout 1998), pp. 225–35.

[64] MGH Conc. IV, no. 9 D, p. 81.

[65] MGH Capit I, no. 15, c. 6, p. 38.

[66] Jussen, 'Der "Name"', p. 156.

[67] B. Kasten, 'Erbrechtliche Verfügungen des 8. und 9. Jahrhunderts', *Zeitschrift des Savigny-Stiftung für Rechtsgeschichte*, Germ. Abt. 107 (1990), pp. 236–338, esp. pp. 254–5.

[68] Wemple, 'Les traditions romaine, germanique et chrétienne', in G. Duby and M. Perrot (eds), *Histoire de la Femme*, vol. 2, Le moyen âge (Paris 1990), pp. 185–216. Frequent remarriages of widows are assumed by P. Toubert, 'Le moment carolingien (VIIIe–Xe siècles)', in A. Berguière, C. Klapisch-Zuber, M. Segalen and F. Zonabend (eds), *Histoire de la famille*, vol. I: *mondes lointains, mondes anciens* (Paris 1986), pp. 333–59.

[69] Regino of Prüm, *Libri duo de synodalibus causis et disciplinis ecclesiasticis*, II, 188, ed. F. G. A. Wasserschleben (Leipzig 1840), p. 287. See Freisen, *Geschichte des kanonischen Eherechts,*

Stepmothers in Frankish legal life

The decrees of the Council of Cividale offer an early example of the efforts of the church to punish forbidden marriage not just with ecclesiastical sanctions but with consequences that would weigh heavily on the guilty parties in secular life – consequences that relied on the secular power for their effective imposition. Still, the control of norms, the investigation of particular cases to determine whether a forbidden marriage was the result of ignorance or disregard of the rules, and the decision to punish: all were basically the bishop's responsibility, even though it might be for the priest on the spot to take initial action.[70]

Characteristic of the Carolingian period, as indicated above, was the withdrawal of kingship from areas of law that we would nowadays designate family law. Remarriage was a case in point. Instead, there were increasing moves to impose ecclesiastical norms and punishments, sometimes backed by the threat of secular penalties. Pippin incorporated ecclesiastical rulings on marriage into his capitularies, and ordered that a stepmother guilty of adultery with a stepson must never marry again, and nor could the stepson, though the betrayed husband and father might do so. People who refused to abandon adulterous relationships were punished with fasts and fines of 60 *solidi* – payable to the king – to bring them to heel.[71] Charlemagne commanded in 802 that those guilty of incest who could not be led by their bishop to repentance and penance, were to be brought before the ruler himself and punished by the royal ban.[72] The close interplay of ecclesiastical and secular control was very clear in the episcopal capitularies of the second half of the ninth century. Isaac of Langres (857–80), for instance, incorporated into his very full regulations on incest a capitulary of Pippin, and the ordinance of the Theodosian Code denying legitimate heirs to incestuous partners. Those guilty of incest could no longer hold public office. Not only the king and his officials but all *fideles* were bound to help in imposing the ecclesiastical rules, by refusing to eat and drink with, or even to kiss or greet, those who known to be guilty of incest.[73] Isaac's regulations, however, remarkable as they are, do not explicitly mention stepmothers. We need to look at other types of evidence to find stepmothers in social action.

---

p. 597; E. Ennen, *Frauen im Mittelalter*, 2nd edn (Munich 1985), pp. 59–63; Wemple, *Women in Frankish Society*, p. 84; P. Stafford, 'Charles the Bald, Judith, and England', in M. T. Gibson and J. L. Nelson (eds), *Charles the Bald. Court and Kingdom*, 2nd edn (Aldershot 1990), pp. 139–53; R. Schieffer, 'Karolingische Töchter', in G. Jenal (ed.), *Herrschaft, Kirche, Kultur*, pp. 125–39, at p. 130–1; Le Jan, *Famille*, pp. 300–1; S. Reynolds, 'Carolingian elopements as a sidelight on counts and vassals', in B. Nagy and M. Sebök (eds), *The Man of Many Devices, Who Wandered Full Many Ways. Festschrift in Honor of János Bak* (Budapest 1998), pp. 340–6.

[70] Council of Orléans (538), c. 11, p. 118; Council of Les Estinnes (743), c. 3, MGH Conc. II, 1, no. 2, p. 7; Council of Mainz (813), ibid. no. 36, c. 53, p. 272; Lotharingian Council of 846, c. 6, MGH Conc. III, no. 12, p. 136.

[71] MGH Capit I, nos 14–16, pp. 34–41; no. 12, p. 31.

[72] MGH Capit I, no. 33, cc. 33, 38, pp. 97, 98.

[73] MGH Capitula episcoporum II, Isaac of Langres, title 4, pp. 207–12. Cf. Cod. Theodos. 3, 12, 2, p. 150, and 3, 12, 3 p. 152.

Stepmothers as mistresses of households

To get behind the mystery of stepmothers' evil reputation, we need to interrogate the narrative sources, even though it is true that they give information only on royal and aristocratic families. A brief glance at the *Histories* of Gregory of Tours (538/9–after 593) reveals some cases in point from the early Merovingian period. Touched by fantasy though these stories are, they possess an inner logic in so far as they correspond exactly to widespread assumptions about the dangerous activities of stepmothers. Two examples will illustrate this. The first is the unnamed second wife of King Sigismund of Burgundy. His first wife had been the daughter of Theoderic, king of the Ostrogoths, but she died leaving a son, Sigiric. Sigismund's second wife maltreated and insulted her stepson *sicut novercarum mos est* ('as is the way with stepmothers'). When the boy saw his stepmother come in, one feast day, dressed in the ceremonial clothes of his dead mother, he was upset and called out: 'You're not worthy to cover your back with those fine clothes, since everyone knows they belonged to your mistress, I mean my mother'. The stepmother, in a fury, urged her husband to take action against his son, telling him that Sigiric had set his sights not only on his father's life and on rulership over the Burgundians, but, beyond that, on the Italian kingdom of his (Sigiric's) grandfather Theoderic as well. Sigismund ordered the boy to be seized while drunk and drowned in a well.[74] The story probably reached Gregory through orally transmitted information stemming from Clovis's widow, Clothild, herself a Burgundian princess who blamed the deaths of her own parents on Sigismund's father Gundobad, and there is also independent written corroboration from Gregory's contemporary Marius of Avenches.[75] One cirumstantial detail lends additional credibility to Gregory's story: according to Burgundian law, a woman's clothes would be inherited by her daughter, and we know that Sigismund did indeed have a daughter by his first wife.[76] Yet Sigiric's accusation, as Gregory reports it, turned on his stepmother's lowly status as a former servant of Sigismund's first wife. The insult was thus an attack on Sigismund himself, who, like the Merovingians, was entitled, as king, to choose a wife regardless of her rank.[77]

The second example is Fredegund, wife of Chilperic I. She intrigued successfully against her stepson Merovech, son of Chilperic's previous (and repudiated) wife Audovera. It is in this context that, for the first and only time, Gregory of Tours terms her *noverca*.[78] After Fredegund's own sons had died in an epidemic, she turned on another of Audovera's sons, Chlodowech, who 'was insulting his stepmother, Queen Fredegund, by saying unfitting things about her'. Her position at this point

---

[74] Gregory of Tours, *Historiarum Libri Decem*, ed. B. Krusch and W. Levison, MGH SSRM I (Hannover 1951), III, 5, pp. 100–1. See Goetz, *Frauen*, p. 231.

[75] Gregory, *Hist.* II, 28, p. 73, cf. C. Nolte, 'Die Königinwitwe Chrodechilde. Familie und Politik im frühen 6. Jahrhundert', in Parisse (ed.), *Veuves et veuvage*, pp. 177–86, esp. pp. 180–1; *La Chronique de Marius d'Avenches*, ed. J. Favrod (Lausanne 1993), p. 70.

[76] *Lex Burgundionum* tit. 51, 3, p. 84; art. Sigismund', by J. Richard, in *Lexikon des Mittelalters* 7 (Munich 1995), col. 1885.

[77] Cf. J. L. Nelson, 'Queens as Jezebels', in D. Baker (ed.), *Medieval Women* (Oxford 1978), pp. 31–77.

[78] Gregory, *Hist.* V, 39, p. 246.

Stepmothers in Frankish legal life

was vulnerable, since she had no living son. She accused Chlodowech of having been responsible for the deaths of her and Chilperic's own sons, and persuaded the king to have him thrown into prison where he was killed on her orders, though she convinced Chilperic that it was suicide. She also saw to it that Chlodowech's following was disbanded, his mother, Audovera, killed, his sister put in a convent, and had his treasure-keeper tortured. Last but not least, all the dead man's possession fell into Fredegund's hands.[79] This ran contrary to Frankish law, since she was no blood relative of Chlodowech. Further, this type of misconduct was one that early medieval legal codes tended to ascribe to stepfathers rather than stepmothers.

What Gregory's two stories of the unhappy fates of Sigiric and Chlodowech show, in the end, is the vulnerability of a royal stepmother. If she lacked a son of her own, her political influence clearly had a time-limit, and even in her husband's lifetime she could not count on either his continued favour or his willingness to accede to any murderous actions she proposed. When all was said and done, a stepmother remained precisely that. The two instances just discussed are in fact the only cases where Gregory explicitly labels a stepmother as such. His reluctance to use the word is an indication of how freighted it was with evil connotations.

Something similar can be seen in four Carolingian cases: Plectrude, Swanhild, Fastrada and Judith. Plectrude, wife of the mayor of the palace Pippin (II) (†714) was first labelled a stepmother, not by near-contemporary chroniclers but by the author of the *Annales Mettenses Priores*, writing c.805.[80] By that time, the descendants of Plectrude's stepson Charles Martel were firmly established as the royal line, and Plectrude could then be blamed for intriguing against Charles with the aim of excluding him from the succession to his father, though Pippin himself had wished to leave him as sole heir.[81] This version of history was false, for the near-contemporary sources clearly state that Pippin had decided sometime before his death to exclude Charles and leave the mayoralty to his and Plectrude's two grandsons. Further, these earlier sources use neutral terms to describe Plectrude: *femina*, or *matrona*.[82]

Swanhild, Charles Martel's second wife, was identified as a stepmother by a contemporary chronicler, Count Hildebrand, the continuator of Fredegar: 'Charles's daughter Hiltrude, on her stepmother's evil advice . . . journeyed across the Rhine to Duke Odilo of Bavaria [Swanhild's kinsman] and married him, against the will and counsel of her [full] brothers'.[83] This was a *scandalum* still remembered in the

---

[79] Ibid., 247.
[80] *Annales Mettenses Priores*, ed. B. von Simson, MGH SSRG in usum scholarum 10 (Hannover and Leipzig 1906), pp. 19–20.
[81] See J. Semmler, 'Zur pippinidisch-karolingischen Sukzessionskrise 714–723', *Deutsches Archiv* 33 (1977), 1–36; B. Kasten, *Königssöhne und Königsherrschaft. Untersuchungen zur Teilhabe am Reich in der Merowinger- und Karolingerzeit*, MGH Schriften 44 (Hannover 1997), pp. 65–6, 80ff.
[82] *Liber Historiae Francorum*, c. 51, ed. B. Krusch, MGH SSRM II (Hannover 1888), 325; *Chronicarum quae dicuntur Fredegarii scholastici libri IV*, Cont. 8, ed. Krusch, MGH SSRM II, 173.
[83] *Cont. Fred.* c. 25, p. 180. See M. Becher, 'Zum Geburtsjahr Tassilos III', *Zeitschrift für bayerische Landesgeschichte* 52 (1989), 3–12, at 4, pointing to the likelihood that Hiltrude was already pregnant by Odilo, who had spent the winter of 740/41 at the court of Charles Martel.

mid-ninth century.[84] Given the bad consequences of Hiltrude's action, the chronicler could be confident that contemporaries would share his view that Swanhild was indeed a wicked stepmother.

Fastrada, Charlemagne's fourth successive wife (†794), was charged retrospectively with having exerted an evil influence over her usually kindly and forgiving husband. It was through her cruelty and Charlemagne's willingness to yield to her, that two rebellions broke out against him: the East Frankish Hardrad's in 785/6, and Charlemagne's own eldest son's (Fastrada's stepson's) in 793.[85] No source identifies Fastrada as a stepmother, however. The fact that she bore Charlemagne only two daughters meant that she did not conform to the conventional stereotype of the wicked stepmother seeking to promote her own son(s) at a stepson's expense. Her strong and ambitious character was clearly what drove her actions, regardless of any specifically stepmotherly motives. In her case, the modern anthropologists' explanatory model of the 'fitness' of the gene, which determines both murderous and altruistic behaviour, does not apply.

Judith was the young and beautiful second wife of the emperor Louis the Pious. He was forty to forty-one at the time of the marriage in 819, while she may well have been the same age as her youngest stepson, Louis the German, born in 805. Judith is not termed 'stepmother' in any of the sources, not even in any of the plentiful documentation for the rebellion of 833–4. Supporters of Louis the Pious's and Judith's son Charles the Bald, such as Nithard, refrained from any accusations against Judith, while her personal opponents, Agobard of Lyons and Wala of Corbie, attributed the conflicts within the royal family not to Judith's embodiment of wicked stepmotherhood, but to her youth and folly. 'She played childishly',[86] and when the ageing Louis's enthusiasm cooled, she sought another sexual partner, and found one in Bernard of Septimania whom Louis had appointed to be his chamberlain and Charles's tutor – posts which necessitated *ex officio* contacts with the empress.[87] Even the loyal Nithard denounced Bernard for having ruined the commonweal with his selfishness and insatiable lust. Bernard fled after the first revolt of Louis's sons by his first marriage. Judith, whom her stepsons had forced into the convent of St Radegund at Poitiers, was restored by the emperor in 831, after clearing herself with an oath, and resumed her influence

---

[84] Astronomer, *Vita Hludowici imperatoris*, c. 21, ed. E. Tremp, MGH SSRG 64, (Hannover 1995), pp. 348–9.

[85] Einhard, *Vita Karoli Magni*, c. 20, ed. O. Holder-Egger, MGH SSRG (Hannover 1911), 26. See F. Staab, 'Die Königin Fastrada', and J. L. Nelson, 'The siting of the Council at Frankfurt: reflections on family and politics', both in R. Berndt (ed.), *Das Konzil von Frankfurt*, 2 vols (Mainz 1997), vol. 1, pp. 183–217, and 149–65.

[86] Agobard of Lyons, *Libri duo pro filiis et contra Iudith uxorem Ludovici pii*, ed. G. Waitz, MGH SS XV (Hannover 1887), p. 276. See E. Ward, 'Agobard of Lyons and Paschasius Radbertus as critics of the Empress Judith', *Studies in Church History* 27 (1990), 15–23.

[87] Nithard, *Historiarum Libri IV*, I, 3, ed. E. Müller, MGH SSRM 44 (Hannover 1907), 3; Thegan, *Gesta Hludowici imperatoris*, c. 36, ed. E. Tremp, MGH SSRG 64 (Hannover 1995), 597. See further P. Depreux, *Prosopographie*, pp. 137–9, 270–86; and G. Bührer-Thierry, 'La reine adultère', *Cahiers de civilisation médiévale* 35 (1992), 299–312, at 301–3.

Stepmothers in Frankish legal life 63

over him.[88] Unlike the stepmothers already mentioned, Judith seems to have been a victim rather than an active agent: victim, that is, of the leading office-holders of the empire, who preferred to see the emperor remarried rather than remaining a widower;[89] victim of her own family, the Welfs, whose obscurity before Judith's marriage in 819 contrasts so strikingly with their rise to power and influence thereafter; victim of the nameless clergy who, according to Agobard, did not blush to take part in the empress's 'games' to please her and so gain influence over her;[90] victim of the unscrupulous Bernard who misused her for his own ends; and finally, victim of her stepsons, especially the co-emperor Lothar, who forced her into the convent on pain of death and likewise tried to exclude her son Charles from a share in the succession to their father's rulership.[91] It was probably this position as victim that prevented even Judith's worst enemies from denouncing her as a stepmother, even though her role was not essentially different from Fredegund's, Plectrude's, or Swanhild's.

A further feature of the Sigiric story as recounted by Gregory was the fact that conflict between stepmother and stepson was sparked off in the context of the stepmother's misappropriation of the mother's estate – the very area, that is, in which the codes had sought to regulate matters. Sigiric's stepmother had worn the clothes of his own biological mother, clothes that ought in Burgundian law to have gone to Sigiric's sister. Sigiric could charge his stepmother with having cheated his sister and himself out of their mother's legacy. Recalling how much stress was laid by later medieval urban legislation on the lawful inheritance of moveables, and the frequency with which townsfolk bequeathed clothes in their wills, we can recognise a pressure point here that was clearly difficult to subject to control whether of the informal or legal kind.[92]

This brings us up against the general question of household management. In the Merovingian and Carolingian periods, the woman's position as manager of the household was clearly an important one, and it was often contested, not only between a husband's second wife and her stepchildren, as in the cases under discussion, but also between wife and concubine, and even mother and daughter – for the mistress of the household had control over its resources, as well as her own personal possessions. This is fairly well documented in the case of Merovingian queens. Fredegund, for instance, provided the treasure with which her daughter Rigunth set off to marry a Visigothic prince. The quantity of this dowry was so large that Fredegund was required to explain where it all came from: she replied

---

[88] E. Boshof, *Ludwig der Fromme* (Darmstadt 1996), pp. 186ff.
[89] Astronomer, *Vita Hludowici*, c. 32, p. 392.
[90] Agobard, *Libri duo*, I, 5, p. 276.
[91] Astronomer, *Vita Hludowici*, c. 44, p. 458.
[92] See G. von Olberg, 'Aspekte der rechtlich-sozialen Stellung der Frauen in den frühmittelalterlichen Leges', in W. Affeldt (ed.), *Frauen in Spätantike und Frühmittelalter. Lebensbedingungen – Lebensnormen – Lebensformen* (Sigmaringen 1990), pp. 221–35, esp. p. 230: 'Die Ausübung einer herausgehobenen Tätigkeit als prestigeförderndes, sozialrelevantes Kriterium wird für Frauen nur innerhalb der Hausgemeinschaft deutlich.'

that it consisted in part of gifts from her husband King Chilperic, in part of her own acquisitions, in part of the income and dues from properties that had been left to her as gifts of the Franks.[93] All that would basically have corresponded to what the codes assigned to a legally endowed and married wife: her own inheritance, and rights of usufruct in betrothal gifts, dower lands, morning gifts and other gifts. Plectrude too was in charge of the Pippinid treasure, at any rate after the death of her husband in 714. She used some of it to buy off the Frisian king Radbod who had besieged her in Cologne. Charles Martel, escaped from the captivity in which Plectrude had left him, attacked Radbod while the latter was retreating, and inflicted heavy losses on him. After the battle of Vinchy (715), Charles Martel in turn besieged Cologne, and compelled her to hand over the rest of the treasure.[94] Until that moment, Plectrude, the *matrona*, had remained the mistress of the household: it was a position for which Martel's mother Alpaida had never been able to contend, perhaps because she was of less lofty rank than the *nobilissima* Plectrude.[95]

The quasi-constitutional position of the married woman as mistress of the household is explicit in the case of the Carolingian queen, as prescribed in the *De ordine palatii*, written by Adalard of Corbie (†826) and revised by Hincmar of Rheims. She, and beneath her (*sub ipsa*) the chamberlain, were responsible for the maintenance of the court in suitable splendour and decorum (*honestas*), especially for the *ornamentum regale*, the royal insignia and equipment, and also for the annual gifts presented by the *milites* of the king's retinue.[96] Agobard's critique of Judith gained its force precisely from such an understanding of the queen's responsibilities: 'if a queen has not known how to rule herself, how will she be able to care for the honourable and seemly state (*honestas*) of the palace, or how will she diligently play her part in the government of realm?'[97]

Yet the functions and activities that society considered tolerable, and actually desirable, in a mother, were the very same things that were laid against a stepmother as criticisms. Thus royal mothers were expected to wield influence and power for the benefit of the family and the realm, whereas stepmothers in the same position were suspected of dishonourable dealings and misuse of power to the disgrace of family and realm. Thus Agobard charged Judith and her entourage with having alienated the emperor from his sons by his first marriage, 'so that he regarded them as his enemies'.[98] The anonymous biographer of Louis the Pious confirms this allegation: those sons believed that their father intended to disinherit

[93] Gregory of Tours, *Hist.* VI, 45, p. 318.
[94] *Liber Historiae Francorum*, cc. 52, 53, pp. 326–7; Fredegar, *Cont.*, cc. 9, 10, pp. 173–4.
[95] See W. Joch, 'Karl Martell – ein minderberechtiger Erbe Pippins?', in J. Jarnut, U. Nonn and M. Richer (eds), *Karl Martell in seiner Zeit*, Beihefte der Francia 37 (Sigmaringen 1994), pp. 149–69; Kasten, *Königssöhne*, pp. 71–2; and more generally, I. Heidrich, 'Von Plektrud zu Hildegard. Beobachtungen zum Besitzrecht adeliger Frauen im Frankenreich des 7. und 8. Jahrhunderts und zur politischen Rolle der Frauen der frühen Karolinger', *Rheinische Vierteljahrsblätter* 52 (1988), 1–15.
[96] Hincmar of Rheims, *De ordine palatii*, ed. T. Gross and R. Schieffer, MGH Fontes iuris Germanici antiqui 3 (Hannover 1980), (c. 5), 72–4, pp. 360–72.
[97] Agobard, *Libri duo*, I, 5, p. 276.
[98] Ibid. I, 1 and 5, pp. 275–6.

them.[99] This brings us back to a final characteristic feature of Gregory's Sigiric story. In that case, as already indicated, conflict over the first wife's bequests, over control of the treasure and over the household, rapidly grew into a struggle for influence over the husband/father and for the social standing that that conferred. When such conflict occurred in the royal family, it escalated into a struggle to the death over the royal succession. Royal stepmothers were considered dangerous because through their control of the household, they were in a position to gain the upper hand in determining who should succeed the king. Their motives for setting aside, violently or otherwise, the stepsons who stood in their way might vary. The nameless Burgundian queen seems to have felt herself dishonoured and threatened in rank and position by her stepson Sigiric. In her case, there was apparently no question of her acting in the interests of a son of her own. Fredegund feared for her own future after the deaths of her own sons and the verbal humiliation her stepson accorded her. Both these women were reacting to positions of extreme weakness.

Plectrude's case was different. Her position in 714 seemed strong. She was grandmother of the young heirs, one of whom was mayor of the palace, and another held the title of duke.[100] Yet her stepson Charles Martel must have enjoyed political support or Plectrude would have seen no need to lock him up. Further, Martel was the only surviving son of Pippin II; and for grandsons to take precedence over an adult of the older generation was highly unusual. Plectrude was able to keep Martel out of the game for a whole year. But that year saw the defeat of her grandsons' armies by aristocratic opponents among the Neustrian Franks – and it was only after that defeat that Charles Martel was able to gain release from imprisonment.[101] Even so, it took two years more for him to force Plectrude to hand over the treasure, and a further five before he was able to deprive her grandsons of power altogether.[102]

Swanhild and Judith were stepmothers who did not seek to exclude their stepsons from power completely, but to gain for their own sons an equal share in the paternal succession. They had to fend off the sons of their husbands by previous marriages, sons whose mothers were already dead. They were thus able to assume the position of mistress of the household. Nevertheless, it was virtually impossible for either to achieve her goal. In Swanhild's case, Charles Martel made arrangements for the mayoral succession in 737 that excluded her son.[103] She resumed the

---

[99] Astronomer, *Vita Hludowici*, c. 48, pp. 472–4.

[100] A useful family-tree may be found in P. Fouracre, *The Age of Charles Martel* (London 2000), p. 197. Plectrude's elder son Drogo had four sons, while the younger, Grimoald, had one.

[101] *Liber Historiae Francorum*, c. 51, p. 325.

[102] *Annales Mosellani*, s.a. 723, ed. G. H. Pertz, MGH SS I (Hannover 1826), p. 49; *Annales Alamannici*, s.a. 723, ed. W. Lendi, *Untersuchungen zur frühalemannischen Annalistik. Die Murbacher Annalen. Mit Edition*, Scrinium Freiburgense 1 (Freiburg 1971), p. 148.

[103] Erchambert, *Breviarium regum Francorum*, ed. G. H. Pertz, MGH SS II (Hannover 1829), p. 328. See Kasten, *Königssöhne*, pp. 110ff.; J. Semmler, 'Bonifatius, die Karolinger und "die Franken"', in D. Bauer, R. Hierstand, B. Kasten and S. Lorenz (eds), *Mönchtum – Kirche – Herrschaft 750–1000* (Sigmaringen 1998), pp. 3–29, at p. 10. Curiously, Fouracre, *Age of Charles Martel*, does not mention the plan of 737.

struggle in 740/1 when her own son Grifo came of age, perhaps with support from her kinsman Odilo of Bavaria and even of a key Frankish aristocrat, Count Gairefred of Paris.[104] In autumn 741, Charles Martel revised his plans, and assigned Grifo a probably equal share in the succession along with his older half-brothers. In the *Annales Mettenses Priores*, Swanhild is not only defamed as a mere concubine but alleged to have aimed at the sole succession of her own son, excluding her stepsons entirely.[105] As remarked earlier, the author of the annals was a supporter of the descendants of those stepsons. Was Swanhild a wicked stepmother? It is clear that Swanhild's position vis-à-vis her husband and stepsons was for many years a defensive one. It may be that the crucial factor in Charles Martel's change of mind in 741 was the pressure of Count Gairefred of Paris in favour of Swanhild and her son; for Gairefred controlled the monastery of St Denis, and that was where Charles Martel very much wished to be buried.[106] Shortly before his death, Charles Martel in his final grant to St Denis committed the powerful monastery to the cause of Swanhild and Grifo, for they, and they alone, confirmed the grant with the marks of their consent.[107]

As for Judith, she too was attacked, and acquired the attributes of a stepmother, as a result of her efforts, necessarily belated, to gain for her young son Charles a share in the succession. Naturally this was opposed by her stepsons and their followers, for the succession had been settled by the *Ordinatio imperii* of 817, with Lothar as main beneficiary, Pippin of Aquitaine and Louis the German as minor legatees. Judith and Louis the Pious at first tried to get Louis's three older sons to agree to Charles's getting a share equivalent to those of Pippin and Louis.[108] Various alternative schemes were mooted in the 830s, as Judith persisted in her attempts to secure a future kingdom for Charles. If no real or lasting agreement was reached, that resulted from the uncomfortable realities of Frankish politics, and can hardly be laid at Judith's door. She manoeuvred skilfully to negotiate a settlement that her stepsons, or at least the eldest of them, Lothar, could accept.[109] Again, her posture was essentially a defensive rather than an offensive one. This was no aggressively evil stepmother.

The evidence considered in this essay shows that in the case of ruling families, second (or third or further) marriages created a problem that simply could not be

---

[104] Becher, 'Geburtsjahr Tassilos'; J. Jahn, *Ducatus Baiuvariorum. Das bairische Herzogtum der Agilolfinger* (Stuttgart 1991), pp. 170ff.

[105] *Annales Mettenses priores*, s.a. 741, 32.

[106] Diploma of Pippin I of 8 July 753, ed. H. Atsma and J. Vezin, *Chartae Latinae Antiquiores*, vol. 15 (Zurich 1986), no. 598.

[107] Diploma of Charles Martel of 17 September 741, MGH Diplomata regum Francorum e stirpe Merowingica, ed. K. A. F. Pertz (Hannover 1872), no. 14, pp. 101–2, now *Die Urkunden der Arnulfinger*, ed. J. Heidrich (Bad Münstereifel 2001), no. 14, pp. 90–2.

[108] A. Angenendt, 'Die Karolinger und die "Familie der Könige", *Zeitschrift des Aachener Geschichtsvereins* 96 (1989), 33–4.

[109] See J. L. Nelson, 'The last years of Louis the Pious', in P. Godman and R. Collins (eds), *Charlemagne's Heir. New Perspectives on the Reign of Louis the Pious* (Oxford 1990), pp. 147–59; eadem, *Charles the Bald* (London 1992), pp. 96–7.

regulated by legal stipulations on inheritance and property rights. For a woman, marriage into a royal family consisting of a husband who already had children entailed tensions and shocks not only within that family but extending into the kingdom as a whole. Because of the position of the woman within the household, the incoming wife acquired tasks and forms of authority which could be neither regulated nor controlled. From her role as mistress of the household, the queen derived a power all of her own. The room for female manoeuvre that opened up as a consequence aroused misgivings against the new woman both within the family and more widely in the realm at large. This was the more inevitable when resources on the scale of a royal treasure were at stake. It may be, in the end, that this rather obvious reason explains why stepmothers – usually unfairly – had and have the reputation of wicked women.

Political ideas in late tenth-century England: charters as evidence

Pauline Stafford

A series of half a dozen English charters in the name of King Æthelred II surviving from the 990s are of especial interest.[1] They date from 993 to the end of the decade. All restore lands and liberties to churches. And a common thread runs through them, namely reference to the king's youth as a period of ignorance and/or of actions which he now wishes to undo. In 993, for example, in a charter for Abingdon, he is presented reflecting on the causes of present ills, among which he highlighted actions undertaken 'because of the ignorance of my youth'. In 997 he refers to earlier usurpations of church land which occurred because of 'the enormous youth of my boyhood', 'whilst I was powerless and unwilling, still in the age of infancy'. He had acted not cruelly but ignorantly, when others took advantage of his boyhood's ignorance. This stage of life is contrasted with one in which the king now finds himself, variously described as 'adult', as a time of 'manly strength' and an age of discernment (*intelligibilem aetatem*) and stability of mind. Simon Keynes has used these documents to periodise the reign of Æthelred, separating the maturity of the 990s from the years of 'youthful indiscretions' in the 980s.[2] They belong in a wider group of charters of the late tenth and early eleventh century which Stenton distinguished from the 'monotonous series' of mid-tenth-century charters because of their 'tendency ... to enlarge upon the history of the property', providing a commentary

---

[1] S. Keynes, *The Diplomas of King Æthelred 'the Unready', 978–1016* (Cambridge, 1980), pp. 176–86. The charters concerned are S. 876: AD 993; S. 885: AD 995; S. 891: AD 997; S. 893: AD 998; S. 937: AD 990 × 1000, ?999. S. 838, for Tavistock, also contains reference to actions in the king's youth, but the date is impossibly early, AD 981. This is one reason for thinking that the text as we have it is not a simple record from 981, see Keynes, *Diplomas*, p. 97 n. 43 and p. 180 n. 101. (Charters are referred to throughout by their number in P. H. Sawyer, *Anglo-Saxon Charters, an Annotated List and Bibliography*, Royal Historical Society Guides and Handbooks, 8 [1968].)

[2] Keynes, *Diplomas*, pp. 176–86, and see also their significance in his 'Crime and punishment in the reign of King Æthelred the Unready', in I. Wood and N. Lund (eds), *People and Places in Northern Europe, 500–1600* (Woodbridge, 1991), pp. 67–81. Patrick Wormald has used them in the dating of I and III Æthelred, 'Æthelred the lawmaker', in *Ethelred the Unready, Papers from the Millenary Conference*, ed. D. Hill, B.A.R., British Series, 59 (1978), pp. 47–80, at p. 61, and P. Wormald, *The Making of English Law: King Alfred to the Twelfth Century*, vol. I (Oxford, 1999), pp. 328–9.

Political ideas in late tenth-century charters 69

on events and 'on relations between the king and some of his leading subjects'.[3] Their utility to the historian of tenth- and early eleventh-century England is substantial, not least for precisely the themes of this collection: for what they reveal about the working of the law and about the collective action and solidarities, lay values and lay political theory in the study of which Susan Reynolds has been such a pioneer. She has encouraged us to use charters more creatively as a source, remarking that

> It is odd that historians . . . will not risk deducing attitudes and values about collectivities from charters, chronicles and laws. . . .[4]

This essay will seek to respond to that encouragement.

In comparison with earlier tenth-century English royal charters, many of those of the 990s are detailed and discursive. For the sake of clarity this detail can be separated into that concerned with the history of the estate in question and that discoursing on the justification and explanation of the grant and the authority with which it was made. A distinctive feature of many of these charters is the incorporation into the formulaic text of the typical mid-tenth-century charter of an account of the legal case, dispute or other circumstances through which the land in question came into the king's or beneficiary's hands.[5] Sometimes these details are brief. A reference to the fact that land granted by the king to Wulfric was held by his mother, Wulfrun, scarcely appears at first sight to be a history of the estate at all. But it may constitute a statement of her right to bequeath, sum up her claims transferred to her son, and vindicate in writing her possession against other claimants – a narrative of claims implicit in a single phrase.[6] In other cases the charter expands slightly on recent holders and their actions or grants. Such brief details are akin to the short statements found in some monastic foundation – or confirmation – charters of this date, where the list of lands is accompanied by a list of the purchases, bequests or legal cases by which they were acquired.[7] At their most developed, however, these charters contain lengthy, detailed accounts of the land's recent history and holders. This may be entered as a virtually freestanding section within the charter; in some cases it is separated off from the Latin text by being recorded in the vernacular.[8] This trait in particular establishes the close

---

[3] F. M. Stenton, *The Latin Charters of the Anglo-Saxon Period* (Oxford, 1955), pp. 66–7, 74–5 and 80.

[4] S. Reynolds, *Kingdoms and Communities*, 2nd edn (Oxford, 1997), p. xxxix.

[5] See e.g. S. 883, 886, 877, 896, 926, 927, 934, listed in Keynes, *Diplomas*, p. 97 and cf. e.g. S. 878, 882, 884, 889, 892, 893, 894, 897, 901, 909 from the 990s and early 1000s – and from slightly earlier, in the 980s, S. 842, 835, 837, 844, 850, 855, 866, 869, 871.

[6] See S. 878; note also that this charter has a vernacular insert in which different holders of the land are mentioned. This makes the statement about Wulfrun, and the absence of statement about others, in the body of the charter even more pointed and significant.

[7] See e.g. S. 911: AD 1005, Eynsham and compare the brief details in S. 884, 889, 892 (in the vernacular boundary clause) and S. 901. There are similar records from about this date from Peterborough, R. 37 and 39–40. (R. + number indicates number in A. J. Robertson, ed., *Anglo-Saxon Charters* [Cambridge, 1939].)

[8] see e.g. S. 877 containing the account of Wulfbold and his crimes and cf. e.g. S. 886.

connection between this group and the vernacular records of disputes, many of which also date from the later tenth century.[9]

In common with these other records, the discursive charters are testimony to the concern at this date with the documentation of decisions concerning land, and thus of the importance of documentary evidence in disputes about landholding.[10] Even the more formulaic elements of late tenth-century English royal charters reveal this concern. They begin to refer regularly and at greater length to the loss of documents and to their replacement. They speak of the relationship of the present charter to those which may survive from the past, usually anathematising the latter.[11] Again the parallels with vernacular accounts are marked. These sometimes tell of the theft of charters, or of the circumstances in which they had changed hands.[12] Concern for documentation of landholding, or, more correctly, with the documents which provided title to land and with a recitation of an estate's recent history, appears to have been at a peak in late tenth-century England. It was not an entirely novel concern. In this as in other ways these charters present an amplification of the terse formulae of earlier charters.[13] They suggest that the standardised forms of Stenton's earlier 'monotonous series' were not all empty verbiage. But clearly in the late tenth century there were new imperatives which inspired both expansions of those earlier formulae, and also departures from them. Before examining the nature of those imperatives, the other characteristics of these charters should be briefly considered.

Typically, the main (Latin) body of the text elaborates some of a number of themes. Lengthy proems or *arengae* fit the king's actions into a story of human history from the Creation to the birth of Christ. These proems are not new, but they become common again in the last decades of the tenth century.[14] In the early

---

[9] see e.g. S. 1454, 1456, 1457 and 1458 = R. 66, 69, 59 and 41. Cf. the *Libellus Æthelwoldi*, a twelfth-century document in Cambridge, Trinity College, 0.2.41, pp. 1–64 and BL Cotton Vespasian A XIX, fos 2–27, but based on a lost register of Ely records from *c*.970 to *c*.990 AD. Similar documents probably lie behind the *Chronicon Abbatiae Ramesiensis*, ed. W. D. Macray, Rolls Series (1886).

[10] See Keynes, *Diplomas*, p. 98 and P. Wormald, 'Charters, law and the settlement of disputes in Anglo-Saxon England', in *The Settlement of Disputes in Early Medieval Europe*, ed. W. Davies and P. Fouracre (Cambridge, 1986), pp. 149–68.

[11] Wormald, ibid., pp. 160–1; in n. 59 he numbers 70 formulae from the period 900–1066 where anathemata envisage 'rivalry of extant texts' and at n. 63 suggests that the increased use of the vernacular is linked to concern with documentation. Keynes, *Diplomas*, p. 88 and especially n. 20 for the prevalence of these formulae for condemning older charters in Æthelred's reign, and dating this from the 980s. See e.g. S. 835, 842, 856, 857, 869, 873, 876, 878, 881, 883, 884, 885, 888, 896, 877, 901, 937, etc. – all from Æthelred's reign. There are earlier examples, and an interesting cluster in the reign of Edmund – S. 460, 469, 488, 496, 470, 474, 475, 487, 491.

[12] See R. 69 and especially R. 59 here.

[13] In addition to e.g. the expansion on notions of consent, which will be dealt with later, the brief details in S. 469, 682, 767, 781, 782, from the reigns of Edmund to Edgar, are of the sort often amplified in the narratives of the 990s.

[14] 'Creation' proems from the 980s and from 990–1004 – see S. 844, 853, 855, 856, 860, 866, 868, 876, 880, 899, 904, 906. Such proems were common in the reign of Athelstan, and again in the reign of Edmund. There are a number from Edgar's reign, though many are in charters debatable in their present form – see S. 673, 745, 761, 784, 786, 788, 812, 819, 821.

years of the new millennium a handful of *arengae* strike a contemporary note, with references to the affliction of enemies and the Last Judgement.[15] Several charters stress the king's own blood family, past and present, presenting a royal dynasty stretching through time.[16] As already noted, the king's own development from youth to maturity is mentioned, usually in the context of explaining his actions and changes in them. Three histories converge: the history of salvation and the working out of the divine plan, the family or dynastic history of the royal house, and the king's own individual life history. Some charters emphasise the advice and counsel which the king seeks and according to which he acts. This may in turn be related to notions of the king's good and that of his people (*gens, natio, populus*).[17] These themes seem at first sight to distinguish the Latin charters from the more terse vernacular accounts. But once again there are parallels, especially in the concern to record the authority of the meetings and counsel with which the king acts.[18] In sum, therefore, there is a stress on kinship, family and inheritance – including that of the king himself; on consultation and advice often with reference to some notion of the public good; and on documentary proofs of ownership: all in the context of a view of history, both dynastic and salvational, and of the king's own bodily history. Much of this is framed by a concern to justify and explain the king's actions; rarely in tenth-century England (or earlier and later for that matter) are 'the reasons which are moving' the king presented in such detail.[19]

One stimulus to all this is clearly the working out of tenth-century ecclesiastical reform. Its developing agenda is another theme of these charters. Restorations of church lands are amongst the spurs to detailed exposition. Charters previously granting church lands are annulled and anathematised. There are references to the free election of abbots, the proscription of royal building on church land and of the taking of royal *pastus*/provisions from it.[20] The hand of reformers is clear in these texts, whether in the extensive recording of details of land history or of the king's actions. But reform was not the sole stimulus. The frequent forfeiture of land into the hands of the king and his officials for crime is another. Forfeiture of land had been determinedly developed and elaborated as a penalty in tenth-century law, and its potential exploited by kings and their officials.[21] There were

---

[15] See S. 894: 998 AD; 895: 998 AD; 899: 1000 AD; 911: 1005 AD.
[16] See especially S. 876: 993 AD; 891: 997 AD; 899: 1001 AD. There are general references to predecessors and successors in S. 842, 856, 860, 861, 849, 854, echoing earlier tenth-century formulae.
[17] See S. 876, 893, 937.
[18] R. 63, the 'micel gemot' and 'micel sinothe'; cf. the various meetings specified in R. 69 with those in the Latin charters, below. Compare the ranking and ordering of witnesses in R. 63 and R. 66, 'eal seo duguth' and 'ealra witena' of R. 69, the 'witan . . . ge gehadodde ge læwide' R. 63, and the 'fela cynges witena' of R. 59 with the 'omnes optimates', 'omnes sapientes utriusque ordinis' of such Latin charters as S. 876 and 891.
[19] Stenton, *Latin Charters*, p. 75.
[20] See S. 838, 876, 881, 884, 895, 904.
[21] See Wormald, *The Making of English Law*, at pp. 160, 363, etc; P. Stafford, 'The laws of Cnut and the history of Anglo-Saxon royal promises', *Anglo-Saxon England*, 10 (1982), 173–90; *eadem, Unification and Conquest, A Political and Social History of England in the Tenth and Eleventh Centuries* (London, 1989), pp. 141, 146, 159–60, 188–9.

other, more short-term, factors. The king's family was growing in size. By 993, Aethelred had four sons and an unknown number of daughters, and a dowager queen alongside his own wife; by 1002 he had married twice, perhaps three times, and produced at least two more sons. Not since the reign of his great-grandfather Edward the Elder at the beginning of the century had an English king been blessed – or faced – with such a progeny, and with the issue of providing for it. Another feature of charters of the 990s is the prominence of this royal family. The dowager queen, Ælfthryth, Æthelred's mother, re-emerged in witness lists now and the king's sons appeared for the first time.[22] Some of the charters of these years were concerned with the issues raised by the growing size and complexity of the royal family.

Family provision was inseparable from the questions of church endowment and reform. There was considerable negotiation c.993 about the land of the king's sons, previously given to Abingdon. The king's mother's dower land was reorganised and a religious community was reformed in memory of the king's murdered brother, Edward, on her land. There was provision for and reorganisation of the land of two nunneries closely connected to the royal family, one of which contained Edward's relics.[23] Family and its lands and monastic endowment were in turn connected to the issues raised by forfeiture. The dowager queen and Abingdon abbey were both compensated using forfeited land. Forfeiture, like monastic foundation, refoundation or reform, led to transfers of land, often in circumstances which might subsequently be debated or called into question. Both encouraged the recording of these circumstances in ways which would justify the title of the subsequent holder – whether through an edited history of the estate or through an underlining of the authority of actions and transactions. The involvement of royal family members and their claims merely increased this pressure to record.

This context of church reform, legal forfeiture and dynastic concerns was thus the stimulus to the English charters of this date. This combination did more than produce a series of detailed estate histories. It called for a definition of good kingship, or rather for explanation and justification of – clearly debatable – royal action which had to be framed within contemporary notions of such kingship. The mounting pressure of external Viking attack sharpened this debate.[24] By the end of the reign these attacks would call Æthelred's kingship fundamentally into

---

[22] See S. Keynes, *An Atlas of Attestations in Anglo-Saxon Charters* (Cambridge, 1995, privately printed), Table LIX and cf. Tables XXXI a–c for the earlier tenth century, where it becomes apparent that such appearances cannot simply be taken for granted. Further analysis of the appearance of royal family in tenth-century charters in P. Stafford, *Queen Emma and Queen Edith, Queenship and Women's Power in Eleventh-century England* (Oxford, 1997), pp. 85–6, 198–206.

[23] See S. 876, 877, 899, 904. There is further discussion of this reorganisation, and of its relationship to reform in my '"Cherchez la femme": queens, queens' lands, nunneries and the foundation of Reading Abbey', *History*, 85 (2000), 4–27.

[24] It is possible that the approaching millennium had its impact too – not least in the sensitivity to history in these charters. For a wide perspective on millennial references and a flavour of the intense debate surrounding them see R. Landes, 'The fear of an apocalyptic year 1000: Augustinian historiography, medieval and modern', *Speculum*, 75 (2000), 97–145.

Political ideas in late tenth-century charters 73

question. In the 990s they must have added fuel to the questions about rule which other developments in England at this date were already posing. The details and terms of this debate can arguably still be heard in these charters. These latter can thus be dissected for the history of law and landholding, for the monastic revival and for contemporary events. But they should also be read as some of our most important surviving sources for English political thought at this date.[25] They debate and justify action and define good kingship within a set of values and ideals which allow examination of the common political discourse of late tenth-century England. As with any discourse, it was a multivocal one, susceptible to interpretation and presentation in a variety of ways. It may have been committed to writing by clerics, but it was one in which both laymen and clerics, and, equally important, reforming clerics, were constrained to present their arguments. These charters provide our clearest insights into the thinking of the elites of late tenth-century England revealed at this critical moment.

Central to that thinking was the belief that the king should act with advice and counsel. Two charters of 993 and 997 respectively detail this process of consultation.[26] In 993 the king ordered a synodal council, consisting of bishops, abbots and the first amongst his great men, to meet to discuss the reasons for the tribulations which had befallen him and his nation (*natio*). He himself addressed them and ordered them to discuss together, 'Deo consulente' and with the inspiration of Christ's grace, what was appropriate and necessary for God, for the spiritual safety of the king's soul and for his royal dignity, as well as what was necessary for (*oportuna*) the English people. When the king decided to act on their decisions, he renewed the freedom of Abingdon 'inspired by grace and at the request of his great men, lay and ecclesiastic, and taking counsel with them'. In 997 the king asserted that he was acting 'informed by the frequent warning advice (*ammonitio*) of his wise men'. Another, undated, Abingdon document, which may be associated with that of 993, or may be dated *c.*999, concerns land disputed between Abingdon and the king's sons.[27] It refers to a series of decisions about the estates, and to the forfeiture and bequest which had brought other lands into the king's hands. At point after point, divine inspiration and action to placate God is invoked. But once again counsel is human as well as divine. Æthelred himself had been given the lands of the king's sons, granted by his father to Abingdon, according to the order and decree of all the great and good (*optimates*), unanimously. These decisions of the great men were controversial – the king will not say whether they acted justly or unjustly, though significantly he did not undo their actions. Such actions had

---

[25] I do not have room here to consider the more systematic thought, as represented e.g. in the works of Ælfric of Eynsham and Wulfstan of Worcester. It might, however, be noted that they share some of the same themes as these charters – e.g. in the stress on counsel, and, in Ælfric's case, a reiteration of a royal past. Perhaps significantly, however, Ælfric's choice of previous rulers differs in some respects from that in these charters – with more of a stress on victorious kings and those remembered for their generosity to churches, rather than on the immediate blood line which is the family highlighted here.
[26] S. 876: 993 AD; 891: 997 AD.
[27] S. 937.

delivered other land into his hands. The land which Æthelred was now giving to Abingdon had been taken from the widow Eadflaed by ealdorman Aelfric in the early 980s. Ælfric's own expulsion and forfeiture had resulted in his lands being decreed to the king by the *optimates* in a synodal council at Cirencester. Amongst the great men were the widow's advocates, who had secured for her a lifetime holding of those lands. Now they were back in the king's hands – and he granted them to Abingdon – acting for the love of Christ but also of those who exhorted him with friendly insistence (*amica assiduitas*) as to what was necessary. The advice and the agreed decrees of the great men are repeatedly cited as constituting authority.

In 993 and 997 that authority was underlined by details of the meetings in which decisions were made. A synodal council at Winchester at Pentecost 993 decided, amongst other things, to restore the liberty of Abingdon monastery. It was followed by another assembly on 17 July in the oratory at Gillingham after mass, where the renewal of that liberty was granted, corroborated and confirmed.[28] In 997 a meeting of 'a great multitude of the wise' took place at Easter at Calne, in the hall of the royal vill, and land was restored there to the Old Minster, Winchester. But permission to draw up the charter for that restoration was 'granted and judged worthy to be corroborated by the authority of many elders (*senes*)' at a later meeting, of the whole army (*exercitus*) and a throng (*caterva*) of bishops, abbots, ealdormen, great men and many nobles at Wantage, which had been called to correct a diverse range of problems.[29] Occasionally counsellors or particular witnesses are singled out by name in the body of the text. The instigators of the undated grant to Abingdon included the abbot, Wulfgar, but also the king's 'beloved servant' Wulfgeat (a member of the king's household and later to be himself a victim of forfeiture) along with Æthelred's maternal uncle Ordulf and his kinsman (*consanguineus*) Æthelmær.[30] The latter two were, like Wulfgeat, prominent household members in the 990s, and in 993 were the specified witnesses of the confirmation with the king's assent at Gillingham.[31] Tenth-century English charters do not regularly record the meetings, sites and timing of councils so explicitly, nor do they specify the particular individuals at whose prompting the king acts. Some of these documents of the 990s, by contrast, do.

This degree of detail and precision is unusual, even by 990s standards, and probably reflects the importance of the meetings concerned. The 993 meeting marks something of a turning point in the reign. A considerable reorganisation of ealdormanries, perhaps driven in part by military considerations, occurred around this time, as, apparently, did a reorganisation of royal family lands that was linked to the emergence of the king's family on to the political scene.[32] The Wantage meeting

[28] S. 876.
[29] S. 891.
[30] S. 937 and cf. for his forfeiture S. 918 and possibly 934, and Anglo-Saxon Chronicle, MS C, D and E s.a. 1006, in *Two of the Saxon Chronicles Parallel*, ed. C. Plummer and J. Earle (Oxford, 1892).
[31] Keynes, *Diplomas*, pp. 187–8 for discussion of their position.
[32] Keynes, *Diplomas*, pp. 186–7; P. Stafford, 'The reign of Æthelred II, a study in the limitations on royal policy and action', *Ethelred the Unready*, ed. D. Hill, pp. 15–46, at p. 29.

of 997 may have been the occasion from which the famous law-code, III Æthelred, derives (above, n. 2). Issues of unity were to the fore, and these were reflected in the code's concern with local practice. It can be no coincidence that the charter which records the meeting is the only one of Æthelred's reign where the witness list specifies the areas of jurisdiction of the ealdormen, as if to stress how far they spoke for, and/or were entrusted to implement decisions in, those areas. But these two meetings, and the charters which record them, voice a concern with counsel, advice and consent which is echoed in many other charters of this date. No fewer than sixteen charters of the period 990 to 1005 mention it explicitly.[33] In two charters the consent of the great men, regularly noted in a general way in the introduction to the witness lists of earlier charters, is given personal voice at the end of the list: 'All of us, the king's great men, have quickly shown our unanimous consent to this royal gift (*unanimen* [thus] *consensum alacriter praebuimus*)', 'all we great men (*optimates*) have consented (*nos omnes optimates consensimus*).[34] The king acts 'using the advice of the great men and with their counsel'.[35] And their legitimate role in the government of the kingdom, which such counsel expresses, is made explicit: they are 'the bishops and all those by whom the sceptre of *imperium* and the government of the kingdom are ruled'.[36] In all this earlier formulae are amplified and elaborated. The 990s did not create new ideas, but they called for clearer statements. Counsel and consent, and the authority which these gave to the king's actions, are leitmotivs of these charters, not least because, as in the cases presented in the Abingdon charters, the justice of those actions was clearly debatable.

That debate articulated the recognition that counsel could be good or bad. Æthelsige was one of those now accused of having given bad counsel – *suasio* is the word chosen – in the 980s. He was an enemy of God and of all the people, a 'public enemy' (*publicus hostis*).[37] These charters suggest that counsel could be categorised within a notion of wider, public interest; the interests (*oportuna*) of the English were its legitimate objects.[38] There were evil men who were offenders against the public good, accused before the king and the nation. Ealdorman Ælfric was exiled because he had committed crimes against God and the king's royal *imperium*,[39] and was accused and found guilty (*reus*) as one who acted against the king and all his people (*gens*).[40] A good counsellor was one such as Bishop Æthelwold, who always looked to the welfare of the king and his *patria*, in contrast with the detestable pride of those who should have looked to that well-being but

---

[33] S. 876, 880, 881, 891, 893, 894, 895, 896, 898, 899, 909, 911, 913, 937, 942, 944; cf. twenty-one charters from the whole of Edgar's reign – at least five of which, S. 816, 817, 825, 826, 827, are probably Winchester forgeries, perhaps to be dated to Æthelred's reign – and rarely so explicit or insistent; cf. ten of Edmund, six of Eadred and thirteen or slightly more of Eadwig.
[34] S. 889 and 893.
[35] S. 876.
[36] S. 881.
[37] S. 893.
[38] S. 876.
[39] S. 896.
[40] S. 937.

neglected it. Since the bishop's death, tribulations had fallen on the king and his nation (*natio*).[41]

The use of the term *patria* is noteworthy. It was not a common word in tenth-century English charters. It only came into regular use from the reign of Edgar onwards.[42] It is associated in time and usage with ideas of England, if not English unity. The vernacular was the 'patria lingua';[43] St Alban was the protomartyr of this *patria*.[44] As early as the reign of Edward the Elder *patria* had been the word chosen in the description of the treachery of Wulfhere in Alfred's reign; he had left homeland and lordship (*patria* and *dominium*) in spite of his oath.[45] It was used again in the charters of Æthelred which gave accounts of the exile of Ealdorman Ælfric, who forfeited his hereditary lands in 984/5 and was expelled from the *patria*.[46] A charter of 1004 notified all those 'living in this *patria*' of events in Oxford related to suspected internal treachery by Danes living 'in this island', i.e. betrayal of the English by Danish settlers or residents to the Danish invaders.[47] The word expresses notions of unity – if not Englishness – in the later tenth century, at least at royal level. It may thus define betrayal not merely of king but also of kingdom, an idea with particular resonance in the context of external attack. *Patria*, however, is also a term redolent of kinship and its values, drawing some of its strength from them and calling them too into play in its notion of unity and the loyalty that should command. Its usage alerts us to a tension in late tenth-century political ideology which made forfeiture especially problematic.

The ideas of a public good explicit and implicit in these charters might suggest a sharp distinction between a public political world and a private one of kinship and family. But this antithesis is not present, at least in any simple form. Family and kinship are a sphere of values in themselves, and one which has a legitimate place in the political world. Æthelred expresses filial piety in a grant for the souls of his father and mother in 1002.[48] But such family piety is not necessarily defined as private. The king himself is made to articulate this in a charter of 1001. In this grant to Shaftesbury, where the king's 'martyred' brother's bones lay buried, Æthelred is made to contrast actions done *privatim* for his own individual benefit and those undertaken for the general safety of his blood family (*genealogia*), already gone or still to come.[49] Helping kin was conceptually distinct from reprehensible 'private' selfishness. The royal kinship of named counsellors like Ordulf and

---

[41] S. 876.

[42] In particular it becomes a common substitute for 'anglice' (itself a significant usage) in the phrase which introduces a place name in the vernacular – 'ab huius patriae gnosticis' 'ab illius patriae gnosticis' in e.g. S. 698, 702, 706, 709, 710, 711, 714, 716, 717, 719, 720, 722, 737, 738, 747, 762, 771, 777, 794, 800, 801, 805.

[43] S. 888 and 889.

[44] S. 912.

[45] S. 382.

[46] S. 896 and 937.

[47] S. 909.

[48] S. 904.

[49] S. 899.

Political ideas in late tenth-century charters

Æthelmær is explicit in charters. Such kinship was apparently not felt to detract in any way from their ability to give good, thus by implication 'public', counsel; indeed it might have been seen as enhancing their advice. Ancestry was a history within which the individual was placed and – at least ideally – constrained. Some charters presented the royal family as a dynasty stretching through time, with the present king referring to and bound by the actions and decisions of his predecessors, and himself in turn binding his successors. Thus Æthelred confirmed the grant of his uncle Ordulf to the church which was the resting place of his own grandmother and where others of his ancestors lay awaiting the trumpet which would call them to the third birth of the resurrection.[50] In 993 he referred to and renewed grants by his predecessors, and identified them by their blood relationship – his father Edgar, his uncle Eadwig and his father's uncle Eadred.[51] In 997 his charter was given a history and ancestry. It was Christian – stretching back to the beginnings of Christianity in Wessex in the person of Cenwalh – but also dynastic, renewing the charters of Edgar, his father, and of that father's uncle, Eadred.[52] In the undated grant to Abingdon in which Æthelred compensated the church for the loss of land which his father had given to it, he acted for love of his father and to avoid bearing his father's curse, as well as for the good of his own sons.[53] Thus a public, political sphere in which treachery and crime of the individual could be defined and punished was not clearly separated from, and seen as superior to, a sphere of family and kinship, which had its own strong and defensible ideals.

It is thus no surprise that kinship, inextricably tied into ideas about inheritance, was a crux of the 990s debates. Dynastic power and authority were rooted here, as the recitations of family history in the charters show. A good king defended such central values, as Æthelred himself did at this date. A remarkable number of cases involving women, in particular widows, and their inheritance, were settled now.[54] As these cases demonstrate, royal power grew as much within as against accepted ideals. Women's claims constituted the most problematic area of family inheritance, and thus one of those most susceptible to external interference and protection by a lord/king. Even as Æthelred asserted his good lordship to protect inheritance he meddled in it, revealing the ambiguities, and thus the room for manoeuvre, which these core values left open. But ambiguities had limits, and basic principles

---

[50] S. 838 – dated 981, but in most respects belonging with the 990s charters, not least in its concern with the king's youth – see above n. 1.

[51] S. 876.

[52] S. 891.

[53] S. 937.

[54] see wills of Æthelflæd, S. 1494 (975 × 991 AD, probably at the end of that date range); of Æthelgifu, S. 1497 (990 × 1001 AD), of Ælfflæd, S. 1486 (1000 × 1002 AD), the inheritance of Wulfrun, on which see S. 878 and 1380, and note the matronymic references to Wulfric as her son, and thus heir, in S. 878, 877 (the latter 988 × 990, but finally recorded c.996). See the disputes involving widows resolved now, S. 1454, Wynflæd and Leofwine (990 × 992 AD), and that over the inheritance as a widow of Ætheric of Bocking's widow, after her husband's alleged treachery, *Anglo-Saxon Wills*, ed. D. Whitelock (Cambridge, 1930), no. 16.2, c.997 AD. The will of Wulfwaru, S. 1538 (984 × 1016) may belong now. See also the case of the widow Eadflæd below.

constantly reasserted themselves. By the 990s forfeiture – and the advance of royal power which it signalled – had combined with monastic reform to raise general but urgent questions about family inheritance and the degree to which hereditary claims should be or could be overridden.[55] A king whose reign had begun with a brother's murder and who was now experiencing mounting external attack faced issues which had been fermenting throughout much of the tenth century. Justifications of dispossession and disinheritance had to be framed within a political discourse in which family and inheritance were deep-seated and pervasive. Tensions inevitably arose, since the debate stretched the old language up to, if not beyond, its breaking point.

It was a language long since appropriated and now again used by reformers themselves. The idea of inheritance applied to heavenly as well as earthly goods. The king acted in order to be heir in heaven, or to secure a patron at the Last Judgement through the use of the earthly inheritances of his patrimony.[56] Christ himself had his inheritance, held through the persons of clerics. Bishop Æthelwold and Abingdon had received freedom 'in eternal inheritance' of which the monastery had been subsequently deprived: the inheritance (*hereditas*) of Christ and his holy mother had been sold and was now to be restored.[57] The transfer of the notion of inheritance from earth to heaven allowed argument about the claims of churches, potentially at odds with those of families, to be argued within the same set of values.

It was similarly within them that forfeiture had to be justified. In the charter concerning the forfeiture of Æthelsige and the transfer of the land to Wulfric, the names they bore are given special attention. The name which his kin had given to Æthelsige had been dishonoured by the crime he had committed, hence he deserved to lose his inheritance, implicitly also received from them. On the other hand the recipient of Æthelsige's forfeit land was still distinguished by the name, Wulfric, which the nobility of his kindred (*parentela*) had given him.[58] Worthiness or unworthiness for inheritance from family also marked out the worthy and unworthy more generally, and unworthiness shown in other respects might thus affect claim on inheritance. Inheritance-worthiness involved judgements which included a notion of the public conceived in kinship terms. The king and people whose well-being was to be ensured could be seen as a *patria* – here literally a fatherland – from which the guilty were exiled. Ealdorman Ælfric was exiled and lost land, including hereditary land, because he became a public enemy. Kin who got involved in such action disinherited themselves – as Ealdorman Leofsige's sister did by helping her brother after his exile.[59] But forfeiture necessarily involved the claims of kin more generally even without such accessory fault. And English people *c*.1000 could distinguish actions done 'privatim', by or for the individual,

---

[55] For comment on the tenacity of notions of inheritance vis-à-vis church land see e.g. P. Wormald, *How Do We Know so Much about Anglo-Saxon Deerhurst?* (Deerhurst, 1993).
[56] S. 888 and 885.
[57] S. 876.
[58] S. 886.
[59] S. 926.

and those with implications for a family, 'genealogia'. Could a single individual embody family claims in such a way as to lose them all? How far could an individual be punished when claims did not end with him or her? Forfeiture, even when expressed in kinship terminology, was deeply inimical to kinship values.

The tortuousness inherent in any attempt to reconcile the two may be betrayed in the wording of the charter describing Ælfric's forfeiture. It enshrines confused if not contradictory meanings of terms for 'hereditary right' and 'inheritance'. Ealdorman Ælfric had taken from the widow Eadflæd her *hereditas*, appropriating it into his own. As a result of judgement against him, which may have involved much larger questions than this misappropriation and which had wider political ramifications, he lost this and everything he possessed by 'hereditary right' (*iure hereditario*).[60] In both cases *hereditas* appears to have its expected meaning as 'that which has been acquired through hereditary claim from family'. Though the land went back for life to the widow, as her *hereditas*, it then passed on her death to the king, who gave it to Abingdon 'from my own inheritance' (*ex mea propria hereditate*) – though clearly here the king was speaking of acquisition via legal processes. In such a dispute, 'inheritance' does not simply mean that which has been acquired from family, though it still clearly possesses that meaning and draws strength from it. The more familiar meaning remained. Both Eadflæd and Ælfric had 'inheritance' which can be assumed to have come to them through kinship. But land was being acquired in other ways as well. 'Inheritance' in this charter seems almost to denote a right to possess and to give, rather than indicating kin as the source of that right. A situation in which land was changing hands rapidly threatened claims on inheritance as traditionally conceived. But here the language of landholding and land-giving seems – deliberately? – slow to respond. The use of inheritance terminology to cover land acquired by the king by political and legal process may indicate how far kinship and its values circumscribed and limited the free growth of royal power.

During the 990s, interlocking questions about royal lands, inheritance, church endowments and forfeiture were thrashed out in a context of external attack, and at the height of a reform movement. Notions of English unity were at stake.[61] The charters of the 990s became more discursive, that is lengthier, as a symptom and consequence of these debates. They therefore became more discursive in the (post)-modern sense, that is, more rhetorical, more ideologically charged. Thus we can read from them statements of beliefs and values, hitherto less articulated, which justified political claims in tenth- and early eleventh-century English culture. Prevailing ideals of kinship and inheritance, of the public good and English unity, of consultation, advice and consent, provided the framework of argument within which the authority for contentious actions was established. Within that framework,

---

[60] S. 896.
[61] On monastic reform and English unity see N. Banton, 'Monastic reform and the unification of tenth-century England', in *Religion and National Identity*, Studies in Church History, 18, ed. S. Mews (Oxford, 1982), pp. 71–85.

Æthelred's rule in the 990s was defined as 'good kingship', in the sense of abiding by traditional values. How debatable that was is indicated by the charters themselves and by later events. Most of these themes were reiterated, but now turned into a critique of the king and his actions, in the 'Coronation Charter' of Cnut, which may itself embody the promises of good lordship/kingship which Æthelred made on his return from voluntary exile in 1014.[62] That shift of voice, from active to passive, from positive to negative, from legitimation to critique was, of course, in part the result of Æthelred's defeat. In the process the 'much-counselled' Æthelred of the 990s became the 'no-counsel' of that king's famous epithet 'Unræd'. The debates of the 990s may have shaped that specific critique. But in the 990s his actions could still be presented in a positive light. These charters not only give us a rare insight into the terms of early medieval English political debate, and into the tensions and contradictions within and between them, but also into their successful deployment within a specific historical context.

The charters in which the debate was recorded were drafted by clerics, and were often grants, restorations or confirmations to religious houses. But the values they articulate are not merely or primarily clerical. These charters do not speak merely the language of reform, though they include that. Rather, clerical cases are made by invoking what might be seen as lay values, or what might, more appropriately, be defined as a shared inheritance. Nor, significantly, did churches always win the argument. Land claimed by the king's sons was not, for example, returned to Abingdon. Abingdon was compensated for its loss, but the aethelings' rightful inheritance was defended and the charter's wording prevaricates on the question of whether the original deprivation of Abingdon had been just or unjust. The notion of a conflict of lay and ecclesiastical ideals may in any case be anachronistic for the earlier Middle Ages.[63] Reform might be considered one of the factors which sharpens the possibility of such confrontation. But in the late tenth century dividing lines were far from simple. Clerics were as likely to be divided as united by reform, and laymen at court were often reform's most ardent supporters. Reform itself, of course, may appear clearer with a historian's hindsight than it did to contemporaries. Polarised divisions may not be an appropriate way of capturing and understanding such a situation.

This essay began with the 'youthful ignorance' charters. Returning to them now suggests how far the ideals of the 990s, albeit recorded in clerically drafted documents, should be seen as shared values, or ones which at least had strong resonance for the laity. In the context of debates which utilised the values of kinship and family, and in which the king was made to place himself and his actions within a dynastic past, a metaphor of the king's reign drawn from his human life-cycle was a very apposite way of presenting what was claimed as a shift in direction and

---

[62] Stafford, 'The laws of Cnut and the history of Anglo-Saxon royal promises', and Wormald, *The Making of English Law*, vol. 1, pp. 361–2.

[63] see J. L. Nelson, 'The Lord's anointed and the people's choice', *The Frankish World* (London, 1996), pp. 99–131, on the possibility of greater consensuality. See also Elizabeth A. R. Brown in this volume.

a king's change of mind. Æthelred was depicted as dissociating himself from the actions of his 'boyhood', 'childhood' and 'youth'.[64] Yet the actions now disowned took place in the later 980s: the period of 'youthful ignorance' dated from c.984, by which date the king was about fifteen, and extended into his late teens.[65] Definitions of 'puer' 'iuvenis', 'infans' were very flexible in the early Middle Ages, but these would have to be stretched far indeed to cover Æthelred during these years. In tenth-century England a man was judged capable of undertaking many aspects of adult life at fifteen.[66] And by the mid-980s Æthelred had apparently gone through one of the defining rites of passage to adulthood, marriage.[67] Indeed 984 is perhaps best seen as the end of a period of regency when the king took over full rule, that is, claimed adulthood. His mother, for example, now disappeared from the charters.[68] The late 980s have some appearance of a distinctive period in the reign – characterised by the clustering of grants to laymen and the absence of abbots from the witness lists. But to label this period retrospectively as 'youth', even 'infancy' is no simple description: the terms look especially loaded set beside the labelling of Edgar, in one of these same charters, as a 'senex' 'old man, elder'.[69] The context stresses Edgar's wisdom; but he was no more than thirty-two at his death. In the cases of both father and son, the human life-cycle, youth and age, is used as an explanatory device rather than as a description of physical reality.

What the discursive charters offer is a debatable, contentious retrospective interpretation of the later 980s as a reprehensible period – and a reversible one. In some ways, especially in the grants to laymen, these years look like the opening phase of other tenth-century reigns – here deferred by a period of regency. The

---

[64] Puer/pueritia – S. 891, 893, 937; infans/infantia – S. 838; iuvenilis/iuventus – S. 876, 886, 891, 893.

[65] Discussion of his likely date of birth in Stafford, *Queen Emma and Queen Edith*, p. 189. n. 127, and Keynes, *Diplomas*, pp. 174–6. The period of pueritia/iuventus referred to seems to have begun about the time of the death of Bishop Æthelwold, see S. 876 – though we need not entirely accept this charter's view that that death was the turning point. S. 891 refers to charters granted in this period of pueritia/iuventus concerning Ebbesborne, at least one of which can be dated to 986, S. 861. S. 893 refers to this period of youth and the actions of Æthelsige and the land at Bromley. The charter granting Bromley to Æthelsige, S. 864, is dated 987.

[66] Later definitions ended pueritia about the age of fourteen, S. Shahar, *Childhood in the Middle Ages* (London, 5 1990), pp. 24–6, though it seems that in the early Middle Ages and later a man might be adolescens or iuvenis even puer or infans until twenty and beyond, ibid., pp. 27–31. Cf. R. Meens, 'Children and confession in the early Middle Ages', in *The Church and Childhood*, Studies in Church History, vol. 31, ed. D. Wood (Oxford, 1994), pp. 53–65 at pp. 53–5. Æthelred's father had been fourteen or fifteen at the date when he was chosen king by the Mercian and Northumbrians and according to the Blickling Homily on St Martin, the hero attained manhood at the age of fifteen and took worldly weapons, *The Blickling Homilies of the Tenth Century*, ed. R. Morris, Early English Text Society, vols 58, 63 and 73 (1880), p. 213. In the laws of Athelstan, however, twelve appears as an age which for some legal purposes was adult, II Athelstan 1, *The Laws of the Earliest English Kings*, ed. F. L. Attenborough (Cambridge, 1922).

[67] The date of his first marriage is debatable – but see the number of children he had by 993, and Stafford, *Queen Emma and Queen Edith*, p. 66, n. 3, and p. 85.

[68] *Atlas of Attestations*, ed. Keynes, Table LIX, and discussion, Keynes, *Diplomas*, p. 176, and Stafford, *Queen Emma and Queen Edith*, pp. 199–206.

[69] S. 937 – where he is also 'plenus dierum'.

disappearance of abbots from the witness lists now does suggest Æthelred's turning away from the pattern of his father's later years, when monastic reform and its products had been prominent at court. A partial return to this pattern in the 990s produced the perspective from which the late 980s were rewritten.[70] By the 990s great play was apparently being made with Æthelred as a 'good king' – taking counsel, protecting the church, defending widows. But how was the shift away from the late 980s to be presented? Not as repentance. Æthelred was to be no Louis the Pious, though the actions from which he was now turning were less serious than those which prompted Attigny.[71] Instead Æthelred (or his spokesmen) invoked the metaphor of the human body and its life-cycle, a process of natural change and development. Such a metaphor had special relevance in a decade when royal family inheritance and the emergence of the king's sons had brought royal youth back to mind – it is difficult to know whether that analysis provoked the re-emergence or vice versa – and when inheritance in general had been at issue. It made special sense alongside a presentation of the dynasty extending through time, an undying body of kingship greater than the individual king, which grew out of the blood links over time of a natural family. A king changing his mind, undoing his own previous actions, was a problematic situation. In the 990s it was managed and naturalised through re-presentation as a shift from youth to maturity, and as a renewal of the actions of Æthelred's predecessors. It was a re-presentation comprehensible and acceptable to cleric and lay alike, underlining the significance of shared ideas of inheritance, kinship and the body in the shaping of early medieval political discourse. If we want to hear that discourse in late tenth-century England, we should listen attentively and above all to charters.

[70] So many of the ecclesiastical accounts of the king's and others' actions now, as in the years after 975, are so *parti pris* that the circumstances, motivation, etc. of these years is difficult to disentangle.

[71] On the latter, and on the extent to which it shaped the later deposition of Louis, see Mayke de Jong. 'Power and humility in Carolingian society: the public penance of Louis the Pious', *Early Medieval Europe*, 1 (1992), 29–52. This too was no simple clerical triumph since penance was conceived in secular terms as a punishment for dishonour – hamscara. Although the murder of his brother, from which Æthelred himself had benefited, may lie in the background of the 990s, there is no indication of direct accusation of the king. Stress on his youth might, however, indirectly cover any such suspicions.

Medieval mentalities and primitive legal practice

M. T. Clanchy

We cannot make sense of the transformation of lay society and government in the twelfth and thirteenth centuries if we start from the belief that people then inherited a purely – or even largely – formalistic, rigid, and magical idea of law from their predecessors.[1]

This argument from *Kingdoms and Communities* explains much of Susan Reynolds's approach to medieval history, both in that book and in *Fiefs and Vassals*. We need to start from beliefs, as we have little certain knowledge about law in early societies which lack documents. But what should we believe? Reynolds departs from the common belief that Western civilisation is a story of progress: 'medieval ideas about kingdoms and peoples were *very like* modern ideas about nations'.[2] This is one of the basic propositions of *Kingdoms and Communities*; I have italicised *very like* to emphasise how Reynolds does not accept that medieval ideas must have been different simply because they were old. Within the medieval period itself the same considerations apply: 'people had been, by and large, just as intelligent and thoughtful in their management of law and government in the tenth century as they were in the thirteenth'.[3] Many fewer texts survive from the tenth century than from the thirteenth; historians should acknowledge this and not attempt to fill what is a vacuum in the evidence with unproven presumptions about early medieval people being primitive in mentality.

The argument from mentalities is circular, as Reynolds points out. The interpretation of early medieval law as 'essentially formal and ritualised depends on assuming that it must have been, because primitive law must by definition be formal and ritualised and because the early Middle Ages look primitive'.[4] Mentalities have been treated as entities with a distinctive life of their own. Earlier in the twentieth century 'the medieval mind' was an acceptable way of characterising medieval culture: 'The Middle Ages! They seem so far away; intellectually so preposterous,

---

[1] S. Reynolds, *Kingdoms and Communities in Western Europe, 900–1300*, 2nd edn (Oxford, 1997), pp. 37–8.
[2] Reynolds, *Kingdoms and Communities*, p. 9.
[3] Reynolds, *Kingdoms and Communities*, p. 338.
[4] Reynolds, *Kingdoms and Communities*, p. 37.

spiritually so strange.'[5] This is the opening sentence of Henry Osborne Taylor's *The Mediaeval Mind*, an impressive two-volume compendium and commentary, which was first published in 1911 and reprinted throughout the 1920s and 1930s. The whole concept of mentalities as entities is challenged by Reynolds in her paper to the Royal Historical Society in 1990.[6] In the same year, independently of Reynolds, G. E. R. Lloyd published *Demystifying Mentalities*, which concludes that talk about mentalities diverts attention away from individual diversities within societies. The same individual may exhibit very different modes of reasoning, depending on the subject being addressed. It is these diverse modes of reasoning which should 'provide the locus of the investigation, not the reasoners themselves nor their supposed mentalities'.[7] Lloyd called for case by case investigations, as the same person may think or do one thing that looks primitive and another that looks advanced.

Later on in this essay I discuss a case which came before the royal judges in the court of King John in 1213, when the prior of Durham's attorney produced a charter with a broken knife attached to it instead of a seal. The attorney was presumably experienced in the business of the court. Why did he rely on this primitive form of proof, which was in fact rejected, when Durham cathedral priory was one of the most advanced and successful corporations in England? Its monks had been reformed, its cathedral was an extraordinarily innovative building, its books had been renewed, its properties reorganised, it should surely have progressed beyond the magical idea of law which authenticating documents with knives implies. On the other hand, all Durham's modernising activities in the twelfth century had been devoted to maintaining a primitive form of religion centred on the miracle-working shrine of St Cuthbert. As this summary discussion demonstrates, deciding which practices are 'primitive' and which 'advanced' is done subjectively in accordance with modern criteria of modernity. This is a circular argument of the same sort as the one Reynolds describes concerning early medieval law.

Historians welcome calls for case by case investigations, as generalising across the centuries is usually now left to sociologists and popularisers. Rare are the historians who are as happy making generalisations as they are recounting details, and this is what makes Reynolds so unusual. Her early publications concentrated on detail, most notably her edition in 1965 of nearly 900 instructions addressed between 1315 and 1330 to Roger Martival, bishop of Salisbury.[8] This is a register in which the bishop's clerks noted down the texts of the royal writs they received day by day. At first sight a gulf seems to separate the detail of Bishop Martival's register and the extraordinarily bold generalisations of *Kingdoms and Communities* and *Fiefs and Vassals*. Perhaps, though, it was the experience of following Martival's

[5] H. O. Taylor, *The Mediaeval Mind*, 4th edn (London, 1925), p. xi (preface to the 1st edn).
[6] 'Social mentalities and the case of medieval scepticism', *Transactions of the Royal Historical Society*, 6th series, 1 (1991), pp. 21–41.
[7] G. E. R. Lloyd, *Demystifying Mentalities* (Cambridge, 1990), p. 145.
[8] *The Registers of Roger Martival, Bishop of Salisbury 1315–30*, vol. 3, *Royal Writs*, ed. S. Reynolds, The Canterbury and York Society, 59 (1965), pp. i–xxxvii, 1–278.

clerks line by line and day by day which gave Reynolds the confidence and ambition – twenty years later – to generalise about how medieval people thought. Another register from Martival's time, that of Jacques Fournier, bishop of Pamiers from 1318–25, inspired Emmanuel Le Roy Ladurie to write his account of life in the village of Montaillou (first published in 1975).

Compiling such registers shows how dependent officials had become on writing by the 1300s. Was this progress? Reynolds concedes that it was in a way, as 'there were far more complicated problems in the thirteenth century . . . However little the fundamental social and political ideas of laymen seem to have been affected by academic advances, their arguments were sharpened – in both senses of the word – by the growth of literacy.'[9] Even this (I think) may be too large a concession to the belief in progress. 'Writing does not always lead to much cognitive development even among the literate', as Reynolds concedes elsewhere.[10] Records provide evidence of how complicated people's problems were and so they look as if they were sharpening arguments for the first time. Whether literacy in itself really does develop a capacity for intellectual argument has been long debated. Famously, Socrates argued for the superiority of orality: writing in his opinion was an Egyptian invention depending on arbitrary symbols to make partial memoranda; this undermined the individual's internal memory and true understanding.[11] Do non-literate societies address far less complicated problems? Or is it only that we as literates, conditioned by our schooling, cannot avoid thinking our ways to be superior?

Perhaps it is not so much medieval people who have been demonstrated to be formalistic and rigid in their thinking, as twentieth-century historians who have imposed inflexible and anachronistic ideas upon them. For Reynolds, the feudal model of society is the prime example of this. Feudalism is described as a concept foreign to the Middle Ages on the first page of *Kingdoms and Communities*, an argument developed in detail ten years later in *Fiefs and Vassals*. Reynolds gives us a memorable metaphor: 'feudalism has provided a kind of protective lens through which it has seemed prudent to view the otherwise dazzling oddities and varieties of medieval creatures'.[12] The Middle Ages has often been seen in terms of light and darkness; illuminated manuscripts and heraldry contrast with dark dungeons and superstitions. A gulf separates the Pre-Raphaelites' Middle Ages, peopled by bright-faced youths and damsels, and the sinister scenes recounted in the fairy tales of the brothers Grimm. Despite all the public lectures and books of John Ruskin and William Morris idealising the Middle Ages, their view remained that of an aristocratic elite. At some undefined time in the nineteenth century the adjective 'medieval' entered popular consciousness as a description of anything really barbaric. At much the same time, largely through the influence of Marx, 'feudalism' came to describe almost any hierarchical and oppressive system. This combination

---

[9] Reynolds, *Kingdoms and Communities*, p. 338.
[10] Reynolds, 'Social mentalities', p. 24.
[11] W. J. Ong, *Orality and Literacy* (London, 1982), p. 79.
[12] *Fiefs and Vassals: The Medieval Evidence Reinterpreted* (Oxford, 1994), p. 11.

of pejorative terms is Reynolds's starting point in *Fiefs and Vassals*. Bosses or landlords who bully their employees or tenants are thought of as 'feudal'. 'If they bully them fiercely they are worse: they are positively medieval'.[13] To describe medieval society as 'feudal' is to subscribe – wittingly or unwittingly – to a theory of the progressive improvement of humanity over the course of time.

This is an old idea, which was familiar to Abelard in the twelfth century, for example. In his imaginary dialogue between a Philosopher, who stands for the classical learning of the ancients, and a Jew, who represents the divine law of the Old Testament, Abelard has the Philosopher deplore the way in which religious faith is excepted from general intellectual progress. The ignorant along with the highly educated are commended equally for their conventional religious faith and no one is encouraged to progress further by making inquiries. 'This is amazing', Abelard's Philosopher comments, 'when through the series of ages and the succession of times human understanding [or 'intelligence' – *intelligentia*] grows in all other things'.[14] The Philosopher's belief in intellectual progress accords with the confidence of Abelard and other twelfth-century scholastics that they were innovative improvers. The concept of 'modernity' (*modernitas*) and the word 'modern' (coined from the Latin *modo* meaning 'now') were first given general currency in the Twelfth-Century Renaissance in order to distinguish 'modern' times and 'modern' authorities from the ancient world, whether pagan or Christian. In this spirit Abelard's teachers, William of Champeaux and Anselm of Laon, were described as 'modern masters' by comparison with St Augustine, Gregory the Great and Bede.[15] Ideas of progressive change therefore existed within the Middle Ages themselves. Nevertheless, the optimism of Abelard's Philosopher was exceptional, as mainstream Christian teaching opposed the idea of the perfectibility of man and, as far as the general public was concerned, there was little to show for the practical benefits of science before the fifteenth century.[16]

It was only with the eighteenth-century Enlightenment that progress began to be generally accepted as a norm. As Reynolds explains, medieval people then became comparable with the primitive 'savages' whom the European nations were busy converting, conquering or enslaving.[17] Until recently ideas of superiority, in one form or another, were commonplaces of European thought. Reynolds points up the paradox in this: 'Intellectuals in the twentieth-century west are themselves

---

[13] Reynolds, *Fiefs and Vassals*, p. 1.

[14] Peter Abelard, *Collationes*, ed. J. Marenbon and G. Orlandi (Oxford, 2001), p. 10 (my translation).

[15] M. T. Clanchy, *Abelard – a Medieval Life* (Oxford, 1997), pp. 79–80. For the origins of the word *modernitas* and *modernus*, see the medieval Latin dictionaries *Novum Glossarium Mediae Latinitatis*, vol. 'M', ed. F. Blatt (Copenhagen, 1961), pp. 671–3, and *Lexicon Latinitatis Nederlandicae Medii Aevi*, vol. 5, ed. O. Weijers and M. Gumbert-Hepp (Leiden, 1994), pp. 3054–5. See also the articles by W. Hartmann and E. Gössmann in *Antiqui und Moderni: Traditionsbewusstsein und Fortschrittsbewusstsein im späten Mittelalter*, ed. A. Zimmerman (Berlin, 1974), pp. 21–57.

[16] See in general J. W. Dean, *The World Grown Old in Later Medieval Literature* (Cambridge, Mass., 1997).

[17] Reynolds, 'Social mentalities', p. 22. See also D. Spadafora, *The Idea of Progress in Eighteenth Century Britain* (New Haven, 1990).

conditioned by the traditional beliefs of their society and the habits of thought inculcated by their professions'.[18] I would illustrate this from the opening sentence of C. S. Lewis's *The Discarded Image* (first published in 1964): 'Medieval man shared many ignorances with the savage, and some of his beliefs may suggest savage parallels to an anthropologist'.[19] 'In a savage community you absorb your culture, in part unconsciously, from participation in the immemorial pattern of behaviour, and in part by word of mouth, from the old men of the tribe'.[20] The 'savage' process of acculturation, which Lewis describes here, is similar to the acculturation of undergraduates in which he participated year by year as a Fellow of Magdalen College, Oxford; he was the grand old man of his tribe. *The Discarded Image* assumes a top-down model of cultural diffusion: ordinary people get their ideas, in a simplified form, from clerics and scholastics. As an overview of the medieval world, it stands at the opposite pole from Reynolds's emphasis on lay collective activity and lay ideas in *Kingdoms and Communities*. In the second edition in 1997 she reiterates that 'intellectuals are not the only people who think. What they think, however innovative and interesting, is affected by what their unintellectual neighbours take for granted.'[21]

In comparing medieval man with a savage, Lewis was not being racist. As he explained, he was using 'savage' in the technical sense of an anthropologist. In 1964 he was right up to date and acknowledging international scholarship, as C. Lévi-Strauss had published *La Pensée sauvage* in 1962. Lévi-Strauss became a cult figure, despite talking about savages, because he maintained that primitive people were as intelligent as Plato and Einstein.[22] The concept of the 'savage mind' had its roots in the heyday of European imperialism. Lévy-Bruhl's *Les Fonctions mentales dans les sociétés inférieures* was translated into English in 1926 as *How Natives Think*.[23] French anthropology of the 1920s has a direct bearing on medieval history because it provided much of the agenda, particularly through the idea of mentalities, which inspired Marc Bloch and the *Annales* school. When Reynolds published *Kingdoms and Communities* in 1984 it was not her purpose to discuss mentalities as such, nor to refute the generalisations in *The Discarded Image*. But she was well aware of these debates: 'In what way the mental processes of people living in "primitive" societies are different from the generality of those in "advanced" ones seems to be a much more debatable issue today than it was when historians first started to study early medieval law.'[24] She cut through a great deal of theorising about medieval mentalities simply by declaring that 'one reason that

---

[18] Reynolds, 'Social mentalities', p. 25.
[19] C. S. Lewis, *The Discarded Image: An Introduction to Medieval and Renaissance Literature* (Cambridge, 1964), p. 1.
[20] Lewis, *The Discarded Image*, p. 5.
[21] Reynolds, *Kingdoms and Communities*, p. lvii.
[22] Ong, *Orality and Literacy*, p. 174. J. Goody, *The Domestication of the Savage Mind* (Cambridge, 1977), p. 4.
[23] Lloyd, *Demystifying Mentalities*, pp. 1–3 and bibliography, p. 164.
[24] Reynolds, *Kingdoms and Communities*, p. 36.

their superstitions and rituals look so strange to us is that they are strange – in the sense of being unfamiliar. We have our superstitions and rituals too, which we take for granted or explain away.'[25]

Making their way back through time, historians are stopped short at the gap where documentary evidence ceases, as they have no expertise of their own to get them any further. This is when they become introspective or speculative. Rather than making assumptions about mentalities, Reynolds advises them to be cautious in these circumstances: 'the historian who makes too big an imaginative leap into the mind of the past may end up as far from it as the one who makes no leap at all'.[26] Is a controlled and informed leap possible? Only if we know the size and shape of the gap to be crossed. As far as medievalists are concerned, two books of the 1990s help here: Richard Britnell's *Pragmatic Literacy, East and West, 1200–1330* and Patrick Geary's *Phantoms of Remembrance*. Britnell points out that 'historians are inclined to take the survival of records as a matter of chance. . . . The irrationality involved in keeping large quantities of bulky matter, of no literary interest, for centuries after it has ceased to have any practical value is a remarkable feature of Latin Christendom.'[27] The registers of Bishops Martival and Fournier (and hundreds of other similar documents) illustrate this. Britnell suggests that the use of parchment in itself encouraged the retention of records. Compared with paper or waxed wooden tablets, parchment was durable, particularly if the pages were bound up into books like bishops' registers. But there may have been more to durability than that. Because writing was primarily used in the Middle Ages to make liturgical and ecclesiastical books, all records took on a providential dimension. Christ in Majesty, opening the Book of Judgement at the Last Day, was one of the commonest images in medieval churches and the Devil likewise was shown keeping records of everyone's sins.[28] Any medieval writing therefore had the potential to be a Domesday Book. Again, we come up against the question of which practices are 'primitive' and which 'advanced'. Was it progressive or regressive to keep records that had no further practical value in this world, though they might have in the next? If there was going to be a Last Judgement, it was not irrational to prepare documentation for it. Reynolds has rightly questioned whether the Middle Ages was an 'Age of Faith', in which all individuals believed in the supernatural, but there is no doubt that the authorities promoted Christian teaching about an afterlife.[29]

Geary, who discusses record-keeping two centuries earlier (his subtitle is *Memory and Oblivion at the End of the First Millennium*), makes a similar point to Britnell's, this time in criticism of my *From Memory to Written Record*: 'Preservation of documentation was seldom random. We thus do not have random samples of either

[25] Reynolds, *Kingdoms and Communities*, p. 36.
[26] Reynolds, *Kingdoms and Communities*, p. 37.
[27] R. Britnell (ed.), *Pragmatic Literacy, East and West, 1200–1330* (Woodbridge, 1997), p. 24.
[28] *Revelation*, chapter 5, verse 1. M. T. Clanchy, *From Memory to Written Record: England 1066–1307*, 2nd edn (Oxford, 1993), pp. 32, 187–8.
[29] Reynolds, 'Social mentalities', p. 25.

the quantity or quality of documentation from different periods of the Middle Ages but rather documents from previous ages selected for particular reasons by subsequent generations.'[30] In *From Memory to Written Record* I do indeed compare the volume of documents from different periods, as if they were random samples, and in the second edition in 1993 I likened my task to that of an archaeologist digging an exploratory trench, as if discovering documents metaphorically buried in books or archives was the same thing as excavating them.[31] The essential difference is that archaeological finds are random samples of past artefacts, whereas historical documents like title-deeds and accounts of court cases were deliberately created to inform or misinform posterity. *Documentum* in Latin (from *docere* 'to teach') does not mean 'evidence'; it means a 'lesson' or 'instruction'.[32]

The inscribed sticks dating from the twelfth to the fourteenth centuries, which were discovered on the Bryggen waterfront at Bergen in excavations between 1955 and 1968, point up the difference between archaeological finds and historical documents.[33] There is no evidence, either implicit or explicit, that they were made for posterity. Many of them are inscribed with runes describing cargoes or cut with notches for counting; they were presumably discarded at the dockside in the process of loading and unloading ships. Why people also dropped, at the same waterfront site, other sticks containing a whole variety of little texts in runes is harder to answer. A number simply record the runic alphabet (the *futhark*), others are the beginnings of the Latin prayers 'Pater Noster' and 'Ave Maria', and as many again contain obscene vernacular insults. When they were dropped at the waterfront, all these sticks had presumably served their purpose in one way or another, as charms or invocations for a safe voyage perhaps, or as curses against an enemy. For the present argument, the point to emphasise is the random and uncontrived element in this archaeological evidence of writing, as distinct from historical evidence.

The tally-sticks from the medieval Exchequer together with the two broken knives preserved at Durham, which I discuss in *From Memory to Written Record*, look at first sight like random archaeological finds, though they really have more in common with historical documents. The tally-sticks date mainly from the thirteenth century; they were discovered in 1908 and Sir Hilary Jenkinson surmised that they were 'a purely fortuitous sweeping together of accidental fragments'.[34] To that extent their existence has a random element like the Bergen sticks. The knives are

---

[30] P. J. Geary, *Phantoms of Remembrance: Memory and Oblivion at the End of the First Millennium* (Princeton, 1994), p. 14. See also M. Innes, 'Memory, orality and literacy in an early medieval society', *Past and Present*, 158 (1998), pp. 3–36 (p. 9 comments on Clanchy).

[31] Clanchy, *From Memory*, 2nd edn, p. 20.

[32] Clanchy, *From Memory*, 2nd edn, p. 54.

[33] I owe my knowledge of the Bergen finds to Dr. T. Spurkland of the University of Oslo. Very little material is accessible in English, apart from *The Bryggen Papers*, Supplementary series no. 2, ed. A. E. Herteig (Bergen, 1988), pp. 1–72. Archaeological evidence of writing is discussed by M. Garrison, 'Send more socks: mentality and the preservation context of medieval letters', in *New Approaches to Medieval Communication*, ed. M. Mostert (Turnhout, 1999), pp. 69–99

[34] H. Jenkinson, 'Medieval tallies, public and private', *Archaeologia* 74 (1925), p. 292. Clanchy, *From Memory*, 2nd edn, plate viii.

not modern finds at all. One of them bears an explanatory label, which was probably written in the twelfth century at the time it was put in the Durham archive, as well as two inscriptions on its haft explaining that it is 'the sign for the chapel of Lowick' concerning 'the tithes of Lowick'.[35] Evidently it was intended to function as a title-deed informing posterity, just like a sealed charter. The other knife, which was produced in the king's court in 1213, concerns Durham cathedral priory's rights in the church of Blyborough in Lincolnshire. This is a more complex case which merits renewed attention in the light of Geary's *Phantoms of Remembrance*. He describes how 'bits of the buried past refused to stay buried. Texts, names, traditions, inscriptions and objects continued to haunt the landscape of the eleventh and twelfth centuries, wraiths of earlier ages that fit uneasily into the constructed pasts of our memory specialists.'[36] Is the Blyborough knife an archaic survival of this sort, a wraith or phantom of an earlier age?

Geary's point is that the deliberate preservation of particular memories meant that older evidence was destroyed or lost, as well as being selectively reshaped. 'As new cartularies were created, old charters were destroyed; as new necrologies were produced, older ones were not copied in their entirety.'[37] The Durham archive illustrates this very well; the rewriting of the history of the cult of St Cuthbert was a complex business, involving the production of numerous new books and documents (some of which were certainly forged).[38] The Blyborough charter to which the knife is attached is probably not a forgery, but an authentic document written by the Durham monks in the year it specifies (AD 1148) and before the witnesses it names, together with 'a very great multitude of men, both cleric and lay, then present at the assembly (*placitum*) in Durham'.[39] This document is one half of a chirograph recording the agreement by which Robert of St Martin gave whatever he had in the church of Blyborough and its lands to Durham. The knife, which is not inscribed like the one for Lowick, is attached to the document by a knotted strip of parchment, which passes through a hole bored in the handle and through two slits cut in the document. Like the Lowick knife, it was presumably offered to the monks by Robert of St Martin as a 'sign' or corroboration of his gift.

In 1148 when the Blyborough chirograph was made, seals were still rare and there are a number of instances of knives being used to corroborate gifts.[40] Like finger rings and other personal possessions, such objects functioned as 'pegs for

---

[35] Clanchy, *From Memory*, 2nd edn, p. 258.

[36] Geary, *Phantoms of Remembrance*, p. 180.

[37] Geary, *Phantoms of Remembrance*, p. 180.

[38] See the articles in *Anglo-Norman Durham, 1093–1193*, ed. D. Rollason, M. Harvey and M. Prestwich (Woodbridge, 1994), and in particular the contribution by D. Bates, 'The forged charters of William the Conqueror and Bishop William of St Calais', pp. 111–24. See also *Symeon of Durham, Historian of Durham and the North*, ed. D. Rollason (Stamford, 1998), and W. M. Aird, *The Church of Durham, 1071–1153* (Woodbridge, 1998).

[39] K. Major, 'Blyborough charters', *A Medieval Miscellany for D. M. Stenton*, ed. P. M. Barnes and C. F. Slade (Pipe Roll Society, new series 36, 1960), p. 206 and plate xv. Clanchy, *From Memory*, 2nd edn, pp. 38–9.

[40] See n. 57 below.

Medieval mentalities

memory' (as Elisabeth van Houts has described them), particularly if they were accompanied by explanations in writing, like the Lowick and Blyborough knives.[41] The Blyborough example is unique in being produced as evidence in the king's court sixty-five years later in 1213. It was rejected there 'because it is not made according to the custom of the realm, nor is there seal on it, but a certain knife which can be put on to or taken off the charter'.[42] This judgement makes clear that authenticating documents with knives was no longer sanctioned by custom and, furthermore, the court objected for the practical reason that the knife was simply tied to the document and not stuck to it like a seal. Solely sealed charters were valid in the king of England's courts, even though seals had only recently been developed for common use.[43] Consequently Durham priory was compelled to negotiate two new chirographs with Roger, the heir of Robert of St Martin. These documents were drawn up in accordance with the very latest custom of the king's court, as they took the form of tripartite chirographs with the third copy being lodged for safekeeping in the royal treasury. This is the procedure which had been introduced in 1195 by the justiciar, Hubert Walter.[44] Among the thousands of third copies of chirographs ('feet of fines' in legal jargon), formerly kept in the treasury and now in the Public Record Office, are the two concerning Blyborough.[45]

Durham priory only kept cartulary copies of these new chirographs and not the originals, but it did keep the original of the chirograph of 1148, with the knife attached to it, even though it had been judged invalid in the king's court.[46] It may have been brought back to Durham with the other documents, which the prior's attorney had exhibited at the king's court in December 1213, and been kept because the new tripartite chirographs were not finally issued until six years later, in December 1218.[47] The years 1213 to 1218 were tempestuous ones: there was no bishop of Durham between 1208 and 1217, the rebellion of the northern barons against King John reached its high point with Magna Carta and the French invasion in 1215, King John's death in 1216 led to the disputed accession of the boy king, Henry III. Possibly – and this is no more than a conjecture – the monks at Durham thought the northern rebellion and the death of King John might invalidate the judgements made in his courts. Durham was a highly privileged jurisdiction which had aspirations to be a law unto itself, as it was the special land of St Cuthbert placed between England and Scotland. King John had compelled exalted litigants like the prior of Durham to follow him across England in pursuit

---

[41] E. van Houts, *Memory and Gender in Medieval Europe, 900–1200* (Basingstoke, 1999), chapter 5, 'Objects as pegs for memory', pp. 93–120.

[42] *Curia Regis Rolls*, 7 (1935), p. 39. Clanchy, *From Memory*, 2nd edn, p. 39.

[43] C. T. Flower, *Introduction to the Curia Regis Rolls* (Selden Society, 62, 1943), pp. 279–80. Clanchy, *From Memory*, 2nd edn, pp. 308–17.

[44] Clanchy, *From Memory*, 2nd edn, p. 68.

[45] Public Record Office, CP25 1/128/14, nos 98 and 99, published as document nos 8 and 10 in 'Blyborough charters', pp. 211–13.

[46] Durham Dean and Chapter Muniments MSS, *Cartularium Vetus*, fo. 61. 'Blyborough charters', pp. 212–13.

[47] 'Blyborough charters', nos 8 and 10, pp. 211–13.

of justice. The hearing of the Blyborough case had been adjourned from Oxford to Reading in 1213 explicitly because 'pleas follow the court'; this was the grievance remedied by clause 17 of Magna Carta.[48] The Blyborough knife became a bit of the past which 'refused to stay buried' (in Geary's phrase) because it had been resurrected by Durham priory in the exceptional circumstances of 1213, when the future of English law and of the English monarchy itself was impossible to predict.[49] It would only have become evident some years after the two new chirographs were issued in 1218 that the knife of 1148 was useless and should be thrown away.

The function of the Blyborough knife as a symbol would have continued to be understood by contemporaries for some time after John's reign. Bracton's lawbook, which dates mainly from the 1220s and 1230s, insisted on the doctrine of 'livery of seisin'.[50] A thing is not transferred 'by the drawing up of charters and instruments, even though they be read aloud in public'.[51] Lawful 'livery' (*traditio*) requires a physical act of transfer: thus a house is transferred 'through its door and by its hasp or handle' and land is transferred 'in the manner commonly called "by staff and by rod"' (*per fustum et per baculum*)'.[52] By making contact with some physical object, Bracton explains, the donor signifies what is in his 'mind' (*animus*) and thus the symbolic object expresses his intention.[53] Bracton does not mention knives among these symbolic objects and this suggests that they were becoming obsolete. Why they were no longer favoured, when the use of staffs and rods continued, is hard to explain. No contemporary tells us what knives in particular had signified in the first place. Were they valued as intimate possessions, because men ate with them and carried them on their persons? I have suggested that the Lowick knife at Durham was the donor's own carving knife.[54] Or, was it the knife's ability to cut which was significant and symbolic of finality? In the Blyborough case was the knife tied on to the document because it had been used to cut the wavy line in the parchment, across the word CIROGRAFUM, which created the two parts of the chirograph?[55] The blades of both the Lowick and the Blyborough knives are broken straight across close to the handle. What was the significance of breaking the knife, which seems to have been done deliberately?[56] There are no certain answers to these questions at present. Scholarship in this area has not advanced much beyond the great collection of references assembled in Du Cange's *Glossarium*

[48] M. T. Clanchy, 'Magna Carta and the common pleas', *Studies in Medieval History Presented to R. H. C. Davis*, ed. H. Mayr-Harting and R. I. Moore (London, 1985), pp. 231–2.

[49] See n. 36 above.

[50] Clanchy, *From Memory*, 2nd edn, p. 260. J. Hudson, *Land, Law, and Lordship in Anglo-Norman England* (Oxford, 1994), pp. 160–4.

[51] *Bracton on the Laws and Customs of England*, ed. S. E. Thorne (Cambridge, Mass., 1968), 2, p. 124, Latin text, unnumbered lines 5–6.

[52] *Bracton*, 2, p. 125, Latin text, unnumbered lines 14, 16–17.

[53] *Bracton*, 2, p. 125, Latin text, unnumbered line 11, and see p. 124, Latin text, unnumbered lines 7, 13, 14.

[54] Clanchy, *From Memory*, 2nd edn, p. 258.

[55] 'Blyborough charters', plate xv, facing p. 206.

[56] Clanchy, *From Memory*, 2nd edn, pp. 258–9.

between 1678 and 1766 and Henry Ellis's additional material for England published in 1814.[57]

Rituals look formalistic and magical because they are unfamiliar to us and yet we too have our superstitions and rituals, as Reynolds points out.[58] In Western culture the wedding ring is the most obvious example of a symbolic object which is still widely used, although the contracting parties may no longer accept that it signifies 'livery of seisin' and the transfer of the bride to the groom. Habits can change very fast without legislation or formal public declarations. Within the last thirty years, for example, the process of writing has been transformed by photocopiers, word processors and e-mail. Former methods of working with carbon paper, typewriters and postage stamps look antiquated, even though most of these things had only been invented in the nineteenth century. Really old practices disappear almost without comment, because only a few historians know how old they are. The use of sealing wax, which the judgement in the Blyborough case already ruled to be customary in 1213, was required for the registration of letters and parcels in England until the 1970s. To use a physical symbol to indicate what is in somebody's mind when making a contract is not irrational, though it may seem primitive or redundant in modern culture. No writing can be a complete representation of thought because it takes words out of their 'natural, oral habitat' (in Walter Ong's metaphor) and places them in an artificial environment.[59] Socrates was right to warn that writing involves losses in understanding as well as gains.[60] Medieval people invented ways of corroborating documents with seals or other symbolic objects, and embellished their texts with enlarged or illuminated lettering, because they were more aware than modern literates of the inadequacy of writing as a representation of acts or of intentions.

The universality of printing and word-processing, compounded by years of schooling, makes us take writing for granted. It is 'so prevalent and so much bound up with our daily habits' (in the words of Pollock and Maitland) 'that we have almost forgotten how much of the world's business, even in communities by no means barbarous, has been carried on without it. And the student of early laws and institutions, although the fact is constantly thrust upon him, can hardly accept it without a sort of continuing surprise.'[61] The modern creation of *The World on Paper* (the title of David Olson's book of 1994) limits our capacity to think critically about writing itself. The problems of understanding fully what we read 'arise not from what texts represent – sounds, words and sentences – so much as from what they fail to represent, the manner or attitude of the speaker or writer to what

---

[57] J. Cherry, 'Symbolism and survival: medieval horns of tenure', *The Antiquaries Journal*, 69 (1989), p. 111, provides an introduction to current knowledge. See also the references indexed under 'knife' in Clanchy, *From Memory*, 2nd edn, p. 396.

[58] See n. 25 above.

[59] Ong, *Orality and Literacy*, p. 101.

[60] See n. 11 above.

[61] F. Pollock and F. W. Maitland, *The History of English Law before the Time of Edward I*, 2nd edn (Cambridge, 1898), 1, p. 25. Clanchy, *From Memory*, 2nd edn, p. 185.

is said'.[62] Because writing cannot express every nuance of speech, still less the body language involved in communication, it requires reinforcement. Seals, knives and other additions to charters functioned as residual evidence of the performance which making a promise involved.[63] Nothing could fully replicate the significance of the ceremony in Durham cathedral in 1148, when Robert of St Martin had solemnly sworn at the altar to give St Cuthbert and his monks whatever he had in the church of Blyborough.[64]

Legal practice in the recording of contracts differs from one society to another, as it is rooted in particular cultural traditions which are sanctioned by custom, though changes may come fast when a new technology obtrudes itself. Equally there can be long time-lags, which make some practices look antiquated and primitive. Thus seals continued to be used for centuries, whereas they were themselves still novel in the twelfth century. At first they were thought to speak for their owners and to have supernatural powers. Their inscriptions declare, for example: 'I cover secrets', or this is a 'sign of God's clemency'.[65] From the thirteenth century onwards the magic of seals wore off, as they became routine legal requirements. By the nineteenth century seals with knights and heraldry on them epitomised the essence of feudalism and medievalism. Medieval practices look primitive because they seem so different from our own and it is difficult to find out exactly how they worked or why they changed over time. Reynolds has challenged many of our most fundamental presumptions about the Middle Ages. Were they ritualistic and primitive? Were they an age of faith? Were they feudal? Has there really been social and intellectual progress? Or have people, by and large, been just as intelligent and thoughtful in the management of law and government at one time as at another? Do whole societies have distinctive mentalities anyway? Thanks to her, medieval history will never be quite the same again.

[62] D. R. Olson, *The World on Paper* (Cambridge, 1994), p. 19.
[63] B. J. Hibbitts, 'Coming to our senses: communication and legal expression in performance cultures', *Emory Law Journal*, 41 (1992), p. 959.
[64] See n. 39 above.
[65] Clanchy, *From Memory*, 2nd edn, p. 314. See also on the significance of seals B. M. Bedos-Rezak, 'Medieval identity: a sign and a concept', *American Historical Review*, 105 (2000), pp. 1489–1533, particularly pp. 1508–10.

The problem of treason: the trial of Daire le Roux[1]

Stephen D. White

During the twelfth and early thirteenth centuries, *chansons de geste*, romances, and other Old French narratives produced in France and England routinely included at least one episode in which a character, by accusing another character of treason, initiates a judicial *plaid*, that is a trial. The earliest imaginary treason trial in Old French is found in the Oxford version of *La chanson de Roland* from around 1100, in which Ganelon is tried for treason in Charlemagne's court.[2] In *c.*1150 the author of *Le roman de Thèbes* supplemented a retelling of Statius's *Thebaïd* with an original episode in which King Eteocles' appeal of treason against his man Daire le Roux is debated in the king's court.[3]

From the 1170s onwards, treason trials were included in several different kinds of Old French stories, including ones that were presumably modelled on older

---

[1] Small portions of this essay appeared in Stephen D. White, 'La traiciǫn en la ficciǫn literaria. Derecho, hecho y ordalįas en la narrativa y épica en francès antiguo', trans. Julio Escalona Monge, *Hispania: Revista Española de Historia*, 57 (1997), 957–80. For a fuller discussion of treason cases, see Stephen D. White, *Treacherous Lords, Duplicitous Knights, and Unfaithful Women: Treason in Medieval French and Anglo–Norman Literature* (forthcoming).

[2] Ganelon's case, *La chanson de Roland*, ed. Frederick Whitehead, revised by T. D. Hemming (London, 1993), lines 3,698–3,974. For brevity's sake I cite trials fully once and later refer to them by name, followed by the number of the note where they are fully cited.

[3] The poem survives in five manuscripts, two identified as 'short' (C, B) and three as 'long' (A, P, and S), all of which include a version of Daire's case. For the version henceforth cited as S, see *Le roman de Thèbes*, ed. and trans. Francine Mora-Lebrun (Paris, 1995), lines 8,261–10,375; for C, see *Le roman de Thèbes*, ed. Guy Raynaud de Lage, 2 vols (Paris, 1971), vol. 2, lines 7,303–994; for a reconstruction of C, see *Le roman de Thèbes*, ed. Léopold Constans, 2 vols (Paris, 1890), vol. 1, lines 7,291–8,162. The Constans edition also includes extracts from other mss., including A's and P's long addendum to the debate on Daire's case. C is taken to be both the oldest surviving version of the poem and the one closest to a lost 'original' dated *c.*1150–5. But because C's version of the debate on Daire's trial deals briefly with the legal issues that its own narrative of the case raises, it reads like a summary of a version resembling the one in S, which, though produced in the late fourteenth century, conserves so many orthographic features of a twelfth-century manuscript that all three modern editors were struck by its 'fidelity' to a very old version (see Mora-Lebrun, ed., pp. 33–4). On dating, see, in addition to the three editions already cited, Douglas Kelly, *Medieval French Romance* (New York, 1993), p. xiv and the literature cited in note 3 (p. 139). For other studies, see the bibliography in Mora-Lebrun, ed., pp. 39–41.

narratives. They appear both in shorter works such as Marie de France's 'Lai de Lanval', the Anglo-Norman *Amis et Amiloun*, several branches of *Le roman de Renart*, and also in such late twelfth-century Arthurian romances as Béroul's *Roman de Tristan* and *Le chevalier de la charette (Lancelot)* and *Le chevalier au lion (Yvain)* by Chrétien de Troyes.[4] From the late twelfth century on into the thirteenth treason trials also figure in numerous *chansons de geste*, including *Girart de Vienne, La chanson de Floovant, Macaire, Gui de Nanteuil, Garin le Loheren, Aye d'Avignon, Doon de la Roche, Raoul de Cambrai, Ami et Amile, Gui de Bourgogne, Florence de Rome, Gerbert, Huon de Bordeaux, Parise la duchesse, Gaydon* and *Renaut de Montauban*. After 1200 treason trials continue to figure, not just in epics, but also in prose romances such as the cyclic- and non-cyclic *Lancelot* and *La mort le roi Artu* and in verse-romances such as Jean Renart's *Le roman de la rose (Guillaume de Dole)* and *Le roman de la violette* by Gerbert de Montreuil.[5]

Proceeding on the commonplace assumption that during the period when these texts were composed, changes in Old French literature were closely correlated with social, political and legal developments, several medievalists have recently treated selected trial scenes as evidence of a major transition during the twelfth and early thirteenth centuries in prevailing views about trial by unilateral and bilateral ordeal as a means of adjudicating lawsuits and in the general 'legal ethos' of French (including Anglo-French) society.[6] A fuller study of imaginary treason trials, however, yields different conclusions partly because, as I have argued elsewhere, it reveals noteworthy continuities throughout this period not just in the motifs and stock characters found in trial scenes but in the manner of representing the bilateral ordeal (that is, a judicial duel or trial by battle) as an effective means of disproving false accusations of treason. In addition, as I hope to show here, the study of trial scenes shows significant continuities in the representation of treason against a lord, not as a clearly definable offence against so-called 'feudal law', but rather as

---

[4] Lanval's case, 'Lanval', in *Les Lais de Marie de France*, ed. Jean Rychner (Paris, 1983), pp. 72–92, lines 259–629; Kay's case, Chrétien de Troyes, *Lancelot or, The Knight of the Cart (Le Chevalier de la Charrete)*, ed. and trans. William W. Kibler, Garland Library of Medieval Literature [henceforth GLML], ser. A, vol. 1 (New York, 1981), lines 4,737–5,053; Lunete's case, Chrétien de Troyes, *Le chevalier au lion*, ed. David F. Hult (Paris, 1994), lines 3,593–765, 4,312–573; Yseut's case, Béroul, *The Romance of Tristan*, ed. and trans. Norris J. Lacy, GLML, Ser. A, vol. 36 (New York, 1989), lines 4,116–261 (Yseut). See also *Le roman de Renart*, ed. and trans. Jean Dufournet and Andrée Méline, 2 vols (Paris, 1985), branches 1, 2, 5a, and 6. Here and in notes 5 and 6 below, I cite only selected cases from selected texts.

[5] Pharien's case, *Lancelot du Lac*, text and trans. François Mosès from the ed. of Elspeth Kennedy (Paris, 1991), pp. 106–111 (also found in the cyclic Prose-*Lancelot*); Guinevere I, Guinevere II, Lancelot, see *La mort le roi Artu: roman du XIIIe siècle*, ed. Jean Frappier, 3rd edn (Paris, 1964), see cc. 62–85, 90–3, 94–158 respectively; the seneschal's case, *Jean Renart, Le roman de la rose or of Guillaume de Dole (Roman de la Rose ou de Guillaume de Dole)*, ed. and trans. Regina Paski, GLML, vol. 92A (New York, 1995), lines 4,602–5,655; Euriaut's case, Gerbert de Montreuil, *Le roman de la violette*, ed. Douglas Labaree Buffum, SATF (Paris, 1927), lines 3,947–4,117, 5,070–332. See also the case of the false Guinevere, *La fausse Guenièvre: Lancelot du Lac*, III, ed. and trans. François Mosès (Paris, 1998).

[6] See R. Howard Bloch, *Medieval French Literature and Law* (Berkeley, 1977), p. 3; see also pp. 10, 11.

a politically and legally problematic category of wrongdoing.[7] To the extent that imaginary treason trials are encoded with an identifiable legal ideology, episodes of this type, far from being literary vehicles for progressive ideas about law, might well be characterised, at least by the thirteenth century, as conservative or even reactionary media for representing judicial processes and complex legal issues from an aristocratic perspective.

Imaginary treason trials produced between c.1100 and c.1240 almost always follow a single legal scenario, which, in two main variants, serves as a kind of megamotif in epics, romances and other kinds of stories.[8] First, the appellant accuses the defendant of committing murder, performing acts of sexual infidelity, or else betraying the defendant's lord by plotting against him or aiding his enemies. In response, the defendant either truthfully denies committing the treasonous act cited by the appellant or else acknowledges committing it but denies that it was treasonous.[9] After the barons of the court discuss the case and determine that it should be settled by battle, a victory in battle by the defendant or defendant's champion establishes that the appeal of treason was false. Aside from a few cases where an ambiguous oath of denial is used to rebut an appeal of treason and the unique case from the Oxford Roland, where the defendant fails to rebut a problematic appeal of treason, imaginary treason trials can thus be divided fairly neatly into two categories: first, false appeals of treason, in which a court finds that the defendant did not actually commit an act that was generally acknowledged to constitute treason; and, second, problematic appeals of treason, in which the appellant, the defendant and the members of the court argue about whether an act that the defendant was generally acknowledged to have committed actually constituted treason.[10]

In cases where a bilateral ordeal is used to test a false appeal of treason, this procedure, though occasionally subject to abuses, is consistently represented in both twelfth- and early thirteenth-century texts as an adequate, honourable means

---

[7] For a valuable discussion, see F. P. R. Akehurst, 'Murder by Stealth: Traïson in Old French Literature', in *Studies in Honor of Hans-Erich Keller: Medieval French and Occitan Literature and Romance Linguistics*, ed. Rupert T. Pickens (Kalamazoo, MI, 1993), pp. 459–73.

[8] For outlines of the procedures, see Wolfgang Van Emden, 'Trial by Ordeal and Combat: The Deliquescence of a Motif', in *Essays for Peter Mayer* (Reading, 1980), pp. 173–93 at p. 181; and Paul R. Hyams, 'Henry II and Ganelon', *Syracuse Scholar*, 4 (1983), 22–35; and Stephen D. White, 'Liars, Bunglers, and Lawyers in Old French Literature: Lying, Mispleading, and Legal Artifice in Imaginary Treason Trials', in Laura Blanchard, ed., *History in the Comic Mode* (forthcoming).

[9] For treasonous killing or murder, see the cases of Guinevere I (n. 7), Huon (n. 6), Euriaut (n. 7), Fromondin (n. 6), Hervieu (n. 6), Parise (n. 6), Richier (n. 6), and Ferraut (n. 6). In the cases of Bernier (n. 6) and Lancelot (n. 7), murder overlaps with political betrayal. For appeals about sexual infidelity, see the cases of Guinevere II (n. 7), Lanval (n. 5), Ami (n. 6), Kay (n. 5), Yseut (n. 5), and the seneschal (n. 7). For betrayal of a lord, see below at n. 23.

[10] The Oxford *Roland* differs in this respect from other versions, where, as I read them, Ganelon's guilt is not problematic. See Leslie C. Brooke, 'Ganelon's Path to Treachery in the Rhymed Versions of the Chanson de Roland', in Linda M. Paterson and Simon B. Gaunt, eds, *The Troubadours and the Epic: Essays in Memory of W. Mary Hacket* (Warwick, 1987), pp. 169–89; and Leslie C. Brooke, 'La Traïtrise et la vengeance: Ganelon dans les versions rimées de *La chanson de Roland*', Actes du XIe Congrès international de la Société Roncesvals, vol. 1, pp. 87–101. I thank Sarah Kay for these references.

of proving a defendant's innocence.[11] Moreover, in cases where the defendant is accused of treasonously committing an act such as homicide that he or she actually committed but did not necessarily perform treasonously, the victor in the duel (almost always the defendant or defendant's champion) almost always has a better case than the loser does, though in several trial scenes, an accord between the two parties would clearly have been preferable to a judgement in favour of either of them.[12] If the history of imaginary trial scenes provided evidence of a movement towards more critical, rational and legally sophisticated thinking about substantive law, procedure and proof, we would expect to find, on the one hand, that the earliest twelfth-century imaginary treason trials typically address simple factual questions that a unilateral or bilateral ordeal answered correctly and, on the other, that later cases are more likely either to pose questions of fact or law to which ordeals provide manifestly wrong answers.[13] The study of cases produced between 1100 and 1240, however, yields no such evidence of growing legal rationality or of increasing scepticism either about bilateral ordeals, which many stories represent as effective devices for disproving false appeals of treason, or about unilateral ordeals, which, in imaginary treason trials, are hardly ever used to determine guilt or innocence.[14] In fact, the earlier the trial scene the more likely it is to problematise treason. From the late twelfth century onwards, appellants who make flagrantly false, legally unproblematic accusations of murder, sexual infidelity and betrayal of a lord consistently lose judicial duels. If, given the difficulties of precisely dating most of these stories, any evolutionary trends can be detected in the history of twelfth- and thirteenth-century trial scenes, the most obvious one is the growing disposition among story-tellers to construct cases in which a defendant falsely accused of treason is acquitted.[15] The trend, however, was resisted by several early thirteenth-century authors, who continued the twelfth-century practice of constructing imaginary treason trials in which treason against a lord is a contested concept that must be debated and negotiated, particularly in cases where the lord is himself a traitor.[16]

From Ganelon's idiosyncratic trial in the Oxford *Roland*, where the defendant, for once, is judged a traitor, to the trial in *La mort le roi Artu*, where Lancelot is acquitted of treason, imaginary *plaids* problematise treason by dramatising disagreements about what it means to betray a lord and about who should be punished as a traitor. In the Oxford *Roland*, after Charlemagne accuses Ganelon of betraying the twelve peers for money, Ganelon acknowledges harming them but denies that he committed treason; and when Thierry later accuses him of betraying Roland,

---

[11] For abuse of the procedure, see Huon's case (n. 6).

[12] See Stephen D. White, 'Imaginary Justice: The End of the Ordeal and the Survival of the Duel', *Medieval Perspectives*, 13 (1998), 32–55.

[13] Ibid.

[14] Ibid.

[15] See the cases of Garin (n. 6), Garnier (n. 6), Gaydon (n. 6), Girart (n. 6).

[16] For an interesting but debatable account of changes in the representation of treason generally, see Adelbert Dessau, 'L'idée de la trahison au moyen âge et son rôle dans la motivation de quelques chansons de geste', *Cahiers de Civilisation Médiévale*, 3 (1960), 23–6.

wronging Charlemagne, perjuring himself and breaking faith, Ganelon's champion Pinabel fights Thierry to prove he is lying. When, in *Le roman de Thèbes*, King Eteocles accuses Daire le Roux of treason for trying to turn over a tower to Eteocles' enemy Polynices, Daire admits the deed but denies that he is a traitor and eventually makes an accord with his lord. In *Le chevalier au lion (Yvain)* by Chrétien de Troyes, Laudine's seneschal charges Lunete with betraying her lady, Laudine, for Yvain, who later defends Lunete on the grounds that she never contemplated treason against her lady. In the trial of Bernier in *Raoul de Cambrai*, Raoul's kin accuse Bernier of treasonously killing his lord, Raoul, while Bernier responds that in killing Raoul he did not do treason.[17]

In the late twelfth century, story-tellers were also creating imaginary treason trials of a very different kind in which the defendant or defendant's champion rebuts a false accusation of political betrayal by defeating the appellant in battle. Here, the real traitor is not the defendant, who is a man or woman of unimpeachable loyalty, but rather the appellant, whose treacherous nature is publicly revealed when he loses a judicial duel with the defendant or defendant's champion. After Bernard de Naisil, in *Garin le Loherain*, falsely accuses Garin of plotting to kill King Pepin, Garin's champion, Begon, kills Bernard's champion, Isor. Falsely accused of plotting to kill Charlemagne in *Gaydon*, Gaydon defeats the traitor Thierry in battle. After Auboin, in *Aye d'Avignon*, falsely accuses Garnier de Nanteuil of plotting to kill Charlemagne, Garnier defeats Auboin, forcing him to confess that he had perjured himself.[18] In an unusually complicated case from the early thirteenth-century prose-*Lancelot*, a woman pretending to be Guinevere falsely accuses Arthur and all his barons of disloyally banishing and disinheriting her and then replacing her with an imposter. During the same period, however, problematic treason cases were also included in both romances and *chansons de geste*. In another episode from the prose-Lancelot, an anonymous knight of King Claudas's offers to prove that Pharien betrayed the king by harbouring the sons of Claudas's deceased mortal enemy Ban; but since Ban had been Pharien's lord, Pharien's nephew argues that Pharien had not committed treason because he had a duty to aid the children of his deceased lord. In a trial from *Huon de Bordeaux* that combines elements of both false and problematic appeals, the traitor Amaury accuses Huon of treasonously killing Charlemagne's son Charlot; but with the abbot of Cluny's support, Huon defends himself by arguing that although he killed Charlot, he did so in self-defence and without recognising the emperor's son. In a case that blurs the distinction between murder and political betrayal, Gawain, in *La mort le roi Artu*, charges that his brothers were treasonously killed by Lancelot, who denies the accusation, while acknowledging that he killed two of Gawain's three brothers.[19]

---

[17] See the cases of Ganelon (n. 2), Daire (n. 3), Lunete (n. 4), Raoul (n. 6).

[18] Garin's case (n. 6), Gaydon's case (n. 6), Garnier's case (n. 6). For a false appeal of murder, see Gui's case (n. 6); for a false appeal of sexual infidelity, see Blanchefleur's case (n. 6).

[19] See also Pharien's case (n. 7) and Huon's case (n. 6). On literary representations of traitors, see Sarah Kay, *The Chansons de Geste in the Age of Romance: Political Fictions* (Oxford, 1995), esp. 178–99; and Michael Heintze, *König, Held, und Sippe: Untersuchungen zur Chanson de geste des 13. und 14. Jahrhunderts und ihrer Zyklenbildung* (Heidelberg, 1991).

In constructing an imaginary treason trial, the story-teller could thus represent a court as an arena for one of two different kinds of debate, one of which addresses the factual question of whether the defendant had actually performed an act acknowledged to be treason and the other which considers the legal question of whether the defendant had acted treasonously and should be executed as a traitor. In a debate of the first kind, the factual question is easy to answer, at least for an audience already familiar with the facts of the case from the preceding narrative. But the legal questions, though not necessarily insoluble, were debatable, as is evident from debates not just among the characters in these stories, but also among modern critics, about whether Lancelot, in *La mort le roi Artu*, killed Gawain's brother Gaheris 'treasonously' or whether, in the Oxford *Roland*, Ganelon's defence to an appeal of treason had any merit at all.[20] The literary law case that explores questions about treason most fully and explicitly is the trial of Daire le Roux, which appears in both a short version of *Le roman de Thèbes* known as C, and in a long version known as S, as well as in several other versions of the poem. Whether C's is the oldest version of the case, which S later expands, or whether it summarises a longer version resembling the one found in S, it seems virtually certain that in the mid-twelfth-century form of *Le roman de Thèbes*, Daire's case was constructed in such a way as to problematise treason.[21] Whereas the narrative, in both versions, transparently represents multiple acts of treason committed by Daire's lord, the treacherous king Eteocles of Thebes, its account of Daire's alleged treason against Eteocles, like the statement of facts in a moot court case, is so complicated and ambiguous that in it the concept of treason becomes almost totally opaque.

Early in the story, Eteocles betrays his brother Polynices and also his own sureties, including Daire, by breaking an agreement to share the kingdom with his brother (C 1,285–1,472; S 1,332–1,557). After Polynices' ambassador Thideüs leaves Eteocles' court, Eteocles commits a 'great treason' (S 1,562) by having him ambushed by fifty knights, who, however, only wound him (C 1,473–1,834; S 1,558–1,911). During the invasion of Thebes that Polynices then launches, an aborted version of Daire's alleged treason is played out when the castellan of Montflor, who is cousin to Eteocles and Polynices, acknowledges Polynices' claim to Montflor and proposes to surrender it to Polynices. But his men insist that to execute the proposal would be treason because the true lord of Montflor, they maintain, is Eteocles, to whom they themselves had sworn oaths of fidelity (C 2,945–3,698; S 2,975–3,780). Later, Thideüs is treacherously killed with an arrow while he is fighting Eteocles, who then tries to prevent his burial (C 6,199–6,896; S 7,259–7,832); and another Greek leader, Parthonopeus, who had been betrothed to Eteocles'

---

[20] See, e.g., R. Howard Bloch, 'From Grail Quest to Inquest: The Death of King Arthur and the Birth of France', *Modern Language Review*, 69 (1974), 40–55; Lynette Muir, 'Further Thoughts on the "Mort Artu", I', *Modern Language Review*, 71 (1976), 26–8; R. Howard Bloch, 'Further Thoughts on the "Mort Artu", II', *Modern Language Review*, 71 (1976), 28–30. For references to alternative views of Ganelon's much debated trial, see Robert Francis Cook, *The Sense of the Song of Roland* (Ithaca, 1987), pp. 114–24, 171–3, where the author's view of treason differs radically from the one taken here.

[21] This position is congruent with the one taken in Mora-Lebrun, ed., pp. 24–6.

daughter, is wounded '*en traïson*' (C 8,595–8,876; S 11,005–38). In his last act as king, the dying Eteocles treacherously kills his own brother Polynices (C 9,763–9,816; S 11,433–66).

In contrast to Eteocles' repeated acts of unambiguous treachery, which express the treason in his heart, Daire's alleged treason is very difficult to assess. Instead of being designed to provide the evidence on the basis of which one can clearly determine whether Daire betrayed his lord, the story must have been intended to provoke the kind of inconclusive debate that the barons of Eteocles' court engage in. Although the barons concur on the main facts of the case, they never reach agreement about various secondary questions about treason that keep arising in their deliberations. As a result, their debate, in both the short and the long versions of the story, reveals how ambiguous a concept treason is. The story also demonstrates how openly politicised treason trials inevitably were by showing how different judges reach different conclusions about why Daire should or should not be punished as a traitor, depending on how they represent what he did, how they construe treason, and what political perspective they have on the case. In addition, by positioning Daire's case in a larger narrative that includes one abortive case of treason very similar to Daire's and several straightforward cases of Eteocles' treason, the storyteller both problematises the whole notion of a man betraying a lord and heightens the ironies of a trial in which a loyal, honourable man, caught in a terrible bind, is accused of betraying a dishonourable lord who breaks his oath, makes his own men perjurers, treasonously harms others, insults his men, and, just before dying, kills his own brother 'en traïson'.

In C, the circumstances of Daire's alleged treason, the debate on his case in Eteocles' court, and the accord that concludes his dispute with his lord are described in a little less than a thousand lines (C 7,291–8,162), while the same tripartite episode is more than twice as long in S (S 8,261–10,375). Even C's relatively brief account of Daire's alleged treason is constructed in such a way as to raise the main questions that are debated more fully in S about whether Daire should be punished for betraying his lord and why. In both versions, Daire commits his act of alleged treason during a war between his lord, Eteocles, the king of Thebes, and Eteocles' brother Polynices who, supported by the Thebans' enemies the Greeks, is invading Thebes, which Polynices claims by right under a sworn agreement he had previously made with Eteocles to alternate each year as lord of Thebes and of Thebans, including men such as Daire. Among the sureties for the agreement, which Eteocles, after ruling for a year, has broken by refusing to give Polynices his biennial turn as ruler, are Daire and other barons of Thebes. Daire finds himself caught between a sworn duty to uphold Eteocles' agreement with Polynices, under which Polynices will be Daire's lord, and a sworn duty to keep faith with Eteocles, who, after breaking the agreement, has also treacherously broken a truce with his brother by ambushing his brother's emissary.[22] Daire, who commands an important tower,

---

[22] For a brilliant discussion of Daire's case that gives full attention to these oaths, see Zrinka Stahuljak, 'Bloodless Genealogies' (Emory University Ph.D. thesis in French, 2000), ch. 2.

comes under additional pressure to support Polynices against Eteocles when Polynices, after capturing Daire's son in battle, exploits the youth's claims of kinship on his father in an effort to gain control of the tower Daire holds for Eteocles. Emphasising how grateful Daire's son should be for being treated well and spared demands for ransom money, Polynices tells him that by settling just one matter, they can confirm their love for each other. The youth responds that he would do anything for Polynices, who, throwing him a smile and putting his arm around him, declares that if he can recover his kingdom, he will give him 'twice as much land as your ancestors held', provided that he can take over the youth's – that is to say, the youth's father's – fortress. Daire's son immediately accepts the bargain and, after promising to return to Polynices, goes to see his father in Thebes (C 7,291–7,394; S 8,261–8,306).

There, Daire undertakes to ransom his son from Polynices' prison, which the son, who conceals his bargain with Polynices and his love for him, mendaciously describes to his parents as so harsh that he would rather die than stay there. Money, he insists, will not buy his release, which can, however, be secured immediately if Daire surrenders his tower to Polynices. Initially, Daire refuses to incur the shame of breaking faith with his lord. But his wife, who considers it pointless to keep either their money or the tower if they lose their son by doing so, argues that because Daire, as surety to an agreement that Eteocles had broken, has already perjured himself against Polynices and cannot keep faith with either of these lords without perjuring himself against the other, he should observe the oath he swore in good faith to uphold Eteocles' original agreement with Polynices, not the oath he had later sworn wrongfully to Eteocles, who, by breaking his agreement with his brother, had already made Daire a perjurer. This argument all but persuades Daire to turn over the tower to Polynices. But because he fears the prospect of defending himself in a judicial duel against a charge of perjury, he tells his son that he will surrender the tower on condition that he can do so in accordance with a plan that he devises to give himself grounds for defending himself against an appeal of treason (C 7,355–7,444; S 8,305–8,524).

While Daire's son returns to Polynices, bringing him gifts from Daire and Daire's message that he will turn over his tower to his lord's enemy, Daire attends a royal council where, by deliberately provoking Eteocles into striking him, he provides himself, he believes, with the justification he seeks for renouncing his ties to his lord. When Daire counsels Eteocles to make an accord with Polynices, the king refuses to make peace or surrender his kingdom to his brother. Eteocles also insults Daire by declaring that he supports peace merely as a cost-free means of securing the release of his son, whom he could ransom with his own money if he wished. Daire retorts that in advocating peace with Polynices, he speaks, not just for himself, but for more than 700 of Eteocles' men whom Polynices' army has captured and for whose sake, Daire contends, Eteocles should make an agreement with his brother Polynices. This course of action, he says, will also benefit Eteocles himself, his brother and their men, who are sureties for the two brothers' agreement to rule Thebes in alternate years and who can be absolved of perjury against

The problem of treason 103

Polynices only if Eteocles gives Polynices his 'right' (*dreit*), that is, the kingdom of Thebes to rule for a year. Infuriated by Daire's reference to perjury, Eteocles is on the point of striking him on the head with a truncheon. But when the king's mother, Jocasta, dissuades him from doing so, he simply insults him once more for supporting peace with Polynices for the sake of liberating his son from prison without paying ransom. Eteocles, moreover, contemptuously gives Daire permission to do his worst to him and says he consents to whatever action Daire might take against him. Promising to himself that he will avenge the shame that these insults have brought him, Daire again accuses the king of making all his sureties perjurers; and when Eteocles denies the charge of perjury, Othon, a baron of Eteocles' and a kinsman of Plato's, reprimands him. Eteocles protests that he had offered part of the kingdom to Polynices, who, instead of accepting it, was now trying to conquer the entire kingdom with an army of foreigners, who were ready to kill the men of Thebes, rape the women and enslave the children. When Daire yet again accuses the king of perjury and again argues for making peace with Polynices, Eteocles gets so angry that, at last, he strikes Daire (C 7,495–7,688; S 8,575–8,792).

Fleeing back to his house, Daire now thinks that he will be in the right if he takes vengeance against Eteocles. In a message to his son, he says that he no longer owes fidelity to Eteocles and will now secure his son's release from prison by turning over the tower to Polynices. Daire's son relays the message to Polynices, who, with the youth's help, devises a plan to take the tower. Later, Polynices' Greek followers capture the tower from Daire's men, who accuse Daire of betraying them. Eteocles' forces retake the tower, capture Daire, and deliver him to the king. Condemning Daire as a traitor, Eteocles wants him burned immediately. But Daire denies being a traitor, arguing that his lord wronged him and then gave him permission to retaliate. After he gave good counsel to Eteocles, he explains, the king struck him and then gave him leave to do his worst to him (C 7,689–7,780; S 8,793–9,134).

In both the long and the short versions of *Le roman de Thèbes*, Eteocles' appeal of treason against Daire and Daire's defence become the subject of a judicial debate, which is cut short when Eteocles' mother, Jocasta, intervenes to arrange an accord between her son, who is to marry Daire's daughter, and Daire, whom Eteocles is to pardon. In C Othon defends Daire against Creon, who argues for punishing Daire as a traitor. In S Othon responds to Itier, Sicart, Salin, Alis and Creon, who all argue for condemning Daire. In an even longer version of the debate, there are ten additional speeches, eight condemning Daire and two defending him (A and P 10,665–12,036). In all versions, where there is no dispute about what actions Daire and Eteocles did or did not take, it becomes clear that the narrative of Daire's alleged treason can be interpreted so as to constitute both an argument for and an argument against punishing him as a traitor. Everyone agrees that Daire tried to turn over the tower to Polynices; that before doing so, he did not defy his lord or ask him for justice; that Eteocles struck Daire after Daire gave him counsel that he was asked to give; that Eteocles told Daire to do his worst and that he consented to it. No one, moreover, disputes that Eteocles broke his agreement with Polynices about ruling Thebes in alternate years, that Polynices had a claim under the agreement to the kingdom, and that Polynices had allied himself with the Thebans' enemies the Greeks. What the judges argue about is what these 'facts' mean. What implications do they have, individually and in various combinations, for the question of whether Daire betrayed his lord or acted justifiably in trying to harm him?

In C, the debate proceeds quickly but still addresses this central issue. Whereas Eteocles initially proposes to execute Daire immediately, Othon persuades him to hold a trial (C 7,787–96). In response to Daire's earlier argument that he did not betray Eteocles because he tried to turn over the tower to Polynices after Eteocles had wronged him and given him leave to retaliate, Creon insists that Daire, having committed a great felony, has failed to justify it. Implicitly rejecting Daire's implicit argument that he was entitled to retaliate against the king and had used no trickery in doing so, Creon argues that even though Eteocles insulted Daire, Daire was not justified in responding to the insult by trying to turn over the tower to Polynices because Daire failed to demand justice, defy his lord, or wait for forty days before trying, in ways to which the king had never consented, to disinherit him and seek his death (C 7,925–62). Othon, who has already restated Daire's defence (C 7,911–24), answers Creon by arguing, in effect, that, under certain circumstances, a man who has been harmed by his lord has a right to bypass these procedures and retaliate immediately against his lord. If, he argues, Daire had simply been disinherited by Eteocles, he would then have been obliged to follow the procedures that Creon considered obligatory in every case where a man eventually brought harm to his lord. But according to Othon, these procedures were unnecessary in the present case because a lord's striking his man has such serious legal consequences. By this act, Othon says, Eteocles broke faith with Daire, lost all rights over him, and made himself liable to vengeance (C 7,963–78). In C's version of the judges' debate, Eteocles' perjury is never cited to justify Daire's break with his lord; but the argument itself is clearly articulated earlier in the case by Daire and his wife (C 7,325–44). Similarly, although, in C, no participant in the debate fully explores either the question of why the dispute between Daire and Eteocles erupted or the question of whether Eteocles, in effect, gave Daire permission to try to turn over the tower to Polynices, both Daire himself and Creon come close to addressing both issues; and, in any case, the narrative of Daire's alleged treason in C includes all of the information necessary for raising them.

In S's version of the debate, the questions about Daire's alleged treason that are raised in C are treated more fully, along with the additional issues just noted. To show that Daire committed a great felony for which he should forfeit his life, Itier, an expert in 'judgement', first argues that when Daire turned over the tower to Polynices, he committed treason because he acted without his lord's permission, failed to show him love or fidelity, tried to disinherit him, and did what he could to see that he would be captured and hanged. In effect, Itier denies that in striking Daire Eteocles lost all rights over him, that Daire was entitled to avenge the insult he received from his lord, or that in telling Daire to do his worst, Eteocles, in effect, gave Daire permission to take the action Daire ultimately took (S 9,393–9,418). In response, Othon first concedes that without the king's permission, it would have been wrong for Daire to surrender the tower to Polynices. But, Othon insists, Daire undertook this action only after Eteocles gave him leave to do so by telling him to do his worst. When Itier protests that the king never intended to grant Daire any such permission, Othon tries, by retelling the story of Daire's exchange with Eteocles at the royal council, to show that whatever his intentions were, he did, in fact, grant such permission (S 9,419–9,548). Sicart, however, criticises Othon's narrative, not for being flagrantly inaccurate, but rather for being seriously incomplete. By starting his own version of the story at the point where the Greeks captured Daire's son and refused to return him, Sicart shifts the focus of discussion away from the altercation between Eteocles and Daire and towards Daire's motives in behaving as he did at the council. Sicart tries to show, first, that Daire's only purpose in supporting an accord between Eteocles and Polynices was to secure his son's release from prison and, second, that Daire deliberately provoked his lord into striking him so as to give himself a justification for turning over the tower to his lord's enemy (S 9,549–9,674). Rejecting this construction of Daire's motives, Othon insists that Eteocles had wronged Daire by striking him when Daire was simply fulfilling his obligation to give good and loyal counsel to his lord. Having asked Daire for advice that Daire had a duty to give and having then found that he disagreed with it, Eteocles should simply have ignored it, instead of getting angry about it and striking the man who gave it. After wondering aloud about how his own counsel in Daire's case would be received by Eteocles, Othon condemns the king's treatment of Daire as unjustifiable and a great wrong (S 9,675–9,770). Salin protests that it was Daire who had done wrong because, in shaming the king by calling him a perjurer, Daire revealed that his sole purpose in giving him advice was not to persuade him to follow it, but rather to enrage him (S 9,771–9,814). Othon counters that Daire was right to call Eteocles a perjurer because the king had, indeed, broken his oath and because, in calling attention to the king's perjury and in advising him to make peace, Daire was counselling him to respect an oath he had taken and then broken (S 9,889–9,922). If, Othon concludes, Daire had asked to be liberated from his oath to Eteocles, he would not have committed treason (S 9,939–64).

According to Alis, who develops the argument made by Creon in C, Daire failed to follow the appropriate procedures for breaking with his lord since he did not defy Eteocles before abandoning him and, before making war on him, did not observe a waiting period. His failure to follow either of these customary procedures, Alis continues, indicates that in advising Eteocles to make peace, Daire was simply trying to provoke his lord into inadvertently providing him with a pretext for betraying his lord and thus for taking an action that led to the capture of 200 of his men (S 9,969–10,064). Othon angrily rejects this line of argument because, he insists, if Daire had tried to follow the procedures that Alis mentioned, then Eteocles, having already wronged Daire, would have simply captured and punished him (9,982–10,020). For the purpose of showing that because Eteocles had never denied Daire justice, Daire had no grounds for abandoning him, Creon now cites Daire's failure to protest at his lord's treatment of him, ask for compensation, or defy his lord. Instead of trying to disinherit and kill Eteocles, Creon maintains, Daire should have demanded compensation from the king and given him time to respond. If, after forty days, Daire had not received justice from Eteocles, he would have been entitled to leave his service, though not to disinherit him or seek his death. Instead, Creon concludes, by immediately seeking revenge against his lord, Daire committed a great felony and should lose life and limbs (10,107–50). In S, Othon argues, as he does in C, that a lord who strikes his man loses all rights over him. For a blow of this kind, the only appropriate compensation is vengeance by the sword (10,151–68). At this point in S, Jocasta intervenes to arrange a compromise between her son Eteocles and Daire, though the debate continues in an another version, as ten other speakers, two of them supporting Daire, intervene in the argument.

The debate on Daire's alleged treason was doomed from the start to be inconclusive. No fully persuasive decision can ever be made about whether he should be executed for betraying Eteocles, acquitted, or reconciled with his lord, or about how to argue convincingly for any of these positions. The concept of treason around which the debate is organised is so ambiguous and hazy that it leaves ample room for disagreement about whether a man has betrayed his lord, particularly in a case as complex as Daire's, many details of which were evidently included for the purpose of bringing out both the ambiguities and the ironies of betraying a lord. These ambiguities and ironies are illuminated throughout *Le roman de Thèbes* and, above all, in Daire's case, where his allegedly treasonous conduct is open to multiple readings, as are the norms in terms of which his dispute with Eteocles and Eteocles' dispute with Polynices can be evaluated. Like the narratives leading up to other problematic appeals of treason, the story of Daire's alleged treason includes certain details that could be used to support Eteocles' accusation of treason against Daire, others that support Daire's defence, and still others that could support either position, depending on how they are represented. As a result, even though there is no doubt at all about the crude factual issues of what actions Daire, Eteocles and others did or did not take before Daire tried to turn over the tower to Polynices, Daire's case is still open to two opposing interpretations, one holding that he betrayed his lord and the other that he did not.

Like other Old French literary and legal texts, as F. P. R. Akehurst has recently explicated them, Daire's case fully confirms F. W. Maitland's much-quoted dictum that 'treason . . . has a vague circumference and more than one centre'.[23] In this imaginary trial, as elsewhere, treason is not simply equated with the act of betraying a lord by harming or plotting to harm him, showing cowardice in fighting on his behalf, or aiding his enemies, usually in return for a bribe; the term can also be applied more broadly to harming, plotting to harm, or perhaps even failing to support a close kinsman, fellow noble, or someone else with a strong claim on one's loyalty. At the same time, the term is used in a different way to refer to harmful acts such as homicide that are performed 'treasonously' (*en*

---

[23] Sir Frederick Pollock and Frederic William Maitland, *The History of English Law before the time of Edward I*, 2nd edn, 2 vols (1898; rept. Cambridge, England, 1968), vol. 2, p. 500.

traïson) in the sense of underhandedly, deviously, surreptitiously, sneakily, and thus dishonourably.[24] Finally, treason can be identified, not as an act at all, but as the defining trait of the 'traitor' – an intrinsically disloyal person who, when identified, merits the direst punishments entailing the destruction of the traitor's body and the shaming of the traitor's kin.

These different models of 'treason' are sometimes applicable to the same act, but not always. In imaginary treason trials, moreover, none of them is clearly defined. What constitutes treason against a lord is unclear partly because of unavoidable disagreements about how broadly to construe the notion of 'harming' a lord, much less 'plotting to harm a lord'. There is also uncertainty about what norms apply to disputes between a man and his lord, particularly ones in which the man's obligations to this lord conflict with his obligations to others, such as another lord or a kinsman. Has a man betrayed his lord if he breaks faith with him before committing an act that would previously have constituted treason? If not, what grounds must he have for breaking faith and what procedures must he follow? Having followed these procedures, are there limits on the harm he may do to his former lord? Answering such questions is bound to be vexing in cases where the man's lord is a traitor.

In practice, such questions are also difficult to resolve because every appeal of treason does more than accuse the defendant of committing acts identified with treason; it also identifies him or her insultingly as a 'traitor' and thus as a particular kind of person. Since, in difficult treason cases, the appellant's characterisation of the defendant's act depends on a claim about what the defendant intended to do, which depends, in turn, on a claim about what kind of person the defendant is, it is hard to know what the fundamental issue in the case is. Whether the defendant betrayed his lord? Whether the defendant is a traitor? Or whether this specific appellant has the right to call the defendant a traitor and demand that he or she be punished as one? If the last question is at issue, then the appellant's own identity, as well as the defendant's, must be at issue as well, in which case the trial provides an arena not just for a lawsuit about the defendant's wrongful acts, but also for a dispute over a matter of honour between appellant and defendant, each of whom will have tried to shame the other. If the appeal initiates both a lawsuit concerned with legally classifying the defendant's conduct and a dispute over honour, the *plaid* must be performed in two different modes simultaneously. Disputing in the first mode requires the use of a quasi-juridical discourse including statements of fact, principles and norms; arguments made in the second mode make use of a wider, more fluid discourse of honour, in which the most crucial issue is not what the defendant has or has not done, but who is entitled to say what about whom publicly. In the juridical mode, the appellant accuses the defendant of causing harm treasonously; the defendant contests the accusation by maintaining either that he did not cause the alleged harm at all or that he caused harm by misadventure or else justifiably (e.g. in self-defence) after openly challenging his victim, with the

---

[24] Akehurst, 'Murder by Stealth'.

victim's knowledge and consent, or in retaliation for an injury he was entitled to avenge.[25] The judges then continue the argument in the same mode. In the mode used to debate honour and shame, the appellant tries simultaneously to brand his adversary as a traitor and to claim honour for himself since, in publicly insulting the defendant, the appellant proclaims himself capable of proving the truth of what he says by his own body against the defendant's. In the same mode, the accused and/or accused's champion sooner or later retaliates by giving the lie (*desmentir*) to his accuser, thereby rejecting the accusation of being a traitor and asserting his own capacity to brand the appellant a traitor incapable of proving his own appeal.[26] In practice, the identification of treason, not as an act of which any noble is capable, but as the crime of a race of traitors, may greatly complicate the conduct of certain treason cases, where, for example, even a defendant who apparently committed treason may avoid punishment by persuading others that he or she is not really a traitor and may not be called one by an appellant who is himself a traitor.[27]

Although there are many questions to be raised about treason, simple treason cases would not bring out so many of them so clearly as does Daire's case. If, in a variant of this case, merciless Greek invaders bent on deposing good King Eteocles and annihilating Thebes bribe Daire to turn over his lord's fortress to them in the dead of night so that they can murder the Theban men, rape the women and enslave the children, an appeal of treason against him would have raised no issue for debate. Since, in this scenario, he would have conclusively revealed himself to be a traitor by deliberately and underhandedly betraying his lord and his people for gain, his trial could have provided no opportunity to explore the ambiguities and ironies of treason. Nor would the trial have served this purpose if Creon, rather than Daire, had turned over the tower under the circumstances just specified but had then accused Daire of doing so. Since, in this scenario, as in the false appeal cases already mentioned, the only issue would have been whether or not Daire committed an act that everyone acknowledged to constitute treason against Eteocles, there would have been no need to argue about what treason was, how to interpret the alleged traitor's conduct, or whether he was a veritable traitor. By contrast, even the simplest version of Daire's case was constructed so as to be deeply problematic, as we can see by examining how incidents from the story of his alleged treason were – or could have been – incorporated into arguments for and against judging him a traitor.

Placing the worst possible construction on selected incidents, Daire's enemies can show that by trying to turn over a tower to the enemies of Eteocles and of Thebans generally, Daire has deliberately brought harm to his lord and his people and threatened them with even greater harm, including Eteocles' death and

---

[25] On these arguments, see White, 'Imaginary Justice'; and White, 'La traicięn'.

[26] Here and elsewhere, I draw on various discussions of honour, including William Ian Miller, *Humiliation and Other Essays on Honor, Social Discomfort, and Violence* (Ithaca, NY, 1993), which cites some of the literature in n. 40 on p. 228.

[27] In a case of this kind, the honour of the judges may also be on trial, as we can see in Ganelon's case (n. 2), where Charlemagne condemns his barons as felons for proposing to let Ganelon go free.

The problem of treason

disinheritance. Daire, moreover, has acted underhandedly and thus treasonably by deliberately provoking an argument with his lord, concealing what were evidently mercenary reasons for promoting peace with Polynices, hiding his desire to secure his son's release, and conspiring by night to bring ruin on Thebes. Daire's partisans, however, can place a construction favourable to Daire on a different selection of incidents from the same story, including ones that Daire's enemies have cited but interpreted differently. By interpreting the blow that Eteocles gave Daire as grounds for a man to immediately disavow all obligations to his lord and also to take revenge against him, Daire's party can show that he could not have betrayed his lord because, at the time when Daire tried to turn over the tower, Eteocles was no longer his lord and Daire, instead, was retaliating justifiably against an enemy who was a legitimate target of vengeance for striking and insulting him. Alternatively, even if Eteocles retained power over Daire after striking him, acts of Daire's that might ordinarily have constituted treason against his lord could not be construed in this way once Eteocles had licensed them; nor were the acts treasonous in the sense of being underhanded or devious since, in telling Daire to do his worst, Eteocles knew that Daire might harm him at any time. Finally, in aiding Polynices against Eteocles, Daire was not betraying his own people because, far from harming them, he was acting in their best interests by helping their rightful lord Polynices to overthrow the traitor Eteocles, who had no right to rule Thebes and had made himself and his magnates perjurers by breaking a sworn agreement with his own brother.

These defences, too, are vulnerable to rebuttal by Daire's enemies, who take a different view of how disputes between a man and his lord should be conducted and who can supplement earlier arguments by again placing pejorative constructions on acts of Daire's that his supporters represent favourably. Because Daire deliberately provoked the argument in which Eteocles struck him, the blow gave him no justification for immediately defying his lord, much less retaliating against him by treasonously making war on him. Nor could the act be justified on the grounds that Daire was aiding one of his lords against the other, since it was his duty to reconcile them. Even if Eteocles incurred liability to Daire by striking him, Daire was still obliged to follow customary procedures before breaking with his lord, at which point Daire was still barred from attacking him, even when acting in aid of his other lord. Eteocles, moreover, could not have licensed Daire to turn over a tower to Polynices because, when he told him to do his worst, he never intended to license this kind of act and thus had no notice of Daire's surprise attack. Finally, Polynices, not Eteocles, was to blame for the Greek invasion he led against Thebes because, prior to it, he had rejected the accord that Eteocles had proposed as a means of making amends for breaking his previous agreement with Polynices.

These counter-arguments, too, are open to rejoinders. Since a man could justifiably abandon a lord who was a proven traitor, Daire should not be blamed for doing so without following customary procedures since, if he had followed them, his lord could have inflicted new injuries on him. Neither should Daire be accused of provoking his lord into striking him when, at Eteocles' request, he was fulfilling his obligation to give him the best counsel he could, which necessarily involved a reference to Eteocles' perjury. Since, as Eteocles' man, Daire retained the right to defend his own honour, he had the right to avenge the unjustifiable blow that Eteocles had given him. Finally, merely by offering his brother an unsatisfactory settlement, Eteocles could not relieve himself of liability for his perjury in breaking his initial agreement with his brother, who had invaded Thebes to claim his rights under it.[28]

Instead of deciding whether Daire betrayed Eteocles or at least identifying the critical issue or issues on which this decision should turn, the debate in Eteocles' court first raises but then fails to resolve numerous questions about the circumstances under which a man should be condemned for betraying his lord and, by implication, about treason and lordship, both of which Daire's opponents construe broadly and his defenders narrowly. Some of the specific questions that the judges debate are about how – or whether – a man may dispute with his lord without betraying him; others concern the position of the man whose two lords have conflicting claims on him; still other questions have to do with how broadly or narrowly to construe treason in the sense of harm caused '*en traïson*', that is, secretly or underhandedly. By reformulating the issues in Daire's case into questions about how to construe 'treason' against a lord, we can see how much this trial differs from the flagrantly false appeals of treason in some Old French narratives, which never raise questions of this kind, and how closely it resembles the other problematic appeals of treason already cited, including the cases of Ganelon in the Oxford *Roland*, Lunete in *Le chevalier au lion*, Bernier in *Raoul de Cambrai*, Pharien in the prose-*Lancelot*, and Lancelot in *La mort le roi Artu*.[29] In these five cases, the facts are simpler and the outcomes more conclusive than they are in Daire's case; the debates are also shorter, less explicit, and less complete in exploring the questions about treason that could have been raised in each case. Still, in each trial treason appears, as it does in *Le roman de Thèbes*, as an ambiguous category of wrong doing about which several questions, sometimes difficult ones, need to be explicitly or implicitly resolved before the defendant can be judged a traitor or acquitted. These questions are generally resolved in accordance with narrow constructions of treason against a lord, except in the case of Ganelon, where a narrow construction is at least thinkable.

The questions raised in these trials do not take precisely the same forms as they do in Daire's case. But they focus on the same overlapping issues. When does causing harm amount to treason against a lord? What are the legal implications of a lord striking his man and of challenges or failures to challenge before attacking? Is it

---

[28] The ironies of Daire's trial are all the more striking if it is read in the light of the beginning of the story of his alleged treason. There, we see that Daire surrendered the tower to Polynices because only by doing so, he believed, could he free his son from an imprisonment worse than death. Betrayed by his own son, Daire did not know that Polynices had seduced the youth and bribed him to persuade his father to turn over the tower. Even then, Daire put aside his scruples about breaking faith with his lord Eteocles only when his wife constructed a justification for his doing so.

[29] See also Huon's case (n. 6).

possible to betray a traitor? What should a man do in a dispute between his two lords, each of whom he is obliged to aid and to avoid harming? What does acting *en traïson* really amount to?[30] In the cases of Ganelon, Bernier and Lancelot, as in Daire's case, the central question is not whether the defendant caused harm but whether, in doing so, he acted justifiably. When Ganelon responds to the accusation that he betrayed the twelve peers by representing the alleged betrayal as an act of revenge, he, like Daire's defender Othon, implicitly invokes the right of a wronged man to retaliate against the man who wronged him and against that man's associates, who are vicariously liable for his misdeeds. When, in Lancelot's case, Gawain accuses Lancelot of treasonously killing Gawain's brothers as they and other men of Arthur's were escorting Guinevere to the place where she is to be executed, the people of Camelot have already justified the killings by condemning as traitors who deserved to die everyone implicated in the queen's condemnation and execution. Accused of treasonously killing his lord, Raoul, Bernier, like Daire, can justify harming his lord by representing him as an enemy against whom he had a right to retaliate.

In Bernier's case, as in Daire's, the account of a man breaking faith with his lord leaves room for debate about when and how a man may take this step. In both cases, a man who accuses his lord of treason for breaking an agreement receives a blow from his irate lord and later aids his lord's enemies. Thus, Bernier's case, like Daire's, leaves room for argument about whether a lord who strikes his man, justifiably or not, immediately loses all rights over him or whether the man may not abandon his lord until certain conditions are met (e.g. until he is denied justice for the blow four times and then defies his lord). Because Bernier, unlike Daire, defies his lord before abandoning him, his position in this kind of case is, in one respect, stronger than Daire's. But because Bernier's lord, unlike Daire's, spontaneously offers him ample compensation for the blow, for which Bernier never seeks justice himself, Bernier's right to abandon his lord is, in another respect, more questionable than Daire's.

The adjudication of an appeal of treason is further complicated in cases where the person allegedly betrayed had no claim on the defendant's loyalty and/or is himself a traitor, as Daire's and Bernier's lords are. Is it even possible to betray a traitor? Can a man be disloyal to someone who deserves no loyalty? Just as the adjudication of several cases of sexual infidelity or treason (Guinevere's and Yseut's, for example) is complicated by the fact that the appellants are themselves 'traitors' or 'felons' who make their appeals out of hatred and spite, several appeals of political betrayal are problematic because the person whom the defendant allegedly betrayed has himself betrayed the defendant.[31] In *Raoul de Cambrai*, Bernier's lord Raoul is arguably a traitor, who treasonously harms Bernier's mother and patrilateral kin. In *La mort le roi Artu*, one of Lancelot's two homicide victims is a

---

[30] Several questions raised in the cases of Lancelot (n. 7) and Huon (n. 6) have no clear parallels in Daire's case but are of comparable complexity.

[31] For examples, see above, n. 12.

traitor who hated and betrayed him, while the other was implicated in treason against Guinevere. In the Oxford *Roland* Ganelon virtually accuses Roland of an act of treason in which the other peers and possibly Charlemagne himself are complicit. If a lord or some other self-styled victim of treason is himself a traitor, how much is his appeal worth?

For the purpose of identifying the defendant as a true traitor, appellants in several of our cases, like Daire's accusers, impute underhanded, treasonous conduct to the defendant, who tries to rebut the accusation or innuendo in several ways. One tactic a defendant can use is to cite his challenge of the victim as evidence, not that he owed him no loyalty, but rather that he did not harm him underhandly or by surprise. A question about the significance of challenging or not challenging the person whom a defendant is later accused of betraying is addressed directly in the cases of Ganelon and Bernier, as well as Daire, and indirectly in Lancelot's trial for killing Gawain's brothers. Bernier easily disposes of the question when he responds to the charge that he killed Raoul treasonously by stating that because he had challenged Raoul before abandoning him and had attacked him openly, there was nothing underhanded or treasonous about his fighting with his former lord. In the Oxford *Roland*, Ganelon argues, inter alia, that he did not act treasonously in the sense of underhandedly because he publicly challenged the victims of his alleged treason and gave them clear notice that he might use trickery against them. In *La mort le roi Artu*, the narrative of Lancelot's killings introduces questions about challenges by showing, on the one hand, that Lancelot did not formally challenge either of his two victims, one of whom did not even see his death-blow coming, and, on the other, that his first victim was a 'traitor' whom Lancelot had grounds for hating mortally, while the second was killed after killing one of Lancelot's men and without Lancelot's recognising him.

Closely related to the question of whether the victim of allegedly treasonous harm was attacked underhandedly or had had notice of a possible attack by the defendant are deeper questions about whether the defendant intended treason, whether any deceit on his or her part was evidence of treason, and, ultimately, whether the defendant was a true traitor. Like Daire's case, which is neatly designed to raise questions about whether the deceit he evidently practised revealed him as a traitor, other imaginary treason cases problematise the notions of acting treasonously and being a traitor. In both *Le chevalier au lion* and *La mort le roi Artu*, the defendant's intentions are at issue since, in one case, a woman accused of betraying her lady and, in the other, of treasonously killing a knight is represented by a champion who defends her by swearing that her intentions in doing something that harmed someone else were not treasonous. In the Oxford *Roland*, the twin questions of whether Ganelon's intentions were treasonous and whether he is a traitor are raised by Charlemagne's accusation that he betrayed the peers 'for money'. One part of his response is, not that he took no money from the Saracens, but rather that because he did not do what he did for money, he was not a traitor who had sold out his lord and people. When Lancelot, in *La mort le roi Artu*, denies killing Gaheris '*en traïson*' because he did not knowingly kill him, he, too, treats

The problem of treason 113

intentions as critical for the purpose of determining whether an act was treasonous and the person who performed it was a traitor. Similarly, when Yvain denies that Lunete betrayed her lady, Laudine, because she did not intend treason, he shifts attention away from the effects of her advice and the deceit she may have used in giving it and toward her benevolent intentions in advising her lady, Laudine.

Because any accusation of betraying a lord presupposes that the defendant violated a duty not to harm him, a partial defence to an accusation of this kind is that the defendant caused this harm in order fulfil a binding obligation to aid someone else. Thus, Daire's wife argues for betraying Eteocles in order to save their son from what she and Daire mistakenly consider a fate worse than death; she also contends that because Daire cannot help betraying either Polynices or Eteocles, he should choose the less dishonourable course of betraying the latter. The conflict of obligations that Pharien confronts is less clearcut, since, in fulfilling his obligation to his dead lord, Ban, by caring for Ban's children, Pharien does not harm Claudas directly; but he still disregards his obligation, as Claudas sees it, to hate what his lord hates. For Bernier, the conflict involved in serving a lord who has killed his man's mother and attacked his kin seems to be resolved when his lord strikes him; but Raoul's kin, like Eteocles and several judges of his court, refuse to treat a blow of this kind as grounds for Bernier abandoning Raoul and later killing him.

In imagining political communities where lords chronically fear betrayal by men who chronically fear treachery by their lords, and where, in the courts of lords, men participate in treason trials as appellants, defendants, sureties, witnesses and judges, the creators of imaginary treason trials such as Daire's case were not representing politics and law in ways that were hopelessly remote from the concerns of twelfth- and early thirteenth-century aristocratic audiences in France and England, where revolts against lords were commonplace throughout the period when these stories were being produced and where the adjudication of treason cases was not uncommon. At this time, according to Matthew Strickland, 'Hostilities arising from baronial insurrection accounted for a high proportion of the warfare waged in England, Normandy and other continental lands of the Norman and Angevin kings';[32] and a study of Capetian territories over the same time-span would yield roughly similar conclusions about the frequency of rebellion.[33] As accounts of Anglo-Norman and Angevin *placita* show, moreover, in the aftermath of such rebellions treason trials were held.[34] Since nobles who supported or resisted these rebellions, avoided them, or switched sides in them were surely alive to the possibility of being accused of treason for turning over a tower to an enemy, retreating in battle, aiding a lord's enemies, abandoning a treacherous lord, or otherwise

[32] Matthew Strickland, *War and Chiralry: The Conduct and Perception of War in England and Normandy, 1066–1217* (Cambridge, 1996), p. 230.

[33] For Philip II's reign see John W. Baldwin, *The Government of Philip Augustus: Foundations of French Royal Power in the Middle Ages* (Berkeley, 1986), pp. 13–27, 77–100, 191–219, 331–54.

[34] See R. C. Van Caenegem, *English Lawsuits from William I to Richard I*, vol. 1, *William I to Stephen* (nos 1–346), and vol. 2, *Henry II and Richard I* (nos 347–665), Selden Society, vols 106–7 (London, 1990–91), nos 7, 134, 143, 183, 265, 407, 421, 490, 540.

acting underhandedly, it is readily understandable why, throughout this period, treason, in various forms, was a recurrent theme in what Sarah Kay calls 'political fictions' set in the archaic kingdoms of Arthurian, Carolingian or Greek rulers, just as it was a theme in the verse-histories of recent times.[35]

Although the preoccupation of vernacular story-tellers with treason is in itself evidence that they were not constructing escapist fantasy worlds for their audiences, it is less clear whether, between *c*.1100 and *c*.1240, their stories about treason underwent changes that can be neatly correlated with other changes or crises in politics and legal culture. Because only two such imaginary treason trials, Daire's (*c*.1150) and Ganelon's (*c*.1100), date from before *c*.1170, while the others are all clustered between 1170 and 1240, cases of this kind provide only sketchy evidence about early twelfth-century literary representation of judicial processes.[36] Such evidence as these two texts provide about what ideas about treason were thinkable for the late twelfth century is, in any case, inconsistent with the narratives about law, politics, and 'feudalism' into which trial scenes in Old French epics and romances have sometimes been integrated. First, the study of these cases reveals that they have nothing to do with 'feudalism', as conventionally defined. Participants sometimes invoke oaths of fidelity, but never feudal 'contracts'. Anxieties about the use of treason trials by traitors against honourable men almost always overshadow worries about treason against lords; and concern with bilateral relationships between a lord and a man is counter-balanced by emphasis on the collective role of a lord's great men in adjuducating his disputes with any one of them.[37]

Imaginary treason trials, moreover, do not clearly corroborate the view that the twelfth century saw a sudden transformation in the basis of political order from kinship to feudalism, kinship to royalism, feudalism to royalism, or anarchy to the state. On the contrary, since only a single imaginary trial, namely Ganelon's, dramatises a man's denunciation and punishment for betraying his lord and does so problematically, imaginary treason trials obviously did not serve primarily as literary vehicles for celebrating lordship (much less 'feudal' lordship) and condemning treason against lords; instead, they ordinarily represent the *plaid* as a potentially abusive political instrument that traitors, supported by weak rulers, could have used against loyal men and women, had it not been for the wise counsel of barons and the bravery of defendants and champions. Although, in certain respects, imaginary treason trials were used differently in texts belonging to different literary genres, the study of them does not confirm the belief that from 1170 on Arthurian romances, in particular, manifest an almost entirely new and distinctive interest in intention, legal ambiguity and the ironies of aristocratic politics. Except for Lanval's trial and the trials of Lancelot and Guinevere in *La mort le roi Artu* (*c*.1230), no

---

[35] See, e.g., Godwin's case, Geffrei Gaimar, *L'Estoire des Engleis*, ed. Alexander Bell, Anglo-Norman Text Society (Oxford, 1960), lines 4,895–5,016. On 'political fictions', see Kay, *Chansons de Geste*, pp. 3–4.

[36] In dating *chansons de geste*, I follow Kay, *Chansons de Geste*, esp. pp. 241–51; in dating romances, Douglas Kelly, *Medieval French Romance* (New York, 1993), pp. xiii–xxiii.

[37] Susan Reynolds, *Fiefs and Vassals: The Medieval Evidence Reinterpreted* (Oxford, 1994).

imaginary treason trial in an Arthurian story matches the complexities found in the cases of Bernier, Ganelon, Huon de Bordeaux and, above all, Daire le Roux.

Finally, particularly if the Oxford *Roland*'s version of Ganelon's trial can be securely dated to *c.*1100 and Daire's to *c.*1150, the history of imaginary treason trials does not support, but rather undercuts arguments linking a general late twelfth- and early thirteenth-century 'crisis of the ordeal' with the sudden appearance of rational law. No crisis of the unilateral ordeal is documented in Old French imaginary treason trials, where unilateral ordeals, which were, in effect, abolished in 1215, are rarely mentioned and fully described only once. By contrast, literary trials repeatedly represent the bilateral ordeal of battle – which remained in use long after 1215 and had its ardent aristocratic defenders – as an almost infallible method of rebutting false appeals of treason. Cases where the outcomes of battles seem problematic merely demonstrate a very traditional idea that problematic cases such as Daire's should be settled by accords, rather than by judgements, whether the judgements were reached by ordeals or by other methods.[38] Daire's case and even Ganelon's show, moreover, that in the earlier twelfth century, what S. F. C. Milsom has called 'the ancient pattern of lawsuit', in which judgements were reached by ordeal, had ample room for legal argument of a kind that he has considered literally unthinkable in trials of this kind and had become thinkable, in his view, only when the establishment of 'rational' methods of proof allowed for a distinction between 'fact' and 'law'.[39] Clearly, the kind of professionalised legal thinking that Milsom has in mind and equates with legal thinking in general differs significantly from the kind of '*resoun*' that the author of *Le roman de Thèbes* attributes to the judges of Eteocles' court and that this author and his audience must have been capable of engaging in themselves. But to the extent that evidence about aristocratic legal discourse can be found in twelfth-century political fictions, it indicates that, instead of assuming that secular legal thought was created virtually ex nihilo by legal professionals, historians should follow Susan Reynolds's injunction to look more closely at 'lay political ideas' and consider an alternative hypothesis: that a certain kind of non-professional legal thinking, in which ideas of honour and shame played an important role, had, by the twelfth century, long been an integral part of medieval legal discourse and, when used in legal argument, became, in a sense, a significant form of medieval legal practice as well.[40] As vehicles for exploring debatable questions about treason, loyalty, honour and shame, the most artfully constructed imaginary *plaids* succeed in ways that are merely obscured by efforts to incorporate them into contestable theories about a sudden twelfth-century transformation from archaic, irrational, or feudal law to modern, rational, or royal law.

---

[38] See White, 'Imaginary Justice'.
[39] S. F. C. Milsom, *Historical Foundations of the Common Law*, 2nd edn (Toronto, 1981), pp. 38–9.
[40] Susan Reynolds, *Kingdoms and Communities in Western Europe, 900–1300* (Oxford, 1984), p. 4.

Between law and politics: the judicial duel under the Angevin kings (mid-twelfth century to 1204)

Jane Martindale

Soon after his succession to the throne 'King John of England' was determined to appeal certain 'barons of Poitou' of treachery towards both himself and his dead brother, King Richard. Roger of Howden's contemporary account suggests that the new king must have taken great care to plan the proposed legal proceedings in advance, since he intended these barons to be appealed formally of treachery (the terms *appellatio* and *proditio* were used by Howden). The appeal was to be a prelude to judicial combat, designed to be the method of proof for testing these barons' guilt or innocence. The king had even gone to the lengths of recruiting 'men expert in the art of fighting in the duel [*in duello*] and chosen from his lands on this side of the sea and beyond'; and this expert band of duellers was to accompany John from Normandy to Poitou. The barons, whom Howden unfortunately did not name, were to appear in a court summoned by the king to a place which was also unidentified: the court was probably convened for early autumn in the year 1201, although the precise sequence of events is not entirely clear.[1] But Howden does make it clear that the whole elaborate scheme came to nothing, because the Poitevins were 'forewarned' of King John's plans and refused to come when summoned, stating that they would only 'respond' to men who could be regarded as their equals (*par*). As a result of that declaration John's carefully planned legal process fizzled out completely.[2]

---

[1] '*Eodem anno* [i.e. King John's third year] *Johannes rex Angliae volens appellare barones Pictaviae de sua et fratris sui proditione, multos conduxit et secum duxit viros arte bellandi in duello doctos, et de terris suis cismarinis et transmarinis electos . . .*', *Chronica Magistri Rogeri de Hovedene* (henceforth *Howden*), ed. W. Stubbs, 4 vols (*Rolls Series*, 1868–71), iv, p. 176. I should like to thank for their help, interest and advice Caroline Barron, Michael Clanchy, John Gillingham, Kathleen Thompson, Nicholas Vincent, but especially my fellow editors. The most difficult aspect of writing this study, however, has been to remember that I could not discuss it with Susan Reynolds.

[2] '*Sed barones Pictaviae inde praemuniti ad curiam illius venire noluerunt, dicentes quod nemini responderent nisi pari suo*', ibid. Stubbs considered that this part of the work was 'contemporaneous' and that the chronicler's 'life was not much protracted after this date', i, preface, pp. lxv, lxxi, xxiv; now D. Corner, 'The earliest surviving manuscripts of Roger of Howden's "Chronica"', *EHR*, xclviii (1983), 297–310; and J. Gillingham, 'Historians without hindsight: Coggeshall, Diceto and Howden on the early years of John's reign', in S. Church, ed., *King John: New Interpretations*, (Woodbridge 1999), pp. 3, 9–20.

Between law and politics 117

'And so, cheated of his desire, the king of England returned to Normandy, and because of this the Poitevins became more hostile to him'.[3]

In his monumental study of *The Loss of Normandy* Sir Maurice Powicke observed that King John's attempt to appeal his barons in 1201 involved 'a somewhat curious method' of trying 'to enforce justice' on the Poitevins; and the supposedly unprecedented legal methods which the king hoped to employ in his court were also commented on by Kate Norgate, and implied in A. L. Poole's account of the affair. In his volume of the Oxford History of England, for instance, Poole wrote that John 'charged them with treason, and proposed to settle the matter by trial of battle, using himself professional champions. They *naturally* [my italics] refused to meet these gladiators, demanded to be tried by their peers . . .' Powicke recognised that an important point of principle was being asserted with the Poitevin barons' refusal to fight in John's court; but the interpretation which he placed on the Poitevins' demand to be matched against their peers was anachronistic. He seems to have interpreted the acute political problems of the Angevin dynasty in 1201 from the viewpoint of John's later conflicts with his English barons in 1215.[4] On the whole modern historians have rarely questioned the assumption that John's plans for judicial combat were novel, although it is certainly not difficult to find precedents for his designs. In the English kingdom after 1066, for instance, a duel between an *appellor* and a man (or men) accused of treachery (*proditio*) had become a traditional and approved method of 'trying' such accusations.[5] Howden certainly did not criticise John's plans on legal grounds, although – as his concluding comment on the affair suggests – he did condemn the king for the serious political consequences which followed his failed plan for judicial combat. And since, as now seems clear from studies of the manuscript tradition of Howden's *Chronica*, his tantalising account of this episode must have been written up contemporaneously with the events – or non-events – he was describing, his reference to 'peers' could not have been retrospectively contaminated by the issues which erupted in the English kingdom around the year 1215. Howden's references to King John's failed 'show-trial' therefore acquire a firmer authoriy than they seem to have been attributed in the past. In John Gillingham's words, Howden's account must have been written 'without hindsight'.[6] Perhaps modern historians who, following Howden, comment on this incident need to make a distinction between King John's use of

---

[3] '*Et sic rex Angliae fraudatus a desiderio suo reversus est in Normanniam, et Pictavi facti sunt ei ex hoc inimiciores*', Howden, iv, p. 176.

[4] F. M. Powicke, *The Loss of Normandy (1189–1204): Studies in the History of the Angevin Empire* (Manchester 1913), pp. 215–16: '. . . the rebels refused to come, saying that they would acknowledge no *judge* [my italics] but their peers . . .'; K. Norgate, *John Lackland* (London 1902), pp. 81–2; A. L. Poole, *From Domesday Book to Magna Carta, 1087–1216*, (Oxford 1951), p. 380.

[5] Below, pp. 125–6, 131–2, 133–8.

[6] The entry relating to John's plans for the Poitevin barons could not have been retrospectively interpolated in the light of the baronial demands of 1215, since on the basis of the authorial MS (Bodleian Laud Misc. 582) Howden was almost certainly dead by 1201/2: Corner, 'The earliest surviving manuscripts', pp. 305, 308–10; Gillingham, 'Historians without hindsight', pp. 12–13.

conventional legal methods and his political ineptitude in alienating members of the regional aristocracy whose support he needed.

This intriguing episode provides an appropriate starting point and focus for an essay dedicated to Susan Reynolds, who has written so eloquently about 'the ideas, values, and assumptions about right and wrong that prevailed in lay society', and who has also insisted on the need for medieval historians to pursue traces of such 'values' and 'assumptions' wherever these can be found – even though the laity often expressed their views in a less articulate or systematic fashion than the more intellectual and literate clergy.[7] Judicial combat was in theory only employed as a method of legal proof in lay courts, and was in any case restricted to the laity – so reflections on the judicial duel should provide an interesting topic to offer to a scholar who has emphasised that 'we . . . need to discuss both ideas and practice, distinguishing them from each other, but also relating them to each other'.[8] At a number of different levels, too, the study of the judicial duel throws light on the operation of lay collective activity and judgement- a topic forming one of the most important and original parts of the discussion of law which is a central theme of *Kingdoms and Communities*. The Poitevin barons' refusal in 1201 to fight in the king's court against men who were not their 'peers' illustrates, for instance, how laymen's ideas about society could be articulated in order to justify collective action in both the legal and political spheres of Angevin government.[9]

Paradoxically this duel which never took place is an important – and incidentally often neglected – episode in the medieval history of judicial combat, but it also interestingly illustrates the closeness of the relationship between law and politics at the turn of the twelfth and thirteenth centuries. That relationship will be the main underlying theme of an essay which is also intended to show the continuing importance attached by the laity to the judicial duel during the years of Angevin government in England, in 'Henry II's patrimonial lands' and in the duchy of Aquitaine, acquired through marriage to its heiress Eleanor.[10] Those were years when procedures which legal historians have comprehensively dismissed as 'irrational' were increasingly coming under attack by learned clergy, and also being replaced at law by methods of proof which did not leave 'to supernatural powers the task of indicating which side was in the right'.[11] But, in spite of these attacks, the judicial duel survived the abolition of other 'irrational' ordeals by Pope Innocent III at the

---

[7] S. Reynolds, *Kingdoms and Communities in Western Europe, 900–1300* (2nd edn Oxford 1997), introduction, pp. lxv–vi; cf. introd. to first edn (included in the 2nd), pp. 5–7.

[8] Ibid. introd. to 2nd edn, p. xliv. Below, n. 62 for the opinion of the twelfth-century canonist, Bishop Ivo of Chartres.

[9] Reynolds, *Kingdoms and Communities*, especially pp. 51–9, and introd. to 2nd edn, pp. xxxvi–viii; and chs 1–2, pp. 12–66; cf. J. C. Holt, *Magna Carta* (Cambridge 1965), pp. 63–6, 226–9.

[10] W. Warren, *Henry II* (London 1973), pp. 55–149; J. Boussard, *Le gouvernement d'Henri II Plantegenêt* (Paris 1956), pp. 17–32, 81–155; John Gillingham, *The Angevin Empire* (2nd edn London 2001), pp. 6–21; idem., *Richard I*, Yale English Monarch Series, 1999, pp. 24–75.

[11] R. Van Caenegem, 'Methods of proof in western medieval law', in his *Legal History, A European Perspective* (London 1991), p. 73; below, nn. 13–16.

Lateran Council of 1215; and, although it is difficult to establish a connection conclusively, it seems probable that this survival was bound up with lay attitudes towards judicial combat. Aristocratic laymen, in any case, apparently regarded the duel as an indispensable part of the legal process during the latter part of the twelfth century; the persistence of this attitude and its implications need also to be considered. It is a happy coincidence that Stephen White's essay in this volume discusses secular aristocratic attitudes towards judicial combat within the broader setting of fictional 'treason trials' of the later twelfth century.[12]

As a legal phenomenon the duel has generally been treated as one of a larger group of 'irrational' procedures which were characteristic of every type of judicial process throughout Europe during the earlier Middle Ages. These 'ordeals' have been described as 'ceremonially administered physical tests used as a form of proof from time immemorial', and have often been regarded primarily as 'judgements of God'. For a number of legal historians the use of ordeals for the settlement of disputes has been interpreted as betraying the signs of a time when law was part of a *zauberpriesterlicher Prozess* (a magico-priestly procedure). All these 'archaic modes of proof' have aroused intense interest among scholars working in different disciplines in recent decades.[13] More particularly, the judicial duel as a 'bilateral' method of proof has been considered a combat 'which does honour to the man who wages it' (*le duel est un combat: il fait honneur à celui qui le livre*), in contrast to 'unilateral' ordeals – memorably described by Dominique Barthélemy as 'suffering passively endured' (*souffrance subie passivement*).[14] Studies have ranged widely over both time and place; but, despite Paul Hyams's comment that 'many English legal historians have cursorily dismissed the ordeal as irrelevant', it might still be asked whether there is any need for yet another general inquiry into any of those testing proofs which in English have been described as 'trials by fire and water' and 'trial by battle'.[15] This investigation has been based on the supposition that further study

---

[12] Cf. also Janet L. Nelson this volume, pp. 41–5.

[13] R. Colman, 'Reason and unreason in early medieval law', *Journal of Interdisciplinary History*, iv (1974), esp. 587–91 (quotation at p. 583); 'magico-priestly proceedings' were contrasted with 'secular trial' by Van Caenegem, 'Methods of proof', p. 73; R. Bartlett, *Trial by Fire and Water, The Medieval Judicial Ordeal* (Oxford 1986), throughout; and discussion by the contributors to Daries and Fouracre, *The Settlement of Disputes in Early Medieval Europe*, esp. pp. 16, 18–19, 221–3; cf. especially White, 'Proposing the ordeal and avoiding it: strategy and power in western French litigation, 1050–1110', in T. Bisson, ed., *Cultures of Power, Lordship, Status and Process in Twelfth-century Europe* (Philadelphia 1995), especially pp. 89–90, and n. 4.

[14] D. Barthélemy, 'Diversité des ordalies médiévales', *Revue Historique*, cclxxx (1988), quotation at p. 12; and his *La Société dans le comté de Vendôme* (Paris 1993), pp. 669–80. Cf. Y. Bongert, *Recherches sur les cours laïques du Xe au XIIIe siècle* (Paris 1949), pp. 211–49; P. Ourliac, 'Le duel judiciaire dans le sud-ouest', in *Etudes d'histoire du droit médiéval* (Paris 1979), pp. 253–8.

[15] 'Trial by battle was a practice akin to the other ordeals and, as the relationship of kindred implies, it exhibited both a family resemblance and unique features', Bartlett, *Trial by Fire and Water*, p. 102, in general pp. 1–3; P. Hyams 'Trial by ordeal: the key to proof in the early Common Law', in M. S. Arnold et al., eds, *On the Laws and Customs of England, Essays in Honour of Samuel E. Thorne* (Chapel Hill 1981), quotation at pp. 4–5.

of the judicial study duel is relevant both for an understanding of the history of law, but also for the conduct of political affairs.

The terminology employed in references to judicial combat conveys a preliminary notion of some of the problems relating to the pursuit of this topic. In the first place the widely used term 'trial by battle' perhaps suggests more regular continuity and institutional development than actually existed in twelfth-century England or Europe, and it has not been used in this essay. As the great Maitland wrote in his discussion of the place of the judicial duel in the English legal system before the late thirteenth century, 'the language of the law . . . has no equivalent to our "trial". We have not to speak of trial; we have to speak of proof'; he did however characterise the duel as a 'sacral process'.[16] Medieval references to the judicial duel, the 'bilateral ordeal', in any case differed considerably: over time the lexicon changed, and terms were not always used with technical precision. For instance, *bellum* (war/battle) was the term used to refer to judicial combat in later eleventh-century England (e.g. in *Domesday Book*), as it was in the early legal treatise known as the *Leges Henrici Primi* (attributed by its most recent editor to the reign of King Henry I, before 1118).[17] By the mid-twelfth century, on the other hand, sources connected with royal and ducal government in England and Normandy applied the more precise term *duellum* (duel) to judicial combat; while in the legal treatise known as 'Glanvill' *duellum* has entirely replaced *bellum*.[18] Learned narrative and hagiographical writers, on the other hand, seemed to have enjoyed varying their vocabulary, referring to judicial combat as *certamen* (conflict/battle) or *monomachia* (single combat/duel).[19] But *bataille, batalha* (battle) were the vernacular forms of the *langue d'oil* and *langue d'oc* used in the twelfth and thirteenth centuries to refer to judicial combat.[20]

Whatever the terms used to describe this method of proof in modern discussion, however, there can be no doubt that these proofs were of great antiquity; and their origins and functions have been much debated. This essay is not directly concerned either with returning once more to those important issues, or with pursuing problems associated with the abolition or elimination of 'irrational' methods of proof in the legal procedures of the English kingdom during the later twelfth century – a

---

[16] F. Pollock and F. W. Maitland, *The History of the English Law*, 2 vols (new edn Cambridge 1968), ii, pp. 596–8, 600. For the views of modern legal historians, F. C. Milsom, *The Historical Foundations of the English Common Law* (London 1969), pp. 110, 111; idem, *The Legal Framework of English Feudalism* (Cambridge l976), pp. 2–3, 66, 76–7; for the eventual fate of the civil duel in England, V. H. Galbraith, 'The death of a champion (1287)' in R. W. Hunt et al., eds, *Studies in Medieval History presented to Frederick Maurice Powicke* (Oxford 1948), pp. 283–97.

[17] *Leges Henrici Primi*, ed. L. J. Downer (Oxford 1972), pp. 166, 188, 190 and commentary on pp. 357, 367; on dating, introd. pp. 34–7, 80.

[18] Below, nn. 67–8. For *duellum* as an appellee's choice *se defendendi per corpus suum* . . . , Bracton, *De Legibus et Consuetudinibus Angliae*, ed. G. Woodbine and trans. S. Thorne, 4 vols (Harvard 1968–77), ii, pp. 385–6.

[19] Below, pp. 136–8.

[20] For occitan, P. Ourliac, 'Le duel judiciaire dans le sud-ouest', in *Etudes d'histoire du droit médiéval* (Paris 1979), p. 254. Below, pp. 146–8.

Between law and politics 121

development which Lady Stenton summed up as forming part of the 'Angevin leap forward' essential to the development of the common law.[21] It is essentially concerned with the nature and context of the judicial duels which persisted throughout the years of Angevin rule, although for many legal historians the development of the common law understandably overshadows every other topic. The search for signs of increasing rationality in legal procedures during this period has tended to obscure the 'values' which were associated with the duel as a means of vindicating reputation or right and possession. But at the highest political levels during the twelfth century those values apparently had an international currency, as emerges with particular clarity from the occasion in March 1177 when the Angevin King Henry II acted as arbitrator in a territorial dispute between the kings of Navarre and Castille. In addition to the ambassadors (*missi*) who were sent to negotiate a peace, each of the kings also sent 'two very strong men' (*duo strenuissimi viri*) to fight 'a duel in the court of the king of England if that should be the judgement '(. . . *ad suscipiendum duellum in curia regis Angliae, si adiudicatum fuerit*).[22] Towards the end of his reign Richard I also maintained 'champions' in Normandy, apparently in the hopes of settling by means of judicial combat his disputes with the Capetian King Philip Augustus.[23] In practice neither of those disputes was settled by judgement obtained by means of combat, and it is worth remembering that ordeals could also be perceived, as in Stephen White's study, as 'instruments of power', part of a 'flexible political process' which might be employed tactically for political ends, rather than as a 'legal institution'.[24]

The chief criticisms levied against judicial ordeals before the ecclesiastical prohibition of the unilateral ordeals in 1215 cast some rather oblique light on why judicial combat survived whereas 'fire and water' did not. Originally combat and the unilateral 'trials by fire and water' fulfilled similar legal functions as methods of proof during the settlement of disputes (neatly indicated for the historian by the coupling and contrast of *bellum* and *judicium* as methods of proof in *Domesday Book*), but the connotations of unilateral ordeals and combat within medieval society would have been very different. In judicial combat, after all, a great layman would employ skills similar to those for which he had been trained, and which he

---

[21] '. . . rational methods of proof dominate the scene henceforth . . .' D. M. Stenton, *English Justice between the Norman Conquest and the Great Charter, 1066–1215* (London 1965), pp. 22–53; Van Caenegem, 'Methods of proof', pp. 83–5; Milsom, *Historical Foundations*, pp. 130–1 (civil procedure), pp. 406–9 (criminal); idem, *The Legal Framework of English Feudalism*, pp. 2–5, 66, 76–7; J. H. Baker, *An Introduction to English Legal History* (3rd edn London 1990), pp. 1–16; cf. T. F. Plucknett, *A Concise History of the Common Law* (5th edn London 1956), pp. 113–18.

[22] Van Caenegem, *English Lawsuits from William I to Richard I*, 2 vols, Selden Soc., cvi–cvii (1990–91), ii no. 494 (pp. 538–49); cf. *Gesta regis Henrici Secundi*, ed. W. Stubbs, 2 vols (*RS*, 1867), i, pp. 138–42, 143–57. For Henry II's role as arbitrator and 'man of peace' in his later years, Warren, *Henry II*, p. 603.

[23] Below, n. 123.

[24] White, 'Proposing the ordeal', quotations at pp. 121, 91; M. Strickland 'Provoking or avoiding battle? Challenge, judicial duel and single combat in eleventh- and twelfth-century warfare', in M. Strickland, ed., *Harlaxton Medieval Studies* VII (Stanford 1998), pp. 326–8.

used in war; and by the twelfth century it seems unlikely that aristocratic laymen would have been expected to carry the hot iron or to plunge their hands into boiling water. Indeed, if the *Vie de Guillaume le Maréchale* is to be believed, a great layman would take pride in the prospect of proving his innocence of 'felony or treason' through judicial combat.[25] 'Fire and water' had not apparently attracted sentiments of this kind from any social group, so that Pope Innocent III's condemnation of those ordeals in the fourth Lateran council led to their elimination from European legal procedures – although on religious grounds the judicial duel was equally objectionable to ecclesiastical authorities.[26]

The scope of this essay will be the judicial duel 'as it was practised in the courts' during the reigns of King Henry II of England (1154–89) and his sons Richard I (1189–99) and John (1199–1216 – in this last instance curtailed by King John's loss of Normandy to the Capetian king Philip Augustus in 1204). Originally it was intended to devote as much discussion to the 'cross-channel' territories of these kings, as to the English kingdom; but the uneven distribution and preservation of sources unfortunately has made it difficult to fulfil that aim, although on a more general level comparisons can – and indeed should – be made.[27] The main focus of the study will be a handful of cases in which the judicial duel raises important questions about the interaction of political issues and the conduct of legal affairs after Henry of Anjou succeeded to the English throne; and all of these – including the abortive Poitevin trial – involved members of the secular aristocracy in Angevin-ruled territories.

Sources for the conduct of legal affairs during these years are far more abundant for the English kingdom than for the other territories ruled by Henry II and his sons. In particular, the financial records of the English and (far less abundantly) the Norman Exchequers reveal that judicial duels were widely employed for the settlement of both civil and criminal pleas during the second half of the twelfth century. References taken from these sources never describe a plea in detail, for they were after all primarily intended to provide records of the 'profits of justice', money obtained for the king or duke – or in some instances to note the expenses incurred by the sheriff or other royal official in the organisation of duels and the punishment of those who were defeated.[28] These terse references supplement the better-known narrative and documentary accounts of lawsuits and supply a context for the 'high profile' disputes which attracted the attention of narrative authors like Roger of Howden and Jocelin of Brakelond. And, despite the significant appearance of more 'rational' forms of proof and judgement than the duel during these years, they nevertheless show that judicial combat remained important in

---

[25] Below, nn. 81–5.

[26] Below, nn. 61–5.

[27] The pioneering nineteenth-century compilation by M. M. Bigelow, *Placita Anglo-Normannica: Law Cases from William I to Richard I Preserved in Historical Records* (Boston 1881, reprinted New York 1971) was only recently replaced by the lawsuits edited by Van Caenegem, *English Lawsuits*.

[28] The legal importance of this material is often undervalued: publications by the Pipe Roll Society will be simply cited by reference to king's regnal year, see below, pp. 144–6 (for Normandy).

the Anglo-Norman realm under the Angevins. These financial entries need to be considered as forming a background for more extended texts – especially because Van Caenegem has described those texts as 'very disparate' and '*membra disiecta*', but in his view, providing 'our only hope of piecing together the history of the law in those days'.[29] From the later years of Richard's reign those 'dismembered limbs' are augmented by official legal records of the *curia regis* and of the activity of itinerant justices which transform historians' knowledge of the operation of royal justice within the English kingdom.[30]

Even though there is far less material of a legal character surviving for other regions within the territories ruled by members of the Angevin dynasty in the years between 1154 and Philip Augustus's conquests in the early thirteenth century, the 'continental' setting within which English law developed during the twelfth century should not be ignored, for – to cite Susan Reynolds again – 'many of the national differences now perceived in medieval institutions seem to . . . derive more from different traditions of historical writing than from anything to be found in the sources . . .' That remark seems to be particularly applicable to a political unit like the 'Angevin empire' which in the second half of the twelfth century was composed of territories stretching from the Scottish border to the Pyrenees. There were undoubtedly considerable regional variations in the law and custom of those territories, but some practices seem to have been almost universal; and, wherever evidence has survived which relates to the settlement of disputes or the administration of justice, judicial combat continued to be a recognised means of legal proof. Furthermore, the political superiority of the secular ruler was normally marked by his control of the conduct of the duel (obviously normally exercised through the administrative officials of the duchies and counties).[31] That is borne out by the regulations of *Les Etablissements de Rouen*, which had a wide currency from the late twelfth century onwards and survive in different linguistic versions for use in Angevin-controlled territories (e.g. Latin, French and Occitan – formerly described as provençal). It also becomes apparent from the relevant sections of the important *Coutumier d'Oléron* – an island which remained under the control of the English crown after most of Poitou and Saintonge came under Capetian rule.[32]

The range of the judicial duel as a method of proof had been more restricted territorially than that of the unilateral 'trials by fire and water'. Judicial combat was after all only introduced into the newly conquered English kingdom by the

---

[29] van Caenegem, *English Lawsuits*, i, introd, p. xiii; 80–90 per cent of the lawsuits are classified as examples of 'civil' pleas, ibid., p. xxix.

[30] See 'Forms and subjects of action', in C. T. Flower, *An Introduction to the Curia Regis Rolls, 1199–1230*, Selden Society lxii (1943), pp. 113–22.

[31] Below, pp. 146–9.

[32] A. Giry, *Les Etablissements de Rouen*, 2 vols, Bibliothèque de l'Ecole des Hautes Etudes, lv (1883) (reprint in 1, Geneva 1975) text clause 31, ii (p. 38). The critical study of the (vernacular) Oléron text is provided by Ch. Bémont, *Le Coutumier de l'Ile d'Oléron* (Paris 1919), pp. 55, 78, 81, 85. The only English translation should be used with care, T. Twiss, *The Black Book of the Admiralty* (RS 1873), ii, pp. 348–51, 353–5, 359–63.

Norman ruler for, although liturgical *ordines* preserve texts for the administration of ordeals in England before 1066, historically the duel seems never to have been employed as part of the legal procedure of Anglo-Saxon England; and Maitland speculated that this might have been due to the 'persistence of extra-judicial fighting'.[33] Fortunately for historians *Domesday Book* shows that this type of proof was widely diffused within the English kingdom within twenty years of the conquest: in disputes over land, for instance, litigants offered to justify possession, or conversely, to advance a claim 'either by judgement (i.e. ordeal) or by battle' (*vel iuditio vel bello* or *per iuditium aut per bellum*).[34] Under the Anglo-Norman regime judicial duels continued to be employed as a means of proof for the settlement of land disputes, although they were never – as some legal historians have supposed – the sole method used to reach a decision or to secure a settlement in litigation over property.[35]

Indeed many disputes over land during the years of Anglo-Norman rule were not in practice settled by formal adjudication, but by amicable agreement or arbitration often reached through collective action or pressure. The author of the *Leges Henrici Primi* for instance – as Edmund King has reminded us – rated 'agreement' and 'amicable settlement' higher than the 'law' and 'court judgement' (*pactum enim legem vincit et amor judicium*).[36]

Nevertheless, the 1130 Pipe Roll shows that, during Henry I's reign at least, judicial combat must have been used as a means of resolving litigation more often than is indicated by the surviving *membra disiecta* of Anglo-Norman lawsuits collected by Van Caenegem. This earliest Exchequer record contains at least fifteen entries recording payments to hold a duel, and one to obtain a 'concord' after the

---

[33] *Die Gesetze der Angelsachsen*, ed. F. Liebermann, 3 vols (Halle 1903–16, reprint 1960), i, pp. 401–16; glossary in vol. ii under *ordal*; Maitland, *History of English Law*, i, pp. 50–1; Bartlett, *Trial by Fire and Water*, pp. 13–35; but on ordeals in Anglo-Saxon England, see especially Hyams, 'Trial by ordeal', pp. 93–5, 106–14.

[34] Van Caenegem, *English Lawsuits*, nos 85, 100, 105, 110, 113, 121, 122. Accounts of three further duels survive for the years between the late eleventh century and 1154, ibid., nos 143, 194, 316.

[35] E.g. 'Both in seignorial courts and in the King's court trial after the Conquest would *normally* [my italics] be by battle, the parties fighting either in person or by champion; the appeal to force was ultimately a an appeal to God, who would ensure that right would prevail', A. W. B. Simpson, *An Introduction to the History of the Land Law* (Oxford 1961), p. 27; cf. 'people resorted to them [i.e. 'archaic proofs, including both unilateral ordeals and combat] readily *the moment the initially selected rational proof turned out to be too difficult*' [my italics again], Van Caenegem, 'Methods of proof', p. 73; contrast Maitland, *History of English Law*, i, pp. 89–91.

[36] *Leges Henrici Primi*, 49, 5a (p. 164), on the dating, pp. 34–7; E. King, 'Dispute settlement in Anglo-Norman England', *Anglo-Norman Studies*, xiv (1991), 116; M. Clanchy, 'Law and love in the Middle Ages', in J. Bossy, ed., *Disputes and Settlements: Law and Human Relations in the West* (Cambridge 1983), pp. 47–67. For France, F. Cheyette, '*Suum cuique tribuere*', *French Historical Studies*, vi (1970), 287–99; S. White, '*Pactum . . . legem vincit et amor judicium*: the settlement of disputes by compromise in eleventh-century Western France', *American Journal of Legal History*, xxii (1978), 281–307; P. Ourliac, 'La *convenientia*' in *Etudes d'histoire du droit médiéval* (Paris 1979), pp. 250–2; J. Martindale, ' "His special friend"? The settlement of disputes and political power in the kingdom of the French (tenth to twelfth century)', *Transactions of the Royal Historical Society*, 6th series v (1995), 47–51, 54–6; and above n. 14.

Between law and politics 125

procedure had got under way; and it seems clear that these entries related to civil procedure.[37] But, as it was rather incoherently expressed by the the author of the *Leges Henrici*, duels might also be waged and fought 'for theft or similar offence . . . or for breach of the king's peace or for those matters [incurring] penalty of death or mutilation'.[38]

That was the background to aristocratic judicial duels of the post-Norman period in the English kingdom: indeed from 1066 onward probably the only means by which a man suspected of treachery could clear himself of the accusation that he was guilty of betraying the king was by judicial combat. There was a complete break with the practices of the Old English kingdom, as can be seen from a comparison between political crises occurring before and after 1066. When the Norman archbishop of Canterbury, Robert of Jumièges openly accused Earl Godwin in 1051 of having been responsible for the murder of King Edward's brother Alfred, Godwine apparently offered to clear himself of that charge by going to the ordeal; but in practice the situation was dominated by the king's anger over Alfred's death and other political issues like the overbearing power wielded by Godwine and his sons. So, instead of being immediately resolved judicially the charge almost resulted in open war; and the flight of the whole Godwin clan precipitated a crisis which indirectly contributed to the Norman conquest of 1066. Outlawry was the only legal procedure which marked the dispute: the whole episode marks out 'English politics [i.e. before the Norman Conquest] as particularly savage'.[39]

The conflicts between the sons of William the Conqueror over the succession to their father seem to bring into the open the difficulties of adapting methods of proof which were then regarded as legally valid to such tangled political situations. In 1096 the aftermath of a revolt of Duke Robert of Normandy's supporters against King William Rufus prompted Geoffrey Baynard in the king's court at Salisbury to accuse Count William of Eu of treachery against the king: a duel followed in which the count was defeated, then blinded and castrated.[40] It is interesting, however, that other suspects from this rebellion were not even given the choice of going to the duel: Count William's steward and kinsman was hanged (unjustly in the opinion

---

[37] See for analysis the rather neglected work by J. Goebel, *Felony and Misdemeanor: A Study in the History of the Criminal Law* (Pennsylvania 1937, reprinted 1976), pp. 418 and n. 285.

[38] *Leges Henrici Primi*, 59,16a (p. 188); 59, 27–8 (for procedure and accusation for such offences, p. 190).

[39] Godwin allegedly . . . *missis legatis regis pacem petivit, legem purgandi* [translated by the editor as 'he offered to purge himself by ordeal'] *se de obiecto crimine frustra pretulit*, *The Life of King Edward who rests at Westminster*, 2nd edn, ed. F. Barlow (*OMT*, 1992), pp. 34–5; idem, *Edward the Confessor* (London 1970), p. 112; P. Stafford, *Unification and Conquest: A Political and Social History of England in the Tenth and Eleventh Centuries* (London 1989), pp. 77–80, 89–92; Gillingham, '1066 and the introduction of chivalry into England' in *The English in the Twelfth Century, Imperialism, National Identity and Political Values* (Woodbridge 2000), pp. 214–16, 221–2 (citation at p. 216).

[40] '. . . a mutilation from which he does not seem to have recovered', F. Barlow, *William Rufus* (London 1983), p. 357 (and pp. 347–56 for the extent of the conspiracy which occasioned the appeal); Van Caenegem, *English Lawsuits*, no. 143; Judith Green, *The Aristocracy of Norman England* (Cambridge 1997), esp. pp. 113, 274–5.

of many): Earl Robert Mowbray died in prison – but unfortunately there does not appear to be any information about whether judgement had preceded his imprisonment.[41] An accusation of treachery in the king's court must have inspired fear, and in Henry I's reign, after Robert de Montfort was charged with 'broken faith', he voluntarily renounced his lands and left for Jerusalem.[42] Political security, social solidarity and the economic foundations of power were all at stake when accusations of treachery were brought by one individual against another; and the magnates assembled in the king's court must have been aware of the repercussions of such charges. Personal motives might affect the outcome: Earl Hugh of Chester was allegedly involved in the harsh punishment imposed on Count William of Eu, against whom he allegedly bore a grudge for deserting his wife (Hugh's sister), and fathering three children by a concubine (*de pelice*).[43] The examples just reviewed suggest that, although combat was regarded as the appropriate method of proof to be employed in such cases, similar charges were not necessarily followed by identical proceedings, or by standard methods of proof. One interesting documentary survival also shows that the opening procedures may even have been quite informal, like the occasion on which in Norwich 'in the garden of the bishop', 'a certain young man called Herbert' stood up in the middle of a joint meeting of the shires of Norfolk and Suffolk, claiming that he had heard two men plotting 'the betrayal and death of the king' (*de tradicione et morte regis*). Herbert said that he would 'prove' (*probare*) his accusation if the two men denied this.[44]

Van Caenegem's collection of English lawsuits for the years 1154 to 1199 includes twenty-three cases in which a duel formed part of the strategy of the legal proceedings, or was actually fought. Eight of these cases concern disputes over land or other property;[45] whereas fifteen resulted from accusations of crime. The majority of the fifteen duels fought following criminal accusations related to theft, but there is one case of wife murder and another of suspected poisoning, in addition to the duel fought by Henry of Essex after he had been appealed for *proditio*. (That will be discussed later.) A high proportion of the proceedings are known only from works of a hagiographical character, and were presumably composed so as to enhance the reputation of the saints by preserving the memory of their miraculous

---

[41] Barlow, *William Rufus*; Green, *Norman Aristocracy*, pp. 166–8, 203–4, 209; but see Gillingham, 'Introduction of chivalry', p. 221.

[42] This Robert acknowledged himself guilty of the charge (*reum*), *The Ecclesiastical History of Orderic Vitalis*, 6 vols ed. M. Chibnall (OMT, 1969–80), vi, pp. 22–4, 100–3; Judith Green, *The Aristocracy*, p. 282. Cf. the apparently unsubstantiated charge *de reatu perfidiae* levelled against the royal chamberlain, Geoffrey Clinton in 1130, *Orderic*, iv, p. 276; Green, *Aristocracy*, p. 289; W. Hollister, 'Royal acts of mutilation: the case against Henry I' in *Monarchy, Magnates and Institutions in the Anglo-Norman World* (London 1986), pp. 291–301.

[43] *Orderic*, iv, p. 284.

[44] The outcome of Herbert's accusation gets lost in an account of how the abbot of Bury St Edmunds justified his privileges which he claimed had been infringed by the assembly, H. M. Cam, 'An East Anglian Shire-Moot of Stephen's reign', *EHR* xxxix (1924), 568–71 (on the dating, probably *c*.1148, p. 568).

[45] *English Lawsuits*, nos 381, 456, 491–2, 526, 555, 598, 619, 648.

Between law and politics 127

powers.[46] The saint's action might be punitive, as when St Cuthbert struck dead a perjurer who, before engaging in judicial combat, had sworn his innocence on a cross made from wood associated with the saint.[47] Other recorded acts of supernatural intervention were more benign, either reversing the effects of mutilations imposed after defeat in a duel, or preserving an innocent man from defeat. Thomas Becket's *Miracles*, for instance, include an account of how the saint saved a man who, during the course of a judicial duel, invoked St Thomas on the battlefield. Against all expectations this petitioner to the saint was victorious, although he had already been lifted off his feet by an opponent far larger and stronger than he was.[48]

The eight accounts in Van Caenegem's collection which concern duels fought for land or other property during this period are more straightforward in their content, even though references to duels are sometimes oblique. A judicial combat 'in the court of the lord king in London' is only known because the victor considered that *pro anima* he should grant part of a church on the land for which he had fought to the monastery of Sempringham;[49] while in another case land obtained 'for the settlement of a duel' (*pro pacatione duelli*) was eventually granted to the monastery of Easby by a lay donor.[50] One complicated, bitter and long-running lawsuit over profitable marshland between two Fenland monasteries shows that judicial combat could still be preferred as a method of proof even after more 'rational' methods became available; and during the course of the dispute the abbot of Croyland regretted that 'he could not choose the duel' because his following at court did not include 'any strong young man' (*duellum non potuit eligere . . . aliquem . . . iuvenem validum*). This abbot obviously did not think much of the supposed advantages of the new 'rational' procedures: in fact he suspected that the prior of Spalding had promised the king forty-five marks 'to have the grand assize' (*pro habenda magna assisa*): presumably he thought that the regional jury would be more favourable to his opponent. This stage of the dispute occurred soon after King Richard's accession in 1189, and despite the reforms to the law so highly praised in 'Glanvill's' treatise.[51]

Entries found on the Pipe Rolls need, however, to be added to the accounts of lawsuits involving judicial combat which are collected among Van Caenegem's

---

[46] Ibid. nos 403, 407, 463, 468–9, 471, 502, 504–5, 513, forfeiture of land after defeat in duel *pro murdro uxoris suae*, 520, 618, 648.

[47] *English Lawsuits*, no. 468 (dated 1173 at the latest); cf. ibid., no. 403 (*c*.1162).

[48] Ibid., no. 502. (My thanks to Dr. Nigel Ramsay and Geoffrey Fisher of the Conway Library, Courtauld Institute, for supplying me with information about the nearly contemporary representation of this duel in the glass of Becket's chapel in Canterbury Cathedral.) For miraculous 'cures' of men mutilated following defeat in a duel, ibid. nos 471, 501, 504.

[49] Ibid., no. 555 (dated *c*.1163 x 84).

[50] Ibid., no. 526 (dated 1162 x 1181).

[51] The text is printed from a lost Croyland MS by Stenton, *English Justice*, see pp. 148–51, 154–211; Van Caenegem, *English Lawsuits*, no. 641 (part only); however this dispute was not settled until 1202, by which time its progress is recorded in the *curia regis* rolls, Stenton, *English Justice*, pp. 189, n. 35, 195, n. 36 and cf. n. 38; and on the possibly inconclusive character of 'rational procedures', Colman, 'Reason and unreason', pp. 590–1.

'*membra disiecta*' for the years after 1154. Those show royal officials accounting for a variety of expenses which were bound up with the administration of duels, in addition to proffers made to the king, and fines incurred by litigants and combatants. The cost of equipping and transporting *probatores* had to be noted, and so did the expense of executions and mutilations which followed some of the duels.[52] Duels were expected to be conducted according to standards whose contravention is noted, although rarely with much precision: these entries normally only refer to the fact that a duel was 'badly held', or 'falsely' judged. In Yorkshire, however, it was noted in the 1165–6 Pipe Roll that a cleric was fined 100s. for having obliged one man to fight two duels on one day (twenty-one other individuals were fined between one and two marks for the same offence); but the county of Somerset in 1176–7 was collectively fined 100 marks because 'they sent a duel to the hundred which ought to have been [held?] in the county'.[53] The single surviving Roll of Henry I's reign had already included a variety of references to duels, while after 1154 considerable sums of money continued to be offered and paid in order to engage in a duel (*pro duello*) during the course of disputes over land and other property.[54] During Henry II's reign there are 103 references in the Pipe Rolls to show that payments were made for a duel to 'have land', but also to gain a peaceful settlement (*pro concordia duelli, pro pacificatione duelli, pro fine duelli*) without the formal procedures being noted.[55] By King John's reign such entries in this type of source have become far less frequent, however, and tend to be restricted to men of baronial status, like Eustace de Vesci.[56] References to an individual offering payments 'for having his duel in the King's court', or 'for having his duel in the justices' presence' suggest that apparently some laymen at least continued to prefer old methods of proof; while in Richard's reign one entry of this type was even more precise, since the sheriff of Dorset and Somerset recorded that a litigant paid 20s. 'for having the duel which is in the county in the king's court at Westminster'.[57]

---

[52] *The Great Rolls of the Pipe of the Reign of Henry II*, 5th to 34th years, 30 vols (Pipe Roll Society, 1884–1925); 2nd to 4th years published Record Commission 1844 – henceforth *PR*. For example *PR* 2–4 *H II*, pp. 113–14; *PR* 5 *H II*, p. 5 ; *PR* 10 *H II*, p. 25; *PR* 12 *H II*, pp. 72, 105–6, 130–1 (included hangings); *PR* 13 *H II*, p. 1 (mutilation and hanging) . . . Cf. *PR* 34 *H II*, p. 19 (6 *probatores* fought fourteen duels); *PR 1 RD I*, pp. 112, 224.

[53] For example *PR* 12 *H II*, p. 47. Cf. *PR* 14 *H II*, pp. 28, 134; 15 *H II*, p. 102; 16 *H II*, p. 100; 17 *H II*, p. 27; 18 *H II*, p. 101; 23 *H II*, p. 20; 25 *H II*, p. 78 – the sheriff of Bucks. and Beds. accounted for 20 marks *de comitatu Bedford' pro duello iniuste iudicato*. Similar entries are found on the Norman Pipe Rolls, below n. 123.

[54] Sums accounted for in the 1130 Pipe Roll varied between 5 and 105 marks, Goebel, *Felony and Misdemeanour*, p. 418, n. 285.

[55] These figures (for which individual references cannot be given in a work of this scope) suggest that, despite the 'Angevin leap forward', the judicial duel continued to play a more important part in the conduct of the law than is often assumed, see e.g. Stenton, *English Justice*, pp. 6, 25–6, 94–5; Milsom, *Legal Framework*, p. 66 'let us get battle out of the way first', pp. 73–7.

[56] *PR* 5 *John*, p. 214 (Yorks) – he owed 20 marks. On Eustace, Holt, *Magna Carta*, pp. 59, 92, 119–20, 130–1.

[57] *PR* 12 *H II*, p. 79; *PR* 18 *H II*, p. 121; *PR* 22 *H II*, p. 21; *PR* 8 *RD I*, p. 218. Cf. the 100s. offered by Ralf Neville *pro duello suo festinando versus Willelmum filium Godrici*, *PR* 24 *H II*, p. 71.

The interests of the royal government in the duel can also be established from the references to fines exacted either for some defect in the procedure (e.g. 'false appeal') or for failure to perform, like 'Yvo the husband of Emma' who in 1184–5 owed 9s. 'because he withdrew from his duel on the day he ought to fight'.[58] And in 1189–90 William FitzIsabel was savagely amerced (£566 13s. 4d.) for taking money from a Robert Chaud whom he allowed to escape, although Robert had been appealed by Jordan *Falsonarius*.[59]

During the twelfth century the methods of legal proof which historians have classified as 'irrational' were increasingly condemned by influential groups of both clergy and laity, although on rather different grounds; and the character of those condemnations needs to be considered briefly here because they provide a context both for the eventual prohibition of the 'unilateral' ordeals of 'fire and water' in 1215 and the survival of judicial combat. Ever since the ninth century the objection had been voiced that a divine judgement would not be manifested 'through detestable combats' because 'God's judgements are secret and impenetrable'.[60] By the late twelfth century general ecclesiastical criticism of all ordeals had grown in strengh and effectiveness, although even in a clerical *milieu* there could be confusion in practice about judicial combat, as emerges from the correspondence of the renowned canonist Bishop Ivo of Chartres (died *c*.1116) who censured the bishop of Orléans for allowing his clergy to organise a judicial combat. Ivo also argued that another case ought to be transferred from episcopal jurisdiction to the 'court of the countess' (i.e. the Countess Adela of Blois, mother of the later King Stephen of England) because 'this cause cannot be decided without judicial combat' (*monomachia*). At the beginning of the twelfth century, therefore, in practice even questions relating to the respective spheres of ecclesiastical and secular jurisdiction might be hazy; but interestingly Bishop Ivo did not wholly condemn the judicial use of the duel, although he deplored in the strongest terms the involvement of the clergy in 'judgement of blood'.[61] Arguments against the employment of ordeals (including the duel) in legal proceedings were now being marshalled by intellectuals, like those from the Parisian 'circle' of Peter the Chanter who argued that involvement in ordeals provided occasion for sin because the

---

[58] *PR 31 H II*, p. 70. On the other hand, in the same year a litigant who had wagered duel for land (*duellum de eadem terra vadiavit*) was obliged to offer 40 marks because he recognised that he actually did not have any right (*rectum*) there, ibid., p. 92. Altogether there are twenty-seven entries of this type in the Pipe Rolls of Henry II's reign and eighteen for Richard's.

[59] *PR 1 RD I*, p. 228 (but the sum was also 'for many other debts'). It seems likely that Jordan was an 'approver' – or at least a professional champion, because an earlier Pipe Roll accounted for the property of William *de Dunewico* . . . whom *Jordanus Falsonarius vicit in duello, PR 28 H II*, 73.

[60] Bartlett, *Fire and Water*, pp. 70–102 (quotation at p. 73 from the works of Archbishop Agobard of Lyon, died. 840); cf. the entry '*Ordalies*' in *Dictionnaire de droit canonique*, ed. R. Naz et al. (1957), vi, cols 119–20.

[61] *Patrologia Latina*, vol. 162, respectively epp. 247 (col. 254), 68 (cols 170–1); see G. Constable, 'The Three orders of society' in *Three Studies in Medieval Religious and Social Thought* (Cambridge 1995), p. 295; also K. A. LoPrete, 'Adela of Blois and Ivo of Chartres: piety, politics, and the peace in the diocese of Chartres', *ANS* xiv (1991), 149, n. 81; Bartlett, *Fire and Water*, pp. 29, 75, 82, 95.

whole process tempted God. Already before 1215 Peter drew attention to the essential part which the clergy played in the performance of ordeals through their guardianship of 'the book' and relics which were used in the sacral preludes to the administration of the ordeal.[62] Theological discussion, in the view of John Baldwin, helped to prepare the way for the official prohibition of the 'rite of boiling or cold water, or of burning iron' which was enacted by Pope Innocent III in 1215 (canon 18 of the Fourth Lateran Council); but some years earlier Pope Alexander III had already castigated the ordeal as a 'forbidden and execrable judgement' (*prohibitum et execrabile judicium*).[63] Nevertheless, Innocent III's official prohibition during the fourth Lateran Council in 1215 did not include any open reference to the duel: it was decreed that no cleric should be present at any judgement when 'sentence of blood' was pronounced – indeed a cleric should not even draw up any written document associated with such a judgement. Since 'ordeals by fire and water' needed a priest to consecrate the inanimate elements of iron or water and to administer the oaths of those who were obliged to submit to the ordeal, those methods of proof could not be enacted without active clerical participation.[64]

Secular criticism of judicial combat was based on different – and more pragmatic – grounds. This criticism is most articulately and coherently expressed in the treatise *On the Laws and Customs of the Realm of England* (probably completed *c*.1184 × 89), and frequently attributed to Ranulf Glanvill, Henry II's chief justiciar from 1180. If Ranulf Glanvill were indeed the author of the treatise which bears his name, historians could be certain not only about many 'ideas, values, and assumptions about right and wrong that prevailed in lay society', but would also have the satisfaction of knowing that that they were expressed by a layman.[65] As a method of

---

[62] J. W. Baldwin, 'The intellectual preparation for the canon of 1215 against ordeals', *Speculum*, xxxvi (1961), 630 n. 107; idem, Masters, *Princes and Merchants: The Social Views of Peter the Chanter and his Circle*, 2 vols (Princeton 1970), pp. 323–32.

[63] Alexander III's undated condemnation is cited, *'Ordalies'*, col. 1121; Bartlett, *Fire and Water*, pp. 82, 94, 97. But clerical participation in pronouncing sentences of death or mutilation had been forbidden in 1075, Goebel, *Felony and Misdemeanour*, p. 412.

[64] The clergy must not 'bless' or 'consecrate' any of the elements in the 'rite' (*purgationi aque ferventis vel frigide seu ferri candentis ritum*): *Constitutiones Concilii quarti Lateranensis unacum Commentariis glossatorum*, cap. 18, ed. A. Garcia y Garcia, *Monumenta Iuris Canonici*, series A, vol.ii (Vatican City 1981), p. 66 (for an English translation, *English Historical Documents*, iii, ed. H. Rothwell [London 1975], p. 654). On the 'aftermath' of Lateran IV, Bartlett, *Fire and Water*, pp. 127–32; Van Caenegem, 'Methods of Proof', pp. 82–5. But 'trial by battle' was not 'condemned at the Fourth Lateran Council' as is stated in the entry 'Battle', *Oxford Companion to Law* (Oxford 1980), p. 119.

[65] Reynolds, *Kingdoms and Communities*, pp. ixv–vi. For *'Glanvill'* (inverted commas are used to distinguish the treatise from the historical figure), *Tractatus de Legibus et Consuetudinibus Regni Anglie qui Glanvilla vocatur*, ed. G. Hall (*NMT*, 1965): on dating and problems of authorship, introd., pp. xxx–xxxiii; on Ranulf's career, Stenton, *English Justice*, p. 53, cf. pp. 75–8; H. G. Richardson and G. O. Sayles, *The Governance of Medieval England from the Conquest to Magna Carta* (Edinburgh 1963), pp. 273–9; M. Clanchy, *From Memory to Written Record, England 1066–1307* (2nd edn Oxford 1993), esp. pp. 231–9 (on lay literacy); R. V. Turner, *The English Judiciary in the Age of Glanvill and Bracton* (Cambridge 1985), pp. 19–30, 40–4. For legal change before 1189, Warren, *Henry II*, pp. 298, 330–61.

Between law and politics 131

legal proof 'Glanvill' condemned judicial combat (which he always refers to as *duellum*) on practical grounds, asserting that justice was unlikely to be reached by combat – 'even after many and long delays'. He also condemned the 'doubtful outcome of the duel', emphasising that the vanquished man invariably incurred 'the reproach of perpetual disgrace (*perhempnis infamie opprobrium*)', adding that he might also suffer 'the torture' of his own 'unexpected and untimely death (*insperate et premature mortis . . . supplicium*)'.[66] That criticism relates only to the duel employed as a method of proof in civil disputes (primarily associated with lawsuits about the possession of land), since 'Glanvill' seems to have taken it for granted that judicial combat was legitimately used in pleas of felony when an accused man had formally denied the charges made against him by an *appellator* (. . . *per omnia in curia legitime negante, tunc per duellum solet placitum terminari*); and this corresponds to what is described at far greater length by Bracton in his early thirteenth-century treatise.[67]

The appearance of 'Glanvill's' treatise has been regarded as a sign of a movement towards rationality and order in the law of England during the later twelfth century – of 'the great leap forward' achieved under Angevin rulers. By criticising the duel as a method of proof in civil pleas 'Glanvill' surely deliberately aimed to accentuate the contrast with new methods of proof which were devised for the use of litigants during the years after 1154. This emerges most clearly from his praise for the 'grand assize' (*magna assisa*) as a 'royal benefit' based on 'equity' which, he wrote, was introduced by the Angevin ruler Henry II into the procedure of his royal courts; and the grand assize was bestowed on his people 'by the clemency of the prince . . . after consultation with his great men . . .'. It was 'equitable', he wrote, because proof and judgement in a plea would be based on 'the oaths of at least twelve men' rather than – as with the duel – depending on an initial oath taken by one man before combat (*tanto maiori equitate nitiur ista constitutio quam duellum: cum enim ex unius iurati testimonio procedat duellum, duodecim ad minus hominum exigit constitutio iuramenta*). The attitudes expressed in this treatise seem to underlie much of the discussion of the older 'disciplinary jurisdiction' by legal historians.[68] Van Caenegem, too, concluded that these developments marked a 'summing up after the first and most creative age of the Common Law in England', although, according to Lady Stenton, 'the years when

---

[66] '*Ius enim, quod post multas et longas dilationes per duellum vix evincitur . . .*', 'Glanvill', ed. Hall, II, 7 (p. 28).

[67] For procedure where the duel was employed in pleas of felony (*in placitis omnibus de felonia*), 'Glanvill', XIV, 1 (pp. 171–3); cf. Bracton, *De Legibus*, ii, pp. 384–94; 394–9; 399–40l; 401–4. See also N. D. Hurnard, *The King's Pardon for Homicide before A.D.1307* (Oxford 1969), pp. 187–9, 342–3.

[68] '*Est autem assisa illa regale quoddam beneficium clemencia principis de consilo procerum populis indultum . . .*' 'Glanvill', II, 7 (p. 28); cf. Van Caenegem, *Royal Writs in England from the Conquest to Glanvill: Studies in the Early History of the Common Law* (Selden Society, lxxvii, 1958–9), pp. 363–4; Stenton, *English Justice*, pp. 32–53; but for a more cautious view of 'Glanvill's' treatment of the duel, Hyams, 'Trial by ordeal', pp. 119–21. Cf. Milsom, *The Legal Framework*, pp. 1–35; P. Brand, '"*Multis vigiliis excogitam et inventam*": Henry II and the creation of the English Common Law', in *The Making of the Common Law* (London 1992), pp. 77–102.

the great leap forward was taken remain, despite the work of many scholars, mysterious'.[69] In practice, even where a litigant 'put himself on the grand assise' (. . . *is qui se in assisam posuit*) and had his suit judged by a jury, that more rational mode of proceeding was still not always preferred to the duel during the late twelfth century.[70] The history of the duel in the later twelfth and early thirteenth centuries bears out Susan Reynolds's observations that 'the relation between theory and practice, ideas and activities, remains problematical', but also suggests that 'asssumptions about right and wrong' and the 'values' embodied in the judicial duel were rather more complicated than might be supposed by modern historians adopting a teleological view of law reform in England, or perhaps convinced of the innate superiority and the 'higher intellectual level' of 'more modern methods of proof'.[71]

Roger of Howden's account of King John's scheme to set in motion legal procedures appealing his Poitevin barons of treachery takes on a rather different meaning when it is set against the background which has just been considered. Powicke's conclusion (already mentioned) that, in planning to put these barons 'to the test of trial by battle', the king chose 'a somewhat curious method' of trying 'to enforce justice' scarcely seems tenable, and was possibly influenced by the view of J. H. Ramsay that the whole affair involved 'a scheme in truth of the most childish character'. Kate Norgate in her detailed account of Angevin politics admittedly showed greater interest in the legal aspects of the affair, but she pronounced John's scheme for judicial combat 'unwarranted by historical precedent'. and commented that it involved 'startling innovation upon feudal tradition and practice'. Presumably she thought that the king was struggling to devise a veneer of legality which would conceal the pursuit of his own political – or even personal – ends.[72] More recent studies have emphasised the king's political ineptitude in 'insulting' great laymen – and principally members of the Lusignan family – who had been deeply offended by John's second marriage; but Howden's statement that John wished the appeal of the barons to be based on the accusation that the Poitevins had betrayed not only him, but also his brother Richard, means that the 'treachery' of which they were accused must have antedated John's succession as king in April 1199. In those circumstances the affair cannot have been occasioned entirely by King John's second marriage to Isabella of Angoulême (in August 1200), or by the

---

[69] Van Caenegem, *Royal Writs in England*, pp. 9–10; Stenton, *English Justice*, p. 25, and in general pp. 22–87. For the survival of battle and the 'underlying structures' of the changes, Milsom, *Legal Framework*, pp. 2–5, 185–6; idem, *Historical Foundations of the Common Law*, pp. 10–11; J. Hudson, *Land, Law and Lordship in Anglo-Norman England* (Oxford 1994), pp. 261–9.

[70] '*Glanvill*', II, 6 (p. 27). Although perhaps some views embodied in the legal reforms of Henry II's reign 'may . . . have been peculiarly those of the king's men, and perhaps out of harmony with the lay nobility', Hudson, *Land, Law and Lordship*, p. 269; cf. pp. 33, 45, 47, 141.

[71] Reynolds, *Kingdoms and Communities*, introd. to 2nd edn, p. lxvi; Van Caenegem, 'Methods of proof', pp. 109, 111.

[72] Norgate, *England under the Angevin Kings*, ii, pp. 401–2; idem, *John Lackland*, pp. 81–2.

hostile reactions of the Poitevin aristocracy to that marriage after the king had deprived Hugh of Lusignan of his expected bride.[73]

Nevertheless, the advance planning necessary to find 'men expert in the art of fighting in the duel, and selected from his lands on both sides of the sea', suggests that John was determined to ensure that these barons should be proved guilty in the duels which he intended to take place. His plans must have meant that each of these barons could have found himself engaged in a duel against a skilled and expert fighter from any part of the huge Angevin empire – and there would have been no guarantee that those 'experts' would have had personal knowledge of the treachery of which the Poitevins were accused. In legal terms that was probably the gravest error committed by the king, for an appellor was meant to be a witness of a suspected traitor's or felon's actions.[74] Unfortunately Howden's failure to fill in the details of the affair – and particularly the names and numbers of those to be appealed – probably accounts for many of the often unverifiable hypotheses put forward to account for it. Because no duel took place the whole episode has been ignored by historians of the law and substantially misunderstood by political historians of the Angevin dynasty.[75]

Far from being a 'curious method of doing justice' in cases of felony in the English kingdom judicial combat was the standard method of determining whether threats had been made against the king's life, or sedition plotted against the kingdom or the army (*de morte regis vel de seditione regni vel exercitus*).[76] The 'law as it was practised in the courts' also shows that during the twelfth century duels were used to establish innocence or guilt for a wide range of criminal offences which often touched the lives of quite humble subjects of the English king. When King John became convinced in the year 1201 that the law should be seen to be done as far as his Poitevin barons were concerned, it would have been widely known that judicial combat would follow an appeal for treachery; for that was the correct procedure according to both law and custom, and Howden's use of the terms *appellatio* and *proditio* suggests that he was careful to employ contemporary legal terminology. Presumably any of the justices attending the king would have given him counsel on the normal legal procedure; and possibly the Poitevins were unwilling even to attend John's court because it was established custom that, if anyone denied such a

---

[73] Nicholas Vincent, 'Isabella of Angoulême: John's Jezebel', in *King John: New Interpretations*, pp. 171–5. The complicated political antecedents of the duel deserve further attention than can be devoted to them here.

[74] 'Glanvill', XIV, 1 (p. 172); cf. Bracton, *De Legibus*, ii, pp. 392–9.

[75] It has been taken for granted that John's accusations were made against the Lusignans, although the only reference is to Howden's narrative in which no names were given, Warren, *King John* (London 1961), pp. 89–90, 319; R. V. Turner, *King John* (London 1994), pp. 117–18 ; while no mention was made of the affair by Sidney Painter, 'The lords of Lusignan in the eleventh and twelfth centuries' and 'The houses of Lusignan and Châtellerault (1150–1250)', in F. Cazel, ed., *Feudalism and Liberty* (Baltimore 1961), pp. 41–89; cf. also his *The Reign of King John* (Johns Hopkins 1949), pp. 48–9. Cf. Martindale (no reference either), 'Eleanor of Aquitaine: the last years', in *King John: New Interpretations*, pp. 137–64.

[76] 'Glanvill', XIV, 1 (p. 171). At an earlier date *infidelitas et proditio* were listed among the king's *iura*, *Leges Henrici Primi*, 10, 1 (p. 109).

serious charge in the royal court (*per omnia in curia legitime negante*), then the truth of the accusation would have to be judged by a duel.[77] One of the most significant aspects of this abortive 'treason trial', however, is that the Poitevin barons apparently accepted without question the king's jurisdiction over them: he was entitled to summon them to 'respond' to a charge of treachery in his court. The Poitevins' refusal to engage in judicial combat on John's own terms, on the other hand, provides historians with a tantalising glimpse of 'lay political ideas' expressed during the course of a serious political crisis. Wasn't a concept of equality being advanced to justify taking 'intelligent collective activity' against the king's attempts to impose (but perhaps also to distort) customary legal procedure to further his own political ends? The arguments advanced by the Poitevin barons undoubtedly drew on a stock of aristocratic attitudes which were widespread throughout his territories and which the king himself had to accept. And – however paradoxical it may seem today – because the barons refused to fight those who were *not* [my italics] their equals, the notion of 'parity' which they advanced was profoundly hierarchical.[78]

Another case of proposed judicial combat which never took place needs to be considered before at last discussing in detail a duel which did actually take place. This strongly reinforces the link between acts of betrayal and the duel, but also sheds a rather different light on lay aristocratic attitudes towards judicial combat. The political and social background to the incident seems clear, and is essential for an understanding of its legal aspects: it concerns the successful warrior and ambitious courtier William the Marshal who was suspected of being the lover of his lord's wife, the young Capetian Queen Margaret – or at any rate those were the rumours which were openly circulating at the Christmas court held by King Henry II at Caen in 1182. According to William's verse-biography – 'the earliest vernacular life of a layman in European history' – he dismissed the allegations as 'false and bitter treason' (*traïson false e amère*); and in order to scotch the rumours he proclaimed publicly that he would do 'battle' on three successive days against 'three of the best' men present at the royal court.[79] With considerable *bravura* he also declared that, if he were defeated in these testing judgements, he would expect to be punished by hanging; but according to this account King Henry II refused to allow any legal proceedings to take place. It is especially interesting that William allegedly argued that the king was directing the royal court to act 'against reason

---

[77] 'Glanvill', ibid. (p. 172). To avoid fighting a duel it might therefore be necessary to think of 'legitimate' grounds for avoiding a court appearance.

[78] Above, nn. 1–3; Reynolds, *Kingdoms and Communities*, esp. pp. 51–9, introd. to 2nd edn, pp. xxxvi–viii, and chs 1–2. Holt, *Magna Carta*, pp. 92–5; and for earlier centuries, Nelson, this volume pp. 41–5.

[79] *L'Histoire de Guillaume le Maréchal*, ed. P. Meyer, 3 vols (Société de l'histoire de France, 1891–1901), ll. 5749–5848; ed. also *English Lawsuits*, no. 540; Gillingham, 'War and chivalry in the *History of William the Marshal*', in *Richard Coeur de Lion, Kingship, Chivalry and War in the Twelfth Century* (London 1994), pp. 227–41 (quotation at p. 227); D. Crouch, *William Marshal: Court, Career and Chivalry in the Angevin Empire, 1147–1219* (London 1990), pp. 44–7, 1–6 (on the source); Warren, *Henry II*, pp. 580–8.

and law of the land' (... *vostre cort m'est trop pendant / Contre raison e lei de terre*) in refusing to allow him scotch these rumours through engaging in judicial combat. Instead the Marshal was eventually granted a safe-conduct to withdraw 'with his company' to the neighbouring county of Le Perche.[80]

David Crouch has doubted 'whether the allegation of adultery was ever really made against' William Marshal on the grounds that he apparently survived an accusation of sexual misconduct with remarkable ease; and since this episode *was* [my italics] written up with hindsight, it has been suggested that the whole episode possibly owes more to the conventions of contemporary romance than it does to sober historical 'fact'. Nevertheless, even if there is no means today of checking its historical accuracy the affair is of exceptional interest for any investigation of the judicial duel. In the first place it confirms that in the king's court 'questions about treason, loyalty, honour and shame' would be provoked by a debate over whether a duel should be fought to repudiate a charge of adultery since, if that concerned the wife of a lord, it would imply (in the words put into William's mouth) 'bitter and false treason'. Secondly this incident shows that without a formal accusation no proceedings could take place; and, because even William's taunts did not produce a response from the courtiers gathered for the Christmas festivities, he was unable to defend himself at law – 'evil tongue dares say what it scarcely dares to prove' (*malveise langue ose dire / Ce qu'el n'ose mie prover*), he angrily declared.[81] The whole episode was written up so that William Marshal would be presented to a contemporary audience in the best possible light, and we are scarcely in a position today to decide whether he intended to fight three opponents to clear his name. Perhaps, in Stephen White's words, he was using the 'procedural possibility' of the duel 'as a threat or instrument of power' to enable him to silence and defeat his detractors.[82] The success of those tactics depended of course upon an individual's reputation as a fighter; and by 1182 William had certainly gained a formidable reputation on the tournament circuit throughout northern France; but any such strategy surely also depended upon a careful assessment of the risks involved, and the possible reactions of a such a formidable ruler as King Henry II. In a potentially dangerous situation the cleverness of William's manoeuvre was that it signalled that he was not to be intimidated and that – unlike the men who would not respond to his taunts – he should not himself be thought a coward. If his opponents were not prepared to 'prove' their accusations, they should keep their mouths shut but he 'did not look like a man who flees, or who is afraid of another knight' was his biographer's conclusion.[83]

---

[80] *L'Histoire de Guillaume le Maréchal*, ll. 5822–3, 5831–40.

[81] *Histoire de Guillaume le Maréchal*, ll. 5805–7; White, 'Proposing the ordeal', p. 91; Crouch, *William Marshal*, pp. 33–4, 173–8.

[82] White, this volume; cf. his 'Proposing the ordeal and avoiding it', pp. 91–7 (although there the discussion is as much concerned with the unilateral ordeals as with judicial combat).

[83] *Histoire de Guillaume le Maréchal*, ll. 5842–3. He apparently employed similar tactics in 1205 and 1210, Crouch, *William Marshal*, p. 46; Holt, *Magna Carta*, pp. 92–4; cf. Strickland, 'Provoking or avoiding battle?', p. 325.

A third aspect of the incident is surely of exceptional interest in terms of late twelfth-century politics and 'assumptions' about the 'values' and behaviour of the lay aristocracy. In some fictional narratives a heroic warrior is found fighting a judicial duel in defence of a woman wrongly accused of adultery or murder: the contemporary Angevin genealogical literature, for instance, includes an entirely mythical episode in which 'a noble matron' (also called the Countess Adela) was cleared of the double charge of adultery and murder of her husband after her godson, Ingelgerius, fought a judicial duel in her defence.[84] And yet in these circumstances it was the marshal, not the young queen, who seemingly needed to exonerate himself. As with King John's later accusations against the 'barons of Poitou', legal procedure and proof were not at this aristocratic level the only – or even the most significant – issues involved in proposing a judicial duel. A layman should feel impelled to fight anyone who voiced charges of treachery, for he must show that he felt no fear; but in the real world the Capetian Queen Margaret had a political importance to her Angevin husband and father-in-law which the marshal at this time had not yet acquired; and it seems unlikely that she would have been sacrificed to satisfy William's honour or dignity. Margaret's marriage to the 'young king' had brought the whole of the much disputed Vexin under Angevin control.[85]

In the year 1163 a duel had taken place between Henry of Essex, the powerful royal constable of England, and his 'kinsman' (*consanguineus*) Robert de Montfort. The 'battlefield' was an island in the River Thames close to the great royal monastic foundation at Reading, and it was to that monastery that the defeated constable eventually retired as a monk after he had been left for dead by his opponent. By comparison with the abortive proceedings of 1201 – which were noted only by Roger Howden – this earlier duel was a *cause célèbre* widely reported and remembered in the Anglo-Norman world; and Robert of Torigny (the well-informed Norman chronicler who was Abbot of Mont Saint-Michel) explained that the judicial proceedings were caused by the constable's 'flight in battle against the Welsh'. Interestingly Torigny used the term *bellum* for judicial combat, which he contrasted with *proelium* to describe the war waged by the royal army against the Welsh: he emphasises that Henry of Essex was disinherited after his defeat by Robert de Montfort.[86] In the later twelfth century the defeat of Henry of Essex in judicial combat was treated as a notable event by the historians Ralph de Diceto and William of Newburgh (the combat was described by them respectively as occurring *certamine singulari* and, by Newburgh, as *duellum*). Both of those authors also realised the significance of the constable's disinheritance by King Henry II,

---

[84] *Chronica de Gestis Consulum Andegavorum*, in *Chroniques des comtes d'Anjou et des seigneurs d'Amboise*, ed. L. Halphen and R. Poupardin (Collection de textes pour servir à l'étude et à l'enseignement de l'histoire, 1913), p. 29; for a much expanded version from the C redaction of this text, pp. 136–9.

[85] Warren, *Henry II*, pp. 88–91, 145, 598. Cf. the actions of Count Philip of Flanders, who brutally killed his wife's lover but did not repudiate his wife, heiress to the important county of Vermandois, Gillingham, 'Love, marriage and politics in the twelfth century', in *Richard Coeur de Lion*, p. 250.

[86] Robert of Torigny, *Chronica*, ed. R. Howlett, in *Chronicles of the Reigns of Stephen, Henry II and Richard I*, (RS, 1884–90), p. 218 (under the year 1163).

Between law and politics 137

but neither they nor Robert of Torigny give the slightest hint that they considered that the outcome of the duel was the result of divine intervention.[87] That cannot be too strongly stressed because the secularity of these accounts is in complete contrast to the famous narrative written by a monk of Bury St Edmunds – almost certainly Jocelin of Brakelond – about twenty years after the duel took place. That was preserved in an autobiographical fragment at one remove: as a monk of Reading Abbey Henry of Essex passed on orally his own version of events to the visiting Bury monk.[88]

The centrepiece of Jocelin's account of the legal proceedings and duel is a vision of Edmund, 'glorious king and martyr' who (as the ex-constable described it to Jocelin) appeared 'armed and as though flying through the air' (*vidit gloriosum regem et martirem Ædmundum armatum et quasi in aere volitantem*); but the saint was also accompanied by another figure whom Henry of Essex recognised as a man – now dead – who in life had been one of his own knights (*milites*). St Edmund showed both 'anger' and 'indignation' against the constable, and effectively deflected Henry's blows agsainst his opponent, so that Henry 'was struck even harder . . . At the end he was overcome and fell . . .' Left for dead on the field of battle, the corpse of Henry of Essex was removed to Reading Abbey for burial: his conversion to a monastic life, it is implied, only occurred after his recovery from the wounds inflicted during the duel.[89] Strangely enough, although Jocelin's account of the 1163 duel might suggest that it was being treated as an essentially 'sacral process', it is certainly not stated that St Edmund's intervention was intended to 'prove' that the constable had been guilty of 'treachery' towards the king and army, the offence of which he was accused. On the contrary, the saint's anger was portrayed as having been aroused by Henry's encroachments on monastic property, and his usurpation of the judicial privileges of the community of Bury St Edmunds. Henry was supposed to have wrongfully claimed jurisdiction over a plea of rape; but he was also criticised for failing in generosity to the 'church of St Edmund' which his *comprovinciales* endowed more liberally. Even less relevant to the constable's deeds on the Welsh campaign was the allegation that he had been responsible for the imprisonment and death of his former knight, who appeared in his vision on the 'battlefield'.[90] The 'coded message' of this narrative seems to be that the duel provided St Edmund with an opportunity for punishing Henry for flouting the saint's authority and attacking his servants – a favourite hagiographical theme which was

---

[87] Ralph gave no explanation for the duel, *Radulfo de Diceto, Ymagines Historiarum*, in *Opera Historica*, 2 vols ed. W. Stubbs (*RS*, 1876), i, pp. 310, 269; cf. William of Newburgh, *Historia rerum Anglicarum*, ed. R. Howlett, in *Chronicles and Memorials*, ii, p. 108.

[88] *The Chronicle of Jocelin of Brakelond concerning the Acts of Samson Abbot of the Monastery of Bury St Edmunds*, ed. H. E. Butler (*NMT*, 1949), pp. 68–71. Butler regarded this as an interpolation into the text, ibid., p. 68, n. 2, but that opinion is not universal, see A. Gransden, *Historical Writing in England c.550– c.1307* (London 1974), p. 382, nn. 8, 15 (I have accepted that Jocelin was the author).

[89] *Chronicle of Jocelin of Brakelond*, quotations from pp. 68 and 71.

[90] Maitland, *History of the English Law*, ii, p. 600; *Chronicle of Jocelin of Brakelond*, p. 69; cf. p. 71 for the knight Gilbert de Cereville, apparently accused falsely of seducing Henry's wife against her will.

of far greater importance to the Bury monks than whether Henry II's army had been nearly routed by the Welsh. This was a miraculous intervention on behalf of the monks, not the vindication of Robert de Monfort, the constable's appellor.[91]

The Bury account of the 1163 duel is nevertheless given a legal setting which is credible. Robert de Montfort's appeal of Henry of Essex is carefully described: he 'stood up against him ... in sight of the princes of the land condemning and accusing him of betrayal of the king' (*insurrexit in eum ... in conspectu principum terre dampnans et accusans eum de proditione regis*); and, as the appellor, gave precise details about the place where Henry of Essex had dropped the royal standard on the campaign against the Welsh. In this spoken appeal Robert alleged, too, that the day would have been entirely lost if 'Earl Roger of Clare' had not once more 'raised up the lord king's standard to strengthen and put heart into the whole army'; and these details have been invaluable for the reconstruction of Angevin politics and military campaigns.[92] The legal procedure described also interestingly agree with the formal requirements laid down by Bracton in the 1220s for appeals of felony, and rather more sketchily outlined by 'Glanvill' in his treatise. According to Jocelin's narrative, as soon as appeal and denial had been made, 'after a little space of time had elapsed it came to bodily duel' (*ad corporale duellum*): that is a sequence which also corresponds to the description of procedure given by 'Glanvill', and it is not until that point in the Bury narrative that what Van Caenegem called the 'magico-priestly' element of the duel seems to take over entirely.[93] Since no other account of this duel places it in such a supernatural setting, it surely needs to be asked whether Jocelin's version should be regarded as reflecting the 'mentality' of the majority of the laity – or indeed clergy – at this stage in mid-twelfth-century England.

The participation of the great laity in the proceedings is also emphasised throughout the whole of Jocelin's account of this duel so that, although the interests of the Bury community are obviously the author's main concern, this narrative could still be accepted as incorporating the recollections of a man who, before his downfall, had been one of the greatest laymen in the kingdom. Firstly, Robert de Montfort's appeal was made 'in the sight of the princes of the land', and the duel is described as taking place before all 'the magnates of England' and the 'multitude of peoples' who flocked to the spectacle of the duel to see 'how the affair would turn out'. Then after Henry's defeat, when he was thought to have been killed by

---

[91] The incident was later extracted from the narrative of Samson's life and included in a 'Book of miracles' devoted to many saints, *Chronicle of Jocelin of Brakelond*, introd. xi–xii. However, for a reference to a visit by Robert de Montfort to Soissons to the shrine of St Drausius *qui ... pugiles qui ad memoriam eius pernoctant reddit invictos*, *The Letters of John of Salisbury*, 2 vols, ii *The Later Letters (1160–80)*, ed. W. J. Millor and C. N. L. Brooke (*OMT* 1979), pp. 110–11.

[92] *Chronicle of Jocelin of Brakeland*, p. 70; cf. Newburgh, *Historia*, p. 108; Warren, *Henry II*, pp. 69–71, 160–2; M. Strickland, *War and Chivalry: The Conduct and Perception of War in England and Normandy, 1066–1216* (Cambridge 1996), pp. 122–3, 339–40.

[93] After a legal response made by the accused man *in curia*, a duel would automatically follow: once that stage was reached *nec aliquo modo nisi de licencia domini regis vel iusticiarum de cetero possunt sibi ad invicem reconciliari*, 'Glanvill', XIV, 1 (p. 172).

Between law and politics 139

Robert in the duel, it was 'at the urgent request of the magnates of England, his kinsmen' that his body was taken for burial by the monks of Reading.[94] This mention of Henry of Essex's aristocratic connections echoed Jocelin's earlier comments on the 'parity' of the two combatants, even though Jocelin wrapped this up obscurely when he wrote that Robert de Montfort was 'related to him [i.e. Henry of Essex] by blood, and not unequal in either birth or strength (*ipsius consanguineus, nec genere nec viribus impar*)'.[95] That allusion surely provides an important point of comparison with Howden's reference to the Poitevin barons' insistence that they would only fight against their peers.

An examination of 'law in action' in the English kingdom during the second half of the twelfth century supports the argument that, in attempting to constrain his 'barons of Poitou' to engage in combat in his court, King John was attempting to get that court to employ methods of proof which were sanctioned by custom, methods similar to those outlined in 'Glanvill's' prescriptive text, or in the earlier and less coherently organised *Leges Henrici Primi*. But for a serious secular offence like treachery, the conduct of legal proceedings was by no means rigid. In the important cases which have just been considered collective attitudes and even collective action could affect the outcome of accusations which seem sometimes to have been raised quite informally: these take on a greater significance after the most prominent cases have been compared. The importance of a notion of 'parity' which was also profoundly hierarchical emerges from Jocelin's account of the combat between Henry of Essex and Robert de Montfort, as much as from the Poitevins' declaration that they would not fight against men who were not their equals in status. It seems possible, too, that the collective pressure of 'the magnates of England, his kinsmen' may have accounted for the leniency shown to Henry of Essex after his defeat by Robert de Montfort; although it also conforms to the changes perceived by John Gillingham of increasingly lenient punishments being imposed for such serious offences by aristocratic laymen during the course of the twelfth century.[96] The lengthy debates which form an integral part of Daire le Roux's 'treason trial' as portrayed in *Le roman de Thèbes* are not unfortunately matched in any narrative historical source of this period, but some hints that discussion would precede the transition to more formal proceedings and the organisation of judicial combat emerges from the account of William Marshal's efforts to exonerate himself by means of a judicial duel from supicions of adultery with his lord's wife. It is also revealed during the course of a dispute over castles in the Auvergne, when, after the day for a duel had been set, 'Peter's men spoke with the men of lord Archembald [of Bourbon] about making peace.' Perhaps in some circumstances formal legal proceedings may have been averted entirely, as on the occasion when Queen Eleanor negotiated a settlement for her youngest son John with his brother

---

[94] *Chronicle of Jocelin of Brakelond*, p. 71.

[95] Ibid., pp. 69–70; Newburgh, *Historia*, also stresses that Henry of Essex, *vir inter primos inclitus, et iure hereditario signifer regius*, was accused *a quodam viro nobili*. (Didn't he know de Montfort's name?)

[96] However his discussions are chiefly concerned with acts of political rebellion, Gillingham, 'Introduction of chivalry into England', pp. 221–4.

King Richard after the king's release from captivity in Germany. Richard had been given written proof of his brother's conspiracy with the Capetian king, and John had already been summoned to attend a council at Nottingham to account for his treachery.[97]

In Neilson's pioneering nineteenth-century work on the judicial duel he described 'Robert de Montford's' appeal of 'Henry of Essex, royal standard-bearer of England' for treason, as taking place 'in Parliament'.[98] Today the idea of a mid-twelfth-century 'parliament' providing the institutional setting for appeal in a 'treason trial' seems so ridiculous that the reasons for its anchronism seem scarcely worth refuting; but in other respects historians appear reluctant to re-examine the contemporary context of the disputes which have just been discussed. In particular, in White's words, it is probable that 'a proposal to hold an ordeal was understood as *both* a legal move in a lawsuit *and* a political bargaining ploy of confrontation' (his italics); but it also seems likely that, in Hyams's view, it was a method of proof used in a 'quasi-political episode'.[99] For instance, although the different strands of William Marshal's audacious proposal for judicial combat in 1182 are difficult to disentangle today, that proposal must all the same have embodied an attempt to secure his own position in the uncertain world of Angevin politics by gambling on his reputation as a formidable fighter.[100] It also seems likely that in 1201 King John hoped to achieve important political ends in Aquitaine through the defeat by currently acceptable methods of legal procedure of men whom he regarded as traitors towards both his brother and himself. That seems to provide a rather more plausible interpretation of this puzzling affair than (as used to be supposed) that he was involved in devising some wild and novel means of bringing suspected traitors to justice. Moreover, if there were greater certainty over the identities of those who were to be appealed it would be rather easier to prove whether John aimed to confiscate the Poitevin barons' honours by this means, or merely expected to rid himself of troublesome political opponents in the hope that they would be killed or defeated in judicial combat. Presumably in this particular case John might not have been able to find any Poitevins to appeal other members of their own social standing, and so he had to find strangers to the region 'learned in the art of fighting in the duel'. That was a tactic which completely defeated the king's purposes, and even provoked a response which was deliberately intended to

---

[97] Martindale, 'Eleanor of Aquitaine: the last years', pp. 146–7 and n. 35. It is intriguing to speculate whether anyone would have been found prepared to appeal John of treachery; Strickland, *War and Chivalry*, p. 232.

[98] G. Neilson, *Trial by Combat* (Glasgow 1898), p. 60. He might have been influenced by reference to Henry II's introduction of the 'grand assise' as 'a peculiar species of trial by jury', 'by consent of parliament', W. Blackstone, *Commentaries on the Laws of England*, 5 vols (5th edn Oxford 1773), bk III, ch. 22 (iii, p. 341, 'of private wrongs'); cf. bk. IV, ch. 27 (iv, pp. 347–8, 'of public wrongs').

[99] Even though they were primarily discussing the unilateral ordeal, these comments are perhaps even more applicable to judicial combat, White, 'Proposing the ordeal', p. 101 (his italics); Hyams, 'Trial by ordeal', pp. 93–5.

[100] Did he perhaps calculate that there would not be three men who would dare to challenge him? Above, nn. 81–2.

emphasise that he was attempting to distort the norms of legal procedure by setting aside the convention that in judicial combat men should meet their peers. John's strategy of 'confrontation' backfired.

With the 1163 judicial duel held at Reading a rather different set of questions is raised. A problem which seems never to have been discussed is why this duel ever took place, since the treachery of which the constable Henry of Essex was accused had actually occurred in 1157, while appeal and duel only followed five to six years later. Since Henry's action in letting the royal standard drop must have been seen by a large body of knights gathered round the king during the attack by the Welsh, there was nothing clandestine about his 'betrayal' of king and army; since he seems to have kept his office of constable throughout the important campaign which the king led against Toulouse in the summer of 1159, it is difficult to explain the time-lag between his act of *proditio* and the legal proceedings taken against him.[101] Perhaps by 1163 Henry of Essex was simply no longer in favour at court; but it also seems possible that Robert de Montfort or King Henry himself had ulterior motives for subjecting the constable to legal proceedings which could have led to his death – and more importantly in the long term – to his disinheritance. Robert de Montfort, for instance, may have hoped to regain family lands forfeited in the earlier twelfth century before the constable's office – together with its extensive lands and power – was bestowed on Henry of Essex; but, if that were so, he does not seem personally to have benefited from Robert's defeat of the constable.[102] The king, on the other hand, benefited considerably: the Pipe Rolls show that Henry II kept the constable's honours in his own hand and direct control over the knights whose fees were grouped on those honours. It seems possible – perhaps even likely – that the 1163 duel was a 'put-up job', undertaken for personal motives which are no longer clear, or more directly for the considerable wealth which would accrue to the royal 'fisc' if Henry of Essex were defeated – as indeed he was.[103] The devastating social and economic repercussions of the defeat of Henry of Essex can be measured by the impact which this had on his daughter's marriage prospects, and the attempts made by her proposed husband to sever marriage arrangements made when she was three years old.[104]

A 'transforming touch of genius', according to Warren, was King Henry II's contribution to the development of the common law in England. This 'genius'

---

[101] Above, pp. 136–7; for his military position in 1159, J. Martindale, '"An unfinished business": Angevin politics and the siege of Toulouse (1159)', *Anglo-Norman Studies* 23 (2001), pp. 129–30.

[102] J. H. Round, *Geoffrey de Mandeville* (London 1892), Appendix N: 'Robert de Vere and the hereditary constableship', p. 327 (although even Round could not pin down a precise genealogical relationship between this man and Henry I's Robert de Montfort); cf. Appendix U, p. 391; above n. 43.

[103] Henry of Essex's land of the honours of Boulogne and Rayleigh continued to be known under his name, and lands of the *honour constabularie* do not seem to have been granted out after 1163, *The Red Book of the Exchequer*, ed. H. Hall, 3 vols (RS, 1896), i, pp. 51–2, 66; ii, pp. 525, 595, 733. No account was rendered at the Exchequer for the *honour Bolonie, de terra Henr' de Essexa . . . quia Rex prohibet per brevem suum . . .* , PR 13 H II, p. 158; and 19; PR 14 H II, pp. 43, 46, 192.

[104] Green, *Aristocracy of Norman England*, p. 358.

was expressed at a 'critical moment in English legal history', during a time when 'English traditions' might have been 'distorted' by the grafting of 'alien institutions' on to the existing mass of customary law. Rather quizzically Warren ends his discussion of Henry's contribution to the expansion of the scope of royal justice in his English kingdom with the comment that 'it is remarkable that what is so often regarded as a characteristically English achievement should have owed its inception to a Frenchman from Anjou'.[105] In recent decades Richard I's achievements as a ruler have been deservedly rehabilitated, so that King Henry II's reputation as the lonely royal genius of legal reform does not seem so convincing as it once did; but few, if any, questions have been asked about the implications for legal history of Henry of Anjou's 'non-English' origins.[106] But in his teens the future King Henry II was already taught by his father that the exercise of comital authority must be closely linked to the doing of justice. Such laymen needed an education in the law, so that they could judge disputes, like the suit between two religious houses settled in Count Geoffrey's presence 'in Angers ... in an audience of many laymen and clerics'.[107] Other earlier twelfth-century texts also imply that the hearing of pleas and acquaintance with different methods of legal procedure formed an essential part of the education of an aristocratic layman, although none is quite so evocative as an example from the neighbouring county of Poitou where, at the age of five, the young son of the duke of Aquitaine accompanied his tutor to watch a judicial duel held just outside the city of Poitiers.[108]

Judicial duels are mentioned in a number of documents issued for Henry II's 'continental empire' at different stages of his career. In the year 1150 × 51 his concessions to the citizens of Rouen included a clause relating to the conduct of judicial duels in the city.[109] After Henry succeeded to Stephen as king in England there is a further scattering of references to the duel as a current method of proof in documents relating to Normandy, Maine, and Anjou and Poitou. Particularly important is the reservation inserted in a grant to the monastery of La Couture in Maine that, if a dispute had to be resolved by duel or ordeal (*bellum sive judicium*), it should be conducted 'in the presence of my bailiffs' (*coram baillivis*

---

[105] Warren, *Henry II*, pp. 360 and 361, citing 'the most renowned of legal historians', Maitland, *History of English Law*, ii, p. 673.

[106] J. Holt, 'Ricardus rex Anglorum et dux Normannorum', in *Magna Carta and Medieval Government* (London 1985), pp. 67–83 (especially pp. 82–3); Gillingham, 'Conquering kings: some twelfth-century reflections on Henry II and Richard I', in *Richard Coeur de Lion*, pp. 106–18.

[107] Martindale, ' "His special friend"?', pp. 56–7, n. 84.

[108] He was the future father of Eleanor of Aquitaine, Henry of Anjou's wife, Martindale, ibid. n. 86; and cf. the evidence from the earliest version of the *Roman d'Alexandre*, cited ibid. n. 85.

[109] *Recueil des actes de Henri II concernant les provinces françaises et les affaires de France*, ed. L. Delisle and E. Berger, 3 vols (Chartes et diplômes publiés par les soins de l'Académie des Inscriptions et Belles-Lettres, 1909–27), i, no. XIV – none of the citizens was to be impleaded outside Rouen, *nisi ante ducem Normannorum*, and none of them was to be obliged to fight a duel against a hired champion – *nullus eorum duellum faciat contra aliquem qui sit pugil conducticius*; cf. Bartlett, *Fire and Water*, pp. 53–69.

meis).[110] The records of the settlement in the 1180s of disputes between two of the most prominent religious establishments of the Loire region and two powerful laymen are even more important for their detailed regulation of problems of jurisdiction and the profits of justice which arose when a judicial duel was waged and fought.

The first of these took the form of a *concordia* arranged in King Henry's presence between the abbess and nuns of Fontevraud and the lord of Montsoreau: its terms made a careful distinction between a duel fought over 'chattels and possessions' (*duellum super catallis et possessionibus et quibuscumque rebus*), and one which might incur punishments of death or mutilation (*si fuerit duellum tale unde contingat hominem destrui, vel quocumque modo detruncari*). In the second case the lord of Montsoreau was always to have 'justice of execution of the body and mutilation of limbs' (*justicia destructionis corporis et membrorum*): the nuns' jurisdiction in such an essentially secular matter depended on whether or not the men involved in the duel lived on land belonging to Fontevraud.[111] An agreement concluded between the count of Vendôme and the abbey of la Trinité in Henry's presence contains similar careful distinctions; but there, if a duel took place between the men of the abbey's bourg 'everything will belong to the abbot' (*totum ad abbatem pertinebit*), while on the other hand, if one of the combatants were a stranger, 'the duel will be in Borchard's [i.e. the secular] court' (*in curia Borchardi duellum fuerit*).[112] The illustrious group of witnesses to the Fontevraud agreement conveys a strong impression that these judicial issues had great significance. Those present 'in my court' at Chinon included the king's two legitimate sons, 'Richard count of Poitou and Geoffrey count of Brittany', but also his bastard 'Geoffrey the chancellor', and the count of Vendôme, together with secular regional officials, like the seneschals of Anjou and Normandy, as well as the bishop of Angers, two English archdeacons and numerous others.[113]

A charter issued independently by Eleanor of Aquitaine while she was still queen of the French also dealt with problems of a conflict of jurisdiction which included the employment of the duel as a method of legal proof. The ever-litigious monks of la Trinité de Vendôme claimed that the queen's secular officials (*servientes seu ministeriales nostri*) had obliged the monks' men on their island-priory of Saint-Georges d'Oléron to go to the duel or to the ordeal of hot water, and this was regarded as one of the 'evil customs' which both Eleanor and her then husband

---

[110] *Recueil des actes de Henri II*, ii, no. DLXXX (at Rouen, undated, probably 1172 × 1173 or 1182): this was the result of an inquisition apparently made in Henry's presence in Rouen. Cf. ibid., no. DXXXII (confirmation *c*.1172 × 1178 of an 1122 charter of King Henry I); no. DCLXXV (*c*.1185 × 1188); for Saint-Evroult (although pronounced suspect) ibid., no. DXIII (dated to *c*.1172 × 1178).

[111] Ibid., no. DCXVIII (although undated this can be attributed to the year 1182 by comparison with an episcopal charter subscribed by the same witnesses).

[112] Ibid., no. DCXLVIII: when one of the abbey's men was defeated in a case involving mutilation or death, the count got *iusticia*: the abbot kept the profits if neither capital nor corporal punishment were involved.

[113] See p. 121, above.

King Louis VII, at the request of three bishops, abolished 'publicly' in the palace at Poitiers in the year 1146.[114] Surviving documents issued in the name of Eleanor's paternal ancestors prove that the duel had indeed been employed as a method of judicial proof in their duchy of Aquitaine; and, where references are found during the course of the twelfth century to 'royal' or 'comital' *ius*, in this huge region, it seems likely that control and conduct of the duel would have been one of the components of that *ius*, even if the different elements were not specifically listed. A comprehensive confirmation granted by Henry II on St Lucy's Day 1156 of the privileges granted by Queen Eleanor's ancestors to the abbey of la Sauve-Majeure and its *salvitas* in the Bordelais is a case in point.[115] Altogether, as is shown by even a brief survey of the surviving material for these regions, it seems clear that throughout the counties and duchies which eventually composed the 'Angevin empire' the judicial duel was virtually ubiquitous as a method of proof for the settlement of disputes and the resolution of more serious criminal affairs. There is no reason to suppose that conditions which characterised the administration of justice before the 1150s were transformed by Henry II's succession to the English throne in 1154.[116]

The few surviving rolls of the Norman Exchequer supply the only information of a quantitative nature on the occurrence of duels for any region of these Angevin-ruled territories: the information which these yield provides a useful background for the rather heterogeneous material to be considered last of all. In fact only two Exchequer Rolls for Normandy have survived for Henry II's reign (for 1180 and 1184 – the second is fragmentary), two for Richard's (1195 and 1198), one for John's (1202–3, also fragmentary). Modern historians have understandably used these above all to investigate the economic and military resources available to the Norman dukes during a period of mounting crisis, in particular after King Richard's release from captivity in Germany, and just before John's disastrous loss of the duchy in 1204.[117]

---

[114] Eleanor's charter survives in original at Blois (Archives Départementales du Loir-et-Cher), ed. Giry, *Etablissements de Rouen*, Documents VI, pp. 72–3 (the place/date is taken from her husband's grant which replicates the contents of hers); cf. J.-M.Carabasse, 'Le duel judiciaire dans les coutumes méridionales', *Annales du Midi*, lxxxvii (1975), 382–403.

[115] Giry, *Etablissements*, no. XXV; cf. Ourliac, 'Les sauvetés du Comminges, Etudes et documents sur les villages fondés par les Hospitaliers dans la région des côteaux Commingeois', in *Etudes d'histoire du droit médiéval*, esp. pp. 31–40, 46–61, 98.

[116] Boussard, *Le comté d'Anjou sous Henri Plantagenêt et ses fils*, pp. 140–9, 152 (duel 'la seule ordalie qui semble rester en vigueur dans la seconde moitié du XIIe siècle'), p. 190; Martindale, ' "His special friend"?', pp. 46–51, but suggesting that in Poitou/Aquitaine before 1137 duels were normally only employed if peaceful methods had failed; Barthélemy, above n. 14; and, although chiefly later in date, G. Guyon, 'La procédure du duel judiciaire dans l'ancien droit coutumier Bordelais', *Mélanges Roger Aubenas, Recueil de Mémoires et Travaux publié par la Société d'Histoire du Droit et des Institutions des Anciens Pays de Droit Ecrit*, ix (1974), pp. 384–409.

[117] *Magni Rotuli Scaccarii Normannie sub Regibus Anglie*, 2 vols, ed. T. Stapleton (London 1840–44), Powicke, *Loss of Normandy*, pp. 5–7; Holt, 'Ricardus rex', pp. 73–7; V. Moss, 'Normandy and England in 1180: the Pipe Roll evidence', in D. Bates and A. Curry, eds, *England and Normandy in the Middle Ages* (London 1994), pp. 185–95; idem, 'The Norman Exchequer Rolls of King John', in Church, ed., *King John*, pp. 101–16; N. Barratt, 'The revenues of John and Philip Augustus revisited', in Church, ed., *King John*, pp. 75–99.

Between law and politics 145

As in the English kingdom, the administration of justice produced its own revenues and incurred its own expenses, so the Norman rolls, too, can be used in the course of an investigation like the present one. Indeed, two references from Richard's reign illustrate exceptionally well the way in which the judicial procedure of the duel was bound up with the exercise of secular power at the highest level. On the first occasion, expenses of £11 11d. were noted on the 1195 roll for work carried out on the bridge over the River Orne, on the fortifications of the castle, as well as for roofing the 'hall' and 'for fencing the field for holding a/the duel' (*et campo hordando ad duellum tenendum*). That was not simply a record of routine administrative repairs, since this expenditure was specifically authorised by the king's writ.[118] Then in 1198 the accounts for Vaudreuil recorded the cost (£30) of taking the king's champions to the Ile d'Andély 'against the king of France' (*In costamento campionum Regis qui fuerunt ducti in Insulam de Andele contra Regem Francie. xxx. li. per brevem regis*). Like King John's plans a few years later for the Poitevin barons, nothing came of this attempt to resolve political and territorial disputes between King Richard and the Capetian King Philip Augustus by means of a judicial duel; but this entry from the Norman rolls surely proves that there was a precedent for the 1201 proposals – and furthermore that those proposals were certainly not innovative.[119]

Below this level of 'high politics' there are numerous references to duels, although unfortunately some are entered so tersely that is not always clear why payment was being made; but, as in England, punitive fines imposed for 'badly held' duels are quite explicit.[120] Entries associated with combat in non-ducal courts raise questions which cannnot be pursued here; but the most intriguing of these suggests that the ducal profits of justice from such cases could be considerable: the 114 individuals (clergy as well as laity, and one woman) 'who were present by night at a duel at Lisieux' were listed as being individually amerced for considerable sums, rising to £50.[121] On the 1180 roll a duel in the court of the count of Evreux is mentioned, and there are further references to duel(s) 'in the court of the count of Meulan'.[122] Individuals paid *pro duello*, to have a 'record' of a duel, but also in considerable numbers *pro concordia duelli*.[123] Twenty-seven references to the 'peaceful settlement of a duel' occur in the 1180 roll but, despite the Powicke's impression that 'the duel ... occurs less frequently in the exchequer rolls after 1180', there are still nineteen explicit references *pro concordia duelli* in the roll of the last year of

---

[118] *Rotuli Scaccarii Normannie*, i, p. 210 (cf. introd, p. clvii).

[119] Ibid., ii, pp. 481; 332 (another reference to payment made *pro campione adducto in curia Regis*); Powicke, pp. 357–8; for the significance of Andély during 1197–8, Gillingham, *Richard I*, pp. 301–20.

[120] *Wachel de Ferrariis debet c.li.pro duello latrocinio male servato in curia sua . . . de Sabriolo*; [gap] . . . *l li pro duello de combustione male servato in curia sua*, *Rotuli Scaccarii Normannie*, i, p. 123; cf. p. 109 (from the 1184 roll).

[121] This is the number of names entered on both the 1180 and 1184 rolls, ibid., i, pp. 87, 89, 95, 103, 122, 265. The context and details of this clandestine-sounding duel would surely repay further study.

[122] Ibid., i, pp. 76, 147, 157 and 162 (a duel at Fécamp – it is unclear whether this was in a non-ducal court), p. 208; ii, pp. 432, 457, 482, 486, 491, 555.

[123] For the 'record' of a duel, ibid., i, pp. 25, 54–5, 76, 88, 97 (twice), 120, 267; ii, pp. 404, 480. For *concordia*, see next note.

Richard's reign – in addition to those entries which, from references to payments for records, show that a duel had actually taken place.[124] Admittedly these rolls do reveal that by the end of Richard's reign considerable sums were being paid in order to have a dispute settled by a jury; and furthermore the future King John, as count of Mortain, paid £50 to 'have the assizes'. Such entries prove the reception in the duchy of new methods of proof; but, as this brief survey has suggested, it would be misleading to suppose that the existence of new proofs automatically meant that the duel and other older, 'testing' methods of proof were being comprehensively swept away by a tide of 'rational' procedure.[125]

In Normandy, as in the English kingdom, duels remained a current method of proof in legal proceedings under all the Angevin rulers. For Angevin-ruled territories beyond Normandy there is no means of assessing the frequency with which judicial duels were fought either in the Angevin lands which made up Henry's patrimony, or in Queen Eleanor's Aquitanian inheritance. Nevertheless the '*membra disiecta*' of those territories of the eleventh and earlier twelfth centuries show that employment of the duel had been widespread – even though not frequent – and that it was normally linked to the exercise of comital power, as it continued to be when these territories were amalgamated under Angevin authority. Eleanor's charter regulating the intervention of her officials in the affairs of the monastery of la Trinité de Vendôme provides a link between the part played by the judicial duel in the territories ruled by her ancestors before 1137 and then by her two husbands. It also establishes proof for continuity of practice which allows it to be compared to Henry of Anjou's concessions confirmed to the citizens of Rouen in his duchy of Normandy during the year 1150 × 51.[126]

The texts described collectively by French scholars of the late nineteenth century as *Les Etablissements de Rouen* illustrate better than anything else in this study the fashion in which methods of legal procedure transcended the territorial boundaries which had marked the political divisions of the Angevin empire before 1154. The *Etablissements de Rouen* are especially interesting because they have been preserved in three versions which regulate the conduct of political, economic and judicial affairs of cities and many other urban agglomerations scattered between Normandy and the city of Bayonne on the southernmost frontier of Aquitaine. Henry II and his wife Eleanor, as well as their two sons Richard and John, all made grants of this type, or confirmed and added to those granted previously.[127] The

---

[124] Powicke, p. 92, n. 4; *Rotuli Scaccrii Normannie*, i (from the 1180 roll), pp. 12–13, 15, 22, 34, 36, 42, 54, 58, 63, 86–7, 95, 97; (from the 1184 roll) pp. 199, 122–3; (from the 1195 roll) pp. 162, 212, 238; (from the 1198 roll) ii, pp. 326, 330–2, 345, 346, 386, 396–8, 404, 409, 411, 413; (from the 1202–3 roll) p. 529. This list does not include entries recording payments for *concordia* without any indication of a duel.

[125] E.g. in 1198 £417 7s. was paid by the count of Eu for a jury, ibid., ii, p. 420 (two other refs. on the same page), cf. p. 465; p. 472 for John's payment.

[126] Above, n. 112 ; cf. Giry, *Etablissements de Rouen*, pp. 27–31 (for subsequent confirmations made by Angevin rulers to the bourgeois of Rouen until the Capetian conquest of the duchy).

[127] Giry, *Etablissements*, pp. 10, 48, 51, 67, 271; Martindale, 'Eleanor of Aquitaine: the last years', pp. 162–3.

texts are linguistically interdependent and were drawn up in Latin, French and Occitan: it seems possible that the vernacular was used in a number of cases because the regulations were being laid down for groups of laity rather for religious communities. *Le coutumier d'Oléron* which – in part at least – can be dated back to the time of these Angevins' rule in Aquitaine was also drawn up in the vernacular, and deals at greater length with many of the same issues.[128]

The *Etablissements* state that in judicial matters collective action would be taken by the mayor with his *jurati* (who were expected to be *pares* and would be regarded as such) at a court to be held each week. As far as the duel was concerned, the relevant clauses reveal traces of the overlapping jurisdictions so characteristic of many medieval 'legal systems'. The mayor's court, for instance, initially had jurisdiction over disputes to be settled by means of a judicial duel but, once gages were given, the affair was to be remitted to the king's bailiff (*ex quo duellum initum est ad ballivum regis pertinet / car puis batailhe es empreze, au bailiu dou rey apertin*); but unfortunately the details of how the *duellum/batailhe* should be conducted are not described (possibly because the procedure was already well known). Nevertheless the clauses devoted to punishment for theft and homicide, together with the division of chattels and property between the 'ville' and the king, are surely relevant to this topic, since a man defeated in a judicial duel would almost certainly be liable to some form of corporal punishment and to confiscation of goods and property.[129] The Oléron customs supply far more detail and, in particular, make a distinction between disputes in which duels could be fought between champions, such as those concerning inheritance and debt and those which followed accusations of 'murder, theft, forgery, or other great matter which is criminal' which could not be fought by champions but must be fought *cors a cors* (*La bataille emprise par ochison de crim, si cum de murtre, ou de larroncin, de traison, de fausseté, ou d'autre mayor choze qui portet crim . . .*).[130]

Many of the legal and political problems associated with judicial combat under the twelfth-century Angevin rulers are brought together in two further cases from the eastern regions of the duchy of Aquitaine. One of these, dated 1178, preserves an account of a duel which took place, as the court of the viscount of Turenne had judged it should (*per la batailia far que la cortz del vescomte avia jutgada*): it ended with the defeat and death of Aimeri de Saint-Ceré who was the chief protagonist and had been appealed for the seizure of a castle (*castel*), but also for the betrayal (*traicio*) of the viscount, his lord. Some of the salient details are missing, but it is seems that Viscount Raymond of Turenne was exercising jurisdiction conceded to him by the count of Auvergne. The protagonists were all members of the laity, and

---

[128] The name of a man who was prévôt of Oléron in 1184 is mentioned in the text, but so are other identifiable individuals of the thirteenth century, Bémont, *Le coutumier d'Oléron*, pp. 10–12; and on the '*variété de langue d'oïl*' employed for this *coutumier*, pp. 13–15.

[129] Giry, *Etablissements*, pp. 38–42: clause 31 (part cited above in text – this regulation applies only to an individual who wishes to lay a claim *de jurato communie/de jurata de le comunie*); cf. pp. 34, 35, 37.

[130] *Coutumier d'Oléron*, LXVII, cls 124–34 (pp. 78–80, citation at p. 79). Criminal causes and procedure are defined LXVIII–IX, cls 135–47 (pp. 80–3).

the court laid down that Aimeri should fight aganst a knight 'who was his peer in wealth and standing' (*ab cavaler que fos sos pars de riqueza e de grandeza*).[131] The political importance of this charter is that it describes the operation of a lay court in a region where the influence of the counts of Toulouse and Auvergne overlapped, although the position of the English king as duke of Aquitaine was apparently acknowledged; but it also shows how widespread in practice was the range of the judicial duel in the late twelfth century. The late twelfth-century charter granted by the count of Auvergne to the inhabitants of Montferrand, for instance, assumes as a matter of course that a duel would be fought there *en la cor[t] al comte*.[132]

The other dispute (also transcribed in the seventeenth century) provides a rare survival of a 'cause' which brought two important laymen before 'their lord King Henry of the English', 'who assigned a day of battle' for them after the complicated charges had been declared by both sides – in fact two appeals seem to have been made, which greatly complicated the procedure to be followed.[133] The parties were Archembald of Bourbon and his man Peter Blot (who claimed to be Archembald's half-brother as well as his *ligius homo*): the disputed property was the castle of Montaigut which Peter claimed had been taken from him 'in wickedness and malice' (*in scelere et in malitia*) when he was Archembald's ward. Burning and violence occurred immediately before some attempt was made to resolve the dispute by legal means.[134] Eventually the litigants' men spoke together about arranging peace (*de pace facienda*), and the king agreed that this should be made, and *Fuit autem pax coram rege hoc modo* . . . An elaborate agreement about the possession and inheritance of the castle follows.[135]

This neglected charter exemplifies many aspects of medieval lay activity to which Susan Reynolds has drawn attention, and which she has regarded as undervalued in many historical investigations. The unnamed laymen who counselled peace to their superiors and who then took their advice to the powerful King Henry II were engaged in collective activity which must have embodied the values of their society – and its priorities. At the same time this remarkable charter also illustrates some of the dangers of reading historical developments backwards from the standpoint of later clearcut national and governmental divisions. The witnesses

---

[131] Its regional and genealogical value was recognised by S. Stronski, *La légende amoureuse de Bertran de Born* (Paris 1914): 'Charte limousine sur un duel judiciaire en 1178', pp. 187–90. (The bulk of the charter is in the vernacular, but proem and dating clause are in Latin).

[132] *Quatre chartes de coutumes du bas-pays d'Auvergne dont trois en langue d'oc*, ed. P. Porteau (Publications de la Faculté des Lettres de l'Université de Clermont), Gap 1943: issued by *Guillhelmes, lo coms de Clarmont, e sa maires* . . . Charte de Montferrand, cl. 20, p. 10 – dated *ante 1199*; cf. also pp. 29, 49, 66 for similar thirteenth-century regulations.

[133] This important charter is not included in Delisle and Berger's collection of Henry II's charters, which probably accounts for its neglect. The only complete surviving edition of it is in the 2nd edn of the *Veterum aliquot scriptorum* . . . *Spicilegium*, ed. L. d'Achéry (Paris 1723), iii, cols 549–50. Pressure of space made it impossible to edit it here as I had originally hoped to do.

[134] Everything was burnt *excepta turre*, ibid. The castle is possibly Montaigu-le-Blin (dép. Allier).

[135] Ibid. Peter renounced his rights *libere et sine querela* and was granted half the *castellania* (which he released in return for the grant of 7000s for seven years).

Between law and politics 149

and guarantors of this 'peace' included not only the king and queen and their son Richard *dux Aquitaniae*, regional laity including the count of Auvergne, but probably also the constable of Normandy, and members of the highest Norman clergy.[136] When this episode is compared with other cases considered earlier, it can be seen how the secular aristocracy of the sprawling Angevin empire was linked by many common attitudes and values, whether these were manifested as convictions about equality, or the need for opportunities to 'defend oneself' by combat against accusations of wrong-doing, or perceived wrong like dispossession or disinheritance. Reactions were apparently similar whether they touched individuals in England, Normandy, Poitou or the Auvergne, and at this stage, indeed 'there was much less difference in social and political organization – not least in its collective manifestations – between different parts of western Europe than seems to be generally thought'.[137]

[136] Ibid. Apart from members of the Angevin dynasty there are twenty-five *videntes et audientes*.
[137] Above, n. 31.

Local custom in the early common law

Paul Brand

Most legal historians would date the emergence of a recognizable English 'Common Law' to the last quarter of the twelfth century. It was during this period that King Henry II and his advisers created the first of a new type of royal court in England: a court where decisions were made by a small group of full-time (and later fully professional) justices appointed by the king, which held virtually continuous sessions over periods of several weeks or months, which exercised a national jurisdiction and whose decisions were recorded in writing. These courts soon began to develop and apply their own set of procedures and substantive rules, a 'law and custom of England', that were common to all the king's free subjects and (for some purposes at least) all of the king's subjects irrespective of their personal status: a development that marks England off from the other countries of Western Europe. Yet legal historians have also long known, in general terms at least, that the early common law courts were not invariably hostile to the continued application and enforcement of various forms of local custom that either supplemented or were at direct variance with the general rules of the common law. This essay attempts to explore in a little more detail just how far that acceptance went.

In the 1299 Cambridgeshire eyre Christine, the widow of Walter the son of William of Pelham, and her second husband, Hubert la Veille, brought an action, claiming her dower share of lands which had belonged to her late husband, against Henry Chamberlain, the guardian of her late husband's lands and of his heir. The pleadings in this case are recorded both in an enrolment, the formal record of proceedings before the eyre justices, and in two contemporary, but unofficial, law reports.[1] Christine's claim was to a half of two acres of arable, one acre of meadow and a rent of fifty-four shillings and thirty capons at Cottenham. In respect of one-third of this holding, Henry pleaded that it was in the tenure of Alice, the widow of Walter's father, and that Walter had never been in seisin of it during the marriage

---

[1] The enrolment is PRO JUST 1/96, m. 10d. The reports are to be found in BL MSS. Additional 31826, f. 156r (as *Alice de la Chambre v. Henry de la Chambre*) (A) and Harley 493A, ff. 214r–215r (as *A lady v. B.*) (H).

Local custom in the early common law 151

and thus could not have endowed Christine with any share in it. This was denied by Hubert and Christine and the issue sent for trial by a jury.[2] In respect of the remaining two-thirds of the holding, Henry's defence was that Christine was only entitled to the standard one-third of the holding as her dower, and not to the one half they were claiming. He also claimed that he had always been prepared to hand over that share, had Christine been willing to accept it. In response, Hubert and Christine said that the land was held in socage and that the custom of the county (*consuetudo istius comitatus*) was that all widows were entitled to a half share of lands held by this tenure as their dower.[3] Henry, however, insisted that 'common dower' in general usage, and as confirmed by Magna Carta, was a one-third share. Christine could only be entitled to more if she could prove that other widows had been endowed of a half of these particular tenements in the past. By implication at least, he was denying that the claimants could simply base their claim on any alleged general local county custom. He went on to deny that these tenements had in the past followed any contrary custom, citing the instances of Alice, the widow of her husband's father (already mentioned as holding one-third of the holding), and of Joan, the widow of Walter's brother Peter, who had also only received one-third of her late husband's holding in dower. One of the reports indicates that the initial response of counsel for the widow (Beaufou) persisted with his claim based on county custom. He argued that the general county custom could not be destroyed by the negligence of other widows in failing to claim their proper customary entitlement in respect of this holding or by their willingness to accept less than that entitlement.[4] Neither reports nor enrolment explain the reasons for his subsequent abandonment of this line of argument and of his initial reliance on the general custom of the county. The most likely explanation seems to be the perceived (but unrecorded) reactions of the justices hearing the case. It left Beaufou with a difficulty, as the widows of previous tenants had evidently in practice received less than a half of their husband's lands in dower. His first response was the ingenious one of asserting that, even if they had received only one-third, this had been by way of satisfaction for their claim to a half.[5] The justices seem to have been minded to allow this plea, though counsel for the guardian argued that it ought only to be allowed if the claimants could show judgments of the king's court in respect of this same tenement, allowing the widows their claim to a half, even if they had then

---

[2] Neither of the reports mentions this preliminary plea.
[3] One of the reports suggests that the custom was not just the custom of Cambridgeshire but also that of the two neighbouring counties of Norfolk and Suffolk: 'par la resun qe le usage est tel en ceste cunte de Cauntebr' cum est aylure en acun pays cum en Norff' e en Suff' de tenemenz tenuz en socage' (A).
[4] '*Beaufo*. Coment qe par aventure celes dames qe vous avez [nomez] eussent la terce partie en dowere saunz plus par negligence ou qe eles sei agrerunt de taunt pur ceo ne ensut il mye qe les autres dames qe solum les usages del counte dreit ount a demander la moyte seyent de lur demande barrees, par qei nous demandom jugement' (H).
[5] '*Beaufou*. Que une tel dame fut dowe de le tierz en nun de la meyte, prest etc.' (A); '*Beaufo*. M, C. e A. furent dowes de la tierce partie de cels tenemenz en noun de moyte, prest etc.' (H).

accepted less.⁶ Eventually, however, the claimants were allowed to assert that the two widows had been endowed (at marriage) with half the said tenements and that the dower they had subsequently been assigned was as that half. They joined issue with the guardian on the truth of this assertion.⁷

Roger de Beaufou, the serjeant who acted for the claimants in this case, clearly did not think it beyond the bounds of possibility to make a successful claim to dower in excess of that allowed at common law on the basis of the custom of a specific county. He may well have known of relatively recent dower cases from two neighbouring counties which might well have suggested this. In 1290 Wynessia, the widow of John of 'Riveshale', had claimed a moiety of a very substantial holding at Hepworth and nine other places in Suffolk against the abbot of Bury St Edmund's in the Common Bench.⁸ The abbot had responded by stating that he always had been ready to hand over the standard one-third of the holding to her. Wynessia had insisted on her half on the grounds that the land was held in socage and so she was entitled to a half share as dower, 'as is the practice and custom in the said parts' (*sicut mos et consuetudo est in partibus predictis*). It is not absolutely clear whether or not she was referring to the custom of the county. She might have been referring to a smaller (or indeed larger) area. But what is clear is that neither the abbot or his counsel nor the justices pressed her to provide evidence that the custom had applied in the past to this particular holding. Although the jury verdict given in the case in 1293 indicates that in the end it was the past history of this particular holding that caused the rejection of her claim, this was for a rather different reason. The jury found that the land was held by serjeanty tenure, not socage, and so the general custom relating to socage lands was not applicable to it. In another case heard in the same court in 1295 Margery, the widow of Alan Colyn, had claimed half of a substantial holding in Little Dunham and thirteen other Norfolk villages as her dower against master Hugh of Palgrave.⁹ Master Hugh had resisted the claim on the grounds that she was entitled only to the common law one-third. It emerged that much of the land concerned had been acquired by Alan from tenants who had held it by knight service. He had, however, evidently acquired it by subinfeudation and to hold it of his grantors in socage. Under these circumstances it was obviously impossible for Margery to rely on the prior history of the holdings to support her claim. She relied instead on the custom of the county (*consuetudo patrie illius*) and insisted that it applied as much to newly acquired (and subinfeudated) lands as to lands traditionally held in socage. The case was adjourned for judgment and none is recorded. The difficulty seems to have been over the applicability of the custom to land which had only just become socage land. It

---

⁶ '*Scoter*. Si les dames eussent recoveryes la moyte en noun de dower par gard de la court le Rey e pus les heirs les eussent dowees de meyns qe la moyte en noun de dowere cum moyte ceo serreit alcune chose . . .' (H).

⁷ Some time later the claimants received permission to withdraw from prosecuting their claim. This probably indicates an out of court settlement of the case.

⁸ CP 40/86, m. 234d.

⁹ CP 40/107, m. 132.

Local custom in the early common law 153

presupposes that there was little problem over the applicability of the customary rule allowing half of socage land to be claimed in dower in the case of lands long so held. Behind these particular cases, moreover, there is a much longer history of the widows of socage tenants in Norfolk and Suffolk successfully (and generally without challenge) claiming a half of the lands their husbands had held in socage as dower in the king's courts from the early years of the thirteenth century onwards. These cases indicate that by the end of the thirteenth century there was a long history of the king's courts accepting local county custom in regard to dower. The early rolls, at least, contain no similar claims in respect of lands in Cambridgeshire. This suggests that the alleged custom was less securely based in the past practice of that county and may explain why Beaufou had to abandon his initial tactic of basing the widow's claim on the county custom: not because local county custom was objectionable in principle, but because this particular county custom was not in fact securely based in the well-established custom of this particular county.

It is, however, striking that it is only in a relatively limited area that any kind of local variation on the standard common law dower is to be found: only in Norfolk and Suffolk and in Kent, a county of many other distinctive local customs.[10] Other kinds of county custom at variance with the rules of the common law, or even supplementary to them, seem to be remarkably rare. One other county or even regional custom at variance with the normal rules of the common law is the alleged custom of counties north of the Trent of treating fleeing criminals beheaded by the hue and cry, when captured, as convicted felons (as if they had been hanged or outlawed or had abjured the realm) with the full legal consequences attendant on this. The king became entitled to their goods and chattels and to hold their lands for a year and a day and their lords to have the escheat of those lands and rendered inadmissible any appeal made in respect of the beheading. When this was asserted as the general custom of these counties in a dower case in the 1292 Westmorland eyre, the plaintiffs denied that the custom had ever received appropriate validation from the king's court but were nonetheless subsequently non-suited in their claim, which may suggest that it was accepted as valid.[11]

The common law was more clearly tolerant of local variation in instances where county custom supplemented, rather than diverged from, the common law. One obvious example was in the rules followed in each county in relation to the *murdrum* fine. It was county custom, as stated to the justices in eyre at the beginning of their session in the county, that determined whether or not the fine was payable in the county and, if it was, whether it had to be paid for accidental deaths as well as deliberate killings (prior to legislation of 1259) and the precise procedure which had to be followed if the individual hundreds or smaller franchisal units which paid the fine were to escape its payment by proving the dead man had

---

[10] Discussed further below, pp. 157, 159.
[11] JUST 1/985, m. 16. But note that in the 1293–4 Yorkshire eyre it was held that the person beheaded had to have been taken with mainour and to have first confessed his crime: *YB 30 and 31 Edward I*, p. 545.

been 'English'.[12] Here each county did indeed follow its own distinct rules for there was no general 'common' law of *murdrum*. A more dubious example of a county custom supplementing the rules of the common law, but enforced through the common law courts, is provided by the county customs allegedly mandating the allotment of a specific proportion of the movable property of a dead person to his widow and his children.[13] Although there may have been some detailed differences between counties on the exclusion of 'advanced' children and what counted as 'advancement', the general rules seem not in fact to have differed from county to county and hence other writs enforcing the same entitlements were based either on Magna Carta or on a more general 'custom of the realm'.[14] That it was by no means inconceivable for the common law to accept other distinctive, but supplementary, county customs, in this case distinctive county customs from Westmorland, is suggested by a series of cases from the years around 1300. In a replevin case heard in 1290 Idonea de Leyburne attempted to justify a distraint made against her tenant John of Greystoke for a relief of £150, equivalent to the annual value of his land, on the basis that relief so assessed was due from all tenants holding by the distinctive regional tenure of cornage under the custom of the county of Westmorland (*talis est consuetudo patrie de Westmerl'*), unless their lords were willing to accept less.[15] The great advantage to her of doing so was that she did not then have to show that she or any of her ancestors had ever received such a sum and was also able to point to the fact that John received a relief so calculated from his own tenants. However, the issue she was eventually driven to accepting was that proffered by John, who offered to prove that his ancestors had in fact always simply paid double the cornage rent. Hugh of Moulton was no more successful eleven years later when he too tried to rely on Westmorland county custom (*consuetudo in comitatu predicto*) when making a similar avowry for relief on his tenant, Eustace de Berewys, though here what Eustace denied was that his father had ever paid cornage.[16] In another Westmorland case relating to cornage tenure the following year the abbot of Shap tried to justify the seizure and appropriation of two horses and the corn they had been carrying under local (county) custom in relation to cornage tenure (*secundum consuetudinem patrie in hujusmodi tenuris*

---

[12] F. C. Hamil, 'The Presentment of Englishry and the Murder Fine', *Speculum*, xii (1937), 285–98; Paul Brand, *The Contribution of the Period of Baronial Reform (1258–1267) to the Development of the Common Law in England* (unpublished Oxford D. Phil thesis (1974)), pp. 246–60.

[13] For ordinary actions of detinue of chattels claiming a fixed proportion of the goods of the deceased for his widow and/or children under county custom see JUST 1/375, m. 6d (and CP 40/98, m. 62d) (Kent); CP 40/143, m. 88 (Lincolnshire); YB 39 E III, f. 6 and possibly CP 40/110, m. 54d (Somerset) and CP 40/113, m. 125d (Hampshire). For special actions claiming such shares under county custom see CP 40/258, m. 403d (Yorkshire); *Reg. Omn. Brev.*, f. 142b (Berkshire) and cases citing the custom of Northumberland, Yorkshire and Kent cited by Robert C. Palmer in *English Law in the Age of the Black Death* (Chapel Hill, 1993), p. 93.

[14] F. Pollock and F. W. Maitland, *A History of English Law*, ii, pp. 348–56; Palmer, *English Law in the Age of the Black Death*, p. 93.

[15] CP 40/86, m. 84d (and reported in BL MS. Additional 37657, ff. 60r–v).

[16] CP 40/135, m. 164d. There are also a number of reports of this case.

Local custom in the early common law 155

usitatam) on the grounds that they had been carrying a load of corn grown on his tenant's land and were going to a mill other than the abbot's own, thereby evading the mill-toll. The case was, however, adjourned for judgement without any definite decision on the validity of this alleged custom, and none is recorded.[17]

Counties were only the largest of the various different kinds of jurisdictional or geographical unit which litigants claimed (and on occasion the courts accepted) as possessing their own distinctive local customs, sometimes in opposition to the rules of the common law, sometimes by way of supplement to them. Even if we look at them as well, however, there is surprisingly little evidence of variant local custom being accepted and enforced by the courts. Other areas whose distinctive custom was asserted in litigation included at least one hundred,[18] several Lincolnshire sokes[19] and Windsor forest.[20] They also included a number of honours,[21] at least one barony[22] and part or the whole of other lordships.[23] In Kent, the practice of partible inheritance between males (as opposed to the normal common law rule of primogeniture among males) in the case of gavelkind tenements was the common custom of the county and can be shown to have been regularly applied and enforced in the common law courts from the time of the earliest surviving plea rolls without the younger sons being required to specifically prove the custom or its prior application to their holdings.[24] This was not the position anywhere else. Elsewhere, younger

---

[17] CP 40/144, m. 94. The case is reported in *YB 30 and 31 Edward I*, pp. 65–9 and in several other MSS.

[18] The only examples I have noted relate to the exceptional Herefordshire border hundred of Archenfield which in 1220 claimed a local custom allowing a killer to compound with the kin of his victim (*CRR*, ix, no. 201) and in 1255 successfully claimed there was no age of majority in respect of land claims within the hundred but that litigation could be brought by and against litigants at any age (JUST 1/300C, m. 8).

[19] For an unsuccessful claim relating to the alleged inheritance customs of the soke of Horncastle in Lincolnshire see *The Earliest English Law Reports, vol. II*, ed. P. Brand (Selden Society, vol. 112), pp. 215–16 (1285.8); for an uncontested assertion relating to the inheritance custom of the soke of Gayton in Lincolnshire see CP 40/105, m. 38d (and CP 40/132, m. 168d) and for a contested claim about inheritance customs within the soke of Grantham in Lincolnshire see CP 40/160, m. 132.

[20] For its allegedly distinctive inheritance custom in respect of female inheritance see CP 40/81, m. 81d.

[21] For the allegedly distinctive custom of the socage lands of the honour of Brittany (in Lincolnshire) with respect to the dower entitlement of a childless second wife see CP 40/47, m. 105; for an alleged entitlement to heriot enjoyed by all tenants of the honour of Tonbridge see *YB 1 and 2 Edward II*, pp. 65–6.

[22] For the claim of the lady of the Cumberland barony of Gilsland to enjoy a customary right of veto over any attempt by her tenants to approve waste lands within the barony see JUST 1/1294, m. 302 and CP 40/91, m. 302.

[23] For the assertion of a customary seignorial right to the wardship of lands held by socage of Hereford cathedral in 1224 see *CRR*, xi, nos 1436, 2191; to the wardship of similar lands held of the fee of Roger de Mortimer in 1260 see KB 26/169, m. 10; to the wardship of lands within Howdenshire held of the bishop of Durham see JUST 1/1194, m. 3d.

[24] See the remarks of Mablethorpe in a case of 1300 in BL MS. Additional 37657, f. 21r and of Warwick in a case of 1307 in BL MS. Hargrave 375, f. 184v.

sons attempting to secure their portion of an inheritance allegedly partible, had to satisfy a twofold test and to be able to demonstrate both that their particular holding had been divided among males in the past and also to show that it was partible 'as of right'. This dual requirement is already visible in the question put to a jury for its verdict in a case of 1200.[25] It is also clearly spelled out in reports of pleading in cases in 1300 and 1301.[26] The initial impression created by the first of these two requirements is that what we are seeing is the enforcement of a custom accepted and valid only at the level of the smallest of all possible units, the individual tenement. That impression is, however, probably misleading. When we can glimpse how lawyers in pleading or juries in their verdicts interpreted the second of the two requirements, what we seem to see is that 'rightfulness' was commonly, if not invariably, interpreted to mean that the tenement should be part of some wider tenurial or jurisdictional unit where partible inheritance between males was the customary norm. In a number of cases the unit seems to have been the lands belonging to the same fee or lordship in a single village. This may have been the relevant unit for the jury in their verdict in a case heard in 1200, though the reference is unfortunately inadequately specific.[27] It was certainly the relevant unit for the claimants in cases of 1294 and 1301.[28] However, in one of the reports of a 1292 case we find a reference to the usage of the hundred(s) of Flegg in Norfolk and in the plea roll enrolment of the same case to the usage followed in other socage lands belonging to the same fee in six other neighbouring Norfolk villages, in both instances as showing that the lands in dispute were not rightfully partible, indicating a wider frame of reference and a wider jurisdictional unit as having at least potential relevance for this purpose.[29] That we are not really dealing with custom applicable at the level of individual tenements is also shown by the way in which the first requirement was applied. Although some claimants do seem to have tried to show that the tenement concerned had indeed been divided between brothers on each occasion within living memory when it could have been or provided some adequate explanation for its not having been divided that did not call the validity of the custom of partibility into question,[30] other claimants seem not to have attempted to do more than provide evidence of a single occasion when this particular tenement had been divided between brothers, to provide evidence that the wider custom had indeed been applied at least once to the tenement in question.[31]

---

[25] *CRR*, i, 137.

[26] BL MSS. Additional 31826, f. 168r and Additional 37657, f. 21r (reports of case enrolled on CP 40/134, m. 37); BL MSS. Additional 31826, f. 115v and Additional 37657, ff. 135r–v (reports of case enrolled on CP 40/135, m. 60d).

[27] *CRR*, i, 137 (*pares illius carucate*).

[28] CP 40/106, m. 142; CP 40/135, m. 60d.

[29] *YB 20 and 21 Edward I*, pp. 321–9; CP 40/92, m. 36d.

[30] For examples see CP 40/92, m. 36d; CP 40/102, m. 209; CP 40/144, m. 245d.

[31] That this was the sole requirement is made clear by Bereford in a case of 1301: 'Si ceus tenemenz fusent partable si covendreit qe en acun tens usent este partiz qe partable ne peunt il point estre sant acun oure estre partiz e mis en usage, mes useez ne mis en usage ne peunt il estre sant estre mis en fet . . .', BL MS. Additional 31826, f. 115v.

The general picture of an early common law that allowed relatively little local variation from its general rules, whether at the level of distinctive county custom or of the distinctive custom of other, smaller units, does require some qualification. All the evidence suggests that the justices of the king's courts in this period found little difficulty about accepting all kinds of variation from the general rules of the common law in individual towns and cities. Some such customs had the sanction of specific royal approval, but the king's justices never made this a precondition for their acceptance and enforcement. Perhaps more surprising was their readiness to accept a relatively large number of divergent county customs in the case of Kent, or rather, to be more precise, in respect of those tenants who held by gavelkind tenure (the local form of socage tenure) within that county. Widows of gavelkind tenants were entitled to claim, and regularly did claim and receive, one-half, rather than one-third, of the lands held by their late husbands in dower on the basis of county custom alone, without any need to prove that the widows of previous tenants of the specific lands in question had been so endowed. In Kent, however, the widow's exceptionally generous endowment was balanced by exceptionally restrictive rules that deprived the widow of all claim to dower once she remarried or if she bore an illegitimate child.[32] Other distinctive county customs at variance with the standard common law rules included partible inheritance among males,[33] entitlement on the part of a widower to only half his late wife's lands though whether or not she had borne him a child (likewise forfeited on remarriage) and the inheritance, rather than escheat, of lands held by those convicted of felony.[34] A clear acceptance of the distinctiveness of Kentish customs is to be found in the record of the visitation of Kent by the baronial justiciar, Hugh Bigod in 1259. During his session at Canterbury the question arose as to whether land held in gavelkind was subject (like other lands) to escheat for felony. The enrolment that tells us of this notes that an inquiry was made of the sheriff and knights of the county as to what the custom of Kent was in this case (*que sit consuetudo Kancie in tali casu*) and that the reason given for this was an acceptance that the 'laws and customs of Kent differed from the customs and laws of other counties' (*quia leges et consuetudines Kancie diversificantur a consuetudinibus et legibus aliorum comitatuum*).[35] No clear view emerged because the knights of the county were not in agreement on the point (*et est dissensio inter milites comitatus*). This is a little surprising because the later rule (that gavelkind land was not forfeited even in these circumstances) had in fact been stated as early as 1223 by eight lawful knights of the county of Kent summoned to advise the Common Bench on the customs or law of Kent, as had also

---

[32] Forfeiture of dower on bearing a child is mentioned as Kentish custom in a case of 1257 (JUST 1/1186, m. 1) and again in 1288, with the child-bearing being said in the latter case to be proved by the raising of the hue and cry (CP 40/75, m. 6). In an intervening case of 1276, however, Kentish custom was said to be forfeiture on remarriage or on proof of fornication, and that it was not necessary to prove that the widow had borne a child: CP 40/14, m. 21d.
[33] Above, p. 155 and note 24.
[34] See below, pp. 157–8.
[35] JUST 1/873, m. 14d.

the widow's entitlement to her dower from the lands of a husband convicted of felony, the matter actually in dispute in that case.[36] It had also been the 'county' of Kent (probably a group of local knights) who had advised the justices of the 1241 Kent eyre of the widower's entitlement under the 'law and custom of Kent' (*lex et consuetudo Kancie*) to half his wife's lands provided he remained unmarried even in the absence of any children to the marriage, something restated by the county for the justices of the 1263 Kent eyre.[37] By 1300 there had already come to be compiled at least two written statements of the county's customs. The earlier of the two is in Latin and the unique version is recorded on a roll now at Lambeth Palace, to which Du Boulay first drew the attention of scholars.[38] It was probably compiled for submission to the justices of the 1279 Kent eyre with two distinct purposes in mind.[39] The primary one was to serve as a collective claim of 'franchises' on behalf of the county to match and complement the individual claims of franchises which all franchise-holders were now being required to submit to the king's justices as a preliminary to the testing of franchise claims in the quo warranto proceedings, specifically to safeguard their distinctive customs against any possible claims that they had been forfeited for non-claim.[40] The subsidiary purpose was to seek a remedy from the justices for what the county community alleged to be two abuses of recent origin in relation to the presentment of Englishry and the amercement of hundreds by the sheriffs of Kent.[41] The second, and better-known, French text may have been produced for the 1293 Kent eyre, perhaps again in order to ensure that distinctive Kentish customs were not forfeited by failure to register a formal claim to them at the succeeding eyre.[42] Even if there is no convincing evidence that these custumals received any kind of formal approval from the king

---

[36] *CRR*, xi, no. 959 (and see nos 529, 1031).

[37] JUST 1/359, m. 6d; JUST 1/363, m. 30.

[38] Lambeth Roll 2068, m. 7d (as noted in F. R. H. Du Boulay, *The Lordship of Canterbury* (London, 1966), at pp. 144–5).

[39] The document refers back to an abuse whose continuation had been specifically forbidden in the 1271 Kent eyre of Roger of Seaton and his colleagues (as well as in passing to the 1248 eyre of Henry of Bath and his colleagues) and so must be of a later date than that. It also refers to the neglect of that prohibition by subsequent sheriffs other than William of Hever, the sheriff of Kent in 1272–4. It was clearly drawn up for presentation to royal justices and the justices of the following eyre visitation seem the most likely candidates. The date is also suggested by its immediate context, an abbreviated version of a custumal and rental made in 1283–5.

[40] D. W. Sutherland, *Quo Warranto Proceedings in the Reign of Edward I, 1278–1294* (Oxford, 1963), pp. 26–7, 190–3. Hence perhaps some of the the wording of the Lambeth document: 'Communitas comitatus Kanc' clamat habere diversas libertates et usus quibus ceteri comitatus non utuntur. Eadem comitatus clamat habere talem libertatem . . . quare petit dictus comitatus libertates et consuetudines suas predictas sibi allocare . . .'

[41] 'Preterea communitas comitatus illius dicit quod ultra modum contra antiquas consuetudines et leges suas gravantur in hoc . . . quare petit dictus comitatus . . . per domini regis justiciarios de hiis duobus gravaminibus statum illorum reformari.'

[42] *Statutes of the Realm*, i, pp. 223–5. The most recent discussions of the text are those by Felix Hull in 'The Custumal of Kent', *Archaeologia Cantiana*, 72 (1958), 148–59 and idem, 'John de Berwyke and the Consuetudines Kancie', *Archaeologia Cantiana*, 96 (1980), 1–15.

or his justices, they do clearly manifest a strong sense of the distinctiveness of Kentish custom and a strong collective will to ensure their preservation and observance. It remains something of a puzzle why the royal courts proved quite so willing to accept and enforce so much divergent local custom in the case of Kent. The sense of Kentish distinctiveness evidently shared by the inhabitants of the county and expressed most clearly in the two statements of Kentish custom must be part of the explanation. But it may also be that the justices of the common law courts had less difficulty about accepting the divergent customs of a single county than they would have had if there had been many other such counties.

The common law courts were therefore clearly not invincibly hostile to the continuance of local custom. Indeed they were willing on occasion to accept and enforce it. That willingness was at its greatest in the case of cities and boroughs, which in any case dealt with much of their own legal business themselves. But custom also survived at the level of individual counties, both where it supplemented the common law (as in the case of the *murdum* fine) and also where it was at direct variance with it, provided the county community itself gave strong and continuing support to that county custom (as in the case of Kent) or where there was good and continuing evidence for its application (as was the case with partible inheritance among males for socage lands in Norfolk and Suffolk). Even where there was some doubt as to whether it was in reality the 'custom of the county' variant local custom might survive if it could be proved to be the custom of a particular holding (as in the 1299 Cambridgeshire dower case) or the custom of a particular holding and other similar holdings in the area (as with partible inheritance among males outside Kent). The general effect of the 'professionalisation' and centralisation of the legal system was obviously a nationwide standardisation of norms, the development of a 'common law' for England as a whole, but the system evidently remained sufficiently flexible to allow the continuance and enforcement of some local custom both at the county level, and at a much more local level, as well.

'Slaves of the Normans'? Gerald de Barri and regnal solidarity in early thirteenth-century England

John Gillingham

In his *Invectives* Gerald de Barri, writing *c.*1200, declared the English to be 'of all peoples under heaven the most worthless; for they have been subdued by the Normans and reduced by the law of war to perpetual slavery (*in servitutem perpetuam belli iure redactam*). . . . In their own land the English are the slaves of the Normans, and the most worthless of slaves.'[1] Prima facie this opinion, one of Gerald's more famous pronouncements, appears to clash with the view of many modern historians who have thought that although after the Norman Conquest, as Susan Reynolds has put it, 'the sense of two separate peoples of separate descents and customs survived well into the twelfth century', by 1200 there had been a recovery of what she termed 'regnal solidarity'. Indeed she has identified Magna Carta as 'the classic statement of regnal solidarity against the king'. The barons of Magna Carta, we are told, 'spoke – and presumably spoke more or less sincerely – on behalf of the community of the realm'.[2] No doubt, but were they really entitled to do this? If Gerald had meant – as prima facie he seems to have meant – that England in the early thirteenth century was still a deeply divided society, and if he was roughly right in that opinion, then clearly they were not so entitled. If, however, Gerald was either wrong, or meant something else altogether, then we need to explain how it was that as late as 1300 an author such as Robert of Gloucester in the preface to his chronicle, famously the first history of the English to be written in the English language since the ending of the Anglo-Saxon Chronicle, could lament that 'the Normans are still among us' and promise that he will 'hereafter in this book tell of all this woe'.[3]

Robert's contemporary Peter Langtoft said something similar in his commentary on the Norman Conquest. 'Since then the English have lived under foreign rule, in servitude and suffering.'[4] By 'foreign rule' Langtoft might, of course, have meant rule by foreign kings rather than by a Norman landowning class. In the

---

[1] 'In terra sua Normannorum servi sunt Anglici et servi vilissimi', Giraldus Cambrensis, *De invectionibus*, ed. W. S. Davies, *Y Cymmrodor*, 30 (1920), p. 93. For the date at which this part of the work was written see below n. 19. This part is translated in H. E. Butler, *The Autobiography of Giraldus Cambrensis* (London, 1937), pp. 209–10.
[2] S. Reynolds, *Kingdoms and Communities* (Oxford, 1984), pp. 254, 262–8.
[3] *The Metrical Chronicle of Robert of Gloucester*, ed. W. Wright, 2 vols (RS, 1887), lines 55–6.
[4] *The Chronicle of Pierre de Langtoft*, ed. T. Wright, 2 vols (RS, 1866–8), i, 288.

story of St Wulfstan as told in a version of the (slightly earlier) *South English Legendary* the kings seem to be the primary focus of concern. Here the Norman Conquest meant the kingdom fell

> Into the hands of foreigners who had no right to it
> and never afterwards did it return to the rightful heirs.
> Even now our kings are non-native heirs.[5]

But whatever Langtoft and the unknown author of the *Legendary* may have had in mind, there is no doubt that Robert of Gloucester meant more than just rule by foreign kings. According to him, 'the upper class (*heie men*) of the country that descend from them (the Normans), stick to the language that they got from them – for unless a person knows French he is little thought of – but the lower class stick to English and their own language even now'. A few lines later Robert explained that the greater part of the high men of the day were descended from the Normans, and he then waxed fiercely indignant at their hypocrisy: they kneel like lambs in church but 'as soon as they have got up and have turned their belly from the altar, they carry out wolvish deeds, tearing the poor bondmen apart'.[6] One possible line of explanation for Robert of Gloucester's feelings is that offered by Sir Walter Scott in *Ivanhoe* and much more recently by Thorlac Turville-Petre.

> It is quite clear – and indeed it is entirely natural – that a large section of the population regarded the post-Conquest nobility as foreigners holding the English nation in subjection. For very obvious reasons, this view is not one expressed by the rulers themselves, and those for whom the history of England is exclusively the history of the powerful have denied the existence of racial resentment expressing itself in nationalistic terms. Up to the end of the twelfth century the new conquerors were sometimes openly contemptuous of the defeated English, but after the loss of Normandy it was clearly in their interests to see themselves as English. Yet it is hardly to be supposed that those who felt they had lost their inheritance and were still excluded from power had any inclination to make their oppressors Englishmen. Even 250 years after the Conquest, they were still able to represent the French-speaking aristocracy as foreigners who held the English in subjection.[7]

In this context the question is: was Robert of Gloucester giving literary form to resentments which had been continuously felt by 'a large section of the population' ever since 1066? Or to resentments which were being given a more nationalistic

---

[5] Wolston, lines 88–90, from *The Early South-English Legendary*, ed. C. Horstmann (Early English Text Society, 87, 1887), p. 73. Cited and translated in T. Turville-Petre, *England the Nation. Language, Literature, and National Identity, 1290–1340* (Oxford, 1996), p. 18.

[6] *The Metrical Chronicle*, lines, 7,538–43, 7,582–3, 7,606–11; cited and translated in Turville-Petre, *England*, pp. 95–6.

[7] T. Turville-Petre, 'Politics and Poetry in the early Fourteenth Century: The Case of Robert of Manning's *Chronicle*', *Review of English Studies*, NS 39 (1988), 17. It is only fair to point out, however, that since 1988 Thorlac Turville-Petre has modified his views, seeing Robert of Gloucester and Manning as two authors not so much addressing a real situation as 'constructing the nation' by invoking an oversimplified logic of development. Hence their 'division into French-speaking lords and English-speaking commoners is an ideological reconstruction of a much more fluid linguistic situation'. See Turville-Petre, *England the Nation*, 91–103, esp. 97–8.

slant in 1300 than they had possessed in 1200? That Gerald de Barri *c.*1200 envisaged a Norman Yoke of the former type is implied by the association which modern writers often make between his view of the English and his own family background. 'Gerald's pride in his Norman, Marcher ancestry had, as its counterpart, a contempt for the English'.[8] Against this, however, I shall argue that when Gerald wrote contemptuously of the English, he meant, not that society in England was still deeply split between a Norman upper and a native English lower class, but rather that the kings of England had reduced *all* their subjects to a condition of despicable servility. In other words in this essay in honour of the creative historian who invented the serviceable phrase 'regnal solidarity', I suggest that in Gerald's anti-English pronouncement we have another example of a 'statement of regnal solidarity against the king'.[9]

In order to put his views of Normans and English into context, it is necessary to begin with a few more words on the old subject of Gerald's own self-identification. Few opinions are more firmly entrenched than the idea that Gerald was part-Norman and part-Welsh; that he was 'born of Norman-Welsh parents'; that 'he found his place in both Norman and Welsh circles'; that he was 'divided by loyalties of race and blood, Norman and Welsh'.[10] According to Sir John Lloyd, 'For the English as a race he was full of contempt; they were born to slavery . . . the noble Norman first claimed his admiration, and, next in order, the freeborn, fearless Welshman, who spoke his mind unabashed in the presence of kings'.[11] It is not surprising then that we should be told that 'the theme of his descent from "both peoples", Norman and Welsh' should 'run through all his work'.[12] However this is not how this English reader reads Gerald's words. In the first preface to *De principis instructione* (*c.*1195) he described his own descent as 'one part Trojan' and 'three parts English and Norman'.[13] It is a passage frequently cited and generally translated

---

[8] R. Bartlett, *Gerald of Wales 1146–1223* (Oxford, 1982), pp. 14, 92.

[9] For 'regnal solidarity' as a 'most servicable phrase' see R. R. Davies, 'The Peoples of Britain and Ireland, 1100–1400: II Names, Boundaries and Regnal Solidarities' *TRHS*, 6th ser., 5 (1995), 1–20, esp. 9.

[10] For some examples see F. M. Powicke, 'Gerald of Wales' in *The Christian Life in the Middle Ages* (Oxford, 1935), p. 109; C. H. Williams in the introduction to Butler, *The Autobiography of Giraldus*, p. 23; J. Conway Davies, 'Giraldus Cambrensis 1146–1946', *Archaeologia Cambrensis*, 99 (1946–7), 86; 'son of a Norman father and Welsh mother', Michael Richter, *Giraldus Cambrensis The Growth of the Welsh Nation* (Aberystwyth, 1972), p. 2, and in his introduction to Giraldus Cambrensis, *Speculum Duorum*, ed. Y. Lefèvre and R. B. C. Huygens (Cardiff, 1974), pp. xxiv–v; L. Thorpe, *Gerald of Wales, The Journey through Wales and the Description of Wales* (Harmondsworth, 1978), p. 9; B. F. Roberts, *Gerald of Wales* (Cardiff, 1982), p. 9; 'the son of the local Norman lord', H. Pryce, 'Gerald's Journey through Wales', *Journal of Welsh Ecclesiastical History*, 6 (1989), 19.

[11] J. E. Lloyd, *A History of Wales*, 2 vols, (London, 1911), ii, p. 555. The title of one of F. X. Martin's articles is revealing: 'Gerald of Wales, Norman Reporter on Ireland', *Studies*, 58 (1969).

[12] Roberts, *Gerald*, pp. 90–1.

[13] 'Tres etenim naturae partes quanquam ab Anglis et Normannis linea contraxerim originali', *Giraldi Cambrensis Opera*, ed. J. S. Brewer, J. F. Dimock and G. F. Warner (8 vols, RS, 1861–91), vol. 8, p. lviii. This preface is preserved only in *Symbolum Electorum*, a collection of favourite pieces made by Gerald *c.*1199 or after 1203 (for discussion of date see Bartlett, *Gerald*, pp. 218–19 and Richter, *Giraldus Cambrensis*, p. 91).

and interpreted as though the word English were not there.[14] Powicke's version was that 'on his father's side he was a Norman, on his mother's side half a Norman'; for Lewis Thorpe, 'the blood in Gerald's own veins was three quarters Norman'.[15] Clearly it is not only the Welsh who have suppressed the English part of Gerald, presumably in the unspoken, and perhaps unconscious, conviction that Gerald cannot really have associated himself with people he held in contempt.[16]

But the word 'English' is there and at least some attempt ought to be made to explain why it is there. In that same preface to *De principis instructione* Gerald referred to his own upbringing and life as *inter Anglos*.[17] Could this merely mean that, although of Cambro-Norman descent, his political ambitions and his hope of obtaining an English bishopric, had led to him spending his active life amongst the English? Not really, given the fact that towards the end of his *Descriptio Kambrie* he set out the case for both English and Welsh precisely on the grounds that he was descended from both peoples, English and Welsh.[18] Where did the English in his ancestry come from? That the Trojan, i.e. British, i.e. Welsh, came from his mother, Angharad, the daughter of Gerald of Windsor and Nest, is clear. This implies that the Englishness in his family came from his father, William de Barri. Indeed Gerald himself made this explicit in *De invectionibus*. Replying to the archbishop of Canterbury's assertion that he was unsuitable as a bishop in Wales because he was related to many of the magnates of Wales (*pleros Wallie magnates*), he wrote that the archbishop would have spoken the truth had he said that he (Gerald) was kin to all the great men of Wales, on his mother's side to the Welsh princes and on his father's side to the English barons (*Anglicis baronibus*) of the king who held the 'incastellated' coast lands of Wales.[19] Since this was written *c*.1200 – at a time when he was fighting on behalf of the claim of St David's to be the metropolitan church of Wales – this means that even here, in his most pro-Welsh phase, he acknowledged the English side of his family background.[20] This suggests that if William de Barri was – as he probably was – of Norman descent, then he was one of those Normans who had

---

[14] E.g., 'was in fact three-quarters Norman and a quarter Welsh', C. Kightly, *A Mirror of Medieval Wales. Gerald of Wales and his Journey of 1188* (Cardiff, 1988), p. 6. For an exception see the description of his family milieu as 'Anglo-Norman knightly circles of the Welsh March', R. R. Davies, *The Age of Conquest, Wales 1063–1415* (Oxford, 1987), p. 102.

[15] Thorpe, *The Journey*, p. 10; Powicke, 'Gerald', p. 109.

[16] In Lloyd's case the suppression is particularly clear, *History of Wales*, ii, p. 555, esp. n. 94.

[17] *Giraldi Opera*, vol. 8, p. lviii.

[18] 'Sed quoniam pro Anglis hactenus diligenter modum et exquisite disseruimus, sicut autem ex utraque gente originem duximus, sic aeque pro utraque disputandum ratio dictat, ad Kambros denuo, in calce libelli, stilum vertamus, eosque de arte rebellandi breviter sed tamen efficaciter instruamus.' *Giraldi Opera*, vol. 6, p. 226; Thorpe, *The Journey*, p. 273.

[19] *De invectionibus*, ed. Davies, p. 86; translation in Butler, *Autobiography*, p. 172. According to Gerald's own later statement this was written at the curia and in the first year of his suit at Rome. This, as Richter has shown, means 1200, Giraldus Cambrensis, *Speculum Duorum*, p. xx.

[20] Y. Wada, 'Gerald on Gerald: Self-Presentation by Giraldus Cambrensis', *ANS*, 20 (1997–8), 242, adduces manuscript evidence to show just how far the process of repackaging himself as a Welshman went. By 1200 at any rate the repackaging had not gone so far as a denial of the English part of his ancestry.

become English by the mid-twelfth century.[21] Taken as a whole the evidence indicates that Gerald acknowledged there was some Norman in his ancestry, but evidently felt he was now more English than Norman. Thus in the speech he put into the mouth of his own maternal uncle, Maurice FitzGerald, he expressed the bind in which the colonists in Ireland in the 1170s found themselves caught in famous, if commonly mistranslated, words. 'Just as we are English to the Irish, so we are Irish to the English.'[22] Schematically then we might think of Gerald's grandfather Odo as Norman, his father, William, as Anglo-Norman and he himself as Anglo-Welsh.

Moreover it is noticeable that when Gerald was at his least English, it was his Frenchness rather than his Normanness that he emphasised. In a speech put into the mouth of Robert FitzStephen, another of Nest's children – though by a different partner (Stephen constable of Cardigan) – Gerald has Robert refer to his Gallo-Trojan, i.e. his Franco-Welsh, descent.[23] In Letter 31 in the *Symbolum electorum* he accused the bishop of St David's, Peter de Leia, of being two-handed (*ambidexter*) in his persecution of him. 'To the French he made me a Welshman and an enemy of the kingdom, but to the Welsh he declared me to be French and their mortal foe in all things.'[24] Here the cleft stick in which he was caught was French–Welsh, not Norman–Welsh. Is this a pedantic distinction? It would be if in Gerald's eyes Normans and French were virtually identical. But this is far from being the case. On the one hand his feelings towards the Normans of his own day were far from friendly, and on the other – as Robert Bartlett has emphasised – he represented a Francophilia not uncommon among twelfth-century scholars.[25] It was the French whom he praised for courage, nobility, intelligence and boldness of speech; it was from the French that he said his kindred obtained their skill in the use of arms.[26] By contrast the Normans – unlike the English – are notable by their total absence from his earliest extant work, the *Topographia Hibernica*, and when they first appear in the *Conquest of Ireland* he criticises them for their arrogance, loquacity

---

[21] Gerald was, as Ifor Rowlands put it, 'uncharacteristically reticent', on the subject of William's father, Odo, I. W. Rowlands, 'The Making of the March: Aspects of the Norman Settlement in Dyfed; *ANS*, 3 (1980–1), 145. On the mid-twelfth-century English see 'Henry of Huntingdon and the Twelfth-Century Revival of the English Nation' in J. Gillingham, *The English in the Twelfth Century* (Woodbridge, 2000) and the literature cited there, especially I. Short, '*Tam Angli quam Franci*: Self-definition in Anglo-Norman England', *ANS*, 18 (1995), 153–75.

[22] *Expugnatio Hibernica*, ed. and trans. A. B. Scott and F. X. Martin (Dublin, 1978), p. 80.

[23] And he used the same pairing – *a Troianis . . . a Gallis* – when referring to the ancestry of his own kindred in Ireland, *Expugnatio Hibernica*, pp. 48, 156. Although the two are obviously related, the distinction between ancestry and present identity should be kept in mind; see my 'The English Invasion of Ireland' reprinted in Gillingham, *The English in the Twelfth Century*.

[24] *Symbolum Electorum*, *Opera*, vol. 1, p. 332; translation taken from Bartlett, *Gerald*, pp. 19–20. It may be that in a letter addressed to the canons of St David's he chose to use the word 'French' as this was the usual Welsh term for the twelfth-century invaders of Wales. Translated as 'too much of a Norman for the Welsh and too much of a Welshman for the Normans' in J. Davies, *A History of Wales* (Harmondsworth, 1990), p. 131. When writing the *Conquest of Ireland* for the royal court the cleft stick was English–Irish.

[25] Bartlett, *Gerald*, pp. 12, 94–5.

[26] *Expugnatio*, pp. 48, 156; *Descriptio*, *Opera*, vol. 6, p. 193.

'Slaves of the Normans'?   165

and boastfulness.[27] This was written in the late 1180s. A few years later in his *Vita Galfridi* he returned to the theme of Norman arrogance and boastful verbosity (*arrogantia pariter et Normannicae verbositatis jactantia*). Since this was in the context of an onslaught on the Norman William Longchamp's character, as well as on his Latin grammar, it is not surprising that he also accused the Normans of a vice which he identified as once characteristic of the French, but now specific to the Normans: homosexuality.[28] All in all it is not immediately obvious that when he wrote of the English as 'slaves of the Normans', he was thinking of the Normans as admirable and noble.

What then did he have in mind when he used the word 'Norman' in the context of English servitude? Did he mean the landowning class of Norman descent, or just the kings? The assumption that he meant Norman lords in general is facilitated by the habit of modern historians – such as myself – of referring to the kings as Angevins. This was not, however, Gerald's usage. He writes only *rex Anglorum* or *reges Anglorum Normannica de stirpe* or *reges Normannorum*. By 1216–17 there had been on his count six or seven Norman kings.[29] Despite his reference to the alleged descent of the current kings from a demon countess of Anjou, they were, in his eyes, 'the Norman tyrants'.[30] He never mentioned Angevin kings, and only once, I think, referred to Angevins. This is in chapter 8 of Book II of the *Descriptio Kambrie* where he wrote that 'the marches of Wales which the English [NB "the English"] inhabit would be better ruled if their kings had relied on the advice of the marchers and the barons of the country rather than on Angevins and Normans'.[31] In chapter 7 he asserted that 'the first three Norman kings' (*primi tres Normannorum reges*) had been able to keep the Welsh in subjection thanks to the military successes achieved by the pre-Conquest rulers of England, notably Harold, but that in the time of the following three kings the Welsh did much better.[32] In analysing the modern (i.e. 1190s) confidence of the Welsh, he explained their recent successes in terms of the 'burdensome overseas commitments of the Norman kings as they tried to cope with the pride of the French'.[33] In these passages it is clear that, no

---

[27] *Expugnatio*, pp. 244–5.

[28] *Vita Galfridi*, *Opera*, vol. 4, pp. 423–4; he returned to the subject of their boastful arrogance in the *Gemma Ecclesiastica*, *Opera*, vol. 2, p. 348.

[29] E.g., *De principis*, Bk I, c. 20, Bk III, c. 31, *Opera*, vol. 8, pp. 138–9, 327.

[30] *De principis*, Bk III, c. 28, *Opera*, vol. 8, pp. 301–2, and on p. 303 a quotation from Boethius: 'all kings of islands are tyrants'.

[31] *Descriptio*, Bk II c. 8, *Opera*, vol. 6, p. 220; for translation,Thorpe, *The Journey*, p. 268, and Bartlett, *Gerald*, p. 25. The whole passage is based on *Expugnatio Hibernica*, p. 246, but with some changes, among them the addition of the reference to Normans and Angevins.

[32] *Descriptio*, *Opera*, vol. 6, pp. 217–18. Thorpe's translation of *trium sequentium tempore* as 'the first three Norman kings' is baffling, *The Journey*, p. 267.

[33] 'Alia quoque, de quibus jactant, operosis regum Normannorum curis, quibus Francorum superbiae in transmarinis tantopere indulgent', *Opera*, vol. 6, p. 217. I don't know how Thorpe managed to translate this as 'The other circumstances about which they boast are to be attributed to the untiring efforts of the Norman kings, who were strongly supported in their invasion by the proud French', *The Journey*, p. 266.

matter how we may choose to label them, in Gerald's terminology Henry II, Richard I and John were Norman kings.

What then does he have in mind by English servitude? By 1216 at any rate it is clear that he meant the subjection of everybody in England to a tyrannical king – and that he hoped that, thanks to the Capetian prince Louis, this was about to end. Robert Bartlett has published and commented upon a political poem which Gerald wrote at this time. 'The madness of slavery now ends; times of liberty are granted; English necks are freed from the yoke'.[34] In chapter 30 of Book III (written 1216) of *De principis instructione* he referred to 'Norman tyranny' (*tyrannica vis Normanorum*) and to the way English necks had been so bent under the yoke and were so given to subjection and servitude that they were always obedient to their ruler'. Chapter 31 ends with an explicit expression of his disappointment that the English kingdom 'trampled so long under tyranny' had not after all thrown off 'the unbearable yoke of long servitude'. The future fate of this dynasty of Norman kings he leaves to others to tell.[35] Here it is explicit that by the tyranny of the Normans he meant the tyranny of kings, not of lords. Indeed in *De principis instructione* Bk III c. 12, so violent and harsh was 'insular tyranny' that even the Normans suffered under *servitutis oppressio* when ruled by kings of England and hence proved less able to resist the free French. It was in these terms that Gerald explained the 'loss of Normandy'.[36]

In a later part of *De invectionibus*, also written *c*.1216, Gerald reflected ruefully that since the English 'had earlier been subjected as slaves, and are now *quasi naturaliter servi*, it is no wonder if they refuse to leave off the long custom of their servile condition'.[37] But much earlier too Gerald had alluded to the English being subjected to a Norman yoke after 1066. In the *Descriptio Kambrie* he had mentioned this in passing in the course of an argument that the English lacked the boldness of speech characteristic of Welsh, Franks and Romans, because they were descended from Saxon ancestors not because of their long servitude, since he had observed that Saxons and Germans suffer from the same defect even though they enjoy freedom (*qui et libertate gaudent*). The implication of his reference in the present tense to Saxon and German liberty is that he thought of the English of his own day as still being in a state of servitude.[38] Yet he wrote this (*c*.1194) when his views were far from being anti-English – indeed at this stage his advice to the English was to starve the Welsh into submission by means of an economic blockade and then expel all the natives in order to make Wales a colony (*de Cambria coloniam*

---

[34] Bartlett, *Gerald*, pp. 97–8, 222–5. 'Servilis rabies iam cessat, libera dantur / Tempora, solvuntur anglica colla iugo.' The yoke re-appears in lines 65 and 79.

[35] *De principis*, *Opera*, vol. 8, pp. 317–18, 328. Some of the passages in chapter 31 must have been written in 1217 when Louis was losing the war.

[36] *De principis*, *Opera*, vol. 8, p. 258; discussed by Bartlett, *Gerald*, pp. 95–6.

[37] *De invectionibus*, ed. Davies, p. 202. For the date see Richter in Giraldus, *Speculum Duroum*, p. xxi. The passage was repeated in *De jure et statu Menevensis ecclesiae* of *c*.1218, *Opera*, vol. 3, p. 223.

[38] *Descriptio*, Bk I, c. 15; *Opera*, vol. 6, p. 193. In Thorpe's translation the implication is made explicit.

efficere), perhaps even turn it into a forest.[39] On the other hand this was also the critical time in his career when his hopes of a promotion through royal service were receding fast – which itself may be significant for the emergence of his doctrine of a tyrannical monarchy.[40] The fact that he could write about English servitude as early as 1194 makes it likely that when he wrote about it in *The Invectives* of 1200 he meant much the same as he would do in 1216–17, that is to say that in calling the English 'the slaves of the Normans' he meant that they stood in a servile relation to their kings.

However in 1200 when he called them the most worthless slaves in their own land, he immediately followed this up with an absurdly one-sided but rhetorically brilliant assertion: 'In our land there are none but Englishmen in the jobs of ploughman, shepherd, cobbler, skinner, artisan and cleaner of the sewers too'.[41] Absurdly one-sided, because in Wales, as in Ireland, the English were also the invaders and would-be conquerors. Indeed one of his own complaints in *The Invectives* (part 5, chapter 6) would be that even the vilest Englishman could get to be a bishop in Wales.[42] The claim that in Wales only English people carried out such menial jobs does not, of course, mean that in England only the English – as opposed to the Normans – carried out such jobs. But the juxtaposition of thoughts is skilfully done – as is plain from the success enjoyed by this association of ideas in modern times. Absurdly one-sided or not, this is the passage always cited by those who claim that Gerald had a low opinion of the English. Taken in isolation this passage tends to reinforce the notion of an author who was proud of his descent from Welsh princes and Norman aristocrats and who despised the English as a lower class engaged in manual and sometimes demeaning work. In fact a more complete analysis of Gerald's usage shows that he thought of all the English, of whatever rank, as being slavishly obedient to Norman kings. It was not that the English were still a majority oppressed in their own country by a Norman minority – as in the late eleventh and early twelfth century they had felt themselves to be. Gerald recognised that at one time there had been hatred between the English and Norman peoples. In his life of St Ethelbert, probably written in the mid-1190s, he referred to 'the inborn hatred between English and Normans', but this is in the course of a miracle story firmly set in the past, indeed one which he had taken from a much earlier life written by Osbert of Clare. In this context, moreover, Gerald called Ethelbert 'our martyr'.[43] But his view of his own time was that all the people of the

---

[39] *Descriptio*, Bk II, c. 9, *Opera*, vol. 6, p. 225 n. 4. Curiously this remarkable passage, which Gerald excised when he subsequently revised the work, has been either relegated to a footnote or omitted altogether by editors and translators.

[40] Although he dedicated the first version of the *Descriptio* to Hubert Walter, he can have had little hope of advancement after he had chosen to support Count John in the failed coup of 1193. On this critical time in his career, Bartlett, *Gerald*, pp. 64–5.

[41] *De invectionibus*, p. 93.

[42] *De invectionibus*, p. 187. (*Invectives*, part 5, cap. 6). Indeed it is clear that in 1200 his opponent at the curia, master Andrew, was another Englishman – and an all too influential one.

[43] M. R. James, 'Two Lives of St Ethelbert, King and Martyr', *EHR*, 32 (1917), 216, 235.

kingdom of England, whether of Old English, Norman or mixed descent, were now oppressed by tyrannical Norman kings. He and Susan Reynolds shared the view that England was a kingdom in which 'a relatively large proportion of the population was frequently and directly exposed to oppression by royal officials'. For him, as for her, there was an 'equality of oppression'.[44] Gerald's description of the English as 'slaves of the Normans' was, in other words, an expression of 'regnal solidarity against the king' – though in his mind a pretty feeble sort of solidarity.

Gerald's attitude to the Norman kings of England was one thing; his attitude to the Normans of Normandy in his own day another. His criticism of Normans for their boastfulness, arrogance and loquacity in the *Expugnatio Hibernica* clearly derives from the situation in which he and his kindred in Ireland found themselves in 1185, being pushed to one side by the Normans in the train of John Count of Mortain.[45] When he repeated this criticism in the *Vita Galfridi*, it reflected another specific political situation, that propaganda war waged against William Longchamp in the autumn of 1191 in which, as Hugh de Nonant's infamous letter makes clear, the unpopular chancellor's French political style and his ignorance of the English language were part of an orchestrated campaign of character assassination in which no tune was left unplayed.[46] In this we can hear the first strains of a new Francophobia, and one which was soon to be given further life by a second propaganda war: that waged in the mid-1190s between the king of England and the king of France.[47] After 1204, of course, dislike of Normans and dislike of French political ambitions tended to coalesce, especially since in England the political humiliation of the loss of Normandy was commonly blamed on 'Norman treachery'.[48] From then on, as is very well-known, recurring fears of a new French invasion, briefly in 1205, then in 1216–17, in the 1260s and again in 1295, contributed to an escalating Francophobia.[49] Clearly in the mid-thirteenth century we have a sharper sense of Englishness than

---

[44] In her view it was this 'equality of oppression' which 'made the barons of Magna Carta sympathise with the lower ranks of society', Reynolds, *Kingdoms and Communities*, p. 268.

[45] See Gillingham, *The English*, pp. 155–6.

[46] *Opera*, vol. 4, pp. 420–2; the text of Hugh de Nonant's letter, which Gerald drew upon in his *Vita Galfridi*, is given in Howden, *Gesta Regis Ricardi*, ed. W. Stubbs (2 vols, RS, 1867), ii, pp. 215–20. Both Hugh and Gerald emphasised the tyranny with which the low-born Longchamp lorded it over all England, though even in such a context as this, Hugh de Nonant acknowledged the force of the concept of 'French liberty'. Significantly it is into the mouth of Count John that Richard of Devizes, who took a more balanced view of Longchamp (see N. Partner, *Serious Entertainments* [Chicago, 1977], pp. 169–71), put the charge that the chancellor had introduced into England the preposterous custom of serving on bended knee, *The Chronicle of Richard of Devizes*, ed. J. T. Appleby (London, 1963), p. 32. The points made here owe much to discussions with John Prestwich.

[47] On this see my *Richard I* (New Haven and London, 1999), pp. 6–7 and my 'Royal Newsletters, Forgeries and English Historians: some Links between Court and History in the Reign of Richard I', *Lacour Plantagenêt*, ed. M. Aurell (Poitiers, 2000), pp. 171–86.

[48] D. Power, 'King John and the Norman Aristocracy', in S. Church, ed., *King John. New Interpretations* (Woodbridge, 1999), p. 119, and the sources cited there, though *Gervase*, i, p. 95 should be ii, p. 95.

[49] See, for example, N. Vincent, *Peter des Roches. An Alien in English Politics 1205–1238* (Cambridge, 1996) and D. A. Carpenter, 'King Henry III's "Statute" against Aliens: July 1263', in his *The Reign of Henry III* (London, 1996), pp. 262–80.

had existed a hundred years earlier, but it does not from this follow that people living in later twelfth-century England and speaking French did not also feel themselves to be English — so long, of course, as — unlike Longchamp — they could also speak English, and were not accused, as Longchamp was, of making derogatory remarks about the English. Thus when Gervase of Canterbury, early in the thirteenth century, wrote: 'William the Bastard brought into England a new form of living and speaking' (*novam vivendi formam et loquendi*), there is nothing in the tone of his other remarks to suggest that he resented the introduction of French.[50] Of course, what poor people felt we have no means of knowing — although upper-class writers believed that they shared their own anti-French feelings in 1217 and in the 1260s.[51] So far as surviving evidence goes, in England linguistic nationalism is essentially a fourteenth-century development.[52] Presumably Chardri, the author of *Le Petit Plet* (The Little Dialogue) of *c.*1200, saw himself as quite English when he wrote: 'Tuz les reaumes ke ore sunt / Passe Engleterre, e savez dunt? / De tuz deduz e de franchise.' (England surpasses all the kingdoms that exist, and do you know in which ways? In all pleasures and in nobility.)[53] But although in the same language, this was evidently exactly the opposite of the kind of song which Longchamp's *de regno Francorum cantores et joculatores* were accused of composing.[54]

It would, of course, be absurd in the light of his anti-Norman sentiments to portray Gerald as 'typically English' — or indeed as 'typically anything'. Nonetheless in the increasingly patriotic atmosphere of thirteenth-century England the matter of Norman identity and the alleged Norman character traits which Gerald had identified came to bear an explanatory weight which they had not possessed in the 1190s. Consider Matthew Paris's explanation of the enmity of Duke Leopold of Austria for Richard I. The quarrel at Acre had been provoked, Matthew said, by the loud-mouthed arrogance and stupidity of one of the king's household knights, a Norman, who behaved in the usual Norman fashion (*more suae gentis*). Consider too his account of the 1196 London demonstration led by William FitzOsbert which includes the detail that William was known as 'cum-Barba' because as a sign of his indignation against the Normans he refused to shave his beard.[55] Neither of these anti-Norman elaborations of two famous stories is to be found in works composed in the 1190s or in Roger of Wendover. Both are indications of the way Matthew was

---

[50] *The Historical Works of Gervase of Canterbury*, ed. W. Stubbs, 2 vols (RS, 1880), ii, p. 60. This is in the *Gesta Regum*, the lesser known of his two substantial works of history, a chronicle covering the period from the arrival of Brutus in Britain to the reign of King John.

[51] Annals of Waverley in *Annales Monastici*, ed. H. R. Luard (4 vols, RS, 1865), ii, p. 287, and see D. A. Carpenter, 'English Peasants in Politics', *Past and Present*, 136 (1992), reprinted in his *The Reign of Henry III* (London, 1996).

[52] T. Turville-Petre, *England the Nation. Language, Literature and National Identity 1290–1340* (1996); R. R. Davies, 'The Peoples of Britain and Ireland, 1100–1400: IV Language and Historical Mythology', *TRHS*, 6th ser. 7 (1997); A. Hastings, *The Construction of Nationhood* (Cambridge, 1997), pp. 44–6.

[53] *Le Petit Plet*, ed. B. S. Merrilees (Oxford, 1970), lines 1263–5. The poet goes on to praise the women of England as well brought up, and English knights and their followers as valiant, courteous and noble — only in their excessive drinking could they be faulted.

[54] Howden, *Gesta Regis Ricardi*, ii, p. 216.

[55] Matthew Paris, *Chronica majora*, ed. H. R. Luard (7 vols, RS, 1872–83), ii, pp. 384, 418.

reinterpreting the past so that it conformed to his own assumptions. As Rebecca Reader has shown, part of this reinterpretation was a more hostile view of the Normans and of the Norman Conquest.[56] According to his *Gesta abbatum*, after 1066 the English had been forced to shave and cut off the beard and long hair which had been a badge of the freedom they had enjoyed since the time of Brutus.[57] In passing it may be worth noting that Matthew probably contributed more than any other historian to the labelling of William I as 'the Conqueror'.[58] He dated the appointment of Paul as abbot of St Albans to the eleventh year of the reign 'Regis Willelmi Majoris scilicet Conquestoris' and earlier still, in his explication of Merlin's prophecies in the *Chronica majora*, he referred to *Willelmus Conquestor* and to *Willelmus primus conquestor*.[59]

Thirteenth-century fears of a new French invasion also led in time to a new and imaginative appreciation of what the Norman Conquest might have meant for the defeated – significantly more so in the minds of authors such as Robert of Gloucester and Peter Langtoft than in the minds of historians writing in the later twelfth century for whom the story of 1066 had no such contemporary resonance. Even a historian such as William of Newburgh, acutely conscious though he was of the injustice and bloodshed of 1066, shows no signs of thinking of the Normans of the 1190s as 'England's enemies'.[60] As Rollason has emphasised, at this date neither the cult of Harold nor the cult of Waltheof regarded their central figures as heroes of an anti-Norman resistance movement.[61] Hence Henry of Huntingdon's early

---

[56] As she points out Matthew's *Gesta abbatum* reflects an 'obsession with the Norman yoke of servitude and English resistance to it' and she naturally links Matthew's 'patriotic championing of the *gens Anglorum*' with 'the escalating xenophobia' of the mid-thirteenth century, R. Reader, 'Matthew Paris and the Norman Conquest', ed. J. Blair and B. Golding, *The Cloister and the World* (Oxford, 1996), especially pp. 137–8, 144.

[57] *Gesta abbatum monasterii Sancti Albani*, ed. H. T. Riley (3 vols, RS, 1867), i, p. 52. A similar story told in his *Historia Anglorum*, ed. F. Madden, (3 vols, RS, 1866–89), i, p. 11. That for Matthew the English followed Trojan custom shows how the History of the Britons had been hijacked by the English.

[58] In attributing the invention of this to Langtoft, Michel de Boüard left Matthew Paris out of consideration, 'Note sur l'appellation "Guillaume le Conquérant"', in C. Harper-Bill, C. Holdsworth and J. L. Nelson, eds, *Studies in Medieval History presented to R. Allen Brown* (Woodbridge, 1989), pp. 21–6.

[59] *Gesta abbatum*, i, p. 52. *Chron. maj.*, i, pp. 201–2. Reader noticed a marginal addition to the *Historia Anglorum* (i, p. 34): *Iste Willelmus conquestor Angliae*, Reader, 'Matthew Paris', p. 129 – a phrase taken up by the author of Burton Annals writing in 1260s, in a famous story in which the tyrannical John was portrayed as the succesor of William the Bastard, conqueror of England, *Annales monastici*, ed. H. R. Luard, vol. 1 (RS, 1864), p. 211. Much earlier, c.1180, the author of the Waltham Chronicle had referred to William as *conquisitor terrre*. This author too regarded the kings of England of his own day as *Normanni reges nostri*, though – unlike Gerald – he praised them: *The Waltham Chronicle*, ed. and trans. L. Watkiss and M. Chibnall (Oxford, 1994), pp. 24, 56.

[60] William of Newburgh, *Historia Rerum Anglicarum*, Bk 1, chapter 1, in ed. R. Howlett, *Chronicles of the Reigns of Stephen, Henry II and Richard I* (RS 1884), i, pp. 22–3.

[61] D. Rollason, *Saints and Relics in Anglo-Saxon England* (Oxford, 1989), pp. 217–19. But it is worth noting that the *Vita Haroldi* of c.1205 takes a more hostile view of the Normans than had the Waltham Chronicler some twenty-five years earlier – hardly surprising after the propaganda of the 1190s and the loss of Normandy. On Hereward the Wake, see H. Thomas, 'The *Gesta Herwardi*, the English and their Conquerors', *ANS*, 21 (1998), 213–32.

twelfth-century perception of the Norman Conquest as the fifth and last of the plagues which God sent to punish the inhabitants of Britain, and as a plague which was still taking its toll in his day, seems to have made no visible impression on the minds of his later twelfth- and early thirteenth-century readers. Even writers who took over Henry's notion of the plagues, such as the unknown author of the *Historia post obitum Bedae* and, following him, Roger of Howden, did not also take on board his interpretation of the Norman plague.[62] It was only after an interval of more than a century and a half that Henry's perception of the Norman Conquest came to be resurrected by Robert of Gloucester and Langtoft.[63] It was in this frame of mind that Langtoft urged all Edward I's subjects to put up with the heavy burden of war taxation because if the war were to be lost the new conqueror (*li novel conqerour*) would bring us all low, no matter of what estate we were, so that in the eyes of proud Frenchman we would be no better than dogs.[64] Langtoft saw French invasion as a threat to English freedom. This was exactly the reverse of the way Gerald had viewed the invasion of Philip IV's great-grandfather, Prince Louis in 1216–17. He supported Louis through thick and thin – unlike the English, who abandoned him once King John was dead. Although by 1215 many English people had come to share Gerald's view of royal tyranny – hence Magna Carta – it was precisely the failure of the aristocratic leaders of English society to continue to support the French prince that led Gerald to suspect that the English were now naturally servile and hence that they would remain what, in his peculiarly jaundiced view, they had already been for generations: slaves of the Normans.

---

[62] Henry, Archdeacon of Huntingdon, *Historia Anglorum*, ed. and trans. D. Greenway (Oxford, 1996), pp. 14–15; Howden, *Chronica*, ed. W. Stubbs (4 vols, RS, 1868–71), i, p. 25, a reference to the plague of Danes.

[63] *Chronicle of Langtoft*, i, pp. 286–90; Robert of Gloucester, *Metrical Chronicle*, lines 44–55. But Robert systematically puts 'England' where Henry had written Britain. For discussion of these matters I am indebted to Ron Greenwald.

[64] *Chronicle of Langtoft*, ii, pp. 212–14. J. C.Thiolier, *Pierre de Langtoft: Le Règne d'Edouard I* (Paris, 1989), pp. 18–19, 279–81.

Kinsmen, neighbours and communities in Wales and the western British Isles, c.1100–c.1400

*Rees Davies**

Susan Reynolds's *Kingdoms and Communities in Western Europe 900–1300* (1984; second edition 1997) is a book with a mission, eloquently and zealously delivered. It set out to demonstrate the centrality of collective, community action at all sorts of levels and in a whole host of forms in the life of medieval Western European societies. As such, part of its target was the overemphasis in much of our historiography on what may be characterised as vertical authority, an overemphasis largely dictated by a too ready surrender to the assumptions and agenda of overwhelmingly royal and seigniorial source material. *Communitas* – in a loose, supple, non-legalistic sense – was to be deployed to redress the preoccupation with *Herrschaft*, *seigneurie* and the centralising, directive and oppressive character of kingship and lordship – especially the preoccupation with state-building, political unification and the institutionalisation of seignorial power which have been such dominant features of the late-modern view of medieval Europe, more especially of and in England.

The stage for Susan Reynolds's bold exploration of this theme was nothing less than the whole (or at least a good part) of Western Europe; the extraordinarily wide and eclectic use of evidence from different parts of the continent has indeed been one of the most distinguishing and exciting features of her scholarship. It has enabled her, with characteristic gusto, to prick some of the portentous bubbles

---

* The following abbreviations are used in the footnotes: CCR: Clun Court Rolls, Shropshire County Record Office, Shrewsbury; DCCC: Court Rolls of Dyffryn Clwyd (or lordship of Ruthin), Public Record Office, London, Special Collections (SC. 2); Davies *CCC*: R. R. Davies, *Conquest, Coexistence and Change. Wales 1063–1415* (Oxford, 1987), reissued as *The Age of Conquest. Wales 1063–1415* (Oxford, 1991); Davies *LSMW*: R. R. Davies, *Lordship and Society in the March of Wales 1284–1400* (Oxford, 1978); Jones Pierce *MWS*: T. Jones Pierce, *Medieval Welsh Society. Selected Essays*, ed. J. B. Smith (Cardiff, 1972); Nicholls *GGI*: Kenneth Nicholls, *Gaelic and Gaelicised Ireland in the Middle Ages* (Dublin, 1972); Rees (ed.) *CAP*: *Calendar of Ancient Petitions relating to Wales*, ed. W. Rees (Cardiff, 1975); Reynolds *KC*: Susan Reynolds, *Kingdoms and Communities in Western Europe 900–1300* (second edn, Oxford 1997); W: Welsh. For Welsh terms see especially *Geiriadur Prifysgol Cymru. A Dictionary of the Welsh Language* (1950–); WL: *The Law of Hywel Dda. Law Texts from Medieval Wales*, trans. and ed. D. Jenkins (Llandysul, 1986). I have cited this translation for the convenience of English readers; but have used the original Welsh law texts myself; Wickham *CCT*: Chris Wickham, *Community and Clientele in Twelfth-century Tuscany. The Origins of the Rural Commune in the Plain of Lucca* (Oxford, 1998).

of English exceptionalist historiography, but equally to call in question whether a handful of magisterial French provincial studies constitute a secure basis for constructing a paradigm which can be imposed on the whole of Western Europe. Indeed one abiding impression left on a reading of her book is that the broad similarity of the issues and challenges facing medieval European societies is more than counter-balanced by the protean individuality of the character and chronology of the response of different communities to them.

One area which, understandably, was omitted from Susan Reynolds's remarkable *tour d'horizon* was the northern and western parts of the British Isles. The reasons for this omission are worth exploring briefly, for they raise issues regarding the concepts, language and assumptions of contemporary historiography (another topic which has frequently engaged Susan Reynolds's attention). The peripheralisation of the western British Isles in medieval historical writing is much more than a matter of the intractability and inadequacy of the evidence and the difficulties of the vernacular languages for these areas. It has also to do with the definition of the canonical concerns and apparent social and political trajectories of English and, to a lesser degree, northern European historiography. Within that cosmos much that seemed to characterise the western British Isles in the Middle Ages seems asymmetrical at best, alien, undeveloped and thereby irrelevant at worst. If to that we add the culpably loose usage of the originally philological term 'Celtic' to cast an air of mystery about anything and everything to the west of Offa's Dyke, we begin to understand why the histories of the western British Isles have been cast into a historiographical oubliette as far as the rest of Britain and Europe is concerned.

It had once been otherwise. In the late nineteenth century in particular, towering scholars (such as Henry Maine, F. W. Maitland, Frederic Seebohm and Paul Vinogradoff) had been fascinated by the evidence for the medieval societies of Wales and Ireland.[1] Their fascination was triggered by their belief that these countries reflected an earlier, tribal, stage in the evolution of human society when kinship bonds and status designations dominated social organisation. As Seebohm put it: 'the Tribal System as an economic stage in people's growth seems to be well nigh universal'.[2] Medieval Wales and Ireland thereby became important showcases in the museum of human evolution; and their significance was enhanced by the pressing concerns of the land problem and concepts of property in both countries, and especially in Ireland, in the late Victorian period.[3]

---

[1] See especially G. A. Feaver, *From Status to Contract. A Biography of Sir Henry Maine 1822–1888* (London, 1969) for Maine's views; F. W. Maitland, 'The Laws of Wales. the Kindred and the Blood Feud'; 'The Tribal System in Wales', *Collected Papers* (Cambridge, 1911), I, pp. 202–29; III, pp. 1–10; F. Seebohm, *The English Village Community* (London, 1883); *The Tribal System in Wales* (1895); P. Vinogradoff, *The Growth of the Manor* (London, 1911); (with F. Morgan), *The Survey of the Honour of Denbigh 1334* (London, 1914).

[2] F. Seebohm, *Tribal System in Wales*, viii, pp. 52, 237.

[3] Clive Dewey, 'Celtic Agrarian Legislation and the Celtic Revival: Historicist Implications of Gladstone's Irish and Scottish Land Acts, 1870–86', *Past and Present*, 64 (1974), 30–70; J. W. Burrow, '"The Village Community" and the Uses of History in Late Nineteenth century England', in N. McKendrick (ed.), *Historical Perspectives. Studies in English Thought and Society in honour of J. H. Plumb* (London, 1974), pp. 155–84.

We may not wish to return to the determinist simplicities of Victorian social evolutionary theory; but there are surely ample reasons for bringing the evidence of the western British Isles in the medieval period fully into consideration when discussing the nature of society and lordship (kingship included) in Western Europe. There is no reason after all why the fastnesses of Wales or Ireland should be any less interesting or rewarding *prima facie* than the high valleys of Catalonia or the Alps – or Montaillou – in the study of the varieties of medieval social organization and consciousness.[4] Nor should the artificialities of a Celtic/Teutonic dichotomy be any longer allowed to serve as a specious pretext for ignoring the 'Celtic' evidence, now that the studies of scholars such as Geoffrey Barrow, Thomas Charles-Edwards, Wendy Davies, Glanville Jones, Robin Chapman Stacey, Patrick Wormald and others have shown the continuum of social and political experience, as well as the differences, shared by these societies.

But there are other, positive, reasons for not ignoring the western British experience. The Irish and Welsh legal sources together 'represent the largest body of pre-twelfth century vernacular material extant from anywhere in western Europe'.[5] Whatever the immense difficulties inherent in this corpus of evidence, it is a body of customary, vernacular, largely lay, and non-ecclesiastical law which allows us to reconstruct some of the theoretical norms, assumptions and procedures of these societies and to do so, in a measure, from a non-lordship angle. Likewise the very differentness, or apparent differentness, of so-called 'Celtic' societies should be a challenge and an opportunity, not a deterrent, to a historiography which has built so much of its typology of social organisation and power, both substantively and chronologically, on a southern English–northern European paradigm. Here in the western British Isles in broad-brush terms we find predominantly (though not exclusively) pastoral societies, a pattern of non-nucleated settlements, low population, extensive lordship (royal and/or seignorial, according to our designations), intensive kinship rights in land and law, small-scale and unstable patterns of political power and loyalties, and very limited opportunities for the wealth accumulation, economic mobility and social differentiation already characteristic of lowland England. Noting the differences, and the apparent variables in the differences, between these two adjacent but markedly contrasting societies surely serves to illuminate both. In particular should it do so at the point – broadly between the eleventh and fourteenth centuries – when these societies came into increasingly close contact and interaction, as English power extended, socially and economically as well as militarily and politically, into Wales and Ireland. The fascination of this period is all the greater as English-trained clerks tried to adjust their formulae of economic and social descriptions and accountability to characterise the very different patterns of social organisation and economic practice of the western British Isles in an age of English conquest. We are, as it were, at the cusp of (at least) two

---

[4] Reynolds *KC*, p. 121; Wickham *CCT*, pp. 192–4, 214–16.
[5] Robin Chapman Stacey, *The Road to Judgment. From Custom to Court in Medieval Ireland and Wales* (Philadelphia, 1994), p. 3.

societies, two sets of vocabularies and assumptions, two paradigms of authority and power; it is a privileged moment for the historian. So likewise is it a privilege to offer this small, marginal, 'western British but mainly Welsh' footnote as an *additamentum* to Susan Reynolds's great book.[6]

How did the Welsh, and for the most part the native populations of the western British Isles (Ireland, Galloway, the Western Isles and Highlands) generally, in the high Middle Ages construct their social world and their place within it? Certainly not as a collection of atomistic, self-contained, individuals. 'Therefore', such are the words placed in the mouth of an early twelfth-century princeling of Powys, 'as a friend (W. *cyfaill*) I beseech you, as a lord (W. *arglwydd*) I command you, as a kinsman (W. *car*) I pray you'.[7] It is a convincing characterisation both in form – for medieval Welshmen had a pathological habit of arranging all life and learning into triads – and in substance. Leaving lordship on one side for the purposes of this essay, it identifies two circles within which the individual – or at least the free-born individual – inevitably orbited – those of friendship or, as we might say, neighbourhood (for the Welsh terms *cyfaill* (friend) and *cymydog* (neighbour) share the same prefix) and kinship. It is with kinship we begin because it was, as it were, aboriginal, natal.

Membership of a kinship group literally identified the individual – be it over recent generations in the patronymic form of his name (e.g. Hywel Fychan ap Hywel ab Einion), or more distantly by allocating him to a membership of a descent group. In the earliest piece of written Welsh to survive – from *c*.830–50 – it is the descent group (W. *llwyth*) which is the social grouping in which the individual is located. Or, to cite a later example, when the Welsh chronicler wished to sing the praises of the Lord Rhys of Deheubarth (south-west Wales) on his death in 1197, it is from the vocabulary of lineage that he borrows his compliments: descent (W. *llin*), kin (W. *cenedl*), captain of the kin group (W. *pencenedl*), the gentility of good birth (W. *bonedd*).[8] Nor was kinship merely a matter of descent and identity; it could be regarded as the primary informing principle in the social and economic relationships of the individual. It was an early Irish law tract which pitched the claims of kinship at their highest: 'Every agricultural partnership, every rent, every sale, every purchase, every exchange, every contract . . . every service is more properly done with a kinsman who is lawful according to the nearness of relationship'.[9]

If kinship was so fundamental, then any notion of collective community action would, in considerable degree, have to operate within its framework. Kinship ties,

---

[6] Each of the themes touched upon in this short essay could be expanded into a long chapter. In the spirit of Susan Reynolds's own work, and conscious that the general reader can only tolerate so much of the detail and terminology of Welsh (and Irish) evidence, I have contented myself with a very broad sketch.

[7] *Brut y Tywysogyon or The Chronicle of the Princes. Peniarth Ms. 20 Version.* Translated by Thomas Jones (Cardiff, 1952), p. 32.

[8] D. Jenkins and M. E. Owen, 'The Welsh Marginalia in the Lichfield Gospels', *Cambridge Medieval Celtic Studies*, 5 (1983), 36–66; 7 (1984), 91–120; *Brut y Tywysogyon*, p. 77.

[9] Quoted in Stacey, *The Road to Judgment*, p. 56.

we now recognise thanks to pioneering work culminating in the magisterial study of Thomas Charles-Edwards, were multiple in form and variable in their demands: they could be, and were, both agnatic and bilateral, 'shallow' and 'deep', ancestor- and ego-centred, concerned with status and 'political' power at one level, with land inheritance and legal responsibilities at another.[10] Their operations are of their very nature 'non-public' and thereby lie overwhelmingly beyond the English and English-type documentation which forms the documentary (as opposed to the literary, including legal text) sources for the study of these societies, especially in the thirteenth and fourteenth centuries. But that is no reason for throwing in the historical towel, for as Chris Wickham has observed recently in another context, 'if we want to understand fully how peasant society worked and changed, we have to study not just how peasants related to lords, but how they related to each other'.[11]

How, therefore, did the centrality of kin bonds in the western British Isles shape the way that free men and nobles (for the two categories were regarded as synonymous) related to each other and inform their communal activities? Social consciousness was in this respect as important as social realities. The world of the west was *envisaged* as a world of agnatic lineages or descent groups – *lignage, progenies, nacio, cognomen, clan*, to choose just a few of the contemporary terms. It was within this world of lineages that the individual found his identity, both in time in his descent from the lineage founder and laterally in terms of his *parentes* and *cognati*.[12] The unity of the lineage was formally expressed in the person of the chief of the lineage – the *pencenedl* of the Welsh law books and record evidence corresponding broadly to the *caput progeniei* of Galloway or the chief of the clan of the Irish annals.[13] In Wales, at least, there is little evidence that the lineage operated effectively and regularly as a social or political force; rather did it give a sense of identity and a source of genealogical prowess to the free nobleman. Yet it defined some of the important communal claims and responsibilities of the individual (as well as, ultimately, his title to land), for it was in respect of membership of the lineage that the free nobleman claimed a share in the easements of the soil (forest, wood, pasture, waste) and paid his contribution to the lord's food renders and circuit dues. Moreover, it was through membership of the lineage that he had a share in the lineage's mills (many mills in Wales were owned by lineages, not by lords, for, as Welsh law had it, the mill was 'one of the three indivisible gems of the kindred'

---

[10] Thomas Charles-Edwards, *Early Irish and Welsh Kinship* (Oxford, 1993). For the practical operation of kinship ties in late medieval Wales, Davies *CCC*, pp. 123–6; Davies *LSMW*, pp. 358–64. The forthcoming study of Llinos Smith will take the issue much further.

[11] Wickham *CCT*, p. 205.

[12] Nicholls *GGI*, pp. 8–12; J. Bannerman, 'The Scots language and the kin-based Society', in D. S. Thomson (ed.), *Gaelic and Scots in Harmony* (Glasgow, 1990); idem, 'MacDuff of Fife', in A. Grant and K. J. Stringer (ed.), *Medieval Scotland. Crown, Lordship and Community* (Edinburgh, 1993), pp. 20–39.

[13] Charles-Edwards, *Early Irish and Welsh Kinship*, pp. 203–11; W. H. D. Sellar, 'Celtic Law and Scots Law. Survival and Integration', *Scottish Studies*, 29 (1989), 1–27, esp. p. 7; *Annals of Tigernach*, ed. Whiteley Stokes (Llannerch Reprints, 1993), *sub annis* 1158, 1159, etc.

(W. *tri thlws cenedl*));[14] in the right of presentation to the kin's churches, the so-called portionary churches of medieval Wales;[15] in the court of the kindred; and even in its obligation to select a member to serve in the lord's army.[16] Such obligations and opportunities suggest that communal activities in Wales, and elsewhere in the west, operated in good part through the channels of kinship ties.

Nor was that all. In societies which constructed social relationships so predominantly in kin terms, it was inevitable that the processes of peace-keeping, dispute resolution and the maintenance of social order should be grounded in a measure in the community of kinsmen. Most spectacularly it was agnatic and cognatic kinsmen to the seventh degree of relationship who were, theoretically, the 'partakers' (in the contemporary phrase) both in prosecuting cases of homicide compensation (W. *galanas*) and in sharing the responsibility for the payment, 'aftyr thyr degrees of their consanguinity or kynred' as one formula expresses it.[17] The survival of the practice well into the sixteenth century – in spite of the vigorous prohibition of English monarchy – showed how deeply rooted were concepts of kin responsibility in Welsh society. Knowing one's kinsmen was important in other directions: compurgators were to be chosen from their ranks; the duties of a co-parcenors (*comporcionarii, co-heredes,* W. *cyd-etifeddion*) with regard to land and its appurtenances were manifold and enforceable; and beyond these, and similar, legal obligations lay a moral world of kindred responsibilities – in arranging marriages or in appointing guardians for minor kinsmen, for example – of which we get the rarest of glimpses from our sources.

Now there is no need, of course, to posit that kinsmen discharged their obligations with the precision and comprehensiveness ascribed to them in the law texts. The multiple forms of kin ties, the practical difficulties of assembling lineages and tracing affines, and the existence of a plethora of alternative bonds of obligation diluted theory often into very anaemic practice. But that is not to gainsay the centrality of kin membership in the construction and practice of social relationships in the western British Isles in the central and later Middle Ages The survival of a rich and finely calibrated terminology of kinship – in contrast with the poverty of the English language in this respect – and the strong traces of the vocabulary and substance of kinship duties in late medieval evidence, especially of the extra-curial and non-official type, suggest as much. Even more striking confirmation that this

---

[14] See, for example, *The Record of Caernarvon*, ed. H. Ellis (1838), pp. 3, 22–33, 37, etc.; Rees (ed.) *CAP*, nos 2174, 2874, 4131–2, 4444; *WL*, p. 113.

[15] Rees (ed.) *CAP*, no. 13367; J. Wyn Evans, 'The Survival of the *clas* as an Institution in Medieval Wales', in Nancy Edwards and Alan Lane (eds), *The Early Church in Wales and the West* (Oxford, 1992), pp. 33–41.

[16] For a rare example of the court held in the name of two lineage groups, National Library of Wales Trovarth and Coed Coch Papers, 6; 'pro toto sanguine ipsius Eden': *Record of Caernarvon*, p. 73.

[17] R. R. Davies, 'The Survival of the Blood Feud in Medieval Wales', *History*, 54 (1969), 338–57. The formula is quoted in Llinos Beverley Smith, 'Disputes and Settlements in Medieval Wales: The Role of Arbitration', *English Historical Review*, 106 (1991), 835–60 at p. 849, CCR 1/34 m. 6. Cf. for Ireland Nicholls *GGI*, pp. 54–6.

was, to a remarkable extent, a kin-constructed world comes from the response of English government and English observers to it. It was different from anything they knew. They might respond to it quizzically as in their recurrent observations on the obsession of the men of the west with genealogy, descent and nobility of blood. Their surprise would have turned to astonishment had they been aware of the sheer volume, complexity and chronological depth of Welsh and Irish genealogical collections. Instead, they took the exercise lightly, quipping that 'Wales is a country in the world's backside where every man is born a gentleman and a genealogist' – thereby revealing their failure to recognise that in this world genealogy was a charter of identity and status, not an antiquarian cult.[18]

But it was in the very act of trying to govern these western societies – and governance and lordship in the Middle Ages was, of necessity, largely self-governance and working with the grain of local society – that the English were to learn how radically different was social organisation in the west and what massive adjustments had to be made to engage with it. Even the business of exploitation turned into a process of education. The manorial survey and extent had done good service in itemising seigniorial resources in lowland southern England; it was of little use – as the inquisitions *post mortem* and the post-conquest extents of 1284 showed in Wales – in a society where manors and rents of assize were virtually unknown (at least *eo nomine*) and in which wealth lay considerably in the renders and tributes of lineage groups. Discovering a language and a documentary format which could somehow capture this world (or at least do so sufficiently for the new lords to have a repertory of their dues and from whom to collect them) was one of the challenges which confronted English surveyors and scribes. The fruits of their response to the challenge are the sequence of great fourteenth-century surveys of north Wales – of which *The Survey of Denbigh* 1334 (which so fascinated Vinogradoff) and *The Record of Caernarvon* 1352 (dealing with the counties of Anglesey and Caernarfon) are the prime exemplars. These surveys put the lineage and its segments (W. *gwely, gafael*) at the centre of their picture for the attribution, allocation and collection of renders and tributes. It was an acknowledgement that this was a lineage-organised society.

It was an acknowledgement which had to be made in other directions. The mechanisms of peace-keeping in medieval England by the thirteenth century were constructed around cohorts of royal officials on the one hand – justices, sheriff, coroners, etc. – and the responsibilities of the locality on the other – be it tithing groups, juries, affeerors, the processes of hue and cry, etc. These peace-keeping mechanisms could be transplanted *en bloc* to English communities in Wales and Ireland, and might even be grafted in some measure on to native societies (as happened in the Statute of Wales in 1284). But there was a limit to the effectiveness of such grafting where the host society organised its social relationships on different principles from those of lowland England. Even the English had to admit defeat.

---

[18] For Wales, Francis Jones, 'An Approach to Welsh Genealogy', *Transactions of the Honourable Society of Cymmrodorion*, 1948, 303–466. The quotation is at p. 429.

So it was that in both Wales and Ireland from the late thirteenth century onwards, the English authorities were recurrently forced to concede that the responsibility for bringing suspected criminals to justice should lie with 'each chieftain of the lineage' or with 'the relatives, kinsmen and nearest relations' of the accused.[19] It was the triumph of the native social landscape and its kin-centred habits. The greatest triumph of that landscape lay in another direction: it captured the English themselves and persuaded them to reconfigure their social organisation in native terms. The most notable example of this process of 'going native' was the remarkable development of Anglo-Irish lineages (*naciones*) in Ireland from the mid-thirteenth century onwards. Their structure, power and activities replicated those of native Irish clans; central to them was the bond of blood, actual or artificial, and clan leadership. One small vignette brings the ambivalences of this world and its social fabric into focus: in 1290 the lineage (*nacio*) of Le Poer assembled before the sheriff of Waterford and were compelled to swear that they would bring one of their members to justice.[20] English, as well as native, Ireland was becoming a world of kinsmen.

But it was also a world of neighbours. It is one of the temptations of our social paradigms that we tend to represent one social bond as exclusive or at least prior and dominant. In reality, of course, men and women inhabit a variety of worlds simultaneously, the bonds of their obligations and opportunities overlapping, interpenetrating, preponderating, waxing and declining in a kaleidoscopic, ever-changing and unreflective manner. Too often we smuggle sets of unexamined assumptions and associations, and an either/or approach to social realities, to simplify and confirm our historical paradigms.

So it is with kinship bonds in the western British Isles. Too often they have been packaged into a self-contained and self-confirming 'tribal system' inhabited by 'free tribesmen'. Our evidence, in fact, suggests a much more complex world. Take the great *Survey of Denbigh 1334* for example: its eloquence on the centrality of agnatic lineages in the inheritance of land and the attribution of dues is matched by the centrality it gives to the vill, the organism of the neighbourhood, as the unit of governance. So it is likewise with the texts of Welsh law: rich they most certainly are in illuminating the dynamics and obligations of kin relationship but by no means to the exclusion of a whole host of non-kindred ties and associations. And

---

[19] Wales: *Calendar of Ancient Correspondence concerning Wales*, ed. J. G. Edwards (Cardiff, 1935), p. 234; *Record of Caernarvon*, p. 131; R. R. Davies, 'Twilight' (as in n. 17) at p. 349. Ireland: H. G. Richardson and G. O. Sayles, *The Irish Parliament in the Middle Ages* (Philadelphia, 1952), p. 292; *Chartularies of St. Mary's Dublin*, ed. J. T. Gilbert (Rolls Series, 1884–6), I, p. 369; *Statutes and ordinances . . . of the Parliaments of Ireland, John–Henry V*, ed. H. F. Berry (Dublin, 1907), pp. 265, 281–91.

[20] Robin Frame, *English Lordship in Ireland 1318–61* (Oxford, 1982), pp. 28–36; Katharine Simms, *From Kings to Warlords. The Changing Political Structure of Gaelic Ireland in the Later Middle Ages* (Woodbridge, 1987), pp. 36–8; C. Parker, 'Paterfamilias and Parentela. The Le Poer Lineage in Fourteenth-century Waterford', *Proceedings of the Royal Irish Academy*, 95 (1995), Section C, pp. 93–117.

when, finally, we enter the documentary clover in post-Conquest Wales, the local court rolls introduce us to a world whose polarities seem to be the individual (be he tenant or litigant) on the one hand and a multiple world of local communities on the other (though we ought to admit that we would not expect otherwise from documents based on English formularies).

Kinsmen and neighbours might, of course, often be the same, as the details of the boundary evidence in deed collections sometimes make clear.[21] But there were at least two good reasons why they might not be so. First, the lands of lineages – as we know from some excellent detailed studies – were often dispersed over several vills and even commotes, sometimes at considerable distance from each other; and so thereby were the lands, or at least the claims to land, of members of the lineage and its segments. Secondly, many, probably most, vills in Wales were inhabited by several lineages simultaneously. In the world of agnatic lineages that meant that many neighbours were *a fortiori* not kinsmen.[22]

But neighbours they remained, and cooperation between neighbours was an economic necessity, not a theoretical aspiration, for the vast majority of medieval communities, those of the western British Isles included. Unexamined assumptions may stand in the way of our acknowledging as much – among them that pastoral and upland communities do not nourish the sort of communal activities associated with lowland arable agriculture, that the small 'Celtic' field hardly fosters the regimented cooperation increasingly prevalent in open and common field 'champion' countryside, and that likewise the well-known dispersed character of human settlement in Wales did not require, or even permit, the close-knit village organisation so common in medieval England. None of these claims in fact stands up to the scrutiny of comparative historical study: it is, for example, from the high valleys and non-seignorialised world of Catalonia and the Alps that some of our earliest surviving evidence for vigorous collective activity survives, while it has been part of the achievement of Susan Reynolds to show the wide range of forms of peasant collective activity (broadly defined) and the very varying circumstances in which it flourished.[23]

But we need not content ourselves with a theoretical defence; the evidence itself speaks eloquently enough, at least for Wales. Collective activity is everywhere. It was bound to be so where good arable land was in such short supply and technological resources inadequate, and where the laws of partibility within lineages and segments divided the land into minute quillets. Microscopic studies of tenurial patterns in areas such as the lower Conwy valley, the plains of Bromfield in eastern Wales or the vale of Clwyd show as much convincingly. Thus at Cadlan in

---

[21] Davies *LSMW*, pp. 371 n. 57, 376; G. R. J. Jones, 'The Llanynys Quillets: A Measure of Landscape Transformation in North Wales', *Trans. Denbighshire Historical Society*, 13 (1964), 133–58.

[22] The classic, and still essential, articles are those in Jones Pierce *MWS*, esp. chap. 7, and the various studies of G. R. J. Jones, including 'The Distribution of Medieval Settlement in Anglesey', *Trans. Anglesey Antiquarian Society*, 6th series, 2 (1992), 221–46.

[23] Reynolds *KC*, chap. 5; Wickham *CCT*, chap. 8; idem, 'Problems of Comparing Early Medieval Societies', *Trans. Royal Historical Society*, 6th series, 2 (1992), 221–46.

Cymydmaen in western Caernarfonshire – that is in furthermost 'Welsh' Wales – in Elizabethan times 76 Welsh acres (W. *erwau*) were shared between twenty proprietors, most of whom held between one and six widely scattered strips.[24] In that context, as well as many others, the detailed section in the Welsh laws on joint-ploughing contracts (W. *cyfar*) and on the responsibilities of the neighbouring or joint landholder (W. *cytiriog*) become meaningful.[25] Nor was cooperation confined to the exploitation of the arable. It extended equally to pasture, woodland, waste, uplands and escheated land.[26] The claim that these were common lands, the property of the community, was a recurrent feature of the struggle between the lord and the community (as elsewhere in Europe) and figures prominently in charters of liberties in Wales. The Welsh word for such land, *cytir*, joint land, was eloquent of its collective status;[27] and when the community was unable to claim it as its own, it often did the next best thing – namely lease it as a community, of the vill or the *patria*, from the lord. Such common or commonly held property required organisation if it was to be exploited efficiently and equitably. And so the Welsh laws speak of the herdsman of the vill (W. *bugail trefgordd*), while the record evidence gives us glimpses of communal cowherds and stock-keepers (*custos averiorum*, *clustor ville*) and of the penalties imposed on those who ignored the community's timetable on transhumance.[28] Such references are surely no more than the tips of an iceberg of community cooperation and regulation, formal and informal, on a wide range of economic matters. They alone made life possible for the great majority of Welsh peasants, free and noble as they might claim to be.

It was the community of neighbours which was also the guarantor of peace and the guardian of acceptable social behaviour. This was proportionately even more so in the western British Isles than in many other medieval societies. This was a face-to-face world where the powers of lords (kings and princes included) were often marginal, where law depended primarily on collective consensus and professional juristic learning, and where the emphasis on status, prowess, honour and vengeance meant that violence lay very near the surface of social relationships. In these circumstances an awesome responsibility lay on the community to establish its own norms of relationships and the mechanisms for ensuring that those norms were broadly observed. It was thereby the best guarantor of peace in the feud. It was the neighbour (W. *cymydog*, literally a man of the same commote or hundred) who was called to stand warranty for a claim to ownership of cattle; it was the duty of everyone 'to serve as a surety (W. *mach*) for another' and the

---

[24] See nn. 21–2 above; Davies *LSMW*, pp. 369–70 (for Bromfield); Jones Pierce *MS*, p. 49 (for Cadlan).

[25] *WL*, pp. 198–202; D. Jenkins, *Agricultural Co-operation in Medieval Welsh Law* (St Fagans, Cardiff, 1982).

[26] Davies *LSMW*, esp. pp. 125–6; Rees (ed.), *CAP*, nos 2598, 5359, 6389, etc.

[27] The sour comment of the surveyor of the lordship of Oswestry in 1602 is revealing: 'They thinke they make no incrochments though they inclose all your Lordships wastes for they stand upon a frivolous term Kyttyr . . . for the world importeth common in Welsh.'

[28] *WML*, p. 62; DCCC 216/2 m. 13; E. A. Lewis, 'The Proceedings of the Small Hundred Court of the Commote of Ardudwy', *Bulletin of the Board of Celtic Studies*, 4 (1927–9), 153–66.

surety system was the backbone of formal relationships in both Wales and Ireland.[29] It was from his neighbours that a man would choose witnesses to verify his contract (W. *amodwyr*) or to assert his claim to land and his unlawful eviction from it (W. *ceidwaid, gwybyddiaid*).[30] The local community was thereby the custodian of knowledge – of fact, contract and opinion. No law-worthy man could operate outside it.

It was also a community of judgement. The rule of custom and collective judgement, as Susan Reynolds has noted,[31] was basic in medieval peasant society. Nowhere more so than in the western British Isles. Professional, hereditary jurists – the *ynad* in Wales, *brehon* in Ireland, the *breitheamh* or *judex* in Scotland[32] – might be the keepers of legal lore, but it was from the local community that the judgement-makers were normally drawn. They might be local good men – the *boni homines* which are such a frequent feature of early rural communes – or elders; they might also, especially in south Wales, be drawn from the ranks of local landholders. Their expertise lay in local knowledge, in appreciating the nuances of social relationships, and in an awareness of the fragility of social concord. 'The law of Wales', it has been observed, '. . . was more concerned with justice and reconciliation than with order and punishment.'[33] This is amply reflected in the evidence in the centrality of arbitration and arbitrators (W. *cymrodeddwyr*) and in the preference that disputes should be terminated 'by the agreement of the parties' (W. *trwy gyfundeb y pleidiau*). Even Edward I felt compelled to concede in the Statute of Wales 1284 that in cases concerning land and tenements in Wales 'the truth may be tried by good and lawful men of the neighbourhood, chosen by consent of the parties'.[34] It was a remarkable vote of confidence in the local community as the guarantors of social peace. It is not without significance that in the earliest recorded piece of Welsh text the aspiration of the 'judges' was to make peace – *gwnawn dangefedd*. The local community was in that sense the moral community; those who flouted its norms and rules – *ordinaciones patrie*, as they were called in the later evidence – were social outcasts.

For it was in the neighbourhood, be it local or regional, as much as, or even more than, in his kin groupings that the individual found his social identity. Discussions of collective activity have perhaps tended to be too severely utilitarian in

---

[29] *WL*, pp. 162, 75. Robin Chapman Stacey, *The Road to Judgment*, is wonderfully illuminating on contract and surety in Irish and Welsh societies and has a significance for the study of early law generally.

[30] *WL*, pp. 79, 86 (and note on pp. 255–6).

[31] Reynolds *KC*, p. 120.

[32] See, respectively, R. R. Davies, 'The Administration of Law in Medieval Wales: The Role of the *Ynad Cwmwd (Iudex Patrie)*', in T. Charles-Edwards et al. (eds), *Lawyers and Laymen* (Cardiff, 1986), pp. 258–73; K. Simms, 'The Brehons of Later Medieval Ireland', in D. Hogan and W. N. Osborough (eds), *Brehons, Serjeants and Attorneys* (Dublin, 1990), pp. 51–76; G. W. S. Barrow, 'The Judex', in *The Kingdom of the Scots* (London, 1973), pp. 69–82.

[33] D. Jenkins. 'The Significance of the Law of Hywel', *Trans. Hon. Soc. of Cymmrodorion*, 1977, 54–76 at pp. 67, 72. See generally Davies *CCC*, pp. 131–5.

[34] The key article is Llinos Smith, 'Disputes and Settlements', as cited above, n. 17.

this respect; there is more to medieval man than law and land, those twin pillars of our documentation.[35] It was the local community which, according to Welsh evidence, could enter into a contract for building or repairing a church or for ensuring that a bridge was kept in good condition. It showed its social concern and solidarity by authorising poor relief for its beggars (W. *commortha*), allowing them to collect sheaves from their neighbours.[36] It was also a community of sociability – organising games or communal feasts and arranging meetings (or 'gaderyngs', as a contemporary source called them) at which minstrels and bards (and wandering monks) – the 'westoures, barthes and rymours' of disapproving English legislation – entertained, and aroused, the people.[37]

These communal gatherings are one of the most remarkable manifestations of collective activity in both Wales and Ireland, all the more interesting because they lie totally beyond the purview of the royal and seignorial evidence and only appear in it to be condemned as seditious and unruly. Open-air assemblies – meeting at a well-known venue such as a hill-top, an oak tree or a township boundary – were probably a feature of most early societies; their agenda of activities were doubtless as broad as their membership was varied. But by the late medieval and early modern period this habit of assembly was seen within the world-view of the well-regulated and tightly controlled English polity as a specifically Welsh and Irish practice and one which was to be deplored. Edmund Spenser's famous characterisation of such public gatherings in Elizabethan Ireland may serve to introduce them:

> There is a great use among the Irish to make great assemblies together upon a Rath or hill, there to parley (as they say) about matters and wrongs between township and township, or one private person and another. . . . To them do commonly resort all the scum of loose people, where they may freely meet and confer of what they list.[38]

It is a description which could broadly be transferred to Wales where references to assemblies (W. *cymanfa*) and public judicial disputations (W. *dadleuoedd*), both in the native evidence and in the comments and condemnations of English observers, lift the veil on their centrality in social life and what would elsewhere be known as public order and dispute resolution.[39]

These assemblies met in the open, often on hill-tops as both the Irish and Welsh evidence suggest: hills had the twin advantage of being traditional venues and

---

[35] For England, see most recently Elaine Clark, 'Social Welfare and Mutual Aid in the Medieval Countryside', *Journal of British Studies*, 33 (1994), 381–406.
[36] DCCC 216/5 m. 26; 218/3 m. 18 (church repairs). Rees (ed.) *CAP*, no. 3263 (bridge repair); CCC 1/6 m. 2, m. 4; 13 (distribution of sheaves).
[37] Rees (ed.) *CAP*, no. 6464 (note); *Record of Caernarvon*, p. 132; *Rolls of Parliament*, III, p. 508; National Library of Wales, Aston Hall, 5835 (prohibition on giving money and clothes to 'those who are called in Welsh *cler*' (= wandering bards).
[38] Edmund Spenser, *A View of the Present State of Ireland*, ed. W. L. Renwick (Oxford, 1970), p. 77.
[39] For references to assemblies, sometimes specifically called *cymanfa*, *Statutes of the Realm*, II, p. 140 (4 Henry IV, c. 27–8); William Rees, *South Wales and the March 1284–1415* (Oxford, 1924), p. 65, n. 3. Cf. also *Record of Caernarvon*, p. 132: 'congregaciones per Wallenses in Northwallia ad consilia aut proposita aliqua facienda'.

locations removed from lowland, English-type authority.[40] Though English authorities viewed them as disruptive and seditious, that reflected the English authoritarian view of the control of the right of assembly. Rather were they occasions when leaders and peoples, and people and people, consulted with each other. That was the nature of the Irish *oenach*, which can be traced from the earliest Irish legal evidence: it was 'the most general gathering of the inhabitants, held at regular intervals for athletic, commercial and legal activities and for the proclaiming of special ordinances by the king in certain recognized emergencies'.[41] In Wales, attendance at such 'popular' assemblies and judicial disputations was regarded as two of the three duties which were attached to land (the third was service to the host).[42] In that sense the habit of assembly, the requirement to take part in collective activity, was a public obligation.

The business of such assemblies, – even when they met unofficially and in the face of English condemnation – was as varied as the community's interests and concerns. Much of their work (as Spenser's description suggests) was judicial or quasi-judicial, so long as our definition of the judicial embraces the arbitrative and the pre- or extra-curial and dispenses with notions of official enforcement. As such they are surely akin to the so-called 'popular courts' which Geoffrey Barrow has traced in Scotland.[43] Even in the later Middle Ages they might be seen as an alternative route to justice: so it is that an accusation could be dismissed because it had been made 'neither in the castle nor in the court, neither in the *congregatio patrie* nor in the presence of bailiffs'.[44] As well as defusing individual disputes, these assemblies (again as Edmund Spenser recognised) were an occasion for addressing inter-communal tensions, a task which was all the more necessary in a deeply fragmented political and institutional landscape. It is against this background that we should view the inter-communal and inter-lordship agreements (W. *cydfodau*) so common in late medieval Wales.[45] It was by community action that social peace was sustained in these societies; assemblies and agreements (the two Welsh words *cymanfa* and *cydfod* share the same prefix of togetherness, *cy(d)*) were mechanisms to that end.

But there was at least one other activity which took place at these assemblies which should inoculate us from taking too utilitarian and prosaic a view of organised collective activity and its social functions in the western British Isles. The issue is best identified from a much-quoted report on north Wales in Elizabethan times:

---

[40] Cf. B. L. Jones, 'Nodiadau amrywiol', *Bulletin of the Board of Celtic Studies*, 40 (1993), 119–22.

[41] K. Simms, *From Kings to Warlords*, p. 60. See also A. P. Smyth, *Celtic Leinster* (Blackrock, 1982), pp. 34–5.

[42] *Ancient Laws and Institutes of Wales*, ed. A. Owen (1841), II, p. 402.

[43] Nerys Patterson, 'Brehon Law in Late Medieval Ireland', *Cambridge Medieval Celtic Studies*, 17 (1989), 43–63, esp. p. 47; G. W. S. Barrow, 'Popular Courts in Medieval Scotland', reprinted in idem, *Scotland and its Neighbours in the Middle Ages* (London, 1992), pp. 217–45.

[44] CCR 1/15 m. 10.

[45] J. B. Smith, 'Cydfodau o'r Bymtheged Ganrif', *Bulletin of the Board of Celtic Studies*, 21 (1966), 309–24; 25 (1973), 128–34; Davies *LSMW*, pp. 244–8, esp. p. 248 n. 72 (for inter-communal agreements).

Upon the Sondaies and holidaies the multitude of all sorts of men women and childrene of evereie parishe doe use to meete in sondrie places either one some hill or one the side of some mountaine, where theire harpers and crowthers singe them songs of the doeings of theire auncestors, namelie, of theire warrs against the kings of this realme and the English nacion, and then doe they ripp up theire petigres at length how eche of them is discended from those their ould princes.[46]

It is a report which echoes an account of a monk more than a century earlier, moving through north and south Wales 'telling chronicles at Commorthaus and other gaderyngs to the motion of the people'. It is also echoed almost exactly contemporaneously in Ireland in the report of Nicholas Dawtry of how the Irish 'delighted in all their assemblies by speech of the people, songs, rhymes and poems . . . [to] hold their pedigrees and genealogies even to prove their descents directly or indirectly . . . from the ancient barbarous kings of that realm'.[47] But for us the value of these reports is different. They lift a corner of the curtain, as it were, on societies which we study otherwise overwhelmingly through the hugely restricting, and even distorting, mirror of seignorial and royal documentation. What we see is a community of culture, entertainment and shared (if also competitive) social memories, to be placed side by side with the communities of agricultural cooperation and the guardianship of social order.

The western British Isles, and Wales in particular, therefore provide ample evidence to support Susan Reynolds's general claim of 'the strength and character of the medieval drive to association'.[48] But community, as Maitland pointed out long ago, is a 'slippery' and 'nebulous' concept.[49] As such it has found no more than fitful favour – with some notable exceptions[50] – in English historiography, deeply attached as it is to its own empiricist, hard-headed, institutional and legalistic ground rules. A natural distrust of woolly (and especially comfortingly woolly) abstract concepts is most certainly in order; so likewise is the need to remind ourselves that tension, hierarchies, cross-currents and individual self-seeking are as much features of medieval (and all other) societies as is collective action. But a healthy scepticism is not a licence for a nominalist reductionism.

Communities certainly defy easy categorisation or definition. They were multiple, plastic and often evanescent. They were frequently based on a short-term identity of interest or need. As Susan Reynolds has put it with characteristic directness:[51] 'people seem to have been ready and able to act collectively in any group that had

---

[46] E. Owen (ed.), *Catalogue of Manuscripts relating to Wales in the British Museum* (1900–22), I, p. 72.

[47] Rees (ed.) *CAP*, no. 6464; D. B. Quinn, *The Elizabethans and the Irish* (Ithaca, 1966), p. 36; J. B. Smith, 'The Last Phase of the Glyndwr Rebellion', *Bulletin of the Board of Celtic Studies*, 22 (1966–8), 250–60 at p. 259.

[48] Reynolds *KC*, p. 77.

[49] F. W. Maitland, *Township and Borough* (Cambridge, 1895), p. 84.

[50] See, most recently, Christopher Dyer, 'The English Medieval Village Community and its Decline', *Journal of British Studies*, 33 (1994), 407–29.

[51] Reynolds *KC*, p. 138.

common interests in the matter in hand', be that matter, one might add, ad hoc, seasonal, annual, long-term or recurrent. They called those collective, overlapping and interacting associations communities (*communitas, universitas*), be they those of status (free, unfree, advowry men, etc.), ethnicity (English, Welsh), locality (vill, commote, lordship, county, region, etc.) or what have you.[52]

Such 'communities' may not have enjoyed the institutional structures of the rural communes of Tuscany, so ably described recently by Chris Wickham. Nor is there any need to deny – why should anyone wish to do so? – that communitarian terminology may often conceal private ambition, especially that of the rich and powerful leaders of the locality. Yet when we find – as we do from the evidence of the court rolls – that a community can prosecute a local officer, appoint proctors to negotiate charters of liberties or the terms of communal fines, summon its members to the local church to share out communal tribute-dues, enter into contracts and appoint its own attorneys, lease land and take over vacant holdings, declare local custom through statutes and ordinances, and even depose a leper from what it portentously called the *collegia communitatis*, we must surely concede that 'communities' in the western British Isles could forge and implement courses of action, however suspicious we may be of the routes by which they reached and implemented such decisions.[53] And they could do all that without entering, or even knowing about, the world of corporations, legally speaking. We may be even more convinced of the case when we recall that during the late thirteenth and fourteenth centuries many of the communities of the English Marcher lordships of Wales won, or were granted, charters of liberties – comparable to village charters of liberties so common in continental Europe (but *not* England) from the twelfth century, but on a much broader geographical base. These charters delimited the powers of their lords, specified the liberties which the community henceforth enjoyed and allowed it to cite the clauses of such charters in its defence.[54] This is the world of Magna Carta and 'the community of the realm' transposed into a different social, geographical and political setting.

Two further reasons may be enlisted, finally, in support of this *apologia* for the study of the communities of the western British Isles. The first relates to lordship. Collective action in medieval societies was not merely or even mainly a response to lordship. Nevertheless the character and changing nature of lordship most certainly helped to shape, and reshape, community. The relationship between king and people, lord (W. *arglwydd*) and country (W. *gwlad*) was an issue which had exercised the societies of the western British Isles from an early date; it evoked some remarkable statements about the relationship of the two.[55] Into this world of dispersed power, intensive kin- and status-rights, and a non-deferential class of free

---

[52] These communities *eo nomine* figure recurrently in, for example, CCC, DCCC and Rees (ed.), *CAP*.
[53] Examples are legion. See, briefly, Davies *LSMW*, pp. 134–5, 163–4, 357, 460–2.
[54] See briefly, with a list of charters, Davies *LSMW*, pp. 562–5.
[55] T. M. Charles-Edwards, 'A Contract between King and People in Early Medieval Ireland? Crith Gablach on Kingship', *Peritia*, 8 (1994), 107–19; J. B. Smith, 'Gwlad ac Arglwydd', *Beirdd a Thywysogion*, ed. M. E. Owen and B. F. Roberts (Aberystwyth, 1996), pp. 237–58.

nobles (as they saw themselves) entered, from the eleventh and twelfth centuries, the claims and assumptions of a very different Anglo-Norman world – a world of an authoritarian kingship, a well-articulated and exploitative lordship, and a habit of individualised power relationships. Part of the fascination of the histories of the western British Isles in the later Middle Ages is the opportunity to glimpse how these two very different paradigms of social consciousness and social and political power negotiated a working relationship with each other. In the process kingship and lordship on the one side and communities on the other had to redefine their claims and relationships.[56] The *modus vivendi* so achieved casts shafts of light on lordship and community in medieval society more generally.

The second issue relates to chronology. Collective action is not the privilege of any period or place. Yet the format, range and character of collective action respond regularly to changing social, economic and political circumstances. In the chronology of medieval communities, historians have recognised the period from the late eleventh century onwards as particularly significant (even when they have made allowances for the rapid increase in documentation).[57] This was certainly a formative period in the history of the western British Isles – in, for example, the definition of lineage rights and local boundaries (lay and ecclesiastical) and in the articulation of the claims of lordship and kingship. If to this we add the galvanising impact of the military, political, economic and commercial power of the Anglo-Norman world, we may recognise that this area may yet hold a particular interest for those who wish to study kingdoms and communities in Western Europe 900–1300.

---

[56] I have explored some of these issues in *The First English Empire. Power and Identities in the British Isles 1093–1343* (Oxford, 2000), esp. chaps 4–6.

[57] Reynolds *KC*, pp. 109, 122–38; Wickham *CCT*, pp. 191, 237.

Lay kinship solidarity and papal law

David d'Avray

Susan Reynolds has rightly rejected any notion of an early Middle Ages where kinship was 'unsupplemented by lordship and by other forms of community',[1] and she has concentrated her own research on other social bonds, but she is convinced nonetheless that 'All that we know of medieval society leaves no doubt of the importance of kinship'.[2] The large bibliography[3] on medieval kinship reflects this importance. One thing that emerges from this scholarly literature is that apart from the rules imposed by the church there was nothing that can be called *the* medieval kinship system. The previous generation of scholars interested in this kind of question argued for a major transformation around the year 1000. According to this theory a system of large cognatic kin groups[4] (i.e. groups including both male and female descendants of the common ancestor) gave way to a patrilineal or agnatic system, which may crudely be defined as one where 'links through the father are emphasized'.[5]

---

[1] *Kingdoms and Communities in Western Europe 900–1300* (second edition, Oxford, 1997), p. 337.
[2] Ibid., p. 4.
[3] To give a few examples – for the Middle Ages in general: G. Duby and J. Le Goff, eds, *Famille et parenté dans l'Occident médiéval* (Collection de l'Ecole Française de Rome, 30; Rome 1977); Anita Guerreau-Jalabert, 'Sur les structures de parenté dans l'Europe médiévale', *Annales. Economies, Sociétés, Civilisations*, 36 (1981), pp. 1028–49; for the early Middle Ages: Alexander Callender Murray, *Germanic Kinship Structure: Studies in Law and Society in Antiquity and the Early Middle Ages* (Studies and Texts, 65; Toronto, 1983); Thomas Charles Edwards, *Early Irish and Welsh Kinship* (Oxford, 1993); Régine Le Jan, *Famille et pouvoir dans le monde Franc (VIIe–Xe siècle: Essai d'anthropologie sociale* (Paris, 1995). For the central Middle Ages: Anita Guerreau-Jalabert, 'Prohibitions canoniques et stratégies matrimoniales dans l'aristocratie médiévale de la France du Nord', in *Épouser au plus proche. Inceste, prohibitions et stratégies matrimoniales autour de la Méditerranée* (Éditions de l'École des Hautes Etudes en Sciences Sociales, 1994); A. Wareham, 'Two Models of Marriage: Kinship and Social Order in England and Normandy', in A.-J. A. Bijsterveld et al., eds, *Negotiating Secular and Ecclesiastical Power: Western Europe in the Central Middle Ages* (International Medieval Research 6; Turnhout, 1999), pp. 107–32; For the late Middle Ages: K.-H. Spiess, *Familie und Verwandtschaft im deutschen Hochadel des Spaetmittelalters. 13. bis Anfang des 16. Jahrhunderts* (Stuttgart, 1993).
[4] On cognatic kin groups see Robin Fox, *Kinship and Marriage. An anthropological perspective* (Cambridge, 1983 edition), ch. 6.
[5] R. Parkin, *Kinship. An Introduction to the Basic Concepts* (Oxford, 1997), p. 15.

Lay kinship solidarity and papal law

Now this theory has suffered a good deal of criticism.[6] The formula 'from cognatic to agnatic kinship' would clearly be a gross oversimplification. Nevertheless there was equally clearly a transformation of some sort. The outcome in northern France and post-Conquest England at any rate was a system which emphasised legitimate succession from eldest son to eldest son, discouraged marriage of younger sons, and allowed for female succession to land in the absence of sons. At the very least this was more clearly defined than in the preceding period.

Differences between regions are as striking as differences between periods, and more relevant to the argument which will be developed in the course of this essay. In some parts of Europe the extended family clan was a major factor in social life. Its members were convinced that they shared common blood. The sign of membership was a common name. Clans were an economic, political, and even a spiritual community. Jacques Heers has the credit of putting clans on the historiographical map. His 'clans' more or less fit the anthropologists definition: 'Higher order units often consisting of several lineages in which common descent is assumed but cannot necessarily be demonstrated'.[7] Heers's seminal *Family Clans in the Middle Ages* (1977)[8] applied a model derived from Genoa to Europe as a whole. It seems to fit Italy fairly well, and it may work for, say, Flanders; but Heers probably generalised too much. For England at least his ideal type does not seem come close to real family structures. There large-scale units of blood kin seem hard to find in the central and later Middle Ages at least.[9] The blood feud is an index of this contrast between different parts of Europe. In Italy and Flanders[10] it is important even in the late Middle Ages. In England by contrast the blood feud and the *wergild* system for which it served as a sanction had disappeared at least by the mid-twelfth century, however it may have been in earlier times.

---

[6] For example, J. Nelson, *Charles the Bald* (London, 1992), p. 175, argues that the 'clans' may have been important in the religious sphere but that their political significance has been much exaggerated; one of the historians who casts doubt on the whole interpretation is C. Bouchard: 'Family Structure and Family Consciousness among the Aristocracy in the Ninth to Eleventh Centuries', *Francia*, 14 (1986), pp. 639–58; Guerreau-Jalabert, 'La Parenté dans l'Europe médiévale et moderne: à propos d'une synthèse récente', *L'Homme*, 110, 1989, XXIX (2), pp. 69–93, at 74, points out that there were always 'cognatic' elements in medieval kinship systems, and that we do not find agnatic 'lineages' in the full sense in which anthropologists of Africa use the term.

[7] Cf. Fox, *Kinship and Marriage*, p. 49.

[8] J. Heers, *Family Clans in the Middle Ages. A Study of Political and Social Structures in Urban areas* (Amsterdam, 1977, a slightly revised edition of the 1974 French edition, *Le Clan familial au Moyen Age*).

[9] B. Hanawalt, *The Ties that Bound* (New York and Oxford, 1986) ch. 5, esp. pp. 83, 89. A lecture by Lee Patterson made me think about this contrast.

[10] Ch. Petit-Dutaillis, *Documents nouveaux sur les mœurs populaires et le droit de vengeance dans les Pays-Bas au XVe siècle. Lettres de rémission de Philippe le Bon* (Bibliothèque du XVe siècle, ix; Paris, 1908) (David Morgan directed me to this important work). Here we find a system of feud and compensation which will look familiar to historians of Anglo-Saxon England. The rules governing the system are an index of kinship structure. Thus the 'Coutume primitive du Franc de Bruges' gives rules (about 'truces' in wars between families) which reveal an ego-centred kindred system of the same sort as that of canon law in the period, though slightly narrower: the kindred includes relatives on either the father's or the mother's side up to the third degree inclusive (so: second cousins) (ibid. p. 58).

Thus medieval kinship structures varied according to period and region. In the course of the Middle Ages, however, a unitary kinship system was increasingly imposed on the laity by the church. Jack Goody's controversial study[11] of medieval kinship has the great merit of recognising that the kinship system which bound together Western Europe as a whole was the set of rules about consanguinity and affinity administered by church authorities. We cannot amputate lay consciousness from the influence of the church, which was by our period enforced by effective power structures. The laity did not necessarily resist this process and probably internalised the church's rules to some extent at least.

This essay aims to answer some precise questions about the rationality of this kinship system. Like most good questions about rationality, these are ultimately derived from Max Weber.

Firstly, we need to ask about the surface rationale propagated by the church. Did it justify the kinship system by appeals to emotion, or tradition, or to instrumental efficacy, or to values, or to some combination of the foregoing? The distinction between 'instrumental rationality' (*Zweckrationalität*) and 'value rationality' (*Wertrationalität*) seems to me especially useful for the study of kinship rules. (The ordinary language of historians can cope with the distinction after a fashion, but fuzzily, without formulating the question with any precision.) In Weber's conceptual scheme these two kinds of rationality were complementary.[12] Instrumental rationality virtually always operates within parameters set by value rationality, and the values which define objectives and 'no-go areas' affect the whole character of common-sense reasoning in a given culture or subculture.[13]

The foregoing all applies to the public justifications of actions: legitimating rationality. We must also ask whether there are different reasons below the surface, on the principle that 'consciousness lies to itself'.[14] Was there an 'agenda' behind the kinship system? This agenda could be hidden from the consciousness of those who imposed the system as well as from those on whom they imposed it. Status groups have a collective cunning in whitewashing their own motives in their own eyes.

Even if there was such an agenda, the first set of questions (about 'legitimating rationality') still need to be asked. Whatever the real motives or causes of a policy,

---

[11] *The Development of the Family and Marriage in Europe* (Cambridge, 1983). The best-known thesis of the book, that the function of the church's kinship rules was to channel property towards the church, is seriously flawed (see below) but the book as a whole has served the field well.

[12] M. Weber, *Wirtschaft und Gesellschaft* (Tübingen, 1972 edition), p. 13: 'Die Entscheidung zwischen konkurrierenden und kollidierenden Zwecken und Folgen kann dabei ihrerseits wertrational orientiert sein . . . Absolute Zweckrationalitaet des Handelns ist . . . nur ein im wesentlichen konstruktiver Grenzfall.'

[13] Incidentally one can find here the elements of an answer to the whole problem of whether rationality is a universal or culturally specific, and to the whole debate about 'how natives think'. Instrumental rationality is a cultural universal but value rationalities are many; values set the agenda and define which means are legitimate; instrumental reasoning is coloured by the value rationality which encloses it and defines its field of operations. Pragmatism is as it were diffracted around the edges by principles, which nevertheless remain distinct.

[14] Claude Lévi-Strauss, Didier Eribon, *De Près et de loin* (Paris, 1988), p. 152: 'je ne conserve des enseignements de Marx que quelques leçons. Surtout celle-ci: que la conscience se ment à elle même.'

Lay kinship solidarity and papal law

the reasons alleged on its behalf can be crucial for understanding why people accepted or tolerated it.[15] And of course one should not assume a priori that there was a hidden agenda. Sometimes the reason given is also the real motive or cause.

Value reinforced by emotion prohibited marriage to near kin. The *Gregorius* story (Hartmann von Aue's poem is the most famous version) shows that incestuous sexual unions were regarded with horror. Here a brother and sister sleep together. The child is sent off in a boat at the mercy of the elements. He is rescued and brought up by monks, but feels an overwhelming 'vocation' to become a knight. He is allowed to do so and rescues a queen from a dangerous unwanted suitor. They fall in love and marry. Then it emerges that he is her son. He performs a penance of unbelievable austerity, thus showing that his after all unwitting offence was thought to be an utterly unspeakable crime. This vernacular story is probably a good guide to lay attitudes. It could not work dramatically unless the evilness of the acts was beyond question.

There is nothing surprising about this. Structural parallels with the Oedipus story are obvious. Most societies frown on brother–sister unions,[16] and perhaps all on the marriage of mother and son. But of course the medieval church's prohibitions of marriage to relatives extended much further. What kind of rationale was advanced for the ban on marriage to less immediate relatives?

A possible answer would be: number symbolism and symmetry. Innocent III at the Fourth Lateran Council decreed that marriage to first, second and third cousins of oneself or of a deceased spouse or sexual partner were out of bounds. In the kinship terminology of the high medieval church this was a ban on marriage in the first four degrees of consanguinity or affinity. Innocent remarked that 'the number four is very appropriate to the prohibition of bodily marriage' because there are four humours in the body, which come from the four elements'.[17] Symbolic reasoning could be taken very seriously in this period. The belief that the union of man and woman mirrored the union of Christ and the church was a principal reason for the medieval papacy's emphasis on indissolubility.[18] However the appeal to symmetry in the 1215 decree does not look like a rational justification of the decree. The phrase '*bene congruit*' should alert us. Innocent is saying that the number four is aesthetically fitting. It would be insensitive to interpret him as asserting a moral absolute. More probably, he had to draw the line somewhere, had no absolute reason for doing so at any particular degree, and did not want to make the new

---

[15] For a seminal statement of this idea, see Quentin Skinner, 'The Principles and Practice of Opposition: The Case of Bolingbroke versus Walpole', in N. McKendrick, ed., *Historical Perspectives. Studies in English Thought and Society in Honour of J. H. Plumb* (London, 1974), pp. 93–128, esp. p. 128.

[16] For an exception see K. Hopkins, 'Brother–Sister Marriage in Roman Egypt', *Comparative Studies in Society and History*, 22 (1980), pp. 303–54.

[17] 'Quaternarius vero numerus bene congruit prohibitioni conjugii corporalis . . . quia quatuor sunt humores in corpore, qui constant ex quatuor elementis', *Corpus Iuris Canonici* X (Decretals of Gregory IX) 4.14.8 (*Corpus Iuris Canonici*, ed. Emil Friedberg (Graz, 1955 reprint), ii, col. 704).

[18] A point which I hope to make elsewhere. For the fundamental importance of symbolism or signification in medieval theological and canon legal thought about marriage see T. Rincón, *El matrimonio misterio y signo, siglos IX–XIII* (Pamplona, 1971).

rule sound totally arbitrary. The *Supplementum* to the *Summa Theologica* of Thomas Aquinas confirms this interpretation. At Q. 54, article 4 the fourth 'objection' is that 'the causes which are assigned to the number of degrees seem altogether irrational, since they have no relation to what is caused: as that consanguinity is prohibited up to the fourth degree because of the four elements . . .', and it is answered thus: 'when such reasons are assigned they are given more by way of fitting symmetry than of cause and necessity'.[19]

The general thrust of the whole decree is that the forbidden degrees are not a matter of absolute value, since the church has the discretion to redraw them. This idea was nothing new. Gratian's *Decretum* made widely available a letter of Pope Alexander II which makes it clear that the forbidden degrees are not a matter of immutable principle: they had been modified for the English so as not to discourage them while they were new to the faith.[20] Much earlier still (726), Pope Gregory II put a similarly relativist spin on the church's rules in a letter to St Boniface. He says that people ought not to marry anyone to whom they were related, but that the rule could be modified for a barbarous people. Four forbidden degrees would be enough for the latter.[21] This appears to be the same boundary that the Fourth Lateran Council would make the general law of Christendom in 1215. According to the 1215 decree 'It should not be judged reprehensible, if *human* statutes should sometimes be varied to suit changing times, especially if urgent *necessity* or evident *utility* demand it' (my italics).[22] The words I have italicised are the language of instrumental rather than value rationality. (The language of instrumental rationality in papal documents deserves a special study, incidentally, and its focus could be sharpened by awareness of modern schools of philosophical ethics.) The absolutes of divine law set the parameters for the discourse of medieval popes, but these parameters left space for (and orientated) a certain sort of ethical consequentialism.[23]

The pontificate of Innocent IV marks a further stage in papal pragmatism. The number of dispensations for marriage increases dramatically. They were granted to papal supporters in the struggle with the Hohenstaufen.[24] More surprisingly,

---

[19] *Sancti Thomae Aquinatis Doctoris Angelici Opera Omnia iussu impensaque Leonis XIII P. M. edita*, xii (Rome, 1906), *Supplementum*, pp. 106, 107.

[20] Decreti Secunda Pars, C. 35, Q. 5, c. 2, Friedberg edn., I, col. 1273, section 6, passage beginning 'Sed sunt quidam . . .'.

[21] 'Igitur in primis legebatur, ut quota progenies propinquorum matrimonio copuletur. Dicimus, quod oportuerat quidem, quamdiu se agnoscunt affinitate propinquos, ad huius copulae non accedere societatem; sed quia temperantia magis, et presertim in tam barbaram gentem, placet plus quam districtione censure, concedendum est, ut post quartam generationem iungantur.' (*Monumenta Germaniae Historica, Epistolae Merowingici et Karolini Aevi*, I (Berlin, 1892), pp. 275–6.

[22] X.4.14.8. (Friedberg edn, ii, col. 703).

[23] Note that the 'consequentialism' differed fundamentally from the modern schools of moral philosophy which would accept the label.

[24] H. Kroppmann, *Ehedispensübung und Stauferkampf unter Innozenz IV. Ein Beitrag zur Geschichte des päpstlichen Ehedispensrechtes* (Berlin, 1937), *passim*. I was stimulated by a paper read by Professor Paul Pixton (at the 1998 Leeds International Medieval Congress) on 'Kissing Cousins: Pushing the Lateran Decree on Consanguinity beyond the Limits'. A difference between us, as I remember his argument, is that he would tend to see the multiplication of dispensations as laxity.

many papal dispensations do not conceal a preoccupation with cementing support against the Hohenstaufen.[25]

The language of pragmatism continued to be used after the Hohenstaufen crisis was over. Popes granted dispensations to kings who supported their interests. The pragmatic reasoning continued to be made explicit in bulls. A bull of Honorius IV to Edward I, sent on 27 May 1286, is a good example. Honorius refers back to a dispensation he had granted to Edward's children, permitting them to marry persons related to them in the fourth degree of consanguinity or affinity. He says that he had granted this, at Edward's urging, 'for a certain reason'. Nevertheless Honorius now wanted to make it clear that the dispensation did not apply to marriages with the family (*cum filiis vel filiabus, nepotibus, neptibusve*) of Peter of Aragon (who was in conflict with the papacy at that time) or with anyone else who was opposed (*indevotis*) to the Roman church.[26] The bull to which he refers, and which Edward regarded as valuable enough to have a notarised copy made of it in 1305, spoke of the problem of finding partners of equal status to Edward's children but not related to them within the forbidden degrees. However it implies that a decisive consideration in the pope's mind was 'the exceptionally devoted affection which you are known to have towards us and the Roman church', which 'has merited that we should honour your person with the fullness of apostolic favour and most benignly allow your petitions to be graciously granted'.[27]

Thus the discourse of papal documents makes it clear that the rules about consanguinity and affinity were not absolute values. To that extent their reasoning can be taken at face value: if someone declares they are following absolute principle we may not believe them, but if they make it clear that they do not feel bound by a principle we are likely to take their word.

So did popes simply use the kinship system in the interests of cynical *Realpolitik*? That would be a misunderstanding. It is hard to avoid if one sees instrumental and value rationality as opposite alternatives. Papal pragmaticism operated within a value framework which it is possible to recover. Religious writings of the period can help us retrace the boundaries between *Zweckrationalität* and *Wertrationalität* in papal manipulation of the kinship system.

A convenient statement of what we need to know can be found in the *Supplementum* to the *Summa Theologica* of Thomas Aquinas (Q. 54, articles 3 and 4). This makes it clear that the ban on marriage beyond the most immediate degrees of relationship was not a matter of principle in itself. Beyond those degrees the function of the prohibition was to link people by social bonds and to increase friendship among them. If men married blood relatives, then the opportunity to create a

---

[25] 'Die Mehrzahl der Dispensen lässt die politische Absicht der deutschen Staufergegner und damit auch der Kurie, den Empfänger für den Stauferkampf zu verpflichten, allzu deutlich erkennen.' Ibid., pp. 79–80.

[26] T. Rymer, *Foedera* (Record Commission edition, 4 vols in 7 parts; London, 1816–69), vol. I.ii (London, 1816), p. 665; for background see P. Chaplais, *English Medieval Diplomatic Practice. Part I, Documents and Interpretation* (London, 1982), ii, p. 481.

[27] I have used the notarised copy, now Public Record Office, London, S.C. 7.36/5.

new social bond would be lost, and so such marriages were banned 'according to human laws and the statutes of the church'. But these laws are sharply distinguished in the text of the *Supplementum* from the natural law prohibition of marriage between child or parent and the divine law prohibition of marriage between other immediate relatives.[28] The rules could be adjusted to fit social conditions: when the social bond between remote relatives had grown weak and needed reinforcing, the ban on the remoter degrees of relationship could be removed.[29]

All this shows that the church's kinship rules were a matter of instrumental rather than value rationality. Or rather, they were instruments in the service of a value – social cohesion, the extension of friendship – but not values in themselves.

So the consanguinity rules were man-made (except where immediate relatives were concerned). Consequently, they could be modified or suspended without violating a principle. In a particular case another good might take priority over them in papal eyes. The rule was a means to a good end but not a value per se. It was believed to extend social bonds in the aggregate, but an extension of social bonds was not essential in any one given case. Other (perceived) goods of the church might have higher priority. Furthermore, in particular cases the rule might militate against the value which provided its main public rationale: the extension of friendship. When Boniface VIII managed to reconcile the warring dynasties of Angevin Naples and the Crown of Aragon, marriage alliances were a crucial tool. But he had to grant dispensations from the forbidden degrees. The families were locked in combat; nevertheless they were too closely related for marriage alliance without papal permission.[30] Preventing or ending discord was a common rationale for papal dispensations.[31] In the last analysis, however, the decision whether to grant a dispensation in a particular case was a matter of calculating the relative utility to the church of heterogeneous effects. The endogamy rules were deemed

---

[28] *Supplementum* to *Summa Theologica*, Q. 54, article 3 'Respondeo' section (*Sancti Thomae . . . Opera Omnia*, xii (1906), p. 106). The idea is an old one. It can be found in Augustine's *City of God* (15, ch. 16). This passage would have been very well known in our period if only because it was incorporated in Gratian's Decretum, Causa 35, Quaestio I, c. 1 (Friedberg edn, i, col. 1262). The idea is developed in an interesting way and with a clear reference to the Fourth Lateran Council a sermon by the thirteenth-century Sienese Dominican Ambrogio Sansedoni: See MS. Siena Biblioteca Comunale T.iv.7, fo. 14ʳ.

[29] Summa Theologica, Suppl. Q, 54 article 4, 'Respondeo' section (*Sancti Thomae . . . Opera Omnia*, xii (1906), p. 107). See also Sansedoni, above: he makes the reference to the Lateran IV decree explicit.

[30] See G. Le Bras, 'Boniface VIII, symphoniste et modérateur', in *Mélanges d'histoire du Moyen Age dédiés à la mémoire de Louis Halphen*, préface de Charles-Edmond Perrin (Paris, 1951), pp. 383–94, at p. 385.

[31] See (as a random example) *Les Régistres de Nicolas III (1277–1280)*, ed. Jules Gay and Suzanne Vitte (Paris, 1938), n. 88 (27 June 1278). A man had married a woman related in the third degree of consanguinity to another woman to whom he had been betrothed. This would have created an impediment of 'Public Honesty'. The pope explains the grounds that would justify validating the marriage: '. . . Verum cum, si forte publice honestatis justitia deposcente inter dictos Alardum et Mariam interveniret divortium, verisimiliter presumatur quod inter ipsius Alardi ex parte una et ejusdem M. consanguineos nobiles et in partibus illis potentes ex altera pacis vinculum super gravibus et antiquis inimicitiis dudum inter partes habitis reformate penitus solveretur et sic graviores antiquis inimicitie ac scandala plurima in illis partibus orirentur . . .' (pp. 25–6).

Lay kinship solidarity and papal law 195

good for church and society on aggregate, but that good might be outweighed in individual cases by other goods, perhaps of a different sort, such as royal support for papal policies.

A conclusion about the surface or 'legitimating' rationality of the kinship rules imposed by the papacy on the laity may now be formulated. The rules were *Zweckrational* rather than *Wertrational*. They were a means of creating new social solidarities. However the means could sometimes frustrate the end. Then rules could be discarded by papal dispensation. Popes could also dispense from the rules for the sake of some other advantage to the church. Pope John XXII summed it up in the early fourteenth century: 'The statutes of the sacred canons should not be mutilated except for the necessity[32] and utility of the church'.[33] 'Necessity' and 'utility' are key concepts in papal *Zweckrationalität*.

We may now turn to the second problem: is the surface rationale the real rationale? The surface rationale is pragmatic, but the pragmatism is explicitly orientated towards values. Did this reasoning mask other and more sinister pragmatic motivations, concealed from the church's public sphere and perhaps from the foreground consciousness of the popes themselves. Was the explicit rationale a false consciousness?

One possibility has been fully explored in recent scholarship: viz., that the 'function' of the forbidden degrees was to channel lay property into church hands.[34] According to this theory the 'forbidden degrees' prevented families from using endogamy to consolidate blocks of family land, with the consequence that it went to the church instead. This thesis has been criticised from many sides. I may be permitted to repeat two objections which have not been answered and which seem to me to be unanswerable.[35] Firstly, the church's rules would not reduce the number of heirs related by blood – a simple but deadly argument against the theory. The second objection is a little less simple. The right to inherit was used as a guide to the forbidden degrees: i.e., the people who have a right to inherit are the people you cannot marry. Thus the rules about the forbidden degrees provided strong reinforcement for and endorsement of inheritance rights. This rule-of-thumb guide seems to have been formulated at least as early as the Pseudo-Isidorean Decretals and to have been repeated in influential canon law collections up to and including Gratian.[36] The canon (beginning *De affinitate*) which immediately precedes this

---

[32] Avoidance of wars and disputes being cases of 'necessity', according to John.

[33] H. Finke, *Acta Aragonensia: Quellen zur . . . Kirchen- und Kulturgeschichte, aus der diplomatischen Korrespondenz Jaymes II (1291–1327)*, I (1908), p. LVIII.

[34] This is the best-known thesis of Goody's *Development of the Family*. As I suggested earlier, the great service of this book was to make medievalists realise that the main kinship system of the Middle Ages was the one the church proposed and gradually imposed, and that this system should be studied in comparative terms.

[35] I sketched out these arguments in 'Peter Damian, Consanguinity and Church Property', in Lesley Smith and Benedicta Ward, eds, *Intellectual Life in the Middle Ages. Essays Presented to Margaret Gibson* (London, 1992), pp. 71–80, at pp. 76–7.

[36] For references see *Decreti Secunda Pars* C. 35 Q. 2 et 3, c. 2, Friedberg edn, i, col. 1264, at note 11.

one in Gratian[37] makes much the same point. (The *De affinitate* canon is found earlier in Burchard of Worms, writing in the early eleventh century. Its origins are obscure but it crops up for the first time in manuscripts of the Pseudo-Isidorean Decretals.[38] It influenced Peter Damian.[39]) So the definition of consanguinity and affinity went hand in hand with a definition of inheritance rights. The more the church stressed the forbidden degrees, the more it strengthened lay inheritance rights. Thus the acquisition of lay property at the expense of lay inheritance rights was probably not a hidden agenda behind the church's kinship law.

There is a more serious possibility: that the forbidden degrees were defined so as to make powerful laymen depend on the pope for favours. The argument would run thus. Even the 'four degrees' rule was a relatively wide prohibition. It put third cousins (and their widows or widowers or ex-partners) in the forbidden zone. Many people today find the idea of marriage to first cousins quite acceptable.[40] (As noted above, in the later Middle Ages popes gave dispensations at their discretion.) This gave them a hold over kings and great nobles, who might need papal permission to marry a moderately remote cousin. The kinship law was an instrument of power.

Theories of this kind are difficult to test. It is easy to suggest that somebody or an institution has an ulterior motive. To prove or falsify the hypothesis can be tricky. Is socialised medicine a form of social control by the modern state? Was the Marshall Plan anything more than a move against Moscow? Were the social reforms of nineteenth-century English governments motivated by fear of violent revolution? The true answer may differ from case to case, but definitive proof will not be easy to find in any of them. The danger is that one's answer will depend on one's temperament, or on one's general feelings towards the power structures in question. Again, actions are commonly 'overdetermined', in the sense that they may be caused by several motivations at once. How can one say which is primary? How can one be sure which would have been enough without the others?

Nevertheless it is possible to go some distance towards an answer. The 1215 decree states that the 'four degrees' rule should be observed strictly: if a couple got married without having the bans read first and subsequently found they were too closely related, they would get no dispensation. In practice it does seem that dispensations were exceedingly rare until the pontificate of Innocent III.[41] Thus the rule substantially antedates the widespread dispensation of it by popes. Can it really have been the intention of Innocent IV and the Fourth Lateran Council to encourage manipulation of lay rulers through the decree? That popes became laxer

---

[37] C. 35. Q. 3 et 3, c. 1 (Friedberg edn, col. 1264).

[38] See H. Hoffmann and R. Pokorny, *Das Dekret des Bischofs Burchard von Worms. Textstufen – Frühe Verbreitung – Vorlagen* (Munich, 1991), p. 208, at VII 16.

[39] See d'Avray, 'Peter Damian', p. 77.

[40] Informal inquiries among my students suggest impressionistically that a substantial minority would consider in principle a marriage to a first cousin: there is no unanimity either way.

[41] Kroppman, *Ehedispensübung*, p. 4: 'während für den friedliebenden Honorius III (1216–1227) nur 3 Ehedispensen nachzuweisen sind, zählt Gregor IX (1227–41) schon deren 18, und unter Innozenz IV. (1243–54) schwillt ihre Zahl mit einem Male auf 272 an!'

later on is easy to explain. No principle was at stake. Friends of the papacy were pressing. Why not say yes? But manipulation was not the original rationale.

Another consideration which points in the same direction is the inflexibility of the popes about dissolving marriages. From the pontificate of Innocent III on it seems to have been hard to get an annulment. So far as one can tell in the light of current research, even a powerful ruler could not succeed unless the law was on his side. Innocent III's refusal to annul the marriage of Ingeborg of Denmark with King Philip Augustus of France is a famous case but not the only one from his pontificate.[42] In the subsequent period it seems to have been hard for a king to get a papal annulment if he did not have a strong case in law and fact. Perhaps the *causes célèbres* of Innocent's pontificate sent a message to queens: your royal husband cannot get rid of you, if you appeal to the pope. Kings too would have become aware of potential problems. The awareness could have deterred them from initiating annulment suits which twelfth-century kings would have pushed through a council of their own bishops.[43] A case which looks like a counter-example is the the marriage of Charles IV of France and Blanche of Burgundy, dissolved by pope John XXII. When one examines the grounds and the evidence John XXII appears to have been in the right.[44] He gave more than one reason for his decision.[45] The simplest is the evidence of a prior 'spiritual relationship' between Charles and Blanche, sufficient to nullify the marriage. It seems that Blanche's mother had been one of the godparents of Charles.[46] No dispensation for this impediment had been granted before the marriage.

If a king asked a pope for a dispensation to get married, he would probably get one; if he asked a pope to get him out of a marriage, he might not get far unless in the right according to the rules. Counterfactually, one could envisage a medieval papacy which claimed the right to grant true divorces in exceptional cases – rather like the House of Lords in England before the nineteenth-century reforms. That would have given popes a splendid hold on kings. But the papal monarchy took a different path. The unbreakability of a consummated marriage between Chritians was treated as an absolute value. Annulments were ultimately limited by *Wertrationalitaet*, whereas dispensations from the forbidden degrees were ultimately a matter

---

[42] For the case of Pere I of Catalonia (II of Aragon) and Marie de Montpellier cf. M. Aurell, *Les Noces du Comté. Mariage et pouvoir en Catalogne (785–1213)* (Paris, 1995), p. 440: Innocent declared the marriage valid, 'contre toute attente'. The excursus 'Zum Eheprozess Philipp Augusts von Frankreich und anderen Eheprozessen unter Innocenz III', H. Tillmann, *Papst Innocenz III* (Bonner Historische Forschungen, 3; Bonn, 1954), pp. 268–81, still has value.

[43] Cf. John W. Baldwin, *Masters, Princes and Merchants. The Social Views of Peter the Chanter and his Circle*, 2 vols (Princeton, 1970), ii, p. 225, n. 181.

[44] For a full summary or paraphrase of the depositions see M. J. Robert de Chevanne, 'Charles IV le Bel et Blanche de Bourgogne', in *Bulletin philologique et historique (jusqu'à 1715) du Comité des travaux historiques et scientifiques*, années 1936 et 1937 (Paris, 1938), pp. 313–50. My thanks Dr Stephen Davies for drawing my attention to this.

[45] I hope to discuss the case in more detail elsewhere.

[46] For examples of the evidence, which does not appear to have been fixed or faked though it is always hard to be sure where the French court of this period is concerned, see de Chavanne, 'Charles IV', pp. 333–540.

of *Zweckrationalität*. This massive distinction is hard to explain if the driving force behind papal marriage policy and law was the desire to make the laity sit up and beg.

Finally, the explicit rationale of the 'four degrees' rule looks strong, provided we place it in an Italian context. Seen in such a context, the rationale is genuinely adequate as an explanation of the law it purports to justify. In theory the rule was supposed to create new bonds of friendship. Now in some parts of Europe, four degrees was overkill if this was the aim. The rule assumes that people are already on friendly terms with first, second and third cousins. In England (for example) that was not particularly likely. More probably, people did not know who their third cousins were. But Italy may have been quite different. Extended clans were a strong feature of social life. These massive clans transcended social class and the gulf between city and *contado*. They extended beyond true blood relationship: they were 'imagined kinship communities' though with a large basis in objective blood relationship. Their potential for social disruption was huge. The 'four degree' rule, however, must have encouraged marriage outside the clan. According to the leading authority on Italian clans the principle of exogamy was in fact practised to a remarkable degree. He is worth quoting:

> Moreover, this family clan, even if it was extremely large, even when it grouped together many hundreds of individuals, remained strictly exogamous. In Pavia, where texts also spoke of *progenia* in reference to nobles, none contracted marriage within his own *progenia*, for such marriages, up to remote relationships, were forbidden by ancient laws. Rather, families sought alliances with other, quite unconnected families, even with adversaries or enemies, which often favoured peace and the end of old vendettas. In Genoa, similarly, out of thousands of documents and tens of thousands of references which enable us to study marriages, one alone, apparently, notes an alliance within a family group, however large. One did not even marry a girl from another branch of the clan: this for the Spinola, Fieschi and Giustiniani families (the last-named being *popolani*); these federations of families which were rather disparate, and originally quite unconnected, strictly forbade internal marriage. The men all behaved as if there really were ties of blood between them all. The simple fact of bearing the same name prohibited matrimonial alliances.[47]

Innocent III, Lothario Segni, presumably knew the social facts reconstructed by Heers. In the light of them, is it surprising that he pegged the number of forbidden degrees at four, rather than reducing them still further? To cut them down more than he did would have been against the grain of Italian social assumptions. Also perhaps of assumptions in other parts of Europe where Heers's model fits. More investigation is needed before the geography of kinship becomes clear. In the meantime we should keep before the mind the obvious fact that the Fourth Lateran Council was held in Italy.[48]

---

[47] Heers, *Family Clans*, p. 56.

[48] For Italian representation at the council, see R. Foreville, *Latran I, II, III et Latran IV* (Paris, 1965), p. 252: 'Avec plus de deux cents représentants – y compris le Pontife romain et dix-neuf cardinaux de curie – les Italiens constituent la moitié du corps conciliaire . . .'.

Lay kinship solidarity and papal law 199

Exogamy was a crude instrument for promoting peace, but perhaps effective. Anthony Molho's study of marriage in late medieval Florence shows that the high-status 'lineages'[49] tended to be linked together by marriage: he speaks much of 'endogamy', but means social rather than clan intermarriage. He quotes a telling passage from the *Della vita civile* of Matteo Palmieri: 'in which he had imagined his city as a set of lineages which . . . "give and receive in legitimate marriages, [and] through their marriage alliances and their love [toward each other] encompass a good part of the city, whence, being related by marriage ['parentela'] they charitably assist each other, conferring upon each other advice, favours and assistance . . ." '.[50] Once the lineages had become interlinked in this way dispensations might be required for the links to be renewed.[51] Nevertheless consanguineous matches may have been rarer than one might expect. Molho investigated one lineage in great detail and remarked that 'perhaps the most important finding regarding consanguinity is its relative rarity among the Rinuccini lineage'.[52] An earlier stage of the process which led to the situation described by Molho – i.e., multiple links between great lineages – has been observed in Carol Lansing's study of thirteenth-century Florentine clans: she shows how marriages were used to bring hostile 'lineages' together.[53] It was not an infallible method,[54] but not only the papal legate[55] but also the communal government itself believed in it: in 1290 it actually paid 1,400 libre in dowries to facilitate marriages linking two hostile lineages.[56]

By this point the system of exogamy begins to look like nothing more than rational common sense of a kind found in very many societies: which is precisely the point of this essay. Still, there was nothing inevitable about this process. Shakespeare's *Romeo and Juliet* provides the perfect counterfactual. Hostile clans do not have to end their differences through marriage alliances. They can discourage 'out-marriage' and exert pressure in the direction of endogamy. The church's law made that hard. The 'four degrees' rule may have been irrelevant to England, but in Italy and in other areas, where clans were the norm, the kinship law regulated by the popes was a powerful force for lay solidarity.

---

[49] Guerreau-Jalabert, 'La Parenté', pp. 71–2 draws attention to the ambiguities of this word.
[50] Anthony Molho, *Marriage Alliance in Late Medieval Florence* (Cambridge, Mass., 1994), p. 344.
[51] Cf. Molho, *Marriage*, p. 265.
[52] Molho, *Marriage*, p. 267
[53] C. Lansing, *The Florentine Magnates. Lineage and Faction in a Medieval Commune* (Princeton, 1991), pp. 125–8. Compare D. Waley, *Siena and the Sienese in the Thirteenth Century* (Cambridge, 1991), p. 121 and p. 143.
[54] Lansing, *Florentine Magnates*, pp. 125–6.
[55] Ibid., p. 127.
[56] Ibid., pp. 127–8.

Laity, laicisation and Philip the Fair of France

Elizabeth A. R. Brown

This volume's title, *Law, Laity and Solidarities in Medieval Europe*, reflects three of Susan Reynolds's chief interests, which she has treated singly and commingled.[1] Here, in homage to a valued friend and intellectual companion, I shall approach the topics from a somewhat different perspective from hers, a perspective that is inspired by her methodological admonitions and that I hope complements her broad vision of medieval society. The chief purpose of this essay is to question the appropriateness of distinguishing sharply between lay (or secular and temporal) and clerical (or ecclesiastical) as we attempt to comprehend the ideas and activities of the people of medieval and early modern Europe. The inclination to establish such boundaries is understandable. Differentiating between lay and ecclesiastical is second nature to those of us who live in times and regions in which the demarcation line between church and state is neatly drawn, and in which religious ideas and institutions and religiously motivated enterprises have lost the pivotal significance they can possess. Religion will, of course, always be with us, and even in our twentieth-century rational, sceptical world, spiritual impulses and motivations remain powerful.[2] The notion of doing God's work and sacrificing comfort and material well-being to advance God's causes continues to have emotional appeal which is sometimes profound. The invocation of Christian morality, generally puritanically defined, continues to influence voters and legislators. Still, in twentieth-century society religion and its various manifestations are less centrally meaningful than they once were. Envisaging a situation in which the reverse is true requires a challenging leap of the imagination.

Among the chief merits of Susan Reynolds's work are her persistence in decrying 'teleological historiography' and her insistence on historians' obligation to refrain from projecting 'our own assumptions and ideas' back on to the past.[3] Hearkening

---

[1] The following abbreviations are used: AN: Paris, Archives nationales; BNF: Paris, Bibliothèque nationale de France.

[2] Rodney Stark and William Sims Bainbridge offer interesting observations, in *The Future of Religion: Secularization, Revival and Cult Formation* (Berkeley, 1985), pp. 1–2.

[3] Susan Reynolds uses these phrases in the introduction to the second edn of her book *Kingdoms and Communities in Western Europe 900–1300* (Oxford, 1997) (first pub. 1984), p. xiii; see also p. xl.

to her caveats, I find myself wondering to what extent treating medieval lay society and ideas as separable from medieval ecclesiastical society and ideas is valid, and to what extent such an approach may lead us to distort the realities of medieval people's activities, and their perceptions of themselves and the world they inhabited.

My feelings of unease are not unique. Michael Camille has warned that '[o]ur modern notion of the separateness of sacred and profane experience' may cause us to underestimate the breadth of medieval culture and the interpenetration of the secular and the spiritual within it.[4] James K. Farge cautions that the modern world's '[deft separation of] the sacred from the secular' makes it hard to comprehend why, in sixteenth-century France, the Parlement de Paris was even more dedicated than the University of Paris to condemning and eradicating religious deviance and dissent.[5] Frank M. Turner has eloquently commented on the barriers to comprehending the intellectual and religious history of Victorian England that the imposition of such distinctions has created. He quotes the observation of Rodney Stark and William Sims Bainbridge, 'At least since the Enlightenment, most Western intellectuals have anticipated the death of religion as eagerly as ancient Israel awaited the messiah', thus suggesting that the premature attribution of distinct secular values to other times may result from historians' desire to find the earliest discernible roots of values they particularly cherish.[6]

With historians of sixteenth-century France and Victorian England emphasising the dangers of drawing neat distinctions between lay and ecclesiastical and between the sacred and the secular, it seems worth considering the possibility that historians of the Middle Ages should also eschew such divisions. In examining this issue I should like first to consider Susan Reynolds's own approach to lay activity and ideas, and then turn to Joseph R. Strayer's hypotheses concerning the laicisation of society and government in the Middle Ages – an approach whose utility I believe he rejected by the end of his life. Finally I shall offer my own appraisal of the relationship between lay and ecclesiastical, church and state, and secular and sacred, focusing on the reign of Philip the Fair (r. 1285–1314), the king of France whose personality and activities have been as intriguing to me as they were to Joseph Strayer. I shall pay particular attention to the king and to Guillaume de Nogaret, one of Philip's ministers, and shall argue that Nogaret and his colleagues shared and reinforced the king's vision of his direct relationship and obligations to God and Jesus Christ, and of his consequent moral and spiritual responsibilities. Following the lead of Ernst H. Kantorowicz, I shall propose that, like the king,

---

[4] Michael Camille, *Image on the Edge: The Margins of Medieval Art* (Essays in Art and Culture; Cambridge, MA, 1992), pp. 63, 69, 90.

[5] James K. Farge, 'Early Censorship of Printed Books in Paris: New Perspectives and Insights', in *Le contrôle des idées à la Renaissance. Actes du colloque de la FISIER [Fédération internationale des sociétés et instituts pour l'étude de la Renaissance], tenu à Montréal en septembre 1995*, ed. Jesus Martinez De Bujanda (Etudes de philologie et d'histoire, 49; Geneva, 1996), pp. 75–91, esp. 75–6.

[6] Stark and Bainbridge, *Future*, p. 1. See Frank M. Turner, 'The Religious and the Secular in Victorian Britain', in his *Contesting Cultural Authority: Essays in Victorian Intellectual Life* (Cambridge, 1993), pp. 3–37, esp. 3.

Guillaume and Philip's other lawyers and officials envisioned their society as an organic, corporeal entity, in which ecclesiastical and temporal power were distinct, but which was animated and protected (and judged) by God, by Jesus Christ, and by the Holy Spirit.[7] I focus on Guillaume de Nogaret not only because he has sometimes been presented as the advocate and implementer of 'centralized secular monarchy',[8] a characterisation I think misleading, but, more important, because of the revealing statements he made about himself and his role in the bitter conflict between Philip the Fair and his arch-enemy, Pope Boniface VIII.[9] I shall end by advocating abandonment of categories that, I believe, pose barriers to comprehending the people of medieval and early modern Europe and distort their vision of the world they inhabited.

Susan Reynolds has devoted much of her considerable scholarly energy to demolishing myths and to challenging interpretations of the medieval past that seem to her erroneous. Her attacks against 'feudalism' have been especially provocative (and welcome). Another of her crusades is directed against the notion of the Middle Ages as an Age of Faith, which she cogently observes 'survives [even among medieval historians] more or less unnoticed, rather like a shabby old chair in our mental sitting-rooms'.[10] She recognises, sometimes with a certain hesitancy,[11] the centrality of the church and its teachings in medieval Europe. She is also determined to demonstrate

---

[7] Ernst H. Kantorowicz analyses the antique and biblical roots and the impact of John of Salisbury's analogy, with special reference to the popularity in France of the notion of the realm as *corpus mysticum*, in *The King's Two Bodies: A Study in Mediaeval Political Theology* (Princeton, 1957), pp. 199–200, 207–10, 218–23, and also 119–22 (the Roman law representation of legists and judges as 'priests of justice').

[8] Franklin J. Pegues, 'Nogaret, Guillaume de', in *Medieval France: An Encyclopedia* (Garland Encyclopedias of the Middle Ages, 2; Garland Reference Library of the Humanities, 932; New York, 1995), pp. 667–8; cf. his more cautious position in the article on Nogaret that he contributed in 1987 to the *Dictionary of the Middle Ages* ed. Joseph R. Strayer, 13 vols [New York, 1982–9], 9 [1987]: 152–3. In a curious article published during the German occupation of France in the Second World War, Carl Schmitt presented Nogaret as the chief of the legists of Philip the Fair who promoted and advanced 'Laizisierung', 'bürgerliche Zivilisation, staatliche Zentralisation und Verwandlung des Rechts in staatliche Legalität': 'Die Formung des französischen Geistes durch den Legisten', *Deutschland–Frankreich: Vierteljahresschrift des Deutschen Instituts / Paris*, 1² (1942), 1–30, esp. 5, 10–11.

[9] It seems to me, as it did to Kantorowicz, that the statements Nogaret wrote in his own defence reflect his own thinking; cf. Pegues, in *Dictionary of Medieval History*, 9: 153 ('Much is known of what Nogaret did, but almost nothing of what he thought or said').

[10] Susan Reynolds, 'Social Mentalities and the Case of Medieval Scepticism', *Transactions of the Royal Historical Society*, 6th ser., 1 (1991), 21–41, at 25; reprinted in her *Ideas and Solidarities of the Medieval Laity: England and Western Europe* (Variorum Collected Studies Series, 495; Aldershot and Brookfield, 1995), no. I. See also her *Kingdoms and Communities in Western Europe, 900–1300*, 2nd edn (Oxford, 1997; 1st edn 1984), pp. xxxii–v (attacking in her introduction what she terms 'the religious/intellectual' focus of the work of Ernest Semichon and others); see also p. xv.

[11] Reynolds, 'Social Mentalities', pp. 38–9 ('most people *probably* accepted the Church's teachings'; 'Much pious behaviour *must have* reflected real faith'; cf. p. 33: 'most people in any society *probably* accept its prevailing beliefs'; italics are mine). In *Kingdoms*, pp. 5–7, she declares, less guardedly, that 'lay society was permeated by Christianity', although she also remarks that 'many people were probably not very religious'.

that doubt and scepticism existed throughout medieval society,[12] and, even more, that lay people (including peasants) were capable of thinking and reasoning, and that such activities were not the monopoly of clerical 'intellectuals' and 'academics'.[13] Susan Reynolds's concern to give medieval lay people their due is reflected in the title she selected in 1995 for her collected essays: *Ideas and Solidarities of the Medieval Laity: England and Western Europe*. In 1997, in the introduction to the second edition of her *Kingdoms and Communities in Western Europe, 900–1300*, she said she wished she had entitled the book 'Lay Collective Activity in Western Europe, 900–1300', emphasising that the true subject of her book was, first, the collective activities of lay people and, second, the ideas 'about the rights and activities of groups' – presumably groups of lay people – that underlay these activities.[14]

Susan Reynolds is hardly alone in distinguishing lay from clerical as she studies medieval society. In 1991, analysing the history of Europe between 1150 and 1309, John H. Mundy presented 'clerks and laymen' as 'the two peoples' on whom he would concentrate. In dealing with the second group he introduced the term 'laicism' to describe the development of 'lay literacy and the lay spirit'. These he believed would one day 'reduce clerical power and authority', although he did not think this was accomplished until 'later during the Reformation and the rise of the national State'. During the time he was considering, he believed, relations between his 'two peoples', were 'often harmonious' but 'never easy'.[15]

The contrast between 'lay' or 'secular' and 'clerical' or 'ecclesiastical' is central to the work of Joseph R. Strayer (1904–87), a historian who resembled Susan Reynolds in being a master generaliser, an enviably clear writer, a hedgehog who was endowed with fox-like acumen.[16] Unlike Reynolds and Mundy, however,

---

[12] Reynolds, 'Social Mentalities', pp. 26–38. In *Kingdoms*, p. 7, she is more restrained, saying that 'although we know that by the twelfth century some suffered from doubts and some flirted with Judaism or Islam, Christianity offered the only ideology available to most'.

[13] Reynolds, *Kingdoms*, pp. 4–5, 9–10, 29, 261, 317, 319, 324–5, 328, 329; and her introduction (1997) to the 2nd edn, pp. xxxix, lvii. See also Reynolds, 'Social Mentalities' (1991), pp. 28, 36; and her preface to her collected essays (1994), *Ideas*, p. vii.

[14] *Kingdoms*, pp. xi–xii, xlvi–vii.

[15] John H. Mundy, *Europe in the High Middle Ages, 1150–1309*, 2nd edn (A General History of Europe; London, 1991), pp. 15–28, esp. 15–16, 27–8. In the final section of his book, entitled 'Church and State' (pp. 399–430), Mundy pits 'the secular State' against 'the Church', although he notes (p. 429) that despite the conflicts in the early fourteenth century between Philip the Fair and what he terms 'Rome', 'little institutional power was surrendered to the secular State'.

[16] On Strayer's life and work, see Norman F. Cantor, *Inventing the Middle Ages: The Lives, Works, and Ideas of the Great Medievalists of the Twentieth Century* (New York, 1991), pp. 245–50, 257–63, 277–85; and Paul Freedman and Gabrielle M. Spiegel, 'Medievalisms Old and New: The Rediscovery of Alterity in North American Medieval Studies', *American Historical Review*, 103 (1998), 677–704, esp. 682, 686–90. Freedman and Spiegel do not discuss Strayer's emphasis on laicisation, although the attention he paid to this topic, like others he treated, clearly reveals his 'desire', as Freedman and Spiegel put it (p. 688), 'to reinterpret medieval governmental history by making it compatible with American democratic principles'. Cantor notes (*Inventing*, pp. 278, 282), 'Strayer's anticlericalism and contempt for Roman Catholicism', and his belief in 'the legitimacy, credibility, and winning capacity of the rationalizing statists in all times and places'.

Strayer was inclined to discount the importance of the laity before the thirteenth century. Then, he thought, lay people came into their own, and lay values began to dominate society and eclipse the values the clergy proclaimed. In 1940, in one of his earliest papers, Strayer argued that during the thirteenth century, 'the church lost much of its influence', and the 'secularization' or 'laicization' (which he termed 'the political aspect of secularization') of society commenced.[17] Focusing on France and England, he argued that the thirteenth century witnessed the emergence of 'a society in which primary allegiance [was] given to lay governments, in which final decisions regarding social objectives [were] made by lay governments, in which the church [was] merely a private society with no public powers or duties'.[18] He attributed to thirteenth-century lawyers a virtual 'theory of the sovereign state' which 'forced a choice between loyalties' to the church and state, and argued that 'royal officials' consciously pursued a 'policy of laicization'.[19] Officials were increasingly laymen, and those who were clerics were so involved in their work for the state that they 'forgot their duty to the church'.[20] After Boniface VIII's clashes with Edward I and Philip the Fair, 'there was no doubt that lay rulers had the primary allegiance of their people' or that lay governments, not the church, controlled society, 'as far as it was controlled at all'. The church was unable 'to regain its old power' and was forced by the lay governments to undertake more 'social service work', thus diverting ecclesiastical wealth from 'purely religious purposes'. Strayer acknowledged that laicisation was not complete in the fourteenth century. In his view, it was 'the next great wave' of laicisation, which he associated with the sixteenth century, that contested the church's role in education and philanthropy.[21] In this article, church and state appear as adversaries, and lay and ecclesiastical as mutually exclusive, antagonistic categories.[22]

Strayer pursued his investigation of laicisation in an essay published in 1969. Far from alluding to this topic, the title of the study, 'France: The Holy Land, the Chosen People, and the Most Christian King',[23] suggested that it would explore the religious elements which figured so prominently in attitudes towards the realm of France. However, in his first paragraph Strayer made clear that, as before, he would be concerned with the emergence of the modern secular state, and the

---

[17] Joseph R. Strayer, 'The Laicization of French and English Society in the Thirteenth Century', *Speculum*, 15 (1940), 76–86, reprinted in John F. Benton and Thomas N. Bisson (eds), *Medieval Statecraft and the Perspectives of History: Essays by Joseph R. Strayer* (Princeton, 1971), pp. 251–65.

[18] Strayer, 'Laicization', p. 251.

[19] Strayer, 'Laicization', p. 258.

[20] Strayer, 'Laicization', pp. 256–7.

[21] Strayer, 'Laicization', pp. 264–5.

[22] Strayer took the same position in his article, 'The State and Religion: An Exploratory Comparison in Different Cultures. Greece and Rome, the West, Islam', *Comparative Studies in Society and History*, 1 (1958), 38–43, reprinted in Strayer, *Medieval Statecraft*, pp. 321–8, esp. 324.

[23] The essay originally appeared in Theodore K. Rabb and Jerrold E. Seigel (eds), *Action and Conviction in Early Modern Europe: Essays in Memory of E. H. Harbison* (Princeton, 1969), pp. 3–16; it is reprinted in Strayer, *Medieval Statecraft*, pp. 300–14.

development of 'primary (though not exclusive) loyalty ... to one secular authority', a primary component of laicisation as he defined the term in 1940.[24] He acknowledged that fostering 'loyalty to a single authority' required 'brute power and administrative skill'. But he believed that 'real loyalty' had to encompass 'genuine respect, admiration, and, if possible, love for the object of loyalty' if it were to last. The Capetian kings, he believed, were virtually unique among medieval rulers in solving 'the problem'. They did this by 'invent[ing] the state which they claimed to rule', a feat they accomplished by cultivating the 'ideas of the sacred king and the holy country'. Strayer gave chief credit for this achievement to Philip the Fair, who aimed, as Strayer saw it, to focus the loyalty of his subjects on 'king and kingdom' rather than on the pope and the church. This was accomplished through 'persuasion and propaganda'. In Strayer's view, Philip the Fair and his 'propagandists' consciously manipulated his subjects' sentiments, or, as he put it, 'rearrang[ed] basic loyalties to concentrate them on king and kingdom'. They made France 'a symbol of the kingdom of heaven' and transformed France into a state in which 'loyalty to [it] was bound to be loyalty to the church, even if the church occasionally doubted it'.[25] Taking no note of the Carolingian roots of the ideas that flowered during the reigns of St Louis and Philip the Fair, Strayer suggested that the French kings' insistence on the sacredness of the realm, its ruler and its people was the product of their calculated ambition to solve a central 'problem of state-building' – rather than any belief on their part in the ideas they and their agents proclaimed.[26] In this, Strayer did not consider France unique. According to him, 'all governments of the period' were 'trying to develop a "political theology" which transferred religious symbols and slogans to the political sphere'.[27]

In his book *On the Medieval Origins of the Modern State*, published in 1970,[28] Strayer contrasted the 'intermingling' of 'secular and religious authority' in the early Middle Ages, with the divergence of the two after the Gregorian reform. In his view,

---

[24] Strayer pursued his investigation of the means by which loyalty to the state was secured in 'Defense of the Realm and Royal Power in France', *Studi in onore di Gino Luzzatto*, 4 vols (Milan, 1949), vol. 4, pp. 289–96, reprinted in Strayer, *Medieval Statecraft*, pp. 291–9. He considered invocation and acceptance of the principle 'defence of the realm' evidence of Philip the Fair's success in encouraging 'the growth of loyalty to the French monarchy', and the principle itself 'one of the foundations on which the new monarchy of the fifteenth century was raised'. Strayer believed that the notion was invoked 'very rarely' in dealing with 'secular persons and holdings', whose loyalty, he said, 'was directed toward a man, not toward a body politic' ('Defense', p. 292). In 1957, acknowledging Strayer's assistance, Kantorowicz demonstrated Guillaume de Nogaret's frequent invocation of the principle, in *King's Two Bodies*, p. 250, and also p. 259.

[25] Strayer, 'France', pp. 313–14.

[26] Strayer's articles 'Laicization' and 'France' appear in a section of Strayer's collected essays (*Medieval Statecraft*) entitled 'Problems of State-Building'. Strayer expressed surprise at the extent of the spokesmen's agreement and the degree to which their pronouncements 'reflect[ed] the common opinion of many Frenchmen': 'France', p. 312. For the Carolingian background, see Ernst H. Kantorowicz, with Manfred F. Bukofzer, *Laudes Regiae: A Study in Liturgical Acclamations and Mediaeval Ruler Worship* (University of California Publications in History, 33; Berkeley, 1946), pp. 56–76, 101–11.

[27] Strayer, 'France', p. 313.

[28] Princeton.

following the changes occasioned by Pope Gregory VII's actions and declarations, 'Kings lost their semi-ecclesiastical character and some of their control over Church appointments'. He concluded that 'the Gregorian concept of the Church almost demanded the invention of the concept of the State' – by which he surely meant the secular state.[29] He focused on monarchies, not the papacy, as, again, he traced the shift of loyalty toward the state, with the clergy forced 'to recognize two sovereigns'.[30] He noted – but did not try to account for – the 'idealization' of the state and the development of the 'cult of the kingdom' in fourteenth-century France. There, he acknowledged, 'a cult devoted to the king' had long existed, with, at its core, royal unction, descent from Charlemagne and the power to heal. Strayer did not elaborate on the relevance of this cult or that of the novel 'cult of the kingdom' to the secular French state. He saw the idealised vision of the realm 'spreading', but he did not say who was responsible for the diffusion, or try to explain why the cult was launched, or why it was accepted and approved. His reticence on these questions suggests that he was having doubts about the validity of the practical, rather cynical interpretation of the motivations and ambitions of the rulers of thirteenth- and fourteenth-century France he had earlier proposed.

Such doubts apparently continued to prick. The France Strayer depicted in his last book, *The Reign of Philip the Fair*,[31] was quite different from the laicised, secular state he had described in 1940. Forty years later, in 1980, Strayer presented Philip as a man who cherished 'the royal dignity' and accepted 'the sacred mysteries of the religion of monarchy', as a pious man, a dedicated Christian. The religion of royalty, Strayer said, was universally accepted, and the king believed to be 'a semi-sacred personage'. No conflict existed 'between the royal religion and the Catholic faith'.[32] Strayer chronicled the royal advisers' dedication to good works and the church, and described the close family ties that bound Enguerran de Marigny, one of the king's chief ministers, to the church.[33] As to Philip's relations with the French church, Strayer acknowledged that its members were fairly treated and were loyal to the king, who strengthened the ties between the realm and the church and advanced the idea of a French, Gallican church.[34] Despite these changes in perspective, some vestiges of Strayer's former outlook remained. He emphasised the hostility he perceived between the clergy, on the one hand, and the nobles and people, on the other, commenting at one point that 'Boniface [VIII] was quite right when he said that the laity had always been hostile to the clergy'.[35] He attributed to

---

[29] Strayer, *Medieval Origins*, pp. 20–2.

[30] *Medieval Origins*, pp. 45, 46, 54. Consult Cantor, *Inventing*, pp. 280–1.

[31] Princeton, 1980.

[32] Strayer, *Philip the Fair*, pp. 387–8. He describes Nogaret as having 'the vision of a convert to a new religion'.

[33] Strayer, *Philip the Fair*, pp. 66–8, 254.

[34] Strayer, *Philip the Fair*, p. 241. Cf. pp. 271–3, where he refers to the clergy as 'caught between two masters' during Philip the Fair's struggle with Boniface VIII, but attributing their capitulation to fear, shows that the clergy stood by the king.

[35] Strayer, *Philip the Fair*, pp. 299–300, 389, 421, 422.

'quarrels among members of the possessing classes' what he presented as restricted clerical participation in the leagues of 1314.[36] As to the nature of Philip's dedication to the religion of monarchy, at the end of the book Strayer again described the familiar components of the cult of king and kingdom as aspects of 'royal propaganda', and presented the assemblies the king convoked as 'exercises in propaganda'.[37] Thus, in the end, he could not bring himself to jettison completely his own antipathy towards the church, or his vision of Philip the Fair as calculating statesman. It seems clear, however, that he no longer believed wholeheartedly in his earlier interpretation. In a short popular article on Philip the Fair published soon after the book appeared,[38] Strayer indicated that Philip himself fully believed the doctrines that Strayer elsewhere termed propaganda. Here Strayer called Philip 'a semisacred person' and said that 'he was imbued with the religion of monarchy'. He implied that, with Joan of Arc, Philip would have believed that 'to attack the king of France was to make war on the Lord Jesus'.[39] Philip he said, 'was not anticlerical: he simply felt that he was a better Catholic than the pope'. Thus, finally, Strayer abandoned his view of Philip as the creator of 'a centralized secular monarchy', although, perhaps because he never explicitly disavowed this reading of the evidence, it has lived on in the work of some of his students.[40]

The interpretation of Philip the Fair that Strayer formulated at the end of his life is, I think, far more convincing than the one he presented in 1940 and 1969. As he wrestled closely with the voluminous evidence for Philip's reign, Strayer seems to have recognised the inappropriateness of the categories he had once invoked. Although Strayer still insisted on the hostility between the clergy and the laity, he showed that, in practice, they lived mostly in harmony, and that the clergy, like the laity, accepted and endorsed the Capetian cult of realm and ruler, many (if not most) facets of which had sacred roots. When he dealt with specific individuals, his accounts of their careers demonstrated the close ties that existed, within individual families, between those who followed careers in the world and those who pursued their fortunes as clerics. Does Strayer's implicit rejection of the pertinence of laicisation and secularisation to the fourteenth-century French state suggest that the distinction between lay and ecclesiastical – or secular and clerical – which I discussed at the beginning of this essay should also be discarded?

---

[36] Strayer, *Philip the Fair*, pp. 296, 421, 422.

[37] Strayer, *Philip the Fair*, pp. 32–4, 46–7, 383–4.

[38] Joseph R. Strayer, 'Vita: Philip the Fair, Christian king: 1268–1314', *Harvard Magazine* (September–October 1980), p. 41. A brief article on Philip that Strayer wrote for the *Dictionary of the Middle Ages*, 9: 554–5, published in 1987 (the year of Strayer's death) presents a straightforward, non-interpretive summary of Philip's accomplishments.

[39] Cf. Kantorowicz, *King's Two Bodies*, p. 255 (drawing the same analogy, which suggests that Kantorowicz's views of Philip the Fair, quite different from Strayer's, may in the end have influenced Strayer).

[40] See the article of Pegues referred to in n. 8 above; and also William Chester Jordan, 'France: 1223–1328', in *Dictionary of the Middle Ages*, 5 [1985]: 166–76, at 170, 171–2.

Unlike other words that historians employ to describe the medieval past, all the terms that are used to designate the two sides of the divide have good medieval roots, and were used long ago to denote meaningful entities. 'Secular', 'temporal' and 'profane' are anchored in this world, whereas 'spiritual' and 'sacred' are linked to the *au-delà*, the realm beyond the terrestrial, the divine. Lay people were those who were not ordained, although the terms *frater laicus* and *miles Christi* shows that the boundaries established by ordination were fluid.[41] The blurring of categories was particularly apparent at the royal level. True, in 1450 the author of *Miranda de laudibus Francie et de ipsius regimine regni* (the legist and prelate Bernard de Rosier) authoritatively declared that no king should arrogate to himself the office and authority of the church and its ministers, citing as a deterrent the example of King Ozias.[42] But in an earlier supplication upholding clerical exemption from taxation, presented to Charles VII at Bourges in August 1440, Bernard appealed to the monarch as 'most Christian king, right arm and protector of the church of God above all kings because of your holy and heavenly unction of your coronation', declaring that in his kingdom he was 'the prime ecclesiastical person'.[43] In 1452, Jean Juvenal des Ursins, archbishop of Reims, compared the king to 'a valiant prelate', and said that he was 'not simply a lay person, but an ecclesiastical prelate, the first in the kingdom after the pope, the right arm of the church'.[44]

---

[41] See Theodore Evergates, 'Historiography and Sociology in Early Feudal Society: The Case of Hariulf and the "Milites" of Saint-Riquier', *Viator*, 6 (1975), 35–49, esp. 42–3. Karl Ferdinand Werner notes that the lay abbacy encouraged the spread of spirituality among royalty and the aristocracy, in 'Il y a mille ans, les Carolingiens: fin d'une dynastie, début d'un mythe', *Annuaire-bulletin de la Société de l'Histoire de France, années 1991–1992*, (1993), 71–89, esp. 88–9, n. 201.

[42] BNF, lat. 6020, fos 1r–12v, at 11r: 'Non debet rex officia & auctoritatem ecclesie dei et ministrorum eius occuppare sibi / Nam rex osias lepra fuit percussus / quia sacerdotale officium occupauit'; for Ozias and his fate, see 2 Paralip. 24, 26.16–21. The tract, which the author dedicated to Charles VII and the people of France, is dated 1 January 1450, the year of Pope Nicholas V's jubilee, although it ends with an epilogue composed in 1465: BNF, lat. 6020, fos 1r, 12r–v. On Bernard de Rosier, see Patrick Arabeyre, 'Un prélat languedocien au milieu du XVe siècle: Bernard de Rosier, archevêque de Toulouse (1400–1475)', *Journal des savants* (1990), 291–326, esp. pp. 305, 314. Bernard was elected bishop of Montauban on 9 January 1450; he became archbishop of Toulouse in 1452.

[43] BNF, lat. 6020, fos 105v–6r: 'Supplicant humiliter prefati prelati & ecclesiastice persone / vt pro dei amore reuerencia et honore / exequendo regale officij vestri / qui estis rex christianissimus / brachium dextrum et protector ecclesie dei super omnes reges ad causam vestre sacre et celestis vnctionis coronacionis vestre in toto vestro regno estis prima ecclesiastica persona'. Patrick Arabeyre discusses the difficult position Bernard held, with allegiances divided 'between pope and king', in 'Un prélat', pp. 306–14; he treats the circumstances under which the supplication was written and presented, on pp. 294, 303–4. The work is entitled, 'Supplicacio christianissimo domino nostro regi francie facta in scriptis in Ciuitate Bituricensi / per Reuerendum patrem dominum Bernardum de Rosergio. vtriusque Iuris doctorem tunc prepositum tholosanum ordinata' (BNF, lat. 6020, fo. 103v).

[44] 'Et est ung roy comme ung vaillant prelat. Car au resgart de vous, mon souverain seigneur, vous n'estes pas simplement personne laye mais prelat ecclesiastique, le premier en vostre royaume qui soit aprez le pape, le bras dextre de l'esglise': in *Verba mea auribus percipe, domine* (written in the spring of 1452), in P. S. Lewis with Anne-Marie Hayez (eds), *Ecrits politiques de Jean Juvénal des Ursins*, 3 vols (Publications de la Société de l'histoire de France, 489, 496, 496A; Paris, 1978–92), 2: 179–405, at 208–9, and, on the work, 3: 83–4.

Similarly, a century later (in December 1547), the eminent lawyer (and future First President of the Parlement de Paris) Christophle de Thou proclaimed that 'kings are not simply lay or profane', particularly the kings of France, whose unction endowed them with a double character, 'both priestly and royal'.[45] Venerable ideas die hard. Likewise, although de Thou, like other people, used 'secular' as a synonym for 'lay', the word *secularis* also designated ordained clergy and ecclesiastics whose mission lay primarily in the world. Thus, the terms lay and ecclesiastical were not rigorously antonymous or mutually exclusive, although their root meanings were essentially different. In practice, how important was the distinction between lay and clerical?

I would propose that the similarities among the activities, interests and assumptions of lay people and ecclesiastics at different levels of society were far more striking and significant than the differences stemming from the fact of ordination, the ceremony that separated clergy from lay. Despite Susan Reynolds's insistence on her concern for the laity, the terms she uses suggest that she is upholding the cause, not of medieval lay people in general, but rather of those members of society who were neither intellectuals nor academics, neither professional philosophers nor expert lawyers. Admittedly, most if not all of medieval intellectuals, academics, philosophers and lawyers were clerics (although this was untrue in later periods). However, early and late, a multitude of clergy were as unintellectual, unacademic, unphilosophical and unlawyerly as any lay people. Think only of Pierre Clergue, the priest of Montaillou whose 'performance of [his priestly] duties was somewhat limited by his constant extra-curricular activities'. Although he had a few books and occasionally acted as notary, he was not a scholar or abstract

---

[45] BNF, Dupuy 702, fos 150r–176v, at 150v–1r (a brief prepared for François II de Dinteville, bishop of Auxerre, in a suit against Pierre de Mareuil, bishop of Lavaur): 'Ceste question depend de scauoir / Si Reges sunt mere Layci / aut persone mere prophane / Quidquid sit In alijs Regibus Lon a tenu que le Roy de France (Lequel a tousiours este estime le Roy des Roys) Etiam par les personnes estranges & Barbares ennemys de ce Royaume qui en ont escript / Quibus fuit magis amica veritas Quem scilicet vnxit deus oleo leticie pre particibus suis) que non erat mere laycus / Et que en sa personne concurrebat duplex qualitas Et sacerdotalis & Regalis / Ce que par toute antiquite aeste attribue aux Roys / Et quod Rex francie non estimetur merus Laycus Combien que es autres Roys lon en ait fait doubte'. De Thou cited numerous authorities before declaring, 'Et sont des Reliques euidentes veteris potestatis pontificalis In Rege francie / Les amortissementz qui se font auIourdhui par lun des choses temporelles qui sont donnees aux esglises Par lesquelz admortissementz le Roy dedicat Res prophanas deo / Et en ses lettres ses secretaires vsent de ces motz / Auons dedie & dedions perpetuellement adieu & alesglise Et de Re prophana facit Rem sacram quod facere non posset / si In sacris ab eo potestas abesset / Et aussi la loy ancienne des Romains escripte par les Iurisconsultes dit / que sacre Res dicuntur que Rite per pontifices deo dedicate sunt / A ceste cause & que le Roy non est mere laycus / quant ores la matiere qui se offre participperoit quelque chose dela spiritualite / que non / Si est ce que le Roy nen est moins Iuge competant. Et aussi la ainsi Recongneu le defendeur. . . . Doncques si le Roy est capable de pouoir congnoistre dela cause qui se offre per seipsum / potuit eam cognoscendam committere etiam personis Laycis & prophanis / Et toutesfois on scait bien que la compaignie presente est composee principallement de ceulx qui maiori honore ecclestice funguntur / et qui tiennent les principaulx benefices & les principales dignitez en lesglise'. For background, see Elizabeth A. R. Brown, 'The Dinteville Family and the Allegory of Moses and Aaron before Pharaoh', *Metropolitan Museum of Art Journal*, 34 (1999), 73–100.

thinker, and like his unordained neighbours and relatives, he too fell foul of the Inquisition.[46]

Lay people and clergy interacted continuously in medieval and early modern times, and examples of the contact between them abound in Susan Reynolds's work. She gives numerous examples of the cooperation of lay and clergy in common enterprises. Although she does not emphasise the importance of familial ties between members of the clergy and their lay relatives, she acknowledges that every cleric was originally lay, and that no ecclesiastic was born ordained.[47] She describes the clergy's participation with lay people in legal judgements.[48] She notes the part ecclesiastics played in associations organised to promote the peace, the religious elements in fraternities, and also the church's use and encouragement of this sort of soldarity.[49] The religious underpinnings of 'the community of the parish' and the interest of the clergy in its activities are self-evident.[50] At higher levels, Susan Reynolds mentions the participation of ecclesiastics in royal councils and acknowledges that 'bishops were not immune from feelings of regnal loyalty'.[51] She suggests that contact between ecclesiastics and lay people in royal assemblies and convocations may have stimulated the exchanges of ideas, and that tactics used by the clergy in their assemblies may have inspired lay people.[52] In indicating that some principles enunciated by theologians simply rationalised 'traditional lay ideas', she alludes to the many and diverse contacts between lay and clergy that promoted such cross-fertilisation – and, implicitly, calls attention to the chicken-and-egg conundrum that bedevils all seekers after the origins of ideas – which came first, the practice or the principle?[53]

As to clerical participation in the alliances formed in France in 1314 and 1315 to protest against royal policies, I have come to believe that the role played by ecclesiastics has been greatly underestimated.[54] As I have tried to show, clerics and lay

---

[46] Emmanuel Le Roy Ladurie, *Montaillou: The Promised Land of Error*, trans. Barbara Bray (New York, 1978), pp. 53–68; and Leonard E. Boyle, 'Montaillou Revisited: *Mentalité* and Methodology', in J. A. Raftis (ed.), *Pathways to Medieval Peasants* (Papers in Mediaeval Studies, 2; Toronto, 1981), pp. 120–2, 127–8, 131–2, 135–7, 139–40. Walter Ullmann contrasted 'the lower regions of society' (or 'the "lower" section of the populace') with the upper, without distinguishing lay from ecclesiastic, in his *A History of Political Thought: The Middle Ages* (Harmondsworth, 1965), pp. 159–61.

[47] Reynolds, 'Social Mentalities', p. 39; Reynolds, *Kingdoms*, p. 7.

[48] Reynolds, *Kingdoms*, pp. 27–8.

[49] Reynolds, *Kingdoms*, pp. 73, 76–7, 90, 118–19 (although cf. pp. 73 and 176).

[50] Reynolds, *Kingdoms*, pp. 79–100.

[51] Reynolds, *Kingdoms*, pp. 304, 328.

[52] Reynolds, *Kingdoms*, p. 317.

[53] Reynolds, *Kingdoms*, p. 328.

[54] On the movement see Elizabeth A. R. Brown, 'Reform and Resistance to Royal Authority in Fourteenth-Century France: The Leagues of 1314–1315', orig. pub. *Parliaments, Estates and Representation*, 1 (1981), 109–37 (esp. 128–37), reprinted in Brown, *Politics*, no. V. See above, n. 36, for Strayer's view. Susan Reynolds notes (*Kingdoms*, pp. 286–8) the prominence of nobles and other lay people in the alliances, but also mentions the participation of the clergy in Burgundy. The stance taken by Edouard

people had often worked together towards common goals, as they did in resisting Philip the Fair's attempts to collect a customary aid when his daughter Isabelle married Edward II of England.[55] The community of interests that encouraged collaboration in fiscal and political matters is understandable. Further, the forms of collaboration and the tactics that were adopted were influenced by the personal bonds between the ordained and the unordained. The ranks of the clergy were filled by the sons, brothers, daughters and sisters of lay families, and the most important families in the realm looked to the church for careers and advancement for their sons and daughters.[56] Of the eleven children of Jean Jouvenel des Ursins and Michelle Vitry portrayed in the family portrait hung in the family chapel at Notre-Dame of Paris in the mid-fifteenth century, two sons were peers and prelates (and both, like two of their brothers and a brother-in-law, royal counsellors), and one daugher was a nun at the elite house of Poissy.[57]

If distinguishing sharply between lay and ecclesiastic, and between secular and clerical produces a misleading image of medieval society, what approach might give a more faithful representation of the notions medieval and early modern people had of themselves and their world? Malcolm Barber treats the history of medieval Europe from the eleventh through the early fourteenth century as the story of Two Cities, focusing on the tensions between the lures of the material world and the desire for salvation, strains that affected all people, whether ordained or not.[58] Stressing the ties that bound people to one another, rather than the classifications that

---

Perroy reflects and has doubtless influenced scholarly emphasis on the role of the lay nobility. In publishing the act by which fifty-four nobles and seven clergy of Forez contracted an alliance, he acknowledged that the confederation consisted of 'nobles et religieux', but he termed it 'nobiliaire' and discussed in detail only the 'nobility of the Forez', without considering the ties, familial and spiritual, that may have linked them to the seven ecclesiastical participants: the abbots of the Cistercian houses of La Bénissons-Dieu and Valbenoîte, the priors of Estivareilles (Benedictine, dependent on Ainay), Firminy (Benedictine, dependent on Ile-Barbe), Pommiers (Cluniac), Rosiers (Cluniac) and Saint-Romain-le-Puy (Cluniac). See his 'La noblesse forézienne et les ligues nobiliaires de 1314–1315', *Bulletin de la Diana*, 36 (1960), 188–221, esp. p. 193; the article is reprinted in Perroy's *Etudes d'histoire médiévale* (Paris, Publications de la Sorbonne [Université de Paris 1], 1979), pp. 183–221.

[55] Elizabeth A. R. Brown, *Customary Aids and Royal Finances in Capetian France: The Marriage Aid of Philip the Fair* (Medieval Academy Books, 100; Cambridge, MA, 1992), esp. pp. 97–176.

[56] Mikhael Harsgor draws uncomfortably sharp distinctions between 'nobles' and 'gens d'église' in his *Recherches sur le personnel du conseil du roi sous Charles VIII et Louis XII*. Thèse présentée devant l'Université de Paris le 25 novembre 1972, 4 vols (Lille and Paris, 1980), esp. 2: 1227–324, at 1227. Laurent Bourquin does not discuss the clerical members of the noble families he studies in *Noblesse seconde et pouvoir en Champagne aux XVIe et XVIIe siècles* (Histoire moderne, 27 [Université de Paris I]; Paris, Publications de la Sorbonne, 1994); see esp. the genealogical table of the Dinteville family on p. 262, which omits ecclesiastics.

[57] Peter Lewis discusses the chapel and the picture, in his edn of Jean Juvenal des Ursins' *Ecrits politiques*, 3: 241–5; Charles Sterling reproduces and comments on the painting, in *La peinture médiévale à Paris, 1300–1500*, 2 vols (Paris, 1987–90), 2: 28–35, no. 1.

[58] Malcolm Barber, *The Two Cities: Medieval Europe, 1050–1320* (London, 1992), pp. 1–2, 421–40.

separated them, Barber's perspective is consistent with the organic metaphor, which compares human society and the human body. Grounded in Aristotelian, Pauline and patristic thinking, elaborated by John of Salisbury, the metaphor was favoured in the fourteenth century and well beyond.[59] This image, I believe, reflects the conception of society accepted by many people, lay and ecclesiastical, in medieval and early modern Europe. Here I should like briefly to discuss its popularity in early fourteenth-century France.

As Ernst Kantorowicz emphasised, the metaphor was critically important in the conflict between Philip the Fair and Boniface VIII. Both king and pope appealed to the image.[60] In *Antequam essent clerici*, which one of Philip's supporters composed in reply to the bull *Ineffabilis amor* of 30 September 1296, the body was the realm and its head the king, and all who refused subsidy and aid – whether clergy, lay, nobles or non-nobles – were declared 'unfitting parts and useless and quasi-paralyzed members', since they were in reality denying support to themselves. Here clergy and lay, like nobles and non-nobles, were joined in corporate regnal solidarity, just as, earlier in the tract, lay people as well as clergy were proclaimed parts of 'holy mother church, the bride of Christ'.[61]

Philip the Fair was concerned for the *regnum*, and the obligation of the clergy and lay people who inhabited it, 'like members truly living together in one body, to have compassion for one another, and to provide mutual aid, spiritually and temporally, for the preservation, defense, and protection of the unity of the kingdom against rebels and all who, through their pride and unbridled power, troubled the peace and quiet of the kingdom'.[62] This statement, formulated in 1305, raised the possibility that lay and clergy alike owed aid *both* spiritual *and* temporal to

---

[59] Cf. Reynolds, *Kingdoms*, p. 326 (denying that John's formulation represented 'a conceptual advance', commenting that such metaphors 'remained just that' and 'did not herald anything like modern organic theories of the state'). For Kantorowicz's discussion of the background of the idea, and the role it played in France through the end of the sixteenth century, see n. 7 above.

[60] Kantorowicz, *King's Two Bodies*, pp. 195, 202, 206, 229, 249, 257–9. Kantorowicz discusses Nogaret's ideas, in *King's Two Bodies*, pp. 250, 255–6 (esp. notes 193, 195), 257, 259.

[61] 'Sancta mater Ecclesia, sponsa Christi, non solùm est ex clericis, sed etiam ex laïcis.... Et quia turpis est pars, quæ suo non congruit vniuerso, & membrum inutile, & quasi paralyticum, quod corpori suo subsidium ferre recusat, quicumque, siue clerici, siue laïci, siue nobiles, siue ignobiles, qui capiti suo, vel corpori, hoc est domino Regi & regno, imò etiam sibimet, auxilium ferre recusant, semetipsos, partes incongruas & membra inutilia, & quasi paralytica esse demonstrant': Simon Vigor and Pierre Dupuy (eds), *Histoire dv differend d'entre le Pape Boniface VIII. et Philippes le Bel Roy de France* . . . (Paris, 1655; reprint Tucson, 1963), *preuves*, pp. 21–2 (and for the bull, pp. 15–20). Kantorowicz discusses these passages in *King's Two Bodies*, pp. 257–8, although his translation of *subsidium* and *auxilium* as 'support' cloaks the terms' fiscal connotations.

[62] 'nouistis plenius qualiter omnes & singuli clerici & laici regni nostri tanquam membra simul in uno corpore vere viuencia sibi debent adinuicem compati mutuumque sibi prestare tenentur auxilium spiritualiter et temporaliter ad conseruationem deffensionem & custodiam uniuersitatis ipsius regni contra rebelles & per sui superbiam atque potenciam effrenatam pacem & quietem ipsius regni turbantes': AN, J 350, no. 5 (a royal letter dated 10 October 1305, addressed to ecclesiastics of the province of Tours, and appended to a commission of the same date to two royal clerks sent to collect a subsidy there). Strayer cited this document and quoted phrases from it, in 'Defense', p. 291.

one another and to the king: the distinction between lay and ecclesiastical was (perhaps purposely) vague. As to Philip's own responsibility to the realm and its inhabitants, there seems no question of his belief that he held the kingdom directly from God, and that he thought himself answerable to God for its governance.[63] The great *ordonnance* of reform issued on 18 March 1303, proclaimed that the kingdom 'had always been subject to God's sway, hand and protection, alone'. The *ordonnance* began by declaring the king's intention to preserve 'the sacrosanct churches, monasteries, prelates and all ecclesiastical persons, of whatever status or condition', and the first articles of the *ordonnance* were dedicated to the rights and privileges of churches and clergy.[64] Philip seems to have come to believe in his calling, transcending the limits of secular rulership, to become king of Jerusalem and leader of a united crusading order.[65]

This conception of royal duty and the king's relationship to God resonates with statements made by Philip's minister Guillaume de Nogaret, who was involved in Philip's most spectacular enterprises but whose notoriety stems from his confrontation with Boniface VIII at Anagni on 7 September 1303. Just as Philip believed that he held his kingdom directly from God, so Nogaret conceived of himself as acting under God's direct control. A letter that he wrote himself, probably as he was journeying to Italy in 1303, reveals his belief that God was directing his actions, and that if his actions displeased God, God would stop him – by death, if

---

[63] Elizabeth A. R. Brown, 'The Prince Is Father of the King: The Character and Childhood of Philip IV of France', *Mediaeval Studies*, 49 (1987), 282–334, at 288, 309, reprinted in Brown, *The Monarchy of Capetian France and Royal Ceremonial*, (Variorum Collected Studies, 345; Aldershot, 1991), no. II. In a response to Emperor Henry VII's summons to his coronation in 1312, Philip declared it 'notorie' that 'a tempore Christi citra regnum Francie solum regem suum sub ipso Jhesu Christo, rege regum et domino dominorum ac omnimode creature dominatore, habuit': see Karl Wenck, *Philipp der Schöne von Frankreich, seine Persönlichkeit und das Urteil der Zeitgenossen* (Marburg, 1905), pp. 71–3, at 72. A memorandum attacking Boniface's memory began by stating that the kings of France 'superiorem, nisi Deum solum, in temporalibus non nouerunt', and proceeded to describe the kings' dedication to the faith and the churches of France: Vigor and Dupuy (eds), *Histoire, preuves*, pp. 317–24.

[64] 'Ut autem Deo propitio reformationem predictam facilius impetremus, & circà eam auxilium & gratias omnipotentis Dei misericorditer habeamus, cujus solius ditioni, manui & protectioni predictum regnum nostrum subjectum semper extitit, & nunc esse volumus, & a quo nobis omnia bona proveniunt; Primò Volumus & intentionis nostre est sacrosanctas Ecclesias, monasteria, Prelatos, & quascumque personas Ecclesiasticas, cujuscumque status, aut conditionis existant, & quibuscumque nominibus censeantur, ob Dei reverentiam & amorem tenere, custodire & conservare in favore & gratiâ, & auxilio condecenti, quibus predecessores nostri retroactis temporibus tenuerunt, foverunt, & etiam servaverunt': Eusèbe-Jacob de Laurière et al. (eds), *Ordonnances des Roys de France de la Troisième Race . . .* , 22 vols and Supplement (Paris, 1723–1849), 1: 354–68, at 357. The first eleven articles are dedicated wholly or in part to ecclesiastical issues.

[65] Heinrich Finke, *Papsttum und Untergang des Templerordens*, 2 vols (Vorreformationsgeschichtliche Forschungen, 4; Münster i. W., 1907), 2: 115–16, 118, no. 75; and his 'Zur Charakteristik Philipps des Schönen', *Mitteilungen des Instituts für österreichische Geschichtsforschung*, 26 (1905), 201–24, esp. 209, 217–19. Strayer knew and cited Finke's work but never discussed this report, which suggests that he discounted, and indeed dismissed, the relevance of the episode to Philip's ambitions.

necessary.[66] Such sentiments are consistent with his conviction that he was obligated – and prepared – to die to defend the *res publica*, the faith, and the unity of the Roman church.[67] The justifications he prepared to defend his actions at Anagni provide access to his ideas about the society in which he lived and his obligations to it and to God. He repeatedly invoked the organic metaphor, but in his apologies it was the body of the universal Catholic church to which he appealed, rather than the body of the kingdom. Echoing declarations about the realm of France made in Philip the Fair's name, Nogaret proclaimed of the church that 'members of this sacred and mystical body, as of the body of any man, owe mutual aid to it, according to apostolic doctrine, to preserve the whole body'.[68] He, Nogaret, had been obliged to intervene, even though he was a private person (*privatus*), because no ecclesiastical or secular power had taken action.[69] 'A private Catholic', he considered himself a '*servus* of Christ', and a 'member of Christ' and of the 'body of the *res publica* of the church of Christ'. His position as *miles*, *vassallus* and *fidelis* of the king of France obligated him to defend the king and kingdom of France, and complemented and reinforced his duty as devout Christian to uphold the faith and the universal church.[70] In Nogaret's eyes, the boundaries of the two bodies, church and kingdom, were virtually coterminous. He envisaged no separation or antagonism between them, whatever divisiveness individuals within them

---

[66] Charles-Victor Langlois edited the letter, written to Etienne de Suisy, Nogaret's predecessor as chancellor, in 'Autographes nouveaux de Guillaume de Nogaret', *Journal des savants*, n. s., 15 (1917), 321–7, at 322–3. In the letter Nogaret declared, 'Domine mi, orate ad Dominum ut si via mea Deo placeat, me in ea diriguat, alias me per mortem vel, ut sibi placeat, inpediat. . . . Adhuc faciam meam dietam, Domino concedente'. Robert Fawtier discusses this letter and Nogaret's mission, in 'L'attentat d'Anagni', *Mélanges d'archéologie et d'histoire de l'Ecole française de Rome*, 60 (1948), 153–79, reprinted in his *Autour de la France capétienne: personnages et institutions*, (ed.) Jeanne C. Fawtier Stone (Variorum Collected Studies Series, 267; London, 1987), no. VIII.

[67] See the defence submitted by Nogaret on 7 September 1304, in Vigor and Dupuy (eds), *Histoire, preuves*, pp. 244 ('militem, qui pro Reipublicæ defensione mortem subire tenetur'), 246 ('volens magis pro defensione Fidei, & vnitatis Romanæ Ecclesiæ cum suo Rege & regno Franciæ mortis subire discrimen'). Kantorowicz analyses other statements of Nogaret, in *King's Two Bodies*, pp. 250, 259.

[68] 'membra huius sacri, ac mystici corporis [vniuersi Catholicæ Ecclesiæ], sicut corporis cuiuslibet hominis, mutuum sibi, iuxta doctrinam Apostolicam, debeant auxilium, ad conseruationem corporis vniuersi': Vigor and Dupuy (eds), *Histoire, preuves*, pp. 243, 244 (a statement Nogaret submitted to the official of Paris on 7 September 1304).

[69] 'in Ecclesiasticæ, & sæcularis potestatis defectum': Vigor and Dupuy (eds), *Histoire, preuves*, p. 243; see also p. 244 ('in vtriusque potestatis, Ecclesiasticæ, & sæcularis, defectum, ad quemlibet Catholicum Christianum, maximè militem, qui pro Reipublicae defensione mortem subire tenetur, vt est ipse Guillielmus').

[70] See Nogaret's declarations of 7 September 1304 ('miles, ac vassallus [Regis Franciæ]') and of 12 September 1304 ('priuatus Catholicus membrum Christi, corpus Ecclesiæ cuius membrum est'; 'seruus Christi, . . . miles dom. Regis Franc. & ideo ad tuendam rem publicam Ecclesiæ Christi astrictus, cuius sum membrum, de patria regni Franc. pro qua pugnare teneor, oriundus, fidelis dicti domini Regis, & ideo ad eius honoris defensionem iure diuino & humano ligatus, zelator fidei Christianæ, vt Catholicus quisque tenetur'), in Vigor and Dupuy (eds), *Histoire, preuves*, pp. 250, 270, 271.

Laity, laicisation and Philip the Fair 215

promoted. Nogaret may have been a cleric at the beginning of his career,[71] but he served Philip the Fair as *miles*, was married, and had children. Nonetheless, his commitment to his faith and the church suggests that, no more than the king, did he consider himself *mere laycus*.

An anonymous sermon given in France in 1315, two years after Nogaret's death, dissolved the tenuous distinction that Nogaret drew between the body of the church and that of the kingdom of France. The sermon focused on the French monarchy and the reigning king, Louis X (r. 1314–16). Applying the organic metaphor to the realm, with the king its head, the preacher announced that 'anyone who assails the king labours against the whole church, against Catholic doctrine, against sanctity and justice and the Holy Land'.[72] Thus, in the preacher's view, the king and his kingdom represented and absorbed the church, the faith and the Holy Land. Taking a more conservative stance, reminiscent of Nogaret's position, the anonymous author of a long poem addressed to Louis X shortly after his death made God the head of the church and its members all *fideles*. It was the king's duty to be loyal to all the members on pain of dishonouring the *chief* (or head) and foreswearing his lord – who was clearly God. Then, in a brisk change of focus, the king became head of the body – now the realm's – and he was admonished not only to attend to all parts of the regnal body, but, even more, to seek wise councillors to be his eyes.[73] The author of the admonition insisted that the king could do nothing 'without clerks and without lay, the wise clerks to counsel you, the lay knights to fight for you'. 'One', the author says, 'is principal, the other accessory', and the poem proceeds to elevate the clergy, while recognising that without the laity the regnal body would perish.[74]

The poet's bias is understandable, since he was in all likelihood one of the clerks who collected the works with which the lengthy *roman* called the *Livres de Fauvel* was joined in a manuscript prepared in the chancery of Philip the Fair's son and namesake, Philip V (r. 1316–21).[75] *Fauvel*, the principal piece in the manuscript,

---

[71] See Robert Holtzmann, *Wilhelm von Nogaret, Rat und Grosssiegelbewahrer Philipps des Schönen von Frankreich* (Freiburg im Breisgau, 1898), pp. 12–13. Ernest Renan discusses Nogaret's background and family, in 'Guillaume de Nogaret, légiste', in *Histoire littéraire de la France*, 27 (1877), 233–371, at 234–7, 303–4, 356–7.

[72] 'Igitur qui contra regem invehitur laborat contra totam ecclesiam, contra doctrinam catholicam, contra sanctitatem et justitiam et Terram Sanctam': Jean Leclercq (ed.), 'Un sermon prononcé pendant la guerre de Flandre sous Philippe le Bel', *Revue du Moyen Age latin*, 1 (1945), 165–72, at 169–70. I discuss the sermon and show that it must have been composed in the summer of 1315, in 'Kings Like Semi-Gods: The Case of Louis X of France', *Majestas*, 1 (1993), 5–37, esp. 10, 23–6.

[73] Walter H. Storer and Charles A. Rochediéu (eds), *Six Historical Poems of Geffroi de Paris Written in 1314–1318, Published in their Entirety for the first time from MS fr. 146 of the Bibliothèque Nationale, Paris* (University of North Carolina Studies in the Romance Languages and Literatures, 16; Chapel Hill, 1950), pp. 38–9 ('Les Avisemens pour le Roy Loys').

[74] Storer and Rochediéu (eds), *Six Historical Poems*, pp. 18–21.

[75] I discuss the manuscript containing this and other poems (as well as the *Livres de Fauvel* and other works) (BNF, fr. 146), in '*Rex ioians, ionnes, iolis*: Louis X, Philip V, and the *Livres de Fauvel*', in Margaret Bent and Andrew Wathey (eds), *Fauvel Studies. Allegory, Chronicle, Music, and Image in Paris, Bibliothèque Nationale de France, MS Français 146* (Oxford, 1998), pp. 53–72.

describes and harshly denounces the corruption that reigned throughout the wicked realm of the horse Fauvel, whose favour everyone wished to curry. All those who dwelled in Fauvel's kingdom, clergy and lay, were vicious and beast-like. He ruled them all, their evil head (*mauves chief*), although they were ultimately subordinate to their creator, God. At the end the author implored the Trinity – God, Jesus Christ and the Holy Spirit – to act with the Virgin Mary in protecting 'the lily and the garden of France', so that God, 'the king of justice', and holy church would be accorded the honour they were due.[76] The clerks who edited this text for the manuscript in which it is preserved shared Nogaret's belief in their God-given calling to act – in their case, to speak out against the corruption of their times, and to advocate reform of the kingdom. Like Nogaret, they rejoiced in Philip the Fair's dedication to combatting, and his eventual triumph over, the Templars. In accomplishing the order's destruction, the king was presented as inspired by God, and the saviour of 'mother church' and her 'spouse', the crucified Jesus Christ.[77]

The seriousness with which Nogaret and Philip V's clerks admonished the ruler and spoke of their duties suggests a conviction that every occupation and calling was sacred, and a belief that salvation depended on the exact fulfilment of the obligations associated with their roles in society, chief among which was, for every person, responsibility for defending the faith and the church. The attitude reflected in their writings and declarations was similar to views Jean Juvenal des Ursins (then bishop of Beauvais) expressed to the three estates of France in 1435.[78] He upbraided them separately – clergy, nobles and common people – for their various sins and shortcomings. These differed from estate to estate, but all estates were united in their dedication to vice and in their failure to heed God's commandments. He called on them all to cleanse themselves of their 'filth and sinning' before beseeching the 'blessed Trinity' for the gift of 'good peace in this most dolorous realm of France'.[79]

In the world of Philip the Fair and Guillaume de Nogaret, as in that of Jean Juvenal des Ursins, the sacred merged with and penetrated the profane, just as, at all levels of society, the secular impinged on, informed and sometimes threatened the spiritual. Through their vocations, clergy differed – and were distinguished – from laity, but lay and clergy were closely tied by bonds of common interest and family relationships, as well as by their concern for and preoccupation with the

---

[76] Gregory Alexander Harrison provides the best available text of the *Fauvel* of BNF, fr. 146, in *The Monophonic Music in the* Roman de Fauvel (Ph.D. diss., Stanford University, 1963), esp. pp. 409, 556; for the organic metaphor, see p. 412. Harrison includes a reduced facsimile of the *Livres de Fauvel* in the dissertation. Edward H. Roesner, François Avril and Nancy Freeman Regalado have reproduced the entire manuscript and provided a valuable introduction and commentary, in *Le Roman de Fauvel in the Edition of Mesire Chaillou de Pesstain. A Reproduction in Facsimile of the Complete Manuscript, Paris, Bibliothèque Nationale, Fonds Français 146* (New York, 1990).

[77] Harrison, *Monophonic Music*, pp. 407, 424–7. See also Kantorowicz, *Laudes Regiae*, pp. 3–4.

[78] For the treatise *Audite celi*, see *Ecrits politiques*, 1: 145–278, and, on the work, 1: 93 n. 1, and 3: 58–9. When he composed the work, Juvenal des Ursins was bishop of Beauvais, a position he held from 1432 until his transfer to Laon in 1444.

[79] Juvenal des Ursins, *Ecrits politiques (Audite celi)*, 1: 145, 238–50, esp. 248, 250.

Laity, laicisation and Philip the Fair

spiritual, the divine and the hereafter. Although the evidence I have discussed is largely drawn from French sources, similar testimony exists for other times and places. The intermingling of sacred and secular that I have described persisted for centuries, longer than, until recently, has been acknowledged. Thus I would propose yet another self-limiting ordinance for historians. I end by encouraging them to exercise as much caution in applying to other times and places distinctions between lay and ecclesiastical as I hope they are doing in using terms connected with the tyrant feudalism.

Lay solidarities: the wards of medieval London

Caroline M. Barron

With characteristic honesty and intellectual rigour, Susan Reynolds has challenged the historians of English medieval towns to move on from the accumulation of evidence and 'to think more about their reasoning, their assumptions, and the concepts that lie behind the words they use...'.[1] She has not, herself, written directly about wards, whether in London or elsewhere, nor, for that matter, has anyone else except the indefatigable Webb partnership more than a hundred years ago.[2] Susan Reynolds's own interests have moved away from English urban history, although her impressive survey volume, *History of English Medieval Towns*, published in 1977, remains a sane and indispensable introduction to the subject which is in constant demand by students and teachers alike. This essay will probably be more empirical than Susan would like, but I hope that its attempt to search for the less visible members of urban society will meet with her approval. Her belief in the essential reasonableness of medieval men and women, and in their ability to act in their own best interests, has been a constant corrective and inspiration. It is in the nature of the surviving records to reveal most about those who were most conspicuous: in the case of London those who became aldermen or held other civic office. Such men were almost always wealthy and it is their views and priorities which may be most easily discerned in the surviving records. But it is possible to trace the concerns and activities of less prosperous Londoners and, when we cannot hear them speak we can, at least, discern the forum in which they came together to express their views. The wardmote, or ward meeting, of medieval London is likely to have been the most important meeting place for the great majority of Londoners: it was here that common attitudes and policies would have been debated and formulated. Although it is rare to hear an individual voice speaking at those distant meetings, yet the fact that the civic records list in detail the manner in which wardmoots were to be held, those who were to be present and

---

[1] S. Reynolds, 'The Writing of Medieval Urban History in England', *Theoretische geschiedenis/Historiography and Theory* 19 (1992), 43–57; reprinted in eadem, *Ideas and Solidarities of the Medieval Laity: England and Western Europe* (Aldershot, 1995), p. 45.
[2] S. and B. Webb, *English Local Government*, 10 volumes (London, 1906–29).

the business to be covered, suggests that they may have had an importance beyond the meagre records of their proceedings that have survived.

Susan Reynolds observed of London government in the twelfth and thirteenth centuries that the city 'also retained subordinate courts in the wardmotes, under the presidency of their respective aldermen. They seem to have been chiefly concerned with policing, defence, public health, and so forth, rather like hundred courts or manor courts with frankpledge jurisdiction elsewhere'.[3] Aldermen were probably already presiding over the city's wards by the early eleventh century,[4] but the wards can be clearly discerned as units of civic government in the 1120s when, in a list of the London properties belonging to St Paul's Cathedral, the properties were divided up according to the wards in which they lay.[5] The aid of 1167–8 was also assessed 'per wardas'.[6] But although the existence of wards is clear from the twelfth century, their separate identities are not clearly distinguished at that time. In the reign of King John we gain our first glimpse of what actually happened in the wards when all men over the age of fifteen were summoned to the wardmotes and instructed in some, at least, of their civic duties.[7] But by 1246 when a team of royal justices visited the city to inquire into purprestures (illegal encroachments on, or enclosures of, land) they conducted their inquiries on a ward by ward basis.[8] At this date about twenty wards may be identified; but of these only three (Portsoken, Cheap [Fori] and Dowgate) were identified by place; all the rest bore the name of their alderman. By the time of the inquiry of 1274–5 which was recorded on the Hundred Rolls, there were clearly twenty-four wards and two more of them, Bassishaw and Langbourne, were identified by their location rather than by their alderman.[9] Finally, by about 1290, or possibly a little earlier, in a list of wards which was copied into the City's Letter Book A, all the twenty-four wards are identified by place and not by the name of their alderman.[10] So, by the end of the thirteenth century the London wards were no longer considered to belong to the alderman who 'ruled' them: rather they were identified by their locations: indeed by the names by which they are still known today.

[3] S. Reynolds, *An Introduction to the History of English Medieval Towns* (Oxford, 1977), p. 119.

[4] S. Reynolds, 'The Rulers of London in the Twelfth Century', *History* 57 (1972), 337–57, p. 339 and n.

[5] H. W. C. Davis, 'London Lands and Liberties of St Paul's, 1066–1135', in A. G. Little and F. M. Powicke (eds), *Essays in Medieval History Presented to T. F. Tout* (Manchester, 1925), pp. 45–59; C. N. L. Brooke and G. Keir, *London 800–1216: The Shaping of a City* (London, 1975), pp. 162–70, esp. p. 163. For a judicious discussion of the early history of the wards, see A. H. Thomas (ed.), *Calendar of the Plea and Memoranda Rolls 1413–1437* (Cambridge, 1943), xxx–xli (hereafter, *CPMR*).

[6] Reynolds, 'Rulers of London', p. 344, n. 35.

[7] M. Bateson, 'A London Municipal Collection of the Reign of John', *English Historical Review*, 17 (1902), 480–511, 707–30.

[8] H. M. Chew and M. Weinbaum (eds), *The London Eyre of 1244* (London Record Society, 1970), pp. 136–52.

[9] [William Illingworth (ed.)], *Rotuli Hundredorum temp. Hen. III & Edw. I*, vol. i (London, 1812), pp. 403–23.

[10] R. R. Sharpe (ed.), *Calendar of the Letter Books of the City of London* (London, 1899), p. 209 (hereafter *CLA*); A. B. Beaven, *The Aldermen of the City of London*, 2 vols (London, 1908, 1913), i, pp. 235–7.

Yet in spite of this development the identities of the wards are hard to discern, unlike the craft and trade associations which were developing in London at the same time (see below), and unlike the parishes. Trade associations (or companies) and parishes both had buildings where members could meet and where records and precious memorabilia could be stored. For this reason, perhaps, over thirty of the London parishes, and some twenty of the city companies have administrative records surviving from the fifteenth century or earlier. The survival of the administrative records of the wards is much more bleak. In the medieval period the wardmoots had no specified meeting place of their own: sometimes they met in the house of the alderman or in some 'borrowed' building (see below) and it would appear that the records of the meetings were presumed to belong to the alderman and, as such, became part of his personal papers. Virtually none of the personal papers of any medieval London alderman has survived and, so far, no collection of private papers has yielded records of London ward meetings, although some records of this kind do survive for the city of York in the late fifteenth century.[11] At the meetings of the wardmotes, among other activities, twelve jurors were chosen (as in a manor court) to make inquiries into what was amiss in the ward and to present the results of such an inquiry to the alderman in the form of an indenture, half to be kept in the ward (by the alderman?) and the other half to be presented by the alderman to the mayor with 'action points' written in. Some of these ward 'presentments' for the years 1373, 1422 and 1423 have survived among the mayor's records in the Corporation of London Record Office.[12] There also survive fifteen presentments for the ward of Portsoken from the years 1465–83 and 1507–8. The ward of Portsoken was unique in that the office of alderman was held, *ex officio*, by the prior of Holy Trinity, Aldgate. The surviving indentures were those kept by the prior/alderman and were preserved at the priory only to be swept up into the Court of Augmentations when the house was dissolved in 1532.[13] Another draft (or possibly a copy) of the presentment for Broad Street ward from December 1523 has survived among the state papers. It seems to have found its way there via the office of Thomas Cromwell whose London house in Throckmorton Street lay in the ward.[14] The inquest return is heavily annotated in Cromwell's hand which is indicative of the extent to which the views of Cromwell's neighbours and, indeed of the ward alderman, were subject to correction by a 'great man'. It is interesting to note, however, that Cromwell thought that the ward meeting was sufficiently important to act himself as one of the twelve ward jurors and, with them, to sign the indenture.

---

[11] See T. Andrew, 'Fifteenth-century Wardmote Courts of York' (unpublished MA dissertation, University of York, 1997).

[12] 1370, presentments for the wards of Langbourne, Portsoken, Aldgate, Castle Baynard, *CPMR 1364–81*, pp. 156–7; 1422, presentments from all 24 wards, *CPMR 1413–37*, pp. 115–41; 1423, presentments for 21 wards, ibid., pp. 150–9.

[13] These are now kept at the Corporation of London Record Office.

[14] PRO, State Papers SP/1/29, printed in *Letters and Papers of Henry VIII*, vol. iii, pt 2, no. 3657.

There are a few other wardmote indentures surviving in scattered places;[15] and, in the sixteenth century the records come a little more thickly on the ground.[16] But, apart from the exiguous records that have survived from the ward administration itself, useful material may be gleaned from custumals, or collections of London custom. It is true that these are 'normative' in that they describe what should happen, and they also represent the view from the centre, from the point of view of the mayor and aldermen, and the city bureaucracy, rather than the view from the men of the ward. But at least the custumals provide a framework. The earliest surviving civic custumal was compiled in the reign of King John and is now in the British Library.[17] This provides information about the conduct of ward meetings and more detailed instructions are to be found in two early fourteenth-century compilations, the Liber Horn and the Liber Custumarum, both associated with the remarkable chamberlain of London in this period, Andrew Horn.[18] Not surprisingly the conduct of wardmotes and ward business was of interest to those who were concerned to reform the way that the city was governed in the later fourteenth century and the 'Jubilee Book' of the 1370s lists the responsibilities of the ward juries.[19] John Carpenter, who compiled the Liber Albus c.1419 provides, probably, the most detailed account of when, and how, the wardmote should be held.[20] Information about the summoning of a ward meeting and about the business to be transacted there also survives in a private collection of material put together for an alderman (possibly Thomas Cook) in the 1480s.[21] This material, spread as it is over nearly three hundred years, can furnish a sense of the evolving role played by the wards in the government of London and, at least, provides a perspective on the

---

[15] See 1342, view of frankpledge for the Holborn precinct surviving among the archives of St Paul's Cathedral, GL 25121/630: I am grateful to Dave Rollenhagen for drawing this to my attention.

[16] The ward of Aldersgate has three indentures surviving from the reign of Henry VIII, GL Ms 1499, 1500, 1501. One of these indentures is partially printed in W. McMurray, *The Records of Two City Parishes* (London, 1925), pp. 29–30. The compilers of the new Aldersgate wardmote inquest book in 1578–9 at that time had in their possession an almost complete set of wardmote indentures dating back to 1460–1. They copied only brief details (the names of the alderman and the jurors) into the new book and then, presumably, disposed of the original returns of which only three have survived, GL Ms 2050/1. The ward of Farringdon Without has a surviving wardmote inquest book for the parish of St Dunstan beginning in 1558, GL Ms 3018/1, and the ward of Cornhill has an inquest book dating from 1571, GL Ms 4069/1.

[17] BL Ms 14252, see Bateson, 'A London Municipal Collection'.

[18] Liber Horn c.1311–28; c.1324 Liber Custumarum, printed by H. T. Riley, *Munimenta Gildhallae Londoniensis* (Rolls Series, 1860), vol. ii, parts 1 and 2; N. R. Ker, '*Liber Custumarum* and other Manuscripts formerly at the Guildhall', *Guildhall Miscellany* (1954), pp. 37–45.

[19] See Cambridge, Trinity College Ms 0.11.3 fos 144–6v.

[20] The Liber Albus is kept at the Corporation of London record Office. It was edited by H. T. Riley, *Liber Albus* (Rolls Series, 1860), vols i and iii; translated by H. T. Riley, *Liber Albus: The White Book of the City of London* (London, 1861), see esp. pp. 32–5, 241, 287–92. All references in this essay will be to the Latin text.

[21] Cambridge, Trinity College Ms 0.3.11. For a description of the manuscript see, L. R. Mooney *The Index of Middle English Prose: Handlist XI: Manuscripts in the Library of Trinity College, Cambridge* (Woodbridge, 1995), pp. 109–11.

purposes which the city's rulers, in particular the aldermen, believed the ward meetings might serve.

In addition to this 'didactic' material, there is much information to be found in the city's administrative and judicial records which throws light, fitfully and indirectly, on how the wards worked in practice. Ward officers appeared before the mayor and aldermen bringing in wrong-doers or, themselves, being accused of misbehaviour. Aldermen were instructed to summon ward meetings for particular purposes. Disputes between neighbours erupted in the wards and were resolved in other courts. And, in times of civic disputes, it is possible to glimpse the 'political' uses to which ward meetings might be put.

The alderman summoned a meeting of the wardmoot when he received a precept from the mayor instructing him to do so. Although in the fourteenth century the alderman was required to hold such meetings at least four times a year, by the fifteenth century the alderman usually received only one precept from the mayor each year. But in 1447 it was decided that, by virtue of the annual precept from the mayor, the alderman might hold as many wardmoots as seemed to him to be necessary during the year.[22] The precept which, until the mid-fifteenth century, was written in French, required the aldermen to investigate not only all the matters listed in the 'Articles of the Wardmote' but also any other issues which were of concern to the mayor and aldermen.[23] So, for example, in 1343, the aldermen were to investigate the inmates of lodging houses, the cleanliness of the streets, and were also to inquire in their wardmoots whether 'the proposed enclosing of St Paul's (i.e. the precinct) was to the prejudice of any in the City'.[24] So the City's rulers saw the ward meetings as a useful source of 'public opinion' which, of course, had also to be controlled.

On receiving the mayor's precept the alderman commanded his beadle to summon the men of the ward to meet him at a stated day, hour and place within the ward.[25] Clearly the place varied from ward to ward. In 1310 the alderman was expected to summon the men of the ward to a specified parish church, or to his own house.[26] In 1423 the wardmoot of Cripplegate ward met in the newly built hall of the brewers' craft (at a charge of 4d.) and the Aldersgate wardmoot used the hall of the Trinity guild.[27]

Who, in fact, was expected to attend the ward meetings? The early fourteenth century custumal, Liber Horn stated that, in accordance with 'ancient ordinances', all the inhabitants of the ward, over the age of fifteen, were to attend the wardmoot,

---

[22] CLRO, Journal 4 fo. 180; the juries were also to serve for a year and if a juryman died during the year then the alderman was empowered to choose another man to fill the vacancy.

[23] In 1437 the precept was written in English, *LBK*, p. 215.

[24] *CPMR 1323–64*, p. 156.

[25] *Liber Albus*, p. 37.

[26] *LBD*, pp. 215–16.

[27] R. W. Chambers and Marjorie Daunt (eds), *A Book of London English 1384–1425* (Oxford, 1931), p. 148; P. Basing (ed.), *Parish Fraternity Register: Fraternity of the Holy Trinity and SS Fabian and Sebastian in the Parish of St Botolph without Aldersgate* (London Record Society, 1982), pp. xxv–xxvi.

take an oath of fealty and enter into frankpledge. Three categories of persons were exempt from attending: knights, clerks and women.[28] John Carpenter, writing a century later in the Liber Albus, adds two further categories to those who are exempt from attending the wardmoot: esquires and apprentices-at-law.[29] Carpenter also makes clear that it is not only householders who are expected to attend but also all hired servants (*omnes viros domos tenentes, etiam et servientes mercenarios*). The beadle was to keep two rolls, one for the freemen who lived in the ward and another for the hired servants and non-freeman (*famulorum mercenariorum et non liberorum*).[30] So, all males over the age of fifteen who lived in the ward, regardless of whether they were freemen or not, were expected to be in frankpledge, attend the ward meeting and contribute to its discussions. In this way, the assembly of the ward was more democratic than the craft or company which included in its deliberations only those who were freemen, but the ward was less inclusive than the parish which comprised all Christian souls within its bounds, whether male or female, adult or child.

There are two detailed accounts of how the meeting of the wardmoot is to be conducted: one written in English in the Jubilee Book of 1378 and the other written by John Carpenter, in Latin, in the Liber Albus of *c*.1419. The earlier account records first that the bakers shall bring in their marks and have them publicly certified at a charge of 4d.; then the constables, scavengers and the beadle are to be chosen by the 'goode men of the warde' and anyone who refused to take up the office was to be fined twenty shillings. Following this 'the alderman ought to make his clerk openly to rede in inglissh the poyntes that ensuen'. These points, known as the articles of the inquest, were the matters about which a ward jury was supposed to inquire. In 1378 there were twenty-nine points, or offences, about which they were to inquire. These were grouped: one group dealt with law-breaking such as curfew-breaking, prostitution, rioters and corrupt officers; another group of inquiries was concerned with the condition and prices at which victuals were sold; another group dealt with building regulations and, specifically, the necessary precautions against fire: another group of questions concerned the condition and cleanliness of the streets in the ward and, finally, the jurors were to inquire whether anyone was concealing the goods of orphans.[31] John Carpenter's account of the wardmoot, written some forty years later, and in Latin, places greater emphasis upon the hierarchy of the ward: the alderman is to take his seat '*cum valentioribus Wardae*', the beadle is to read out the names and to fine absentees, and the articles of the wardmoot are to be read out, although Carpenter does not specify that this is to be done in English.[32] The articles are much the same as those listed in 1378,

---

[28] CLRO, Liber Horn, fo. 232; the exemption of clerics was extended also to laymen who lived within sanctuaries, see H. M. Chew and M. Weinbaum (eds), *The London Eyre of 1244* (London Record Society, 1970), pp. 51–2; M. Weinbaum (ed.), *The London Eyre of 1276* (London Record Society, 1976), pp. 42, 52, 71.
[29] *Liber Albus*, p. 38.
[30] Ibid., p. 37.
[31] Trinity College, Cambridge, Ms 0.3.11 fos 144v–6v.
[32] *Liber Albus*, p. 37.

although there are some interesting omissions from Carpenter's list: he does not include questions about the concealing of orphans' goods, nor those about food which was unwholesome or over-priced. On the other hand Carpenter's list requires the jurors to investigate craftsmen and labourers who were being paid more than allowed by the Statute of Labourers and to report on usurious bargains.[33] These wardmoot inquiry lists provide an interesting insight into the preoccupations of the city's rulers and inhabitants at different periods. The third list of wardmote articles dates from the 1470s when there is less concern about excessive wages, but a new anxiety about disreputable priests, neglected chantries, citizens who covertly sold the goods of strangers for them and those who lived out of the city and so escaped civic charges.[34] The jurors were given a day on which to report all the offences, concealments and negligences that they could find in the ward to the alderman. It was then the responsibility of the alderman, presumably, to have the jurors' findings drawn up in an indenture to be delivered to the mayor. The alderman was expected to correct those matters which fell within his purview and to inform the mayor about other matters of wider concern such as, presumably, the neglect of chantries or usurious practices.[35]

Thus far the business of the wardmoot seems to have been to note the local bakers and their marks, to appoint the ward officers and to select a body of jurors to make inquiries about malpractices in the ward. Presumably the point of selecting the jurors in the open wardmoot was to ensure that they were known and so complaints and information could be conveyed to them. Carpenter describes further business that was transacted in the wardmoot: those who were not already in frankpledge were to take the oath, paying a penny for the privilege, or a four-penny fine if they absented themselves. The writ of 1465 in which the mayor instructed the aldermen to summon their wardmoots clarifies the business to be transacted. Apart from electing ward officers (a beadle, scavengers, constables, raker and aleconners) and selecting a panel of jurors, the wardmoot was to make provision for keeping the watch during the Christmas season and providing lights, and was also to elect men to serve as common councilmen for the ensuing year.[36]

From the late thirteenth century the wards seem to have formed the constituencies, on occasion providing 'probi homines' to assist the aldermen.[37] Although the city crafts in the 1370s had challenged the wards as constituencies for the election of the common councilmen, in 1384 it was decided that it should be in the wards that men were chosen every year for the Council.[38] It is clear that the same men might continue to serve as common councilmen for a number of years, although it would appear that they had to be re-elected each year at the

---

[33] Ibid., pp. 334, 338.
[34] Trinity College Cambridge, Ms 0.3.11 fos 83v–4.
[35] *Liber Albus*, pp. 38–9.
[36] Trinity College Cambridge, Ms 0.3.11, fo. 82v–3.
[37] *LBA*, pp. 209–10; *LBE*, p. 174.
[38] *LBH*, p. 227; *Liber Albus*, pp. 462–4.

wardmoot.[39] The meeting of the wardmoot included men who were householders or residents of the ward but not necessarily freemen. Yet those elected to Common Council had to be citizens and, one might presume, that those who elected them would also have had to be citizens.[40] But the city records are silent on this point, and it may be that non-citizens had some say in the choice of the members of the Common Council. This suggests, again, that the wardmoots may have played a more political role than the city's discreet custumals suggest. But if this grassroots democracy ever existed it seems to have been snuffed out early in the sixteenth century. In 1536 when the inhabitants of Walbrook ward asked to be allowed to elect their own common councilmen 'freely' they were told by the court of aldermen that 'the election belonged to the aldermen' and their choice was simply to be confirmed by the wardmoot.[41]

But it looks as if the ward may have retained more control over the choice of their own ward officers, indeed it was one of the duties of the wardmoot meetings to choose the ward officers and to arrange (presumably by some form of local taxation) for their remuneration. The most senior officer, and certainly the one who appears first in the records, is the ward beadle. The earliest references suggest that his tasks were primarily concerned with keeping the peace and preventing 'immorality' in the ward; objectives that were not always compatible. In 1300 the beadle of Farringdon ward led a posse of neighbours (including the vicar of St Sepulchre's church) to the house of William Cok, a butcher in Cokkes Lane who had been indicted in the wardmote for keeping a brothel and had refused to mend his ways. Clearly the beadle and his gang had warmed to their task for they had brought hammers and chisels and had torn down eleven doors and five windows in pursuit of the offenders.[42] It may be that William Cok was running a substantial business. But the role of the beadle as chief law enforcement officer in the ward, and agent of the wardmoot, is clear. When the city was preparing for the great royal inquiry in 1321 the aldermen were instructed to ensure that their beadles were wearing 'their best coats and surcoats' and they were not to be in any way feeble or infirm, but well able to act as door-keepers or messengers or to fulfil any of the commands of the 'Mayor and Barons [i.e. the aldermen] of the City'. It was the responsibility of the aldermen to ensure that the beadles were 'smart, handsomely turned out, freshly shaven and shorn'.[43] So, it is clear that the beadles were

---

[39] The four men who served as common councilmen for Portsoken ward in 1460 were still serving in 1466. CLRO, Portsoken ward presentments Ms 242a. One of the Portsoken common councilmen, William Stallon, was still serving in 1483.

[40] In 1410, the mayor's writ to elect common councilmen simply specified that they should be 'sufficient', *LBI*, pp. 89–90; in 1427 membership of the Common Council was restricted to those who were free of the city by birth, apprenticeship or office. Those who had paid for the freedom could not be common councilmen, 20 February 1427, CLRO, Journal 2 fo. 90; this was confirmed, 3 March 1446, CLRO, Journal 4, fo. 119v.

[41] CLRO, Repertory 9 fo. 233: I am grateful to Dr Penny Tucker for this reference.

[42] A. H. Thomas (ed.), *Calendar of Early Mayor's Court Rolls 1298–1307* (Cambridge, 1924), pp. 218–19.

[43] Helen M. Cam (ed.), *The Eyre of London 14 Edward II A.D. 1321* (Selden Society, 1968) 2 vols i, pp. 8–9.

also seen, on occasion, as useful civic employees funded by the ward communities. The beadle's oath, dating in its earliest form from the early fourteenth century, provides a detailed job description: he was to prevent law-breaking, eject immoral women from the ward, to inform the alderman (or if he was inactive, the mayor), the chamberlain and the sheriffs about wrong-doers. He was responsible for finding jurors for coroners' inquests, and for cases in city courts; he was to ensure that food was sold in accordance with civic precepts, and he was not himself to engage in the sale of food while he held office.[44] But his duties were not confined to those prescribed by his oath. Sometimes, particularly in the earlier part of the period, the beadles were instructed to assist other ward officials in keeping the streets clean, although this was not their usual duty.[45] There was only one beadle in a ward and he stood at the apex of the local 'civil service'. Surprisingly few of them (compared with the constables) got into trouble, or were reported for abusing their office. But not all were above reproach. Richard Gryndere, the beadle of Billingsgate ward in 1386 entered the house of Joan Garton, a brewster, on the grounds that she was 'harbouring' a married man. Richard brought with him, as his assistants, Hugh Bryseville, a butcher, and John atte More, a brewer. Joan took the case to King's Bench and complained about the attack which she claimed was motivated by economic rivalry: she had been accustomed to buy beer from John atte More for retail sale, but had transferred her custom elsewhere on finding cheaper and better suppliers. She claimed that John was angry at this loss of custom and so persuaded the beadle to break into her house. When they did so they found no evidence of immorality.[46] It is possible that Richard Gryndere was the unwitting dupe of John atte More, but one of his successors as beadle in the same ward in 1461, William Mayle, ran a successful protection racket: when he discovered a case of adultery, instead of bringing the offender to court he accepted a bribe of 16s. 8d. which he shared among his associates and spent the rest on food and drink. He ended up in prison.[47] The jurors at the wardmote inquest at Aldersgate in 1510 declared that few, or none, of them were content with the services of their beadle, Thomas Borne, who was indiscreet and gave 'suspicious persons' warning of impending visits from the constable or the men of the watch, so that they were unable to make arrests.[48]

The duties of the ward constables were more strenuous and physical than those of the beadle. It is possible that, in the late thirteenth century, when these ward officials first appear, the chief 'law enforcement' officer in the ward may have been

---

[44] Copies of the beadle's oath are to be found c.1340 (French), *LBG*, p. 126; (French), *Liber Albus*, pp. 313–14; fifteenth-century (French and English versions), *LBD*, pp. 10, 193; late fifteenth century (shortened English version), Cambridge, Trinity College Ms 0.3.11, fos 85v–6.

[45] 1332, 1345, 1366, 1372, 1417, *CPMR 1323–64*, p. 97; *LBF*, p. 125, *LBG*, p. 208; *CPMR 1364–81*, p. 150; CLRO Journal 1, fo. 39.

[46] Morris S. Arnold (ed.), *Select Cases of Trespass from the King's Courts 1307–1399*, vol. i (Selden Society, 1985), p. 170. The case of Joan Gawton has been recently discussed by Cordelia Beattie, 'Women's work identities in post Black Death England', in James Bothwell, P. J. P. Goldberg and W. H. Ormrod (eds), *The Problem of Labour in Fourteenth-Century England* (Woodbridge, 2000), pp. 1–19, esp. pp. 15–18.

[47] 6 May 1461, CLRO Journal 6, fo. 53v.

[48] McMurray, *Records of Two City Parishes*, p. 30.

variously called either a beadle or a constable. When Sybil Child, 'a common prostitute and scold' who quarrelled with other women, was ordered by the Bishopsgate wardmote in 1309 to leave the ward and live outside the city walls, it was the ward constable who was instructed to take Sybil to the sheriffs when she failed for the third time to comply with the ward's decision. Sybil resisted arrest and later sued the constable, and three women who had helped him, for damages in the King's Bench.[49] It may be that the constables had a particular responsibility towards the sheriffs. By their oath, they were sworn to arrest peace-breakers and bring them to the sheriffs' prisons, and to raise the hue and cry if they needed help. They were also expected to look out for those in the ward who contravened city ordinances and to report them to the mayor.[50] It is clear that constables were distinguished from beadles by 1365 and from that date onwards they appear frequently as maids of all work in the wards.[51] There were, by the early fifteenth century, about two hundred constables operating in the city at any one time. In 1422 the small ward of Bassishaw had two constables and the large extramural ward of Farringdon Without had twenty-one.[52] Like the beadles in earlier times, constables were often found breaking into houses, although it was decided in 1440, perhaps because constables had exceeded their powers, that such forcible entries should only be executed in the presence of an alderman.[53] In 1465, William Willoughby, a constable of Bread Street ward had to pay twenty shillings to a man whose doors he had broken down and then unjustly imprisoned.[54] Clearly considerable physical demands were made upon the constables: Thomas Darlington was rejected by the mayor and aldermen after he had been chosen as a constable by the men of Langbourn ward because he had a malformed hand.[55] The roles played by both the beadles and the constables in pursuing wrong-doers, in particular fornicators, prostitutes and adulterers, must have exposed them to a good deal of abuse and hostility.[56] It is hard to assess the attitude to such arrests: it is not at all certain that the people of the ward were always on the side of law enforcement.

A new ward officer, known as the scavenger, appears in 1364, perhaps in response to the devastations of the plague which were known to be aggravated by dirty living conditions. It was the duty of the scavenger to ensure that the pavements in the ward were repaired and kept free of dung and filth, and that houses were built of fire-proof materials.[57] In the 1290s the city had required wards to elect four men to look after the pavements and in the early fourteenth century the

---

[49] Arnold, *Select Cases*, p. 19.
[50] Oath (French), *Liber Albus*, pp. 312–13; (French and English versions), *LBD*, pp. 10, 192–3; shortened English version in Trinity College Ms 0.3.11 fo. 85v.
[51] *LBG*, p. 198.
[52] *CPMR 1413–37*, p. 116.
[53] CLRO, Journal 3, fo. 41v.
[54] CLRO, Journal 7, fo. 103.
[55] CLRO, Journal 5, fo. 52v.
[56] Between 1400 and 1460 there were 98 recorded arrests, many of them of unbeneficed priests, see *LBI*, pp. 273–87; CLRO Journals 1–6, passim.
[57] Oath (French), *Liber Albus*, p. 313; oath (French and English), *LBD*, pp. 10, 192; briefer English oath in Trinity College Ms 0.3.11, fo. 85v.

oversight of the city's streets was delegated to six specially elected paviours.[58] But by 1365 the responsibility for the cleanliness of the city streets had been returned to the wards. As with constables, the number of scavengers varied from ward to ward: in 1421 Bassishaw and Lime Street wards each had only two scavengers whereas Farringdon Within had thirteen.[59] To assist them, the scavengers had the services of a raker whose office was considered to be so lowly that he was not required to take an oath to perform it competently and honestly. He was, however, chosen for his office by the men of the ward and paid by them. But rakers make only fitful appearances in the city's records. They are first mentioned in 1357 when, it is clear, they are simply street-sweepers.[60] Sometimes the precept to the aldermen to hold wardmote meetings specifies the need to elect rakers, and sometimes not. They are not listed with other ward officers in 1422, but the surviving Portsoken wardmote indentures list the raker along with the other ward officers. In the sixteenth century the ward records from Aldersgate and Farringdon Without (St Dunstan in the West) make no mention of the election of the raker, but the Cornhill wardmote book of 1571 lists him alongside the other ward officers.[61] It was his task to sweep away rubbish and to ensure that water could flow freely down the channels in the streets. Although the civic authorities tried to provide tips to which rubbish from the wards could be taken in tumbrel carts, the rakers often found easier solutions to their problems. Richard Mayllour, the raker of Cheap ward, and his fellow conspirator, John Marchaunt the raker of Bassishaw ward, had to provide surety to the city chamberlain that they would not in future cast dung into Colmanstreet ward, nor place rubbish in the channels in rainy weather so that the force of water would carry it into the neighbouring ward, and that they would remove all their ward rubbish from Colmanstreet ward.[62] These men, like other ward officers, were paid by some form of local taxation, but they were also able to earn extra money by carrying out additional rubbish-clearing exercises. The churchwardens of St Mary at Hill paid the raker 8d. a year as a form of salary until 1517 when the sum was raised to 16d., but they also paid him additional sums for removing dung from the churchyard (2d.) or, in 1559 for carrying away 'all the rubbish of the altars that did lie at the church door' (16d.).[63] On the other hand the scavenger appears only rarely in the surviving churchwardens' accounts. In 1477–9 the churchwardens at St Mary at Hill had to pay the scavenger 8d. because a pavement belonging to the church had been indicted, i.e. it had been the subject of a complaint at the wardmote and they were required to pay the scavenger to

---

[58] *LBA*, p. 183; *LBC*, p. 115; *LBD*, p. 312; *LBE*, p. 55.

[59] *CPMR 1413–37*, p. 116.

[60] H. T. Riley (ed.), *Memorials of London and London Life in the XIIIth, XIVth and XVth Centuries* (London, 1868), p. 299.

[61] GL, Ms 4069/1, fo. 5v.

[62] *CPMR 1381–1412*, p. 71.

[63] H. Littlehales (ed.), *The Medieval Records of a London City Church (St Mary at Hill)* (EETS, 1905), pp. 67, 412. Cf. payments to the raker by the churchwardens in 1469–72, C. Burgess (ed.), *The Church Records of St Andrew Hubbard Eastcheap c.1450–c.1570* (London Record Society, 1999), pp. 18–19.

The wards of medieval London 229

repair it.[64] It would seem, therefore, that whereas scavengers may have been paid by some central ward mechanism, rakers collected annual sums from the churchwardens of the parishes in the ward and then made what extra they could. It must have been a hard life and it is not surprising that they tried, on occasion, to push the rubbish from their ward over the boundary into someone else's responsibility.

The final ward officer had a rather different task to perform. The aleconners (or aletasters) took an oath to ensure that all ale brewed in the ward was of the right quality, sold in the correct measures and at the right price. No ale could be sold or 'outed' in the ward until it had been tasted by the aleconners.[65] They are first named in 1377, but not all the precepts to the aldermen required them to be elected.[66] Aleconners are not recorded among the ward officers listed in 1422 and in 1440 the Common Council asked that aleconners might be elected 'as hitherto accustomed' which may suggest that the practice had lapsed. Their election is recorded only once among the Portsoken wardmote records of the reign of Edward IV, yet all the surviving ward records for the sixteenth century record the elections of men, now known as tipplers rather than aleconners. The ward of Aldersgate listed forty-six tipplers in all in 1510.[67] Moreover their numbers had, by that date, been augmented by the election of a small number of brewers. It is possible that the brewers tested the beer produced by the professional brewers in the ward while the tipplers were responsible for the home-made ale.

It seems clear that, at least until the late fifteenth century, the wardmotes were responsible for the choice of the men who represented the ward at meetings of the Common Council, and for the election and remuneration of their local ward officers. But a crucial aspect of ward democracy remains to be considered: how was the ward alderman chosen? Originally wards had been passed from father to son like pieces of property and in the middle of the thirteenth century the hereditary clashed with the elective principle in determining succession to aldermanries. But by 1249 the elective principle was firmly established: the 'probi homines' of the ward made their choice and presented the man to the mayor and other aldermen.[68] If he was acceptable to them he was sworn and admitted.[69] The presumption was that the alderman so chosen would then remain in office for life. However, the royal charter of 1319 specified that aldermen should be annually elected and not re-elected; but this proved to be unworkable and soon lapsed in practice.[70] Aldermen

---

[64] *Medieval Records of a London City Church*, p. 89. By 1590 it appears that, for example, the churchwardens of St John Zachary paid an annual salary of 2s to the ward scavenger, McMurray, *Records of Two City Parishes*, p. 375.

[65] Oath in French, *Liber Albus*, p. 316; English and French, *LBD*, pp. 10, 201; shortened version of the English oath in Trinity College Ms 0.3.11 fo. 85v.

[66] *LBH*, p. 71; *CPMR 1364–81*, p. 256.

[67] GL, Ms 1499.

[68] G. A. Williams, *Medieval London: From Commune to Capital* (London, 1963), pp. 30, 34.

[69] 1293, the aldermen were to be elected by the 'wealthier and wiser' men of the wards, *LBC*, p. 11. This procedure can be seen in practice in the case of Bassishaw ward in 1310, *LBD*, p. 14.

[70] W. Birch (ed.), *The Historical Charters and Constitutional Documents of the City of London* (rev. edn, 1887), p. 46.

continued to serve for life until the radical reformers of the 1370s managed briefly to restore the annual election of aldermen from 1376 until 1394.[71] But it is not easy to find out how the 'probi homines' of the ward set about finding, or electing, their new alderman. The Jubilee Book drawn up in 1378 during the period of the annual election of aldermen specified that the alderman was to be chosen by the ward of which he was to be alderman, 'and be his name presented to the mayor by the greatest part of the good men with the ministers of the same ward and then be received and take his charge'.[72] The good men of the ward had to choose a new incumbent within fifteen days or the right of choice lapsed to the mayor. Men who were chosen for office and refused to take it up were condemned to lose their freedom.[73] Moreover aldermen could not move from one ward to another without the consent of Common Council.[74] In the 1370s, therefore, it was envisaged that the men of the ward would exercise considerable freedom in their choice of alderman, although their chosen man had to be presented to the mayor who could, presumably, refuse to accept him. But as the 'conservatives' in city government reasserted themselves in the 1390s it was decided that, 'by reason of the headstrong, partial and imprudent elections of the Aldermen', in future the men of the wards should select two candidates from whom the mayor and aldermen would choose one.[75] In 1402 the number of candidates to be presented was raised to four, and this seems to have remained the practice throughout the fifteenth century.[76] The Court of Aldermen claimed, and exercised, the right to reject all four candidates presented by a ward. Sometimes the court maintained that none of the candidates was 'sufficient'[77] and in 1448 the Court rejected the four candidates presented by the ward of Lime Street on the grounds that since not all of the candidates were of sufficient standing, the choice of the Court was restricted.[78] In this incident one can detect, perhaps, a deliberate attempt by the freemen of the ward to control the election of their alderman, but it was resisted by the Court of Alderman who were anxious to retain control over those who joined their meetings.

Once elected an alderman appears to have been able to move quite easily to a different ward, although the Jubilee Book in the 1370s had specified that this could only be done with the consent of Common Council. In the fifteenth century it was customary for the men of the ward to include the names of one or two serving

---

[71] Beaven, *Aldermen of the City of London*, i, pp. 392–402.

[72] Cambridge, Trinity College, Ms 0.3.11 fo. 143.

[73] John Carpenter writing in the early fifteenth century describes a very similar procedure but states that it is customary for the mayor to visit the vacant ward and ask the beadle to summon all the freemen of the ward (NB not the householders) and there they should choose a new alderman or appoint a day to do so when he should be chosen by the 'maiorem et saniorem partem illorum', *Liber Albus*, p. 39.

[74] Ibid., pp. 143–4.

[75] 1397, *LBH*, p. 436; Riley, *Memorials*, p. 545.

[76] *LBI*, p. 18, reiterated in 1420, ibid., p. 241.

[77] 24 July 1444, *LBK*, pp. 295–6; 29 November 1456, 22 November 1457, 12 February 1458, 17, 26 November 1460, CLRO, Journal 6, fos 87v, 185v, 192v, 268.

[78] 1 April 1448, CLRO Journal 4, fo. 213v.

aldermen among the four names that they presented to the Court. In August 1451 the men of Farringdon Without ward presented William Hulyn and William Deer, both of whom were already aldermen, and Richard Alley and Thomas Davey who were not. Hulyn and Deer were asked if they would like to move to become alderman of Farringdon Without and, when they both declined, the Court chose Richard Alley.[79] On another occasion, in 1438, Nicholas Yeo, the alderman of Farringdon Within, asked the Court if he could have the vacant aldermanry of Candlewick Street, and this appears to have been granted to him without any reference to the men of the ward. But sometimes the freemen of the ward flexed their muscles. In March 1446 William Whetenhall, a grocer who had been alderman of Farringdon Within ward since 1438, was chosen by the mayor and aldermen for the vacant ward of Walbrook. It appears that the men of the ward were not consulted and were unhappy with the new alderman. In April seventeen men of the ward came to the Court of Aldermen and protested. Their leader, John Wasshawe, asserted that as greatly as the men of Farringdon Within rejoiced at Whetenhall's departure, so greatly would the men of Walbrook grieve over his coming. In the end, eleven of the seventeen men agreed to accept Whetenhall and the protest fizzled out.[80] But this incident shows that the men of the wards did not always acquiesce in the transfer of aldermen between wards, and that it mattered to them who their ward alderman was. It is not clear, also, whether the men of the ward were consulted when their alderman appointed a deputy. Although by the sixteenth century it was the normal practice for an alderman to appoint a deputy who was often, unlike the alderman himself, resident in the ward, in the medieval period aldermen seem only to have appointed deputies for specific periods of time.[81] When Robert Tatersale, the alderman of Broad Street, planned to be away from London on business in 1425, he asked the Court of Aldermen to accept Thomas Ayer and John Whatele as his deputies.[82] There is no suggestion that the men of the ward were consulted.

The spirited intervention of John Wasshawe in representing the views of the men of Walbrook ward about their choice of alderman serves to remind us that wardmotes were not always as firmly under the control of the Court of Aldermen as the surviving records might suggest. We know something about how the mayor and aldermen expected the wardmotes to be conducted, and we have a few of the wardmote indentures which largely conformed to the expectations of the aldermen. But, just occasionally, the voice of the men of the wardmote breaks into the deliberations of the Court of Aldermen, as in the case of the Walbrook protesters in 1446. It is clear that the wardmote could on occasion, and probably on more occasions

---

[79] CLRO Journal 5, fo. 62; in October and November 1458, Ralph Josselyn was offered both Coleman Street and Langbourne wards but chose to remain at Cornhill, CLRO Journal 6, fos 233v, 221v.

[80] 16 March, 7 April 1446, CLRO, Journal 4 fos 121, 124v.

[81] I. Archer, C. Barron and V. Harding (eds), *Hugh Alley's Caveat: The Markets of London in 1558* (London Topographical Society, 1988), pp. 83–4; I. Archer, *The Pursuit of Stability: Social Relations in Elizabethan London* (Cambridge, 1991), pp. 67–8.

[82] 13 June, 28 July 1425, CLRO, Journal 2, fos 44v, 48v.

than we know, provide the scene for political protests. In the 1430s and 40s there was a sustained protest movement in London led by the alderman and tailor Ralph Holland and inflamed by the craft rivalry between the drapers and the tailors. In the course of the protest, many issues relating to the way in which the City was governed were aired and debated. In May 1444, Holland was finally dismissed from the bench of aldermen and the protest movement began to die down.[83] But just at the end of the protest there was an interesting sputtering of radicalism in the wards. In January 1444 John Farndon was sent to Newgate because at the wardmote of Bishopsgate he had presented 'an unsuitable and scandalous' bill criticising his alderman, the mercer Thomas Chalton. Farndon asserted that Chalton had perverted the course of justice by 'delay, favour and negligence'.[84] But Farndon was not alone: similar bills had been presented at the wardmotes of Bread Street, Broad Street, Queenhythe, Cornhill and elsewhere. In these wards the aldermen had also come under attack. They were accused of being usurers and supporters of robbery and adultery. The City chamberlain (at the time the grocer John Chichele) was charged with having appropriated the common land of the city and the recorder (Robert Danvers) was accused of having forced men to enter into obligations of £20 to observe ordinances which they considered to be unjust. The bills claimed that, in the city, there was one law for the rich and another for the poor.[85] The evidence considered by the Court of Aldermen in January and February 1444 suggests that there had been a serious attempt to use the wardmotes in a synchronised protest movement. This had been articulated by written 'bills' to be read out at meetings of the men of the ward. It is unlikely that John Farndon's methods for disseminating radical information and organising a protest movement were unique, but information about the use of wardmotes for political discussions rarely penetrates the surviving records.

Even if ward meetings might explode into protest and anger about civic matters which extended well beyond the bounds of any particular ward, yet it is clear that the ward might also be a focus of loyalty and, indeed, affection. Thomas Aleyn, a mercer but not an alderman, who lived in the parish of St Lawrence Jewry in the ward of Cheap left a residual bequest of money to be used to help the poor of his ward to pay their contributions to royal taxation.[86] John Hatherley who had, since 1437, served as the alderman of Queenhythe ward where he lived, left money for the poor of his ward when he drew up his will in 1459.[87] The wards of medieval London may have been both political and affective units within the complex jigsaw of civic government.

---

[83] for a discussion of the movement, see C. Barron, 'Ralph Holland and the London Radicals, 1438–1444', in R. Holt and G. Rosser (eds), *The Medieval Town: A Reader in English Urban History 1200–1540* (London, 1990), pp. 160–83.

[84] 16, 24 January 1444, CLRO Journal 4, fo. 13.

[85] CLRO, Journal 4, fos 14, 16v, 17v.

[86] R. R. Sharpe (ed.), *Calendar of Wills enrolled in the Court of Husting, London 1258–1688* (London, 1890), vol. ii, pp. 514–15.

[87] CLRO, Husting Roll 195 (44).

There is some evidence that the ward not only survived into the sixteenth century, but also flourished. It was, of course, challenged by the developing role in city government played by the crafts and companies. There is no doubt that the companies became the focus of concerted economic and political action and they certainly engaged the hearts and loyalties of their members. But their membership was confined to freemen and so their base was narrower, less democratic, than that of the wards.[88] Moreover the dramatic growth in the size of London, from some 50,000 in 1500 to 200,000 in 1600, meant that the ward became too populous to be a successful single unit of administration. In consequence the wards were broken down into their constituent parishes, and it was the men of the parish vestries who administered poor relief and social control. The older intimacy of the ward had been destroyed by massive demographic growth. Yet wardmote petitions continued to be important in influencing the policies of the Court of Aldermen and they constituted one of the many channels of communication between the governed and the governors. It has been argued that it was the effectiveness of these channels which ensured the unexpected stability of London in the sixteenth century.[89] But it was in the medieval period, when the voice of the wardmotes can be only fitfully heard, that those procedures and practices were developed which were to enable the city to hold together in the testing years of the sixteenth century.

[88] S. Rees Jones, 'Household, work and the problem of mobile labour: the regulation of labour in medieval English towns', in Bothwell, Goldberg and Ormrod (eds), *The Problem of Labour*, pp. 132–65.
[89] Archer, *Pursuit of Stability*, pp. 52, 257–60.

Language, laughter and lay solidarities: an inquiry into the decline of pilgrimages and crusading

Charles T. Wood

When attempting to deepen our understanding of the Middle Ages, Susan Reynolds has frequently posed shrewdly penetrating questions, all of them designed to demonstrate the extent to which even cherished views often lack evidentiary support. She has enlarged on the point by further arguing that the most common reason for going astray – about the nature of lay solidarities and their collective activities, for example – lies in a thoughtless tendency to use historically inappropriate concepts when forming our interpretations of the past. She will permit no such sloppiness. Because Miss Reynolds has either consciously or unconsciously accepted the proposition of historians of philosophy that ideas travel on the back of terms, she is ferociously enthusiastic in her opposition to concepts like feudalism, terms the interpretive understandings of which came into being long after the phenomena on which they claim to shed light. As a result, in so far as such terms convey ideas not present in the original sources, their use is to be avoided at all costs.

It might appear, then, that *Entia non multiplicanda sunt praeter necessitatem* must be the one axiom of medieval philosophy on which Miss Reynolds would always insist. Yet, clearly, she is not a nominalist. She may reject all terms not validated by the historical record, but she has no difficulty accepting the real existence of *entia* such as kingdoms, towns and other corporate communities. She is, rather, more accurately to be viewed as a positivist whose frequently legal or quasi-legal approach leads her to stress the matching of language to evidence, interpretation to documentable facts. Nevertheless, precisely because she has done so much to demonstrate how inappropriate concepts can distort our understandings of the past, in seeking to honour her it may not be inappropriate to expand her argument by exploring the extent to which changes in language may themselves be a vehicle of change.

As it happens, I saw Miss Reynolds most recently at a meeting of the Medieval Academy of America, an academic conference of the variety that David Lodge, a novelist well represented on her shelves, sees as resembling 'the pilgrimage of medieval Christendom in that it allows the participants to indulge themselves in all the pleasures and diversions of travel while appearing to be austerely bent on self-improvement'.[1] That assessment of both phenomena explains, perhaps, why this

---

[1] David Lodge, *Small World* (New York, 1984), p. vii.

inquiry will focus on pilgrimages and, to a lesser extent, on their armed cousins the crusades in an attempt to grasp the role played by language in what appears to have been their inexorable decline. In the high Middle Ages, after all, they had been two of the most popular lay solidarities, their corporate identities proclaimed by the symbols displayed by each member – from the palm fronds of Jerusalem's pilgrims or the cockleshells of Santiago's to the more universal cross worn by all crusaders – but only a few centuries later both movements had effectively ceased to exist.

The place to begin is with 'A Pilgrimage for Religion's Sake', a colloquy that Erasmus first published in 1526. By that point, crusades – and especially successful ones – had become a thing of the past. Thirty-four years earlier, even the Reconquista, that most enduring monument to crusading fervour, had come to a successful end, and in this colloquy Erasmus now brought under satirical attack all those pilgrim experiences that had long capped the whole medieval penitential system. Indeed, satire itself – the genre within which Erasmus so typically operated – was about to be temporarily killed off, at least in its religious form, by that Reformation Martin Luther had launched in 1517. For after Luther, satire internal to any faith would become highly suspect and not, as with Erasmus, a vehicle for renewal. In short, to begin with 'A Pilgrimage for Religion's Sake' is to start with a tale in which religious ideals are expressed in a language that may help us better to understand the incipient decline of pilgrimages as a form of lay solidarity. Before turning to Erasmus, however, a brief look at traditional modes of expression may be in order, to set the scene.

In July 1174, Henry II revisited his kingdom for the first time since Alexander III had canonised his late archbishop – or, for that matter, for the first time since Becket's unfortunate martyrdom. In the words of Gervase of Canterbury,

> the king returned to England at the beginning of July. Taught by good advice, he postponed dealing with nearly every matter of State, and immediately on landing set out with a penitent heart to the tomb of St. Thomas at Canterbury. Accordingly, on Saturday, 12 July he left the church of St. Dunstan, which is sited a good distance outside the city, and walked barefoot and clad in a woollen smock all the way to the martyr's tomb. There he lay prostrate for a great while and in devout humility, and of his own free will was scourged by all the bishops and abbots there present and each individual monk of the church of Canterbury. There he remained, constant in prayer before the holy martyr all that day and night. He neither took food nor went out to relieve nature, but, as he had come, so he remained, and would not permit a rug or anything of the kind to be provided for him. After lauds he made a tour of the altars in the choir of the church and the bodies of the saints interred there, and then returned to the tomb of St. Thomas in the crypt. At dawn on Sunday he heard mass. Last of all he drank of the water of the holy martyr and was honoured with the gift of a phial. So he departed from Canterbury rejoicing, reaching London on the Sunday.[2]

---

[2] Gervase of Canterbury, ed. W. Stubbs, *Chronica de tempore regum Angliae Stephani, Henrici II et Ricardi I* (London, Rolls Series, 1879), 1: 248–9, as translated in D. C. Douglas and G. W. Greenaway, eds, *English Historical Documents 1042–1189* (Oxford, 1953), 2: 775–6.

Such, in brief, was Henry's pilgrimage to Canterbury, and even though the scourging would not have been a required part of the penance endured by the hundreds of thousands of others who were soon to take this pilgrimage annually, in other respects Gervase gives an accurate sense of what their total experience would have been like. First there is the penitential walk from St Dunstan's followed by a vigil at the martyr's tomb. The tour of the altars in the cathedral and of the bodies interred there then follows, after which there is the return to the tomb of the martyr himself. Strikingly, too, Gervase's description seems almost unconsciously designed to heighten the reality of Becket's living presence, for whilst the other saints visited are called 'bodies ... interred there', Henry remains 'constant in prayer before the holy martyr' himself, not just his body or tomb. Indeed, monks and priests who later tended the shrine made much the same point when offering pilgrims water from the martyr's well that was fortified with a trace of his precious blood. This tincture, they claimed, came packaged in leaden ampules because the greatness of its curative powers might split the mere wood from which similar vessels were elsewhere made.[3]

Be that as it may, consider now what happens in 'A Pilgrimage for Religion's Sake' when Erasmus's character Ogygius tells his friend Menedemus about his own penitential journey to Canterbury, one that began, like all others, at the south entrance to the cathedral or, in other words, on its salvation side:

> When you enter, the spacious grandeur of the building is disclosed. This part is open to the public. . . . Iron screens prevent you from going any farther, but they permit a view of the space between the end of the building and the choir. . . . [On the north side,] a wooden altar sacred to the Holy Virgin is shown . . . [where] the holy man is said to have spoken his last farewell to the Virgin, when death was at hand. On the altar is the point of the sword with which the crown of the good bishop's head was cut off, and his brain evidently smashed to make death come more quickly. Out of love for the martyr we reverently kissed the sacred rust of this sword.
>
> Leaving this place, we went into the crypt. It has its own custodians. First is shown the martyr's skull, pierced through. The top of the cranium is bared for kissing, the rest covered with silver. . . . The hair shirt, girdle, and drawers by which the bishop used to subdue his flesh hang in the gloom there – horrible even to look at, and a reproach to our softness and delicacy. . . .
>
> From here we return to the choir. On the north side mysteries are laid open. It is wonderful how many bones were brought forth – skulls, jaws, teeth, hands, fingers, whole arms, all of which we adored and kissed. This would have gone on forever if my fellow pilgrim, a disagreeable chap, had not cut short the enthusiasm of the guide. . . . An arm was brought forth, with the bloodstained flesh still on it. He shrank from kissing this, looking rather disgusted. The custodian soon put his things away.[4]

Somewhat later Ogygius and the disagreeable pilgrim (a figure modelled on John Colet) are shown a wooden chest in which the remainder of Becket's body is reported to rest and within which another chest is discovered, this one of gold.

---

[3] With no little embarrassment I have to confess that, though I have many times seen these specifics reported in print, I cannot now find an appropriate reference to cite. They are, however, of no real importance to the argument as a whole.

[4] Desiderius Erasmus, trans. C. R. Thompson, *Ten Colloquies of Erasmus* (New York, 1957), pp. 80–2.

Language, laughter and lay solidarities　　　　　　　　　　　　　　　　　　237

The value of its contents threatens to stun the startled pilgrims. As Ogygius reports the scene: 'The cheapest part was gold. Everything shone and dazzled with rare and surpassingly large jewels, some bigger than a goose egg. Some monks stood about reverently. When the cover was removed, we all adored.'[5] By way of contrast, however, at the very end of the tour the pilgrims enter the sacristy where they are shown a chest with black leather cover within which are found:

> Some linen rags, many of them still showing traces of snivel. With these, they say, the holy man wiped the sweat from his face or neck, the dirt from his nose, or whatever other kinds of filth human bodies have. At this point my friend Gratian [i.e., Colet] again displayed imperfect manners. To him, since he was English, and a well-known person of considerable standing, the prior kindly offered one of the rags as a gift, thinking he was giving him a present that would please him very much. But Gratian was hardly grateful for it. He touched the piece with his fingers, not without a sign of disgust, and put it back scornfully.... [T]he prior, no stupid man, pretended not to notice this incident, and after offering us a glass of wine dismissed us kindly, for we were returning to London.[6]

Even the most insensitive of readers will here recognise that Erasmus has views on the pilgrimage experience that differ substantially from those of Gervase of Canterbury or, in all probability, most other medieval believers. Yet isolating and proving these differences can prove surprisingly difficult. In Erasmus's account, the wealth associated with Becket's relics has become almost beyond measuring, a development he finds flatly repellent and a clear source of abuse. As a protagonist explains in another colloquy, 'The Godly Feast': '[T]hose who adorn monasteries or churches at excessive cost, when meanwhile so many of Christ's living temples are in danger of starving, shiver in their nakedness, and are tortured by want of necessities, seem to me almost guilty of a capital crime.'[7] Nevertheless, if Erasmus documents this view by immediately citing 'St. Thomas's tomb laden with innumerable precious jewels in addition to other incredible riches', he is quick to add: 'I'd rather ... decorate the tomb with branches and flowers; this, I think, would be more pleasing to the saint.'[8] It would appear, then, that relics and pilgrimages were not, in and of themselves, the principal cause of his ire.

It is true, of course, that Erasmus was a man who sought to reform current religious practice by subjecting it to satirical review, the laughter-inducing specifics of which were intended to encourage other Christians to mend their ways. And within this context relics had obvious potential in so far as almost every religious foundation owned not a few of them, some of which could, in the hands of the right author, be made to appear ridiculous. For example, Glastonbury Abbey was proud to possess not just of the bones of Arthur and Guenevere, manna from the Wilderness, and fragments of the barley loaves with which Christ had fed the five thousand; rather, it also laid improbable claim to 'part of the hole where the Holy Cross was placed

---

[5] Ibid., p. 86.
[6] Ibid., p. 87.
[7] Ibid., pp. 161–2.
[8] Ibid., p. 162.

on the hill of Calvary', *de foramine ubi posita fuit sancta crux in monte Caluarie*.[9] As described by Erasmus, Canterbury's rags and bones were scarcely the equal of these treasures, but another point to note is that nowhere does he subject them to the kind of ridicule that their counterparts at Glastonbury were to experience during the Reformation. The relics, it seems, are not his principal target. Instead, he and his character Gratian merely find them distasteful. In other words, and to put the point a bit more speculatively, even though Erasmus surely wants the very unpleasantness of Canterbury's rags and bones to provoke rueful smiles, in no way does his outlook suggest that he would have favoured Cromwell's subsequent destruction of Blessed Thomas's shrine and the burning or dispersal of all that went with it. For him, decoration with 'branches and flowers' would have been preferable by far.

Moreover, if Gratian makes it clear that venerating the disgusting detritus of saints fails to inspire him, it does not follow that in 1526 Erasmus could have expected many of his fellow Christians readily to accept the idea that the chief characteristic of relics was, in the negative sense, their sheer awfulness. On the contrary, a surprising amount of evidence at least down to the time of his birth repeatedly demonstrates that, far from being put off by such holy artefacts, most people were drawn to them almost in direct proportion to the disgust they would otherwise have engendered as purely temporal objects. The greater the awfulness, apparently the greater the mysteries conveyed, a point that was not easily grasped by non-believers.

During the thirteenth century, for example, a Jewish author wrote an anti-Christian polemic, the so-called *Vikkuah Leha Radaq*, that is usually attributed to a Narbonnese rabbi named David Kimhi. Its argument concentrates on some of the logical absurdities and unpleasantly physical realities that any Jew of any century would find in a faith based on scriptures that tell of a God who became man and dwelt here amongst us. Kimhi starts with the popular belief, commonly accepted among Christians, that the Holy Spirit had impregnated the Virgin through her ear, certainly a physiological improbability, and yet not an entirely implausible hypothesis for those knowing that Jesus the Christ was also the Incarnate Word. Nevertheless, because Rabbi Kimhi knows no such thing, he counters with temporal experience and the teachings of science:

> [E]very intelligent person knows that the young of all creatures, whether man, animal, fowl or beast, leaves the mother's body from the place where the semen entered. Therefore, Jesus should have left through the ear through which the holy spirit entered her womb. Yet he did not leave from there but from the place where all others [leave].[10]

---

[9] *The Chronicle of Glastonbury Abbey, An Edition, Translation and Study of John of Glastonbury's Cronica sive Antiquitates Glastoniensis Ecclesie*, ed. J. P. Carley, trans. D. Townsend, revised edn (Woodbridge, 1985), pp. 22–3.

[10] Quotation as translated in David Berger, 'Christian Heresy and Jewish Polemics in the Twelfth and Thirteenth Centuries', *Harvard Theological Review*, 68: 3/4 (1975), p. 289. I am indebted to Professor Berger for graciously sending me an offprint of this article. In a covering letter dated 12 June 1998 he cautions that he believes 'the work in question . . . was probably not actually written by . . . Rabbi David Kimhi', but my ensuing argument depends on the apparent religion of the author, not on his specific identity.

Warming to the subject and fortifying his case with medical views taken from classical antiquity and, possibly, even Isidore of Seville, he then goes on to argue:

> It is well known to all, even to fools, that every woman from the age of thirteen on undergoes menstruation. . . . When she becomes pregnant, she does not have this blood, for the foetus is nourished on [it] . . . during the nine months he is in the womb. Furthermore, when a woman gives birth, that menstrual blood goes to the nipples of the woman . . . and turns into milk. . . . I shall make an additional point . . . that the menstrual blood is a virtually fatal poison. The wonders of the Lord are so great that the foetus is nourished on that blood for nine months without being harmed. However, it does make the child somewhat weak, so that when he leaves the mother's womb, he does not have the strength to walk on his feet. This is not the case with animals, for . . . animals have no menstrual blood. . . . If then Jesus' mother conceived him by the holy spirit, so that he was not nourished in his mother's womb on that corrupt blood, he should have walked on his feet the day he was born and he should have spoken and been as wise as he was when he reached the age of thirty. Instead, he left [her body] from the customary place, was small like other infants, and performed his needs as do other children.[11]

In a secular age, neither the specifics of Mary's reproductive processes nor the reality of a Christ Child with soiled nappies seems likely to inspire much spiritual uplift. To the modern mind, these topics are as offputting as that 'arm . . . with the bloodstained flesh still on it' that Gratian refuses to kiss. Moreover, because the concrete details – especially those relating to menses – would have been even more disturbing within the context of Levitican taboos, Rabbi Kimhi was being entirely logical in assuming that his specifics would prove an effective vehicle for arguing against Christianity itself.[12] Unhappily for him, however, parallel Christian evidence shows that these assumptions rested on false premises.

As demonstrated by the widespread popularity of *De secretis mulierum* (at least eighty-seven manuscripts survive, many wrongly attributed to Albertus Magnus[13]), educated Christians were no strangers to all of the wilder myths about the dangers posed by menstruating women and their poisonously life-threatening menses. As a result, because menstruation was assumed to be one of the curses that God had placed on Eve for her transgression in the Garden, as the Virgin's Immaculate Conception became increasingly accepted in the course of the twelfth century,

---

[11] Berger, 'Christian Heresy', p. 293. For classical views as they carried over into the Middle Ages, Roy Porter, *The Greatest Benefit to Mankind: A Medical History of Humanity from Antiquity to the Present* (London, 1997), pp. 77, 130–1; for Isidore on milk as menses transformed, itself one of the Greek theories, *Etymologiae* 11.1.77 (*Lac*) as translated in Ernest Brehaut, ed. and trans., *An Encyclopedist of the Dark Ages* (New York, 1912), p. 217.

[12] In a letter dated 15 August, 1999, Professor Berger stresses that while 'Jews did refer to the notion that God spent nine months in a womb full of menstrual blood as an anti-Christian argument', the author here is being highly atypical. That is, because he assumes that Christians believed that the Virgin neither menstruated nor had menstrual blood (issues to be covered below), he concludes that Jesus' very normality undercuts basic Christian beliefs about the nature of the Incarnation. See also David Berger, *The Jewish-Christian Debate in the High Middle Ages* (Philadelphia, 1979), Appendix 2, pp. 350–4.

[13] H. R. Lemay, ed. and trans., *Women's Secrets* (Albany, NY, 1992), p. 1.

one might have assumed that, in so far as it freed her from the burden of sin as transmitted in the generative act, it would therefore have liberated her from the curse of menstruation too. Strikingly, though, things failed to turn out so neatly, attractive though this possibility must initially have appeared to presumptively celibate theologians who were more than a little wary of female carnality in any form. Because Jesus had to be both God and man in order to accomplish his salvific mission, Christology dictated that Mary had to conceive in the normal way. If she did not, she would fail to make her dogmatically necessary physical contribution to his humanity, a maternal contribution that could in no way depend, like his paternity, on the miraculous intervention of God. As a result, experience having taught that women without periods did not have babies, it followed that she had to menstruate. So much, then, for anti-Christian arguments based on menstrual taboos, a point that takes unexpectedly concrete form in a pilgrimage relic still exhibited at the Church of the Annunciation in Nazareth: the *mikveh* ritually used by the Virgin to wash away her periodic Levitican defilement.[14]

Indeed, as I pointed out some twenty years ago, these beliefs provide the unseen foundations for much more familiar phenomena, notably the unexpected rise to prominence of the lactating Virgin whose maternal outpourings were to fill the reliquaries of so many pilgrimage sites. As it happens, the Dominicans were her principal sponsors, and that sponsorship was rooted in their opposition to the Immaculate Conception. They feared, in brief, that a Mary conceived without sin might also lack that menstrual cycle so critical to Christ's humanity. On the other hand, even supporters of the Immaculate Conception recognised that she had nursed her child while Dominicans knew, as did Rabbi Kimhi, that 'when a woman gives birth . . . menstrual blood goes to the nipples of the woman . . . and turns into milk'. In other words, what this Dominican sponsorship was slyly arguing was that if Mary had milk, she had menses, and if she was subject to that curse, she was no more the product of an Immaculate Conception than anyone else.[15]

In fairness, though, Christian tolerance did have its limits when confronted by other aspects of Mary's sexuality. Galenic theory held that conception involved the *in utero* joining of two eggs, the male *homunculus* with the female *menstruum*, and this was the view also endorsed in the writings of Albertus Magnus and Thomas

---

[14] C. T. Wood, 'The Doctors' Dilemma: Sin, Salvation, and the Menstrual Cycle in Medieval Thought', *Speculum*, 56 (1981), 717–23. When this article first appeared, some found its subject matter offputting, but in a discussion devoted to change in verbal forms of communication, it provides much more cogent testimony than does a seemingly logical alternative, the necessarily non-verbal evidence of art – potentially just as offputting but more discussable in 'polite society' – first presented by C. W. Bynum in 'The Body of Christ in the Later Middle Ages: A Reply to Leo Steinberg', *Renaissance Quarterly*, 39 (1986) and then more fully explored in her later books, *Fragmentation and Redemption: Essays on Gender and the Human Body in Medieval Religion* (Cambridge, Mass., 1991) and *The Resurrection of the Body in Western Christianity, 200–1336* (New York, 1995). Besides, the Bynum evidence does not speak as directly to the reasons why the specifics of Rabbi Kimhi's polemic were likely to prove ineffective.

[15] Wood, 'Doctors' Dilemma', p. 721.

Aquinas.[16] Nonetheless, Galen further taught that the female egg entered the uterus at the moment and in consequence of orgasm, and for the Virgin that was an obvious source of difficulty. Because Aquinas seems to have found it impossible to think of her as having had either orgasmic experience or the necessity for it, to obviate the problem he reverted to his more accustomed Aristotelian approach, arguing that in Christ's conception the Holy Spirit had simply imposed male form on the formless matter of Mary's menses, a function more normally performed by mortal seed, the *homunculus*. Still, even though he implied (though never explicitly stated) that in all likelihood she had had a normal menstrual cycle, he stressed that hers had been no ordinary menstrual blood, nor could it have been, given the fact that the usual kind 'gets tainted with lust inasmuch as by sexual intercourse the blood is drawn to the place apt for conception'. In her case such carnality was inconceivable because, as he elsewhere put it, 'her sensual appetites were always completely under the control of reason'.[17]

Be that as it may, Aquinas's rejection of a fully sexual Virgin should not obscure the deeper point, the general theological insistence that she had shared, and had had to share, gynaecological attributes that in other women gave rise to male fears, disgust and prejudice. In so far as these attributes demonstrably failed to dampen Marian devotion, by extension there is little reason to believe that Erasmus would have thought that the sheer awfulness of Canterbury's relics would alone have provided sufficient grounds for meaningful reform.[18] Here, though, a modest caveat should be entered. After all, Mary was the mother of God, and that mysterious conjoining of the human and the divine made her a very different being from the sainted archbishop whose martyrdom attracted so many pilgrim visits to his shrine. Therefore it could well be that while the very mystery of the Virgin's normality contributed to the devotion she inspired, the equivalent normality of the decaying remains left by Becket and other saints could still be used to cause horror, disgust and outright rejection.

Yet familiar church teachings pose an immediate objection to that hypothesis, for they held that relics were like the Virgin in being objects in which the divine was ever present. They may have been wholly material in substance, but their participation in the eternal was proclaimed by every miracle for which they – or, really, the saints whose continuing presence they quite literally substantiated – were

---

[16] Albertus Magnus, ed. Auguste Borgnet, *Beati Alberti Magni . . . Opera Omnia* (Paris, 1890–99), 12: 98ff: *De animalibus*, 15, *Tractatus II, De natura spermatis*; Thomas Aquinas, ed. Roland Potter, OP, *Summa Theologiae* (London, 1964–81), 52: 52–5 (3a, qu. 32, art. 4).

[17] Aquinas, *Summa Theologiae*, 52: 26–9, 52–5 (3a, qu. 31, art. 5, and 3a, qu. 32, art. 4); Thomas Aquinas, *Scriptum super libros Sententiarum magistri Petri Lombardi* (Paris, 1929–47), 3: 168 (dist. 4, qu. 2, art. l); Thomas Aquinas, *Compendium Theologiae*, as quoted in Hilda Graef, *Mary: A History of Doctrine and Devotion* (London and New York, 1963–65), 1: 280; Wood, 715–17; J. F. Benton, 'Clio and Venus: An Historical View of Medieval Love', *The Meaning of Courtly Love*, ed. F. X. Newman (Albany, NY, 1969), p. 32; C. W. Bynum, 'The Body of Christ', p. 421.

[18] Here the Bynum artistic evidence cited in note 14 above does become relevant since its subject matter further demonstrates that people were unlikely to abandon relics simply because of their unpleasantness.

so frequently responsible. Moreover, that saintly presence shows that relics were never mere symbols, to be understood only as such. Still, because medieval vernacular languages were late to develop the conceptual and evocative vocabulary needed to discuss the non-material realities of a religion whose God, as pure Spirit, transcended the confines of space and time, one senses that for ordinary people relics must always have had a quasi-symbolic linguistic function based on their ability to stand for, and hence to express, ideas and beliefs for which the spoken language lacked alternatives of equal power. In effect, if the Word had become flesh, believers worshipped him in return by making what once had been flesh into a substitute for words. That being the case, when viewing relics medieval pilgrims would have been not unlike the William Blake who famously claimed that when he saw a cherry tree, he did not see the cherry tree, only a host of Cherubim crying 'Holy, holy, holy'.

Under the aspect of eternity, then, relics were not what they seemed. They had a duality of being, though a duality that was equally capable of being found in sordidly mundane phenomena, often to the laughter of those unexpectedly discovering it. By way of illustration, consider the second story of the first day of Boccaccio's *Decameron*, a tale that opens with the attempts of a Parisian merchant to convert his Jewish friend Abraham for his salvation's sake. Worn down by pleas of friendship, the still unconvinced Abraham finally agrees to consider the matter, but only after he has first made an exploratory pilgrimage to the court of Rome. Fearing the worst, the merchant tries to talk him out of it, but to no avail, so upon Abraham's return it is with a heavy heart that he asks

> what sort of an opinion he had formed about the Holy Father and the cardinals and the other members of the papal court. Whereupon the Jew promptly replied:
>
> 'A bad one, and may God deal harshly with the whole lot of them. . . . [N]obody there who was connected to the Church seemed to me to display the slightest sign of holiness, piety, charity, moral rectitude or any other virtue. On the contrary . . . they were all so steeped in lust, greed, avarice, fraud, envy, pride, and other like sins and worse (if indeed that is possible), that I regard the place as a hotbed of diabolical rather than divine activities. . . . [Y]our pontiff, and all the others too, are doing their level best to reduce the Christian religion to nought and drive it from the face of the earth. . . .
>
> 'But since it is evident to me that their attempts are unavailing, and that your religion continues to grow in popularity . . . I can only conclude that . . . it deservedly has the Holy Ghost as its foundation and support. So whereas earlier I stood firm and unyielding against your entreaties . . . I can tell you quite plainly that nothing in the world could prevent me from becoming a Christian.'[19]

In the Middle Ages, although few miracle-producing relics were the source of such humour, fraudulent ones most certainly were, and nowhere more clearly than in the person of Chaucer's Pardoner, a man of few illusions whose pig's bones and other marvels produce the income needed to slake the thirst of a remarkably cynical avarice.[20] And no better, surely, was Boccaccio's 'Saint' Ciappelletto, a ruthless

---

[19] Giovanni Boccaccio, trans. G. H. McWilliam, *The Decameron* (Harmondsworth, 1972), p. 85.

[20] Geoffrey Chaucer, ed. R. M. Lumiansky, *The Canterbury Tales* (New York, 1960), pp. 14, 287–9.

notary serving even more ruthless Lombard bankers who offers up such a piteously winning deathbed confession that he convinces an unwary friar that he is indeed in the presence of a saint.[21] Nevertheless, what Chaucer leaves unsaid is that in so far as the Pardoner participates in the Canterbury pilgrimage without once engaging in any of his nefarious activities, he is transformed into a penitent whose actual conduct suggests a man genuinely expecting, or at least hoping for, remission of sin. In other words, he is not the denier of numinous reality that he claims to be. Similarly, Boccaccio ends Ciappelletto's story by having its supposed narrator offer the following reassurances to those fearing the inefficacy of prayers offered to a fraudulent intercessor:

> I say that this fellow should rather be in Hell, in the hands of the devil, than in Paradise. And if this is the case, we may recognize how very great is God's loving kindness towards us, in that it takes account, not of our error, but of the purity of our faith, and grants our prayers even when we appoint as our emissary one who is His enemy, thinking him to be His friend, as though we were appealing to one who was truly holy as our intercessor for His favour.[22]

Such evidence demonstrates that, limited in their ability to express the ineffable though medieval people may frequently have been, they had no difficulty distinguishing between this world and the next. Clearly, too, when they saw relics, they saw both of those worlds simultaneously, the one of here below often giving rise to laughter or disgust, but a laughter or disgust that was balanced by the salvific promise of the other world to come. We moderns may also be no strangers to doubleness, but our version tends crucially to differ from that of the Middle Ages, as illustrated by an example found in the records of Dartmouth College, the American institution Miss Reynolds once graced as a visiting professor.

George Ticknor, Dartmouth class of 1807, set out for Europe in 1815, hoping to experience some of the glories that had so kindled the imaginative spirit of those writers to whom he would later devote the better part of his life as America's first significant literary scholar. In 1816 (this tour was indeed a grand one, lasting almost five years), he came to Spain, and that it remained in his mind very much the land of the Reconquista and Cervantes is nowhere better shown than in his journal entries for the year. Nevertheless, one of those entries gives pause. It reports that while on a walk one day, like Don Quixote he had seen a flock of sheep in the distance. Yet, not content with leaving it at that, Ticknor closes the entry with: 'They looked like an army to me, too.'[23]

While that insight may show a doubleness of vision, it is surely not that of the Middle Ages. Ticknor may want only to confirm the validity of Don Quixote's perceptions, but he does so in a way that is totally blind to the profound, yet lovingly satiric ways in which Cervantes used his hero to explore all the uncertain ambiguities that underscored his own day's loss of very different medieval realities.

---

[21] Boccaccio, *Decameron*, pp. 68–81.
[22] Ibid., p. 81.
[23] Dartmouth College, Baker Library, Jones Microtext Centre, Microfilm 2337r, f. 87v.

In Cervantes's frame of reference, Don Quixote becomes the classic example of the errant knight who through his very errantcy transforms himself into the unexpected knight errant; in Ticknor's, however, he becomes merely an erring human being who has made an understandable perceptual error not unlike those we all make every day. Only later, when writing his *History of Spanish Literature*, did Ticknor come to appreciate that Quixote's were not everyday adventures, that it was their skewed form of a lost medieval doubleness that made his adventures immortal.

With that observation, the grounds for Erasmus's rejection of relics begin to come into sharper focus. Gratian may have 'scornfully' rejected the prior's proffered rag just as, 'looking rather disgusted', he had earlier refrained from kissing the repellent arm, but by themselves this scorn and disgust provide no explanation for Erasmus's hostility. What the discussion above suggests, however, is that in a larger sense he had become ensnared in, and accepted the logical consequences of, something analogous to Ticknor's difficulty – in his own case an inability to see relics as temporal objects simultaneously capable of being seen as concrete vestiges of divine mysteries elsewhere hidden from mortal view. As a result, because they had lost their numinous powers, for him they retained only their physical being, nothing more. That is the real point lurking behind Gratian's 'imperfect manners', a conclusion that Erasmus drives home by having the bone custodian respond to those manners by quickly putting away 'his things', *res sua*.

Nevertheless, if Erasmus found that relics spoke only in a language of the here and now, that does not make him the harbinger either of modernity in general or of modern science, a fundamental premise of which is that things incapable of being measured do not exist. No more plausibly is he an ancestor of the Dr Johnson whose empirical response to Bishop Berkeley was a vigorous kick to a gatepost after hearing that his philosopher-friend now doubted whether the existence of matter could ever be proved. Erasmus was no secularist, after all, nor could he have been. The sixteenth century was a time of religious renewal, not decline, and the author of 'A Pilgrimage for Religion's Sake' was himself among the first to stress its necessity. What his satire really documents is the extent to which medieval ways of conceptualising religious ideas had lost their power to communicate effectively, a change that, in so far as it coincided with the decline of pilgrimages and crusading, becomes an attractive candidate for having at least partially caused that decline. If so, though, what replaced the medieval reliance on the concrete, and how, specifically, did the new ways express the religious yearnings that had hitherto led Christians enthusiastically to join such lay solidarities as crusades and pilgrimages?

A satisfyingly complete answer to that question lies beyond the scope of this essay, but the key to one would appear to lie in the changed outlook of Felix Fabri, a German Dominican who made a pilgrimage to the Holy Land in 1480. Four years later, he published his massive *Evagatorium in Terrae Sanctae, Arabiae, et Egypti Peregrinationem*, the 1,300 pages of which make it clear that in Fabri's mind pilgrimages had already become something of a mixed blessing:

> Good and simple Christians believe that if they were at the places where the Lord Jesus wrought the work of our redemption, they would derive much devotion from them; but I say to these men of a truth that meditation about these places, and listening to descriptions of them, is more efficacious than the actual seeing and kissing of them. . . . Such people as these shed many futile tears at the holy places, and make a howling at almost all of them, not because of the power which the place exercises over them, albeit the places do certainly tend to devotion, but because of the ease with which they weep. But I have no doubt of this, that were there ten good Christians in my cell at Ulm, who had a desire to see the Holy Land and the places sacred to the Lord Jesus, I could rouse their devotion and stir up their souls more deeply by my talk about those places than if they were actually lying bowed to the earth in the holy places themselves.[24]

At first glance there is nothing unusual about a Dominican who believes in the efficacy of preaching, for it was the bedrock on which his order had been founded. On further reflection, though, Fabri's observations become new and distinctly unusual in their preference for meditating on purely verbal descriptions to 'the actual seeing and kissing of' the holiest sites in Christendom. Because Dominic himself never went that far, in all likelihood Fabri's proclivity for words reveals one of the long-term consequences of mendicant preaching, Franciscan even more than Dominican: the gradual creation of a vernacular that for the first time had the evocative powers needed to move ordinary believers much more effectively than had the inexpressible forms of communication earlier possessed by relics.

To put the argument another way, it looks as though the symbolic power of concrete objects and places, not to mention the related need to experience them directly, decreased almost in response to, and as a result of, written and spoken language's growing ability to articulate beliefs that previous generations had had to express in non-verbal ways.[25] For some, of course, this transformation also depended on a growing sophistication gained from formal education, while for others it owed not a little to the late medieval appearance of a popular literature that created new vocabulary and forms of expression to impart reality and immediacy to worlds unknown to everyday experience. Nevertheless, important as these contributions may have been, neither of them changes the crucial point, that people like Erasmus and Fabri found themselves turning away from a faith mired in the concrete because they now had a more compelling alternative. Like other reformers and humanists who sought renewal by rallying to the cry of '*Ad fontes, ad fontes!*', they responded more ardently to textual sources than to the martyr's well at Canterbury.

That said, it becomes easy to see why crusading, like pilgrimages, should have gone from high medieval popularity to late medieval decline. As the cliché has it,

---

[24] Quotation as translated in Donald Howard, *Writers and Pilgrims: Medieval Pilgrimage Narratives and their Posterity* (Berkeley, 1980), p. 44.

[25] I recognise, of course, that as far back as the twelfth century St Bernard had transformed Latin's ability to convey mystical thought and complex emotions, but in as much as I am concerned with language as it relates to the decline of two lay solidarities, it seems preferable to see relevant change as beginning with the mendicants, men whose frequent use of the vernacular had much more impact on the laity.

crusades were little more than armed pilgrimages. Moreover, because their goal, the Holy Land, alone possessed what Fabri called 'the places where the Lord Jesus wrought the work of our redemption', crusaders understandably conceived of that goal as nothing less than the largest, geographically immovable relic on earth. In 1095, Urban II himself reflected that mode of thought when he first called on Europe's warriors to use fighting for the holy places overseas as a way of escaping the papal anathemas he had just placed on distressingly popular private warfare at home:

> Let the deeds of your ancestors move you and incite your minds to manly achievements. . . . Let the holy sepulchre of the Lord our Saviour, which is possessed by unclean nations, especially incite you, and the holy places which are now treated with ignominy and irreverently polluted with their filthiness. . . . Enter upon the road to the Holy Sepulchre; wrest that land from the wicked race. . . . Jerusalem is the navel of the world; the land is fruitful above all others, like another paradise of delights. This the Redeemer of the human race has made illustrious by His advent, has beautified by residence, has consecrated by suffering, has redeemed by death, has glorified by burial. . . . Accordingly undertake this journey for the remission of your sins, with the assurance of the imperishable glory of the kingdom of heaven.[26]

As with the relics of pilgrimage sites, it is again the concrete that Urban assumes will communicate most effectively, physical proof of God's merciful intent that will, when attained, assure all pilgrim warriors remission of their sins. It goes without saying, too, that no one had more awareness of the penitential parallels than did this pope, a man whose peroration also shows that he knew how best to call upon the non-verbal aspects of the faith of his age in order to recruit and create a lay solidarity whose sole activity was to be the freeing of the Holy Land:

> Whoever, therefore, shall determine upon this holy pilgrimage and shall make his vow to God to that effect and shall offer himself to Him as a living victim, holy, acceptable unto God, shall wear the sign of the cross of the Lord on his forehead or on his breast. When, truly, having fulfilled his vow he wishes to return, let him place the cross on his back between his shoulders. By this two-fold action he will fulfill the precept of the Lord, as He commands in the Gospel, 'He that taketh not his cross and followeth after me, is not worthy of me.'[27]

Nonetheless, if crusades owed their appeal to a visceral belief that they offered cross-wearing warriors a more congenial opportunity to gain their salvation than did boringly peaceful pilgrimages, both kinds of journey shared that doubleness of vision which mixed laughter with piety, this world with the next. Joinville's *Life of Saint Louis* reports, for example, that whilst Louis's army was camped near Acre, his biographer had encountered a group of pilgrims anxious to see the crusading king. Here is what happened next:

[26] Clermont speech of Urban II in Robert the Monk's version as translated in Edward Peters, ed., *The First Crusade: The Chronicle of Fulcher of Chartres and Other Source Materials*, 2nd edn (Philadelphia, 1998), pp. 27–8.

[27] Robert the Monk's version, with last sentence slightly modified for clarity, from Peters, *First Crusade*, p. 29.

Language, laughter and lay solidarities 247

I went in to the king, who was sitting inside his tent, leaning against its center pole. And he was sitting on the sand without a carpet or, for that matter, anything else under him. I said to him: 'Sire, there is a large group of people from Great Armenia outside, all going to Jerusalem, and they pray me, sire, to cause the sainted king to be shown to them. But I have no desire as yet to kiss your bones.' He laughed aloud, and told me to go and fetch them; and so I did.[28]

It may not be immediately apparent, but this passage is deceptively complex. Joinville began *The Life of Saint Louis* as part of the canonisation campaign of the 1270s, but he completed it in its present form only twelve years after Boniface VIII had proclaimed Louis's sainthood in 1297. In other words, Joinville as author knew that he had had a saint on his hands near Acre that day, though only a confessor, alas, and not a martyr. Yet, rather than trying to pretend that he, like the pilgrims, was already awed by the holiness of Louis's living presence, he admits freely and without a trace of self-consciousness that he had told the king that he wasn't prepared to kiss his bones – *and* that Louis had laughed.

What makes for the humour of the scene is the fact that both participants, saint and sinner alike, turn out to have an acute awareness of the absurdity inherent in trying to treat sentient flesh as though it were a relic worthy of veneration. Only when flesh is no longer animated by its immortal soul can it acquire the ability to attract devotion. To put the matter a bit colloquially, though in a way that would presumably have been familiar to the always blunt-spoken Joinville, 'Kiss my bum' is normally an insult, but it would not so appear if the request came from beyond the grave. Small wonder, then, that after the long-dead Louis appears to Joinville in a dream, this non-kisser of living flesh finds it insufficient merely to dedicate an altar in his chapel to his departed friend. Rather, he implies that full satisfaction will come only when he receives a favourable response to the plea underlying his later statement that it would be 'agreeable to God' if Louis's great-grandson 'procured relics of the true holy body and sent them to the said chapel . . . so that those who come hereafter to the saintly king's altar may have the greater devotion'.[29]

Two hundred years later, if it was becoming increasingly difficult to take a pilgrimage for religion's sake, so too were crusades falling from favour, and for much the same reason. Vernacular languages with growing conceptual and evocative powers were helping to transform potential candidates for membership in two of the greatest medieval solidarities into individual believers. And just as new kinds of language were undercutting the need for relics, so were they also eliminating the need for visits to, or physical possession of, the Holy Land. To repeat Felix Fabri's most striking point: 'I have no doubt of this, that were there ten good Christians in my cell at Ulm, who had a desire to see the Holy Places and the places sacred to the Lord Jesus, I could rouse their devotion and stir up their souls more

---

[28] Translation, slightly modified for accuracy and style, from Sir Frank Marzials, ed. and trans., *Memoirs of the Crusades* (London, 1908), p. 277. Note, incidentally, the extent to which Joinville's carpetless Louis resembles Gervase of Canterbury's Henry II, also a king who 'would not permit a rug or anything of the kind to be provided for him'. Humility, too, had its forms of symbolic expression.

[29] As translated in Marzials, *Memoirs*, p. 326.

deeply by my talk about those places than if they were actually lying bowed to the earth in the holy places themselves.'

Although this essay starts with the pretence of being an inquiry into the role played by language in the declining fortunes of pilgrimages and crusades, perhaps at its end it is better to be viewed as no more than the halting journey of one pilgrim historian through the arcana of the past. Still, as Susan Reynolds has taught us, each age really does communicate in separate ways, and in the Middle Ages those ways involved transcending the limitations of spoken vernaculars by relying on a kind of symbolic doubleness that was especially needed in order to convey the meaning of those instances where God had attempted to reveal his divine purposes to the world of human experience. The primary intent of such language, verbal or not, may have been the heightening of faith, but the temporal realities involved could also lead to laughter of the sort that inevitably arises when mere mortals are absurdly forced to confront some of the less endearing aspects of their mortality. And, inevitably, when language changed, so did the collective activities of those who no longer responded to the old ways of communicating. Whether these conclusions have provided all the pleasures and diversions of travel is not for an author to judge, but in so far as they have, then surely Dame Alice of Bath deserves most of the credit, having prepared the way with single pilgrimages to Rome and Cologne, Santiago and Bologne, not to mention the three to Jerusalem. These are undoubtedly the right places to visit if one's purposes include both laughter and faith, as so often they did in the world of medieval solidarities.

Lay/clerical distinctions in early India

Romila Thapar

The differentiation between the laity and those who have received ordination in a religion is not characteristic of all religions. In some it is demarcated, in some it is not to be found, and in yet others the differentiation is blurred. I would like to contrast the recognition and concern for the laity in Buddhism with the other major religion of early India, Hinduism, which tends either to leave it fluid or as in some sects, gives it no recognition. Votive inscriptions from Buddhist sites in the Deccan, the northern part of the Indian peninsula, during the period from the first century BC to about the third century AD provide the data. This was the period of the initial spread of Buddhism, not as a royal cult but through extensive support from a large community of traders, artisans and small-scale landowners. These votive inscriptions provide a glimpse of the nature and range of this support. There is a tight interconnection between the location of the Buddhist centres along trade routes and the patrons of these centres who are involved in the creation and exchange of items of trade.

A contrast to this is provided by a lengthy inscription recording the building of a temple to Surya, the Sun-god, nearby in central India by Hindu devotees, in the fifth century AD, when various Hindu sects came to be established. In both cases the donations are from well-to-do middle-level professionals associated with production and trade, but the relationship of the communities with the two religions differs. A comparative study raises questions relating to the dissonance between caste and social relations, particularly for lower-caste groups and women in their role as patrons of religion.

The teaching of the Buddha goes back to the sixth century BC and is associated with the middle Ganges valley from where it gradually spread in various directions after his death. By the end of his life he had established a community of monks (*bhikkhu*s) which constituted the institutional authority of Buddhism and was known as the Sangha – literally, the assembly. He did eventually concede that an order of nuns (*bhikkhuni*s) could also be a part of the Sangha. A series of Councils of the Sangha were held to regularise what were believed to be the teachings of the Buddha and the functioning of the Sangha. Inevitably differences of opinion at these gatherings led to sectarian splits and the sects began to establish their own rules.

What did however remain reasonably constant was the relationship between the Sangha and the lay followers. The distinction is embedded in what the Buddha taught, maintaining that renunciation – the renouncing of social obligations and joining an order of monks or nuns – is the ideal path to *nirvana*, or the termination of the cycle of rebirths. However since this choice is not open to everyone it is possible for laymen (*upasaka*) and laywomen (*upasika*) to support the Sangha and thereby acquire merit, the acquisition of which would help towards the termination of rebirths.

The term *upasaka* is derived from a root meaning to sit by the side of, to serve, to respect: in short all that is required of the lay person. To serve is to give and this is the reverse of the *bhikkhu* who is the receiver of alms. The elaboration of the meaning of *bhikkhu* has to do with breaking away from bad qualities. The relationship focused on gifts given by the lay person to the monk – generally necessities since wealth was prohibited – and the reciprocity of the monk performing rituals for the lay person. These were ceremonies tied to rites of passage. But such obligations were restricted to lay persons and did not extend to non-Buddhists. There were categories of gifts which in effect determined the nuances of reciprocal actions.

Before the rise of what has been called 'monastic landlordism' by Max Weber, Buddhist monks were dependent for their food on the alms they collected from the village or town in the vicinity of the monastery. Gift-giving (*dana*) was therefore emphasised as a primary duty of the lay follower and is referred to as the most meritorious act, particularly the gifting of alms or robes or any necessity to a monk. Gift-giving therefore was imbued with a sacred quality quite apart from its mundane function of maintaining the monk.

Support for the Sangha could take the form of contributing towards the building of monasteries or parts thereof and embellishing the monuments which were often part of a monastic complex. Buddhism adopted the local relic cult involving the building of small enclosures (*chaitya*s) around the relics of those who were venerated or trees or locations held sacred. This was also tied into the cult of previous Buddhas as well as the one who is yet to come, the Buddha Maitreya. The monument most frequently associated with Buddhist sites was the *stupa*, the cult of which is generally traced to constructing small mounds, often funerary, also known from the time of the Buddha. Archaeological survivals of these from earlier times are rare and their conversion into large structures date to the turn of the Christian era, a change which is not unconnected with the increasing and impressive patronage received by the Sangha from its lay following. This was also the time when the image of the Buddha was first sculpted, and gradually images were to become an item among donations.

When a sacred site came to be associated with the Sangha in the form of a *stupa*, its adornment was seen as a gift to the Sangha. Maintaining the Sangha was a form of maintaining the faith and implicitly the monk. The symbol of the power of the Sangha comes to be vested in the *stupa* and this draws to it the devotion of the worshipper. Gift-giving was therefore one link between the lay follower and the monk or nun. In exchange for the gift the lay follower acquired merit. Where the gift came from a collective such as a guild, there presumably all its members shared in the merit. The importance of acquiring merit increased when some Buddhist sects stated that merit could not only be accumulated but also transferred to another person.

In the construction of monasteries and *stupas* in the Deccan, there was initially less royal patronage and more donations from the wider lay community. The votive inscriptions which are the major guide to patronage at this time, carry a smattering of references to donations by local rulers such as the Satavahana dynasty and what might be described as the local aristocracy – erstwhile chiefs of clans now moving into positions of administrative importance and marrying into royal families.

The major monasteries were either rock-cut monasteries, clustered around the passes on important trade routes commanding the descent from the plateau of the Deccan to the trading centres of the west coast, or else the freestanding monasteries further east on the plateau. Rock-cut architecture did not lend itself to the construction of the *stupa* complex. Here, the halls of worship, with smaller symbolic *stupa*s, are the most spectacular expressions of lay patronage. Elaborately sculpted, they stand out in sharp contrast to the austere walls and bare cells of the monastic complexes. Gifts to the rock-cut monasteries could also take the form of the excavation of a cell in the rock face or of a cistern and channels to bring and store water. Such a gift might carry a small inscription on the upper ledge at the entrance to the cell. This was an almost particularised act of piety on the part of the lay donor and virtually a private act, since visitors to the rock-cut monasteries would be fewer than those on a pilgrimage or a visit to the *stupa* sites.

On the plateau itself, as at Sanchi and Bharhut, the monumental *stupa*s were circular in plan with a dome-like elevation and were surrounded by a circumambulatory path enclosed by a railing and gateways, the latter demarcating the sacred space. The railing and gateways were donated through cooperative effort and provided the space and the occasion for sculptured embellishment in low-relief as well as surfaces for the inscribing of votive inscriptions. Pillars and other decorative features could be from individual donations. This would have required considerable coordination between the local Sangha and its lay supporters. When the laity helped construct the monument symbolising the Sangha, it could be said to be calling upon the protective power of the Sangha. Implicit in the gift is not only the accumulation of merit, and calling on the Buddha for protection, but also a claim to a respected social status as a donor to the Sangha.

The visually more accessible surfaces generally carry the inscriptions of those socially more privileged although the number of these is limited. A gateway at Bharhut carries an inscription from a family of chiefs known from the second century BC.[1] Donations from royal families tend to occur more frequently in the rock-cut monasteries, such as the donation of Ushavadata the Kshatrapa, who gave a permanent endowment of money to be invested in two guilds of weavers in the

---

[1] E. A. Hultzsch, 'Bharhut Buddhist Pillar Inscription', *Indian Antiquary*, XIV (1885), pp. 138ff.; ibid., XXI (1892), p. 227.

town of Govardhana, the interest from the larger investment to be used for the purchase of robes for the monks,[2] encapsulating a link between the royal family, the guild of craftsmen and the Sangha. Incidentally it also points to the weavers being held in esteem which contradicts their low status in the Brahmanical social codes. In another inscription Ushavadata made lavish grants of cows and villages to brahmans.[3]

The inscriptions inform us that the majority of the donations are from artisans, guilds of craftsmen, traders, and small-scale landowners, donors who seem not to have been among the richest, although some wealthy merchants are mentioned. Donations by monks and nuns in large numbers are also recorded. The identity of the donor becomes important when the act of donation is public. Sometimes the patrons are the craftsmen who actually work on the object of patronage, as in the case of the ivory-carvers guild from Vidisha in central India who sculpted a part of the gateway at Sanchi.[4]

Patronage from artisans was a departure from the normative Brahmanical texts on caste and social functioning, where artisans are listed as low in status. The inscriptions suggest a certain degree of upward social mobility at least in areas where trade and the production of items for trade was important. Possibly some were wealthy, and wealth provided status in routine social functioning. Artisan guilds are a noticeable feature of urban life at this time. Some were so well defined that they came to function as castes (*jatis*). Occupational stipulations on castes and the rigidity of the regulations regarding marriage circles, encouraged the overlap between guild and caste. Guild donations therefore carry a flavour of caste donations.

The identification of the donor is not essential to an act of piety, but where the donor is identified, as was often the case, it becomes a public declaration of belief and faith and also a statement on affluence. Votive inscriptions were also intended to be read by posterity, thus giving a certain immortality to the donor. Communities which do not bury their dead in graves with tombstone inscriptions take recourse to other means of being remembered. These were also ways of advertising one's achievements either as individuals or as a collective, such as a guild. The mention of individual names could signify the growing importance of family identities in a region where earlier the identity of the clan had been dominant.

Wealthier individuals such as the *setthi-gahapati*s – the financiers and landowners were the larger patrons. Urban professionals which included ivory-carvers, weavers, potters, makers of perfumes, bead-makers and garland-makers are mentioned frequently, some taking credit for individual actions. Thus Ananda, the foreman of the artisans of the Satavahana king is thought to be taking credit for having carved the top architrave of the south gate at Sanchi.[5] Often the donation is by one person, perhaps a woman, on behalf of the family. Such donations include families

---

[2] Nasik Cave Inscription No. 10, *Epigraphia Indica*, VIII (1905–6) (New Delhi 1981, reprint), p. 78.
[3] Nasik Cave Inscription No. 12, ibid., p. 82.
[4] No. 200, *Epigraphia Indica*, II (Varanasi 1970, reprint), p. 378.
[5] Luder's List in *Epigraphia Indica*, X (1909–10) (New Delhi 1960, reprint), 'A List of *Brahmi* Inscriptions from the Earliest Times to about AD 400', No. 346.

of small-scale landowners. That the donation is made by a female member of the family suggests a different picture of social relations from those depicted in the Brahmanical normative texts.

Among the donors mentioned repeatedly by name are monks and nuns. This is surprising on both counts. In a community of the Sangha, individual identities are preferably blurred and the association of monks and nuns with wealth sufficient to make a donation is somewhat surprising considering that they were not expected to have access to wealth once they had been initiated into the order. Was this the wealth which they brought with them when entering the monastery or nunnery and which they donated to the institution – a one-time donation at the point of ordination? Or did they continue to hold shares in family property which would have come to them by way of inheritance? Or did the location of the monasteries along trade routes and the welcome patronage of those connected with commerce and exchange, lead the monks to invest in trade – perhaps on behalf of the monastery, and donate their profits? The belongings of a deceased monk were generally sold and the income divided among the other monks. Possibly in some cases an ailing monk may have stipulated that the income from his belongings was to be donated to the Sangha on his death. There is a striking though gradual increase in the number of such donations sometimes reaching half the total number and in some cases even exceeding this.[6] Some of these monks and nuns were doctrinal specialists and the gift may have come from those whom they instructed. Perhaps their donations to the cult of the *stupa* and later to that of images, both unknown to pristine Buddhism, legitimised the cults and encouraged lay persons to make donations.

This tendency would have been further enhanced by the introduction among some sects of the concept of transference of merit, when the merit acquired by a person making a gift could be transferred and could accrue to someone else, such as parents. This was not entirely a new facet of Buddhist thought and may well have evolved from the emphasis which the Buddha placed on caring for and respecting parents and on the welfare and happiness of all beings. Interestingly this was also the period when the accumulation and transference of wealth had become an essential activity in commerce and the parallel is striking. In the case of such donations, the identity of the person making the gift is mentioned as also the relationship of the recipient to the donor. In the transferring of merit there is no exchange transaction between the lay person as donor and the recipient of the merit.[7]

The participation of monks and monasteries in trade provides another dimension to the relations between laity and the Sangha.[8] Deposits were made in favour of monasteries for their maintenance and these deposits had to be invested so that the interest could be used. This created a nexus between the donor, the monastery and the institution where the donation was invested. Such donations, described as

---

[6] G. Schopen, *Bones, Stones and Buddhist Monks* (Honolulu 1997), pp. 23ff.

[7] Schopen, *Bones, Stones*, pp. 58ff.

[8] D. D. Kosambi, 'Dhenukakata', *Journal of the Asiatic Society of Bombay*, 30 (1955), 2, pp. 50–71. G. Schopen, 'Doing Business for the Lord: Lending on Interest and Written Loan Contracts in the Mulasarvastivada *Vinaya*', *Journal of the American Oriental Society*, 114 (1994), 4, pp. 527–54.

akshaya or literally exempt from destruction, implied that the capital which was a gift of money was to be left intact, and that the donation continued even after the death of the donor.

A detailed bond was written and witnessed twice, stating the date, the persons involved and the amount donated and the interest expected.[9] The bond was sealed with the monastic seal. The monastery was represented by designated monks such as the elder and the provost. Such legal documents, together with manuscripts and with money, were stored in a special room in the monastery, the word for which – *koshthika* – suggests a treasury. If there was a likelihood of the monastery being looted as it sometimes was in areas of uncertain governance, the money and the treasures could either be hidden by a devoted monk or else placed in the safe-keeping of a reliable layman.

This introduces a new feature in the relationship between the Sangha and the laity where the layman could virtually become the manager of the monastery's finances. It also required monks to be trained in the administration of finance, a qualification which had other ramifications when land started being granted to Buddhist monasteries.[10] Monks had now to be familiar with the technicalities of building and construction, the supervision of food and clothing and the curriculum of recitations from the Buddhist canon. Taking up secular functions such as these would also have involved a relationship between the monks and those normally concerned with such functions and presumably this relationship was mediated through lay persons. This is suggested in an inscription from Amaravati which refers to an elder as an overseer of works. He is also the teacher of the nun who records the donation, and she mentions her daughter and two other friends.[11] The building of a *stupa* in its first phase required raw materials, financial resources and commissariat arrangements for the architects, builders and masons; and in the second phase a close coordination between the professionals and the supervisory monks since railings, crossbars and gateway panels were separately donated, although perhaps not separately sculpted, and had to be integrated into their proper place in the larger plan. This would have brought the monastic administration close to a variety of artisan guilds and other professionals. That the monks drew upon the existing lay community is suggested by reference to members of the *ghoshthi* and *nigama*s – professional groups which probably assisted in the administration of the monasteries.[12]

The centrality of the lay presence is indicated by the choice of subject for the relief carvings. The most obvious theme was the biography of the Buddha since it was familiar to those who visited the site and was viewed as an act of piety. Equally common was the depiction of *Jataka* stories, which pertained to the previous lives

---

[9] Ibid.

[10] Mathura Lion Capital inscriptions, ed. S. Konow, *Corpus Inscriptionum Indicarum*, II.1 (Varanasi 1969, reprint), pp. 48–9.

[11] Luder's List No. 1250, *Epigraphia Indica*, X, p. 148. V. Dehejia, *Discourse in Early Buddhist Art* (New Delhi 1997), p. 170.

[12] Bhattiprolu Casket inscriptions Nos 3, 5, 6, 8. *Epigraphia Indica*, II, pp. 327–8.

of the Buddha and were heavily imbued with the folk and popular narratives of the time.[13] As such they would have been recognised by lay worshippers, although at some sites such as Bharhut labels were inscribed which helped in identifying the narrative. Donors could choose their theme, perhaps with a little nudge from the monks. The narratives tend to cover a range of routine activities of the kind of people who would have formed the lay community, so the message of the story would be accessible to them.

Gift-giving was not confined to donations for the beautification of the *stupa*. Gradually and over time, monasteries were permitted to employ labourers and servants or even to own bondsmen and slaves.[14] These were gifted to the monastery and used as attendants in the monastery and for the maintenance and repair of buildings; and in later times as labour on the land which monasteries acquired as grants. It is thought that in the earlier period monks had done the manual work; but this now changed. This category of gift required a different form of contract from the earlier donations. The donor had to prove his right of ownership over the slaves donated to the monastery, and the new ownership had to be established as vesting either in the monastery or in an individual monk.

Votive inscriptions at *stupa* sites point quite clearly to the participation of women as donors, both as laywomen and as nuns. Women from royal families or the wives of local chiefs as donors were by now well established. The Ikshvaku dynasty of south India seems to have preferred a gender demarcation where the men were patrons of the Vedic Brahmanical sacrifices and the women made donations to the Buddhist Sangha. This was one way of balancing socio-political factions and pressures. But the women in the votive inscriptions from the *stupas* are generally of lesser social status and seem to command greater independence. They constitute between one-third to a half of the donors. Some are wealthy enough to donate a fully carved pillar, others donate crossbars of a railing, lengths of coping or a decorated slab of stone, all part of the adornment of the *stupa*, or alternatively, cells and cisterns in rock-cut monasteries. Some are from the wealthy families of financiers and large landowners. Others come from lesser artisan households. Laywomen either make individual gifts or often do so on behalf of their families. Thus the laywoman Kama, daughter of the housewife Kanha and the householder Ida, gifted a length of coping to the *stupa* at Amaravati together with her relatives.[15] Gifts by men sometimes include mention of wives, sisters, daughters, sons-in-law and sons.[16]

Donations by nuns are not that surprising. Some women became nuns at an early age and some after they had raised a family and there are others who have daughters who are also nuns. Their donations could have been donations of their

---

[13] E. Hultzsch, 'Bharut Inscriptions', *Indian Antiquary*, XXI (1892), pp. 225ff.

[14] D. C. Sircar, *Successors of the Satavahanas in the Lower Deccan* (Calcutta 1939), pp. 328–30; G. Schopen, 'The Monastic Ownership of Servants or Slaves: Local and Legal factors in the Redactional History of the two Vinayas', *Journal of the International Association of Buddhist Studies*, 17 (1997), 2, pp. 145–73.

[15] Luder's List No. 1252, *Epigraphia Indica*, X, p. 148.

[16] For example Luder's List Nos 1209, 1210, 1207, *Epigraphia Indica*, X.

stri-dhana, literally the woman's wealth, the wealth which is given to a daughter (apart from her dowry) and which in theory is solely hers to use as she pleases. Married women may have had a problem with donating it to the Sangha, but widows and unmarried daughters may have found it somewhat easier. It is unlikely that they would have donated their dowries since this was wealth given only at the time of the marriage of the woman, and once she was married the dowry tended to be viewed as the wealth of her husband.

The impressive patronage of women as donors at Buddhist sites would suggest that Buddhism was liberal in encouraging the participation of women in this patronage and more so than many Hindu sects. Nevertheless it is also a reflection of women from urban social backgrounds with access to some wealth being given greater visibility as lay followers of Buddhism.

The inscriptions also provide evidence of networks of geographical contacts, which relate to the distribution of the lay community. Donors from clearly identifiable towns are fewer than those from places which now cannot be identified and which may have been market centres,[17] also mentioned frequently in the Buddhist canon. Tapping these and also receiving donations from landowners was in effect a reaching-out to rural areas as well. Inscriptions from Bharhut record donors from Vidisha, Pataliputra, Bhojakata, Bhogavardhana and Nasik, which was an extensive geographical reach.

A contemporary text refers to merchants and goods from Bactria, China and Alexandria.[18] Some votive inscriptions refer to Yavanas – people from west Asia and the eastern Mediterranean – some coming overland from Hellenistic commercial centres and some through the maritime trade with Roman Egypt, who identify themselves as lay followers of Buddhism.[19] Buddhism being dominant among the traders of the Deccan at this time, and the Sangha providing facilities to merchants and merchandise through the monastic network, meant that traders from elsewhere may have found it more convenient if they were also of the same religious persuasion as their Indian counterparts. Thus the lay community of the Buddhist Sangha may have extended into pockets of west Asia.

The social groups discussed above continued to provide lay followers of Buddhism, as also did some royal families. Commercial activities, however, were profitable in northern and western India in the mid-millennium and this may well have affected the material support for the Sangha from traders and craftsmen. But there was also for the latter the attraction of other religious sects. An example of this is the silk-weavers guild which was the patron of a temple to Surya, the Sun-god and unconnected with Buddhism.

Normally one would have expected a silk-weavers guild to have been Buddhist. Its patronage of the Sun cult is curious. It has been argued that declining support for Buddhism towards the mid-first millennium AD was accompanied by a

---

[17] Luder's List Nos 986, 988, 995, 998, 1000, 1001, 1005, 1013, 1014, *Epigraphia Indica*, X.

[18] *Milinda-panho*, T. W. Rhys Davids (ed. and trans.), *The Questions of King Milinda* (New York 1963), 5.4; 6.21.

[19] *Epigraphia Indica*, VIII, No. 17, p. 90.

Brahmanical renaissance. Vedic Brahmanism dating back to about 800 BC, focused on rituals of sacrifice and became increasingly the religion of the upper castes. In the early Christian era, partly as a parallel to Buddhism, Jainism and what are generally called the Shramanic religions, or the more heterodox in relation to Brahmanism, there emerged a form of Hinduism now labelled as Puranic Hinduism. A particular deity was worshipped as an image and came to be housed in a temple. Donations towards the building of a temple was one aspect of worship but more important was devotion to the deity or *bhakti*. The mythology involved in the creation of a particular deity and the ritual of its worship was often described in a text, one category of which were known as the *Puranas*. Part of the attempt was to relate multiple deities to a framework of cosmology, mythology and worship.

Surya was one such deity. The silk-weavers may have chosen him because of his popularity in western India. Indian sources frequently associate sun-worship with Iran which has a long tradition of a fire cult and state that the brahmans associated with sun-worship come from there. The silk-weavers are likely to have had commercial connections with Iran.

The guild migrated from Lata in western India to the town of Dashapura in central India in about AD 436. Possibly there was a decline in the silk trade between India and the eastern Mediterranean with the opening up of the central Asian silk route. The intervention of the Huns in north India was a further obstacle to contacts with central Asia. The town the guild chose to migrate to at the invitation of the local king, appears to have had alternate professional employment for some members of the guild, and was a felicitous choice judging by references to the improved prosperity of some members of the guild and not just through weaving silk. At Dashapura they financed the building of a temple to Surya as a cooperative effort of the erstwhile guild. Some members of the guild ceased to weave silk and took to a variety of professions, such as archery, soldiering, astrology, and some had become professional commentators on religious discourses, whereas the rest continued to function as a guild.

The statement on the temple is contained in a lengthy inscription composed in verse.[20] The inscription although in essence a votive inscription is very different from those found at Buddhist sites in the Deccan. A poet was commissioned and paid to compose a poem commemorating the temple and the guild. Being a hack poet he plagiarised liberally from the better-known compositions of the famous Kalidasa.[21] His own contribution is noticeably ridden with the clichés of the current poetic style. The inscription is composed in Sanskrit, the language of high culture. This is a contrast to the votive inscriptions at Buddhist sites being in Prakrit, the commonly spoken language. The attempt therefore is less to record the individual aspirations of each devotee and more the collective aspirations of the guild. The latter point to some attempt at using the temple, the inscription and the cult

---

[20] Mandasor Inscription, J. F. Fleet (ed.), *Corpus Inscriptionum Indicarum*, III (Varanasi 1970, reprint), pp. 79ff.
[21] A. L. Basham, 'The Mandasor Inscription of the Silk Weavers', in B. L. Smith (ed.), *Essays on Gupta Culture* (Delhi 1983), pp. 93–105.

to claim upward social mobility. Reference is made to the ruling king Kumaragupta of the Gupta dynasty and to the governor of Dashapura. This nails down both chronology and political allegiance relating to the time when the temple was first built. Since the temple has not survived, barring the inscription and a scatter of stones, it is difficult to determine its architecture or its sculptural adornment. In medieval times it was replaced by a temple to Shiva.

The inscription refers to the building of the temple and then its renovation thirty-seven years later after it had fallen into disrepair. The dates are mentioned with considerable precision, a precision which parallels the requirement that the start of any activity – in this case the building of the temple – be at the most auspicious moment. This is a contrast to the Buddhist votive inscriptions, many of which are undated. The inscription provides the briefest summary of the history of the guild and the temple, and in spirit is entirely different from the Buddhist votive inscriptions. Despite the migration from Lata to Dashapura and some guild members taking on other professions, the identity of the guild continued since they came together to finance the renovations. That they took to other diverse professions could point to some change in caste status for some, but that they identified themselves as the original guild thirty-seven years later would suggest that the guild may have been in the process of being transmuted into a caste.

Gift-giving is again a major aspect of faith. This was not merely an imitation of the Buddhist practice since the concept goes back to earlier times. Hindu priests, frequently brahmans, could in theory only receive gifts from the upper castes. This rule was presumably set aside in situations where the lower-caste donors were wealthy as they sometimes were. Servicing a temple built by weavers would not have been correct for a brahman, going by the book of rules. That it was a community of silk-weavers who were the donors of the temple is particularly striking given that in the texts incorporating social codes at this time, such as the Manu *Dharmashastra*,[22] weavers were given a low-caste status, a status which they could not circumvent in the codes. In founding a temple they were emulating the upper castes.

In contrast to the Buddhist concept of the lay followers, there is here no institution or organisation intervening between the worshipper and the object of worship. In comparison there is a striking absence of the concept of laity. Sacred space was demarcated in the temple housing an image. The temple was financed and built by the guild without the intervention of any ecclesiastical authority. At most it required a priest to conduct the worship and possibly guild members may even have performed this function. A small offering is gifted to the deity at the time of worship, and part of it returned to the worshipper after it has been blessed. The real gift was implicit in the actual building and maintaining of the temple. Whereas in Buddhism, given the absence of deity, the highest form of worship lay in observing the precepts of the Buddha, in the case of Puranic Hinduism, the intensity of the devotion of the worshipper was what mattered.

---

[22] Manu, 4.84ff.; 186ff.; 10.32ff.; 74ff.

The demarcation between those who have received ordination and the laity hardly exists in this case. The temple is a local place of worship. Presumably the image and the structure followed the canons of image-making and temple architecture, although this was not a necessary condition. Little is said about priests performing the ritual. Yet ritual was a form of orthopraxy, although not mediated by an ecclesiastical organisation. The guild continues to see itself as a guild, even if not functioning as a guild, and it is as a guild that it carries out the renovations, and not as laity in relation to a religious order. The renovations also become a form of donation.

In the concept of the laity in Buddhism there are no tangible boundaries defining the laity socially, whereas in the case of the guild the limitations of membership in a professional organisation bind those that donate and worship, even if worship is open to others. In the former case there are a variety of identities such as language, custom, region, which intersect with religion and where in the context of the Sangha the religious identity has priority. In the case of the silk-weavers, persons other than members of the guild are not mentioned as participating in this activity nor other worshippers of Surya. The act of patronage is common to both but not the establishing of a recognised laity.

One of the reasons for the differentiation in Buddhism between those of a religious order and the laity, was the existence of an order of renouncers who were maintained by the laity. In the case of Hindu sects, orders of renouncers, as district from the individual, emerge in the early second millennium AD, by which time it was common for those in high office to grant land to such orders for their maintenance. The dependence on the laity was substituted by these substantial grants which ensured the maintenance and freedom of the grantee. Furthermore, renunciation in the Hindu tradition was associated only with a late stage in life, and renunciation on the part of the young met with disapproval. The entry into an alternate way of life by becoming a monk supported by the lay population as in Buddhism was initially less acceptable to the Hindu tradition.

An important difference between the Buddhist and the Hindu attitude to the laity as evident from these two examples is the attitude towards caste. Buddhism does not address itself to any particular caste nor does its forms of worship exclude particular castes. The lay persons supporting the Sangha belonged to a range of castes. Admittedly brahmans were few but the rest are well-represented. Theoretically the caste of the *upasaka* was of no importance and this appears to have infiltrated into religious practice. Hindu sects were frequently caste-bound. Although the same deity could be worshipped across castes, the actual act of worship was limited to particular castes and many of the more important temples denied entry to members of the lower castes and the untouchables. There was a recognisable distinction between the religion as practised by the upper and lower castes. For Hindu sects, therefore, the caste within which a particular religious sectarian movement had its roots, would remain the 'laity', as it were, of that religious sect. Buddhism attempted to cut across caste and this may have been one of the causes of its eventual decline, defeated by the growing strength of caste society in India.

The intervention of caste did not prevent the laity of religions such as Buddhism to share in Hindu worship and vice versa as long as there was an approximate caste conformity between sect and laity. The donors to the Buddhist *stupa*s of the Deccan could also have worshipped at the shrines of the local Hindu deities. The incorporation of the latter is evident in the history of all the religions of India. Equally well, the silk-weavers of Dashapura could have made a pilgrimage to Sanchi, although this is nowhere mentioned. This does not imply that there was complete harmony between the different religions. Conflicts, sometimes violent, are on record especially between the Buddhists and Hindu Shaivas. Nevertheless, although some religious sects had a well-developed notion of laity and others did not, this difference did not constitute a boundary of segregation.

This is also reflected in royal and state patronage. It was expected of rulers that they would make donations and provide patronage to a variety of religions. This was not merely to keep a balance but was often a reaction to the political and religious conditions of the time and is reflected in what is commonly referred to by historians as 'the religious policy' of virtually every ruler of significance. It is said, for example, of King Harshavardhana of the seventh century AD that both the Buddhists and the Shaivas claimed him as a royal patron, so even-handed was his patronage. Even with the entry of Islam into the sub-continent, apart from the definitive identity of much of the ruling class, wherever Islam was practised among the populace it was a religion which evolved at the intersection of Islam and Hinduism.[23]

The relationship between the laity and the Sangha was not static. What the laity proposed to finance and support was in part determined by the needs of the ecclesiastical institution and in part the image which the laity wished to propagate of itself. Hence the choice of donation and the message intended. Transmutations also took place when historical needs changed. The gifts of earlier times – monastic cells and sculptured panels – gave way to providing land and labour. This reflects a change in the concerns of the laity and the Sangha. It also reflects a change in the social composition of the laity with a greater dependence on a lay community whose income came from agrarian revenue and would have included an intense competition among various religions for patronage. Thus ruling castes in later times were known to give gift land more frequently. Where donations were at second remove as it were – as, for example, a person financing part of a gateway which was actually sculpted by another – the donation could come from anyone irrespective of caste. Where the donation was a direct gift to a monk, there the caste of the donor could have mattered a little more.

The inscription of the silk-weavers guild points to the absence of both a definitive laity and an ecclesiastical institution. Migration is encouraged by political considerations but economic well-being is not ignored. The temple symbolises the donation and is maintained, but only as long as the identity of the guild lasts. This is a more narrow and closed identity of donors than is the case of Buddhist sites in

---

[23] R. Thapar, 'The Tyranny of Labels', in *Cultural Pasts* (Delhi 2000), pp. 990–1014.

Lay/clerical distinctions in early India 261

the Deccan. There is an implicit attempt at advertising the guild and the worship of Surya, but this is not a matter of primacy. Donations from women are conspicuously absent, the assumption being that the male members of the guild 'spoke' for them. Gift-giving was now increasingly becoming a ritual requirement.

Lay collective activity in early India varied according to religion and among sects within the same religion. I have tried to suggest that, although the concept of laity was a necessity in Buddhism, it was far more blurred if not absent in some of the Hindu sects. This was not merely due to religious formulations and requirements but also hinged on the interface between religious belief and practice and social forms.

A bibliography of Susan Reynolds's work (to 1999)

compiled by Pamela Taylor

1955

'Leicestershire: Table of Population, 1801–1951', in *The Victoria History of the Counties of England. A History of the County of Leicester*, 3, London, Oxford University Press for the Institute of Historical Research, pp. 176–217.

1956

'Pleas in the Liberty of the Abbot of Battle at Bromham', in N. J. Williams (ed.), *Collectanea*, Wiltshire Archaeological and Natural History Society Records Branch, 12, pp. 129–41.

Sections on 'Charities' in all twenty-six parishes in *The Victoria History of the Counties of England. A History of the County of Essex*, 4, London, Oxford University Press for the Institute of Historical Research.

1959

'The City of Cambridge: Schools', pp. 141–6; 'Almshouses', pp. 146–7; 'Other Charities', pp. 147–8, in *The Victoria History of the Counties of England. A History of the County of Cambridge and the Isle of Ely*, 3, London, Oxford University Press for the Institute of Historical Research.

1962

Ed., *The Victoria History of the Counties of England. A History of the County of Middlesex*, 3, London, Oxford University Press for the Institute of Historical Research; author of contributory chapters: 'Staines', pp. 13–33; 'Stanwell', pp. 33–50; 'Teddington', pp. 66–82; 'Isleworth Hundred', pp. 83–4; 'Heston and Isleworth', pp. 85–139; 'Twickenham', pp. 139–66; 'Cowley', pp. 170–7; 'Hanwell', pp. 220–37; 'Harlington', pp. 258–75.

1964

'The City of Birmingham: Manors', with L. F. Salzman, pp. 58–73; 'Agriculture', pp. 246–51; 'Markets and Fairs', pp. 251–3; 'Roman Catholicism', pp. 397–411; 'Schools', pp. 501–

Bibliography of Susan Reynolds's work 263

49, in *The Victoria History of the Counties of England. A History of the County of Warwick*, 7, London, Oxford University Press for the Institute of Historical Research.

1965

Ed., *The Register of Roger Martival Bishop of Salisbury 1315–1330. Vol. III Royal Writs*, Canterbury and York Society, 59.

1966

Review of A. Fremantle and the editors of *Time-Life* Books, *Age of Faith*, in *The Brown Book*, Oxford, Lady Margaret Hall, p. 59.

1967

Review of M. Aston, *Thomas Arundel: A Study of Church Life in the Reign of Richard II*, in *The Brown Book*, Oxford, Lady Margaret Hall, pp. 49–50.

1969

'The forged charters of Barnstaple', *English Historical Review*, 84, pp. 699–720; reprinted in *Ideas and Solidarities*, 1995.
'Oxford Letter', in *The Brown Book*, Oxford, Lady Margaret Hall, pp. 3–6.
Review of M. Chibnall (ed.), *The Ecclesiastical History of Ordericus Vitalis, vol. ii*, in *The Brown Book*, Oxford, Lady Margaret Hall, pp. 51–2.
Review of W. George, *Animals and Maps*, in *The Brown Book*, Oxford, Lady Margaret Hall, pp. 54–5.

1970

'Oxford Letter', in *The Brown Book*, Oxford, Lady Margaret Hall, pp. 3–5.
Review of N. D. Hurnard, *The King's Pardon for Homicide before AD 1307*, in *The Brown Book*, Oxford, Lady Margaret Hall, pp. 50–1.

1971

'Oxford Letter', in *The Brown Book*, Oxford, Lady Margaret Hall, pp. 4–7.

1972

'The Rulers of London in the Twelfth Century', *History*, 57, pp. 337–57; reprinted in *Ideas and Solidarities*, 1995.

1973

'Henry I's Charter for London', *Journal of Society of Archivists*, 4, pp. 558–78; with C. N. L. Brooke and G. Keir.

Review of H. M. Jewell, *English Local Administration in the Middle Ages*, in *The Brown Book*, Oxford, Lady Margaret Hall, pp. 62–3.

1975

'The farm and taxes of London, 1154–1216', *Guildhall Studies in London History*, 1, pp. 211–28; reprinted in *Ideas and Solidarities*, 1995.
Review of K. M. Briggs, *The Folklore of the Cotswolds*, in *The Brown Book*, Oxford, Lady Margaret Hall, pp. 41–2.

1977

An Introduction to the History of English Medieval Towns, Oxford, Clarendon Press.
Review of G. Tindall, *The Fields Beneath*, in *The Brown Book*, Oxford, Lady Margaret Hall, pp. 53–4.

1980

'Decline and decay in Late Medieval Towns: A look at some of the concepts and arguments', *Urban History Yearbook*, pp. 76–8; reprinted in reformatted version in *Ideas and Solidarities*, 1995, pp. 1–4.

1981

'Eadric Silvaticus and the English Resistance', *Bulletin of the Institute of Historical Research*, 54, pp. 102–5; reprinted in *Ideas and Solidarities*, 1995.
'Law and Communities in Western Europe, c.900–1300', *American Journal of Legal History*, 25, pp. 205–24.
Review of G. U. S. Corbett (ed.), *Ancient and Historical Monuments in the City of Salisbury*, 1, in *English Historical Review*, 96, pp. 842–4.
Review of M. Chibnall (ed.), *The Ecclesiastical History of Ordericus Vitalis*, 1, in *The Brown Book*, Oxford, Lady Margaret Hall, pp. 38–9.

1982

'Medieval Urban History and the History of Political Thought', *Urban History Yearbook*, pp. 14–23; reprinted in reformatted version in *Ideas and Solidarities*, 1995, pp. 1–13.

1983

'1483: Gloucester and Town Government in the Middle Ages', in N. M. Herbert et al. (eds), *The 1483 Gloucester Charter in History*, Gloucester, Alan Sutton, pp. 40–51; reprinted in *Ideas and Solidarities*, 1995.
'Medieval *origines gentium* and the Community of the Realm', *History*, 68, pp. 375–90, reprinted in *Ideas and Solidarities*, 1995.
Obituary of Georgina Rosalie Galbraith (Cole-Baker) 1894–1982, in *The Brown Book*, Oxford, Lady Margaret Hall, pp. 39–40.

1984

Kingdoms and Communities in Western Europe, 900–1300; Oxford, Oxford University Press (2nd edn 1997).

Review of C. V. Wedgwood, *The Spoils of Time: A Short History of the World, 1: From the Earliest Times to the Sixteenth Century*, in *The Brown Book*, Oxford, Lady Margaret Hall, p. 44.

1985

'What do we mean by "Anglo-Saxon" and "Anglo-Saxons"?', *Journal of British Studies*, 24, pp. 395–414; reprinted in *Ideas and Solidarities*, 1995.

'The Idea of the Corporation in Western Europe before 1300', in J. Guy (ed.), *Law and Social Change in British History*, London, Swift Printers for Royal Historical Society, pp. 27–33.

Review of J. A. Raftis, *A Small Town in Late Medieval England: Godmanchester, 1278–1400*, in *English Historical Review*, 100, pp. 168–9.

Review of A. R. Bridbury, *Medieval English Clothmaking: An Economic Survey*, in *English Historical Review*, 100, pp. 373–4.

1986

'Chertsey, Surrey and Laleham, Middlesex' and 'Staines, Middlesex', in R. A. Skelton and P. D. A. Harvey (eds), *Local Maps and Plans from Medieval England*, Oxford, Clarendon Press, pp. 237–43, 245–50.

Review of *The Survey of London, 41: Southern Kensington: Brompton*, in *English Historical Review*, 101, pp. 758–9.

Review of *The Victoria History of the Counties of England. The County of Somerset*, 5, in *History*, 71, p. 114.

Review of U. Priestley (ed.), *Men of Property – An Analysis of the Norwich Enrolled Deeds 1285–1311*, in *Journal of the Society of Archivists*, 8, pp. 130–1.

Review of M. Chibnall, *Anglo-Norman England*, in *The Brown Book*, Oxford, Lady Margaret Hall, p. 44.

1987

'Towns in Domesday Book', in J. C. Holt (ed.), *Domesday Studies*, pp. 295–309, Woodbridge, Boydell and Brewer for the Royal Historical Society; reprinted in *Ideas and Solidarities*, 1995.

'More about Feudalism', review article of T. J. Byres and H. Mukhia (eds), *Feudalism and Non-European Societies*, and E. Leach, S. N. Mukherjee and J. Ward (eds), *Feudalism: Comparative Studies*, in *Peasant Studies*, 14, pp. 250–9.

Obituary, with H. Pike and K. M. Lea, of Naomi Day Hurnard 1908–86, in *The Brown Book*, Oxford, Lady Margaret Hall, pp. 33–4.

Review of R. H. Britnell, *Growth and Decline in Colchester, 1300–1525*, in *History*, 72, p. 162.

Review of J. Haslam (ed.), *Anglo-Saxon Towns in Southern England*, in *English Historical Review*, 102, p. 462.

Review of *The Survey of London, 42: Southern Kensington: Kensington Square to Earls Court*, in *English Historical Review*, 102, pp. 457–8.

1988

Ed., with W. de Boer and G. MacNiocaill, *Elenchus fontium historiae urbanae*, II, 2; Leiden, E. J. Brill.

1989

'Magna Carta 1297 and the legal use of literacy', *Historical Research*, 62, pp. 233–44; reprinted in *Ideas and Solidarities*, 1995.
'The History of Group Litigation', review article of S. Yeazell, *From Medieval Group Litigation to the Modern Class Action*, in *UCLA Law Review*, 37, pp. 421–32.
Review of R. Fuchs, *Das Domesday Book und sein Umfeld: zur ethnischen und sozialen Aussagekraft einer Landesbeschreibung im England des 11. Jahrhunderts*, in *History*, 74, p. 117.
Review of F. Opell, *Stadt und Reich im 12. Jahrhundert (1125–1190)*, in *English Historical Review*, 104, p. 1009.
Review of R. D. Sack, *Human Territoriality: Its Theory and History*, in *American Historical Review*, 94, pp. 103–4.
Review of A. Hudson, *The Premature Reformation*, in *The Brown Book*, Oxford, Lady Margaret Hall, p. 48.

1990

Guest editor with B. Pullan, 'Towns and townspeople in Medieval and Renaissance Europe: Essays in Memory of J. K. Hyde', *Bulletin of the John Rylands University Library of Manchester*, 72: 3.

1991

'Bookland, Folkland and Fiefs', *Anglo-Norman Studies*, 14, pp. 211–27.
'Social Mentalities and the Case of Medieval Scepticism', *Transactions of the Royal Historical Society*, series 5, 41, pp. 21–41; reprinted in *Ideas and Solidarities*, 1995.
'Organizzazione dello spazio e del tempo nelle città medioevali inglesi', in P. Bonora (ed.), *La città: dallo spazio storico allo spazio telematico*, SEAT, Turin, pp. 97–102; revised English version, 'Space and Time in English Medieval Towns', in *Ideas and Solidarities*, 1995, pp. 1–7.
'Hypotheses rather than models: settlement and society in Medieval Europe. A Review Article': of C. J. Wickham, *The Mountains and the City: The Tuscan Appenines in the Early Middle Ages*, and A. Everitt, *Continuity and Colonization: The Evolution of Kentish Settlement*, in *Comparative Studies in Society and History*, 33, pp. 630–4.
Review of W. George and B. Yapp, *The Naming of the Beasts*, in *The Brown Book*, Oxford, Lady Margaret Hall, pp. 45–6.

1992

'The writing of medieval Urban History in England', *Theoretische Geschiednis/Historiography and Theory*, 19, pp. 43–57; reprinted in *Ideas and Solidarities*, 1995.
Review of L. Genicot, *Rural Communities in the Medieval West*, in *History*, 249, pp. 104–5.
Review of M. Chibnall, *The Empress Matilda*, in *The Brown Book*, Oxford, Lady Margaret Hall, p. 39.

1993

Review of D. Abulafia, M. Franklin and M. Rubin (eds), *Church and City AD 1000–1500: Essays in Honour of Christopher Brooke*, in *Journal of Ecclesiastical History*, 44, pp. 302–3.
Review of O. Brunner, *Land and Lordship: Structures of Governance in Medieval Austria*, in *History*, 78, pp. 294–5.
Review of H. Swanson, *Medieval Artisans: An Urban Class in Late Medieval England*, in *American Historical Review*, 98, pp. 1231–2.

1994

'Christopher Elrington and the V.C.H.', in C. R. J. Currie and C. P. Lewis (eds), *English County Histories: A Guide*, Stroud, Alan Sutton, pp. 1–4. 2nd edn published 1997 as *A Guide to English County Histories*.
Fiefs and Vassals: The Medieval Evidence Reinterpreted, Oxford, Oxford University Press.

1995

'English towns of the eleventh century in a European context', in P. Johanek (ed.), *Die Stadt im 11. Jahrhundert*, Münster, Institut für vergleichende Städtegeschichte an der Universität Münster, pp. 1–12; reprinted in *Ideas and Solidarities*, 1995.
Ideas and Solidarities of the Medieval Laity, Aldershot, Variorum.
Review of R. H. Hilton, *English and French Towns in Feudal Society. A Comparative Study*, in *English Historical Review*, 110, p. 691.
Review of P. Matarasso (ed.), *The Cistercian World: Monastic Writings of the Twelfth Century*, in *The Brown Book*, Oxford, Lady Margaret Hall, p. 83.

1996

'English Towns', in A. Havercamp and H. Vollrath (eds), *England and Germany in the High Middle Ages*, London, German Historical Institute, and Oxford, Oxford University Press, pp. 271–82.
'The Authorship of the Fonthill Letter', with M. Boynton, in *Anglo-Saxon England*, 25, pp. 91–5.

1997

Kingdoms and Communities in Western Europe, 900–1300, 2nd edn, Oxford, Oxford University Press (1st edn 1984).

'The historiography of the Medieval State', in M. Bentley (ed.), *Companion to Historiography*, London and New York, Routledge, pp. 117–38.

'La diversidad de enfoques y la problema de la especialización en historia medieval', review article of T. N. Bisson (ed.), *Cultures of Power: Lordship, Status and Process in Twelfth-Century Europe*, and W. Davies and P. Fouracre (eds), *Property and Power in the Early Middle Ages*, in *Hispania: Revista Española de Historia*, 57, pp. 329–37.

'Debate: Susan Reynolds to Johannes Fried', in *Bulletin of the German Historical Institute*, 19: 2, pp. 30–40.

Review of M. Bellomo, *The Common Legal Past of Europe, AD 100–1800*, in *Speculum*, 72, pp. 431–2.

1998

'Nationalism and the idea of a nation: modern or old?' (translated into Japanese by H. Tsurushima and M. Tanaguchi), *Rekishi Hyoron*, 584, pp. 5–22.

'Our forefathers? Tribes, Peoples and Nations in the historiography of the Age of Migration', in A. C. Murray (ed.), *After Rome's Fall: Essays Presented to Walter Goffart*, Toronto, University of Toronto Press, pp. 17–36.

Review of B. Pipon (ed.), *Le Chartrier de l'Abbaye-aux Bois (1212)–1341*, in *French History*, 12, pp. 93–4.

1999

'Carolingian elopements as a sidelight on counts and vassals', in B. Nagy and M. Sebök (eds), *The Man of Many Devices, Who Wandered Full Many Ways: Festschrift in honour of Janos M. Bak*, Budapest, Central European Press, pp. 340–6.

Index of topics

The main purpose of this index is to amplify and complement the editors' introduction, encouraging readers to pursue themes and ideas encountered in one particular essay across the rest of the volume. It is not a comprehensive index of subjects treated, let alone those only mentioned in passing. It is highly selective, especially because it (mostly) omits the subjects which are historically specific to the different essays and instead highlights the 'words, concepts and things' which form their authors' underlying concerns. 'Words, concepts and things' is a favourite formulation of Susan Reynolds, and the content and arrangement of the index also owe much to the inspiration which the indexer has found in Susan's own books, essays and conversation.

The primary arrangement follows the three broad areas indicated in the main title of the book, adding sections on kinship and family (which might, perhaps, have come under laity) and on words and language. Under the subheadings the arrangement is alphabetical. There are necessarily many connections and overlaps between the different sections.

I LAW AND POLITICS
A PROPERTY RIGHTS AND RELATIONS
B CRIME AND PUNISHMENT
C LEGAL PROCEDURE
D POLITICAL AND LEGAL NORMS

II LAITY
A LAY VALUES
B NATIONAL IDENTITIES AND CHARACTERISTICS
C THE LAITY AND THE CHURCH

III KINSHIP AND FAMILY
A KINSHIP SYSTEMS
B PARTICULAR RELATIONSHIPS
C WOMEN

IV SOLIDARITIES AND COLLECTIVITIES
A TYPES OF COLLECTIVITY

B EXPRESSIONS AND ACTIVITIES OF COLLECTIVITIES

V WORDS AND LANGUAGE
A MEDIEVAL WORDS
B MEDIEVAL LANGUAGE, LITERACY AND SYMBOLS
C MODERN HISTORIOGRAPHICAL IDEAS

I LAW AND POLITICS

IA PROPERTY RIGHTS AND RELATIONS
property rights in general 18–20, 26
church lands
    granted to laymen 17–18
    grants by laymen to the church 68–82, 90–2
    leased to laymen 18–19

communal 181
  belonging to lineages 177–8
disputed 35, 124–7
dower 2, 8, 150–3, 155n.21, 157–8
dowry 49, 51–3, 256
inheritance 2, 8, 196; *see also* IIA: inheritance
in law codes
  barbarian 50–4
  ecclesiastical 54–9
  late Roman 48–50
in marriage and stepfamilies 48–53
tenure (types)
  cornage 154–5
  gavelkind 155, 157
  serjeanty 152
  socage 152–3, 155n.21, 155n.23, 156, 159

IB CRIME AND PUNISHMENT
crime in general 71, 126, 133, 144, 147, 153
bad counsel (as an offence) 75
homicide 97, 98, 99, 101, 105–6, 111–12, 136, 155n.18, 177
incest 4, 6, 8, 191, 194; *see also* IIIA: consanguinity; IIIB: marriage, incestuous
perjury 101–5, 109–10, 127
punishment
  beheading 153
  forfeiture of land 71–2, 73–4, 76, 78–9
  murdrum fine 153–4
sexual infidelity and misbehaviour 97, 98, 111, 135, 136, 225–7
treason 5, 76, 95–115, 116–17, 125–6, 132–3, 134–6, 139–41, 147

IC LEGAL PROCEDURE
legal procedure in general 84
accords, arbitration and agreements 98, 115, 124–5, 139–40, 145–6, 182, 184
debates in and out of court 3, 101, 103–6, 139, 183
defiance 105–6, 107, 111
frankpledge 223, 224
jurisdiction
  clerical and lay participation in judgement 210
  communal judgement 182

judges 3, 150, 157
juries 152, 156, 220, 223–4
oaths 100–1, 105
  denial in court 97
  fidelity 38, 100, 114, 223
  jurors' 131
  mutual 34, 36–7, 38, 39, 40
  at ordeals 130, 131
ordeals 6, 98, 115, 118–19, 121–2, 123–4, 129–30, 142, 143
  ecclesiastical censure 129–30
  see also trial by battle
peace-keeping and dispute resolution 4, 101, 177, 178–9, 181–2, 210, 222, 225–6
professional law and lawyers 115, 159, 182, 204
treason, procedure for accusation 138
trial by battle (judicial duel) 4, 6, 96, 97–9, 102, 115, 116–49
  ecclesiastical censure 129–30
  intervention by a saint 137–8
  jurisdiction over outcome 143
  lay censure 130–1
  medieval terms 120, 136
  procedure 128–9, 138–9, 145
trials
  actual 113
  fictional 95–101, 107, 110, 113–15

ID POLITICAL AND LEGAL NORMS
legal norms
  English common law 141–2, 150–9
  law-codes 27, 75
  legal education for future rulers 142
  local custom 3, 5, 150–9
  papal 191–9
  Welsh and Irish 174, 178
government and administration 4, 218–33
  aldermen 219–20, 222, 223–7, 229–32
  councils 74–5
  government officials 33, 35, 85, 150–5, 157–8, 174
  kingship *see* IIA: kingship
politics 116–49, 200–17
  political ideas, values and discourse 6, 68–82, 115, 118, 134, 136, 193–6, 204–5, 213–15

Index of topics

war and violence 4, 21–2, 24–5, 35, 72
  armies and soldiers 13, 16, 18, 40–1, 45
  crusades 245–6
  foreign conquest 15, 165, 170–1, 174
  hostage-taking and ransom 102–3, 105
  military leadership 24, 25, 165, 170
  military service 13, 17–18
  rebellion 113–14
  within the family 15, 24–5
  see also IC: trial by battle

II LAITY

IIA LAY VALUES
ideals and thought in general 2, 7, 80
attitude to consanguinity 190–1
attitude to relics 238, 242–4
attitude to treason 113
attitude to trial by battle *see* IC: trial by battle
counsel *see* IVB: counsel
fidelity 2, 38, 41–3, 95–115, 214–15
honour and shame 6, 7, 10, 107–8, 115, 119, 122, 135–6, 181
inheritance 77–9; *see also* IA: inheritance
kingship 15, 21, 26, 27–8, 44, 72–3, 80, 82, 185, 246–7
  kingship as tyranny 165–8, 171
  sacral 206–9
laicisation 6; *see also* VC: modern historiographical ideas
medieval mentalities 83–4, 87–8
rank 27–8, 44, 46
religious scepticism 2
vertical relationships
  dual lordship 110–11, 113
  king–subject 28, 42–3, 214
  lord–community 181, 186–7
  lord–man 102–11, 113–14
  lordship in Wales 172–87

IIB NATIONAL IDENTITIES AND CHARACTERISTICS
national identities in general 5, 76
Angevin 165
English 11, 75–6, 160–1, 165–70
  Francophobia 168–9, 171
  in Ireland 164, 167
  in Wales 162–4, 167
Frankish 21–2, 166
French 164–6, 168
  in Wales 164
German 166
Norman 168
  in England 160–1, 165–70
  in Ireland 164–5, 168
  in Wales 162–4
Roman 166
Saxon 166
'Trojan' (i.e. Welsh) 162–4
Welsh 162–6, 175

IIC THE LAITY AND THE CHURCH
church lands *see* IA: church lands
church reform 71–2, 80, 206
false monasteries 33
lay–clerical distinctions and relations 3, 7–8, 10, 29, 200–17, 220, 249–61
religious patronage by kings 68–82, 260
three orders of society 27–8, 216

III KINSHIP AND FAMILY

IIIA KINSHIP SYSTEMS
chiefs of kin groups 176, 179
clans ('imagined kinship communities') 4, 9, 189, 198, 251, 252
common European kinship system 190–1
consanguinity 190–9; *see also* IB: incest; IIIB: marriage, incestuous
differences between regions of Europe 189–90
dynasties 71, 82
family piety 76
feud 189
genealogy 178, 185
involvement in disputes 113
kin relationships in general 175, 179–80
kinship systems and family in general 4, 5–6, 8–9, 9–10
kinship terminology 177

political solidarity of Carolingians 15,
    22–4, 36, 61–2
provision for royal families 72, 74
relations between kin groups and lords
    175, 176–7
supposed transformation from cognatic to
    agnatic 188–9
surnames 189
Welsh and Irish 173–4, 175–6
youth and maturity 68, 71, 81

IIIB PARTICULAR RELATIONSHIPS
children
    care of 47, 68
    posthumous 48
    sons of remarried widows 51
    stepchildren 47–67
    stepdaughters 49, 56, 58
    stepsons 51, 56, 59
    stepsons of widows 52
    younger sons 155–6
godparents 197
husband's kin 53
marriage and concubinage 23, 33, 63, 81,
    191–9
    divorce and annulment 58, 197
    endogamous and exogamous 195, 198–9
    incestuous 49, 51–2, 54–7, 59; see also
        IB: incest; IIIA: consanguinity
    papal dispensations for marriage 192–7,
        199
    second and subsequent marriages
        48–54, 57–9
paternal uncles 51
stepfathers 48–52, 56, 58, 61
stepmothers 8, 47–67
    in legislation 47–59
    medieval terminology 47–8n.3, 60–2
    political influence 60–7
widowers 49–51, 157–8
widows 48–9, 50, 51–4, 58, 154
    property see IA: dower
    widow-burning 50

IIIC WOMEN
in general 9–10
abduction 55
in Buddhism 249–50, 252–3, 254, 255–6

chastity 54
clerical attitudes 239–41
control of household property and
    clothing 60, 63–7, 154
criminals 34–5
excluded from public sphere 223
guild members 37, 39
in Hinduism 261
property rights and inheritance 69, 74, 77,
    79; see also IA: dower
in ruling families 23–4, 25

IV SOLIDARITIES AND
COLLECTIVITIES

IVA TYPES OF COLLECTIVITY
solidarities and collectivities in general 1, 3,
    4, 172, 187
caste 259–60
craft guilds
    India 251–2, 256–9
    London 220, 223, 224, 232, 233
criminal gangs 4, 34–5, 37, 40, 41
crusade (as a form of lay solidarity) 235,
    245–6
cultic 8
family 76–7, 176, 188–99, 211, 252–3,
    255
friendship 32–3, 74, 175, 193–5, 198
king's advisers 71, 73
neighbourhoods (village) 4, 33–6, 179–83,
    186
    charitable social provision (fraternities)
        4, 36, 37, 38, 40, 210
    military self-defence 39, 45
peace-keeping associations 210
pilgrimage (as a form of lay solidarity)
    235–6, 244–5, 251
regional 3–4, 5, 21–2
regnal 3, 5, 210
    English 160, 162, 168
    French 205–7, 210–11, 212–13
    see also IIB
seminars 11
sociability 183–5; *see also* IVB: convivial
    drinking
urban parishes 220, 223, 233

Index of topics 273

urban wards 218–33
    attendance 222–3
    conduct of meetings and elections 221–4, 231

IVB EXPRESSIONS AND ACTIVITIES OF COLLECTIVITIES
agricultural co-operation 4, 175, 178, 180–1
assemblies 28, 33–4, 38, 53, 90, 183–5, 218–33
convivial drinking 4, 36–8, 40, 41, 45, 59
counsel 3, 7, 10, 73–5, 77, 82, 103, 105, 110, 113, 114, 148
elite formation 20–1
mutual oaths *see* IC: oaths, mutual
parity (as a medieval concept of equality) 29
peers 3–4, 27–46
    angels 43
    baronial and knightly 4–5, 116–18, 134, 139
    bishops 31–2
    Charlemagne's twelve 98, 111, 112
    combatants in judicial duel 139, 141, 148
    counts 28
    courtiers 33
    elite soldiers 41–2
    humanity before God 29–31, 223
    inhabitants of London 222–3
    lord's men 3, 114
    magnates of England 139
    mayor and *jurati* of towns 147
    peasant soldiers 41
    of the realm (as Carolingian ideal) 42–5
    servi 36
shared memory 4

V WORDS AND LANGUAGE

VA MEDIEVAL WORDS
aequales, aequaliter 29–31
appellatio, appellator 116, 117, 131, 133
bataille, batalha 120, 129
bellum 120, 121, 124, 136, 142
beneficium 18
boni homines 5, 35, 182
certamen 120
conjuratio, conspiratio 36–9
consortes 33, 36
conspiratio see conjuratio
consuetudo 151–2, 154; see also *lex et consuetudo*
convenientia 36–8, 40, 42
cultus 30–1
cymydog 181
documentum 89
duellum 116, 120, 127, 128, 131, 136, 138, 143, 145, 147
equales see aequales
fideles 42
frater laicus 208
gens 31, 32, 71, 75, 169
hereditas 78–9
judicium 121, 124, 130, 142
laicus see frater laicus
lex et consuetudo 157–8
miles Christi 208
modernitas 86
monomachia 129
mos 152
nacio, natio 71, 73, 76, 179
natura 31
ordo 31
pares (Latin), *pairs* (French) 28, 30, 32–3, 35, 37–8, 41, 43, 45
patria 10–11, 75–6, 78, 152, 154, 184
placitum 90, 131
populus 71
precaria 17, 18–19
proditio 116–17, 126, 133, 141
proelium 136
progenia 198
secularis 209
societas 43
traïson 111, 134
viri sapientes 35

VB MEDIEVAL WRITING, LITERACY AND SYMBOLS
authentication of documents 89–94
Bible as read and quoted in Middle Ages 29, 42, 51, 55–6, 86

bilingual societies 161, 169, 257
classical texts as read and quoted in Middle
    Ages 43–5, 86
documentary production and retention 2,
    6, 8, 20–1, 85, 88–92, 178
documents as title to land 19–20, 69–70
hagiography 16–17
history-writing 17, 70–1
number symbolism 28, 191–2
human body and life-stages as metaphor
    for society 10, 68, 80–2, 211–15
legends and traditions 12, 16, 22
orality 2, 6, 85, 93
relics 6, 236–8, 241–2, 250
religious satire 235, 237–8, 244
ritual 6, 235–6
    marriage 53–4
    oath-swearing 38, 45
    punishment 36
    requests for pardon and favour 27
use of vernacular 95–7, 115, 120, 147, 245,
    247–8
writing 88–9, 93–4

VC MODERN HISTORIOGRAPHICAL IDEAS
acculturation 5, 13, 20–2, 26, 87, 174,
    178–9
'Celtic' obscurantism 173
cultural diffusion 2
the difference of the Middle Ages 2–3, 7,
    83–94
English exceptionalism 3, 172–4
'feudalism' 1, 3, 5, 13–14, 17–18, 85–6, 114
French normativism 3, 173–4
progressivism (the idea of progress from
    'primitive' to 'modern') 1, 2, 6, 83, 86
    belief in growth of laicisation in later
        Middle Ages 203–7
    modern secularism 201
state-building and political unification 1